The International Firm

A study of management across frontiers–
trade and investment

Text and Selected Readings
Written and Edited by

Michael Z Brooke
M.A., Ph.D.
Director of the International Business Unit and
Senior Lecturer in Management Sciences,
University of Manchester Institute of Science and Technology

and

H Lee Remmers
B.S, Ph.D.
Professor of Finance at the Institut Européen
d'Administration des Affaires, Fontainbleau

Pitman

PITMAN PUBLISHING LIMITED
39 Parker Street, London WC2B 5PB

Associated Companies
Copp Clark Ltd, Toronto · Fearon–Pitman Publishers Inc, Belmont, California · Pitman Publishing Co. SA (Pty) Ltd, Johannesburg · Pitman Publishing New Zealand Ltd, Wellington
Pitman Publishing Pty Ltd, Melbourne

First published in Great Britain 1977

Text set in 12/12½ pt Photon Times,
printed by photolithography and bound in Great Britain
at The Pitman Press, Bath

ISBN 0 273 01119 7

Contents

List of figures

List of tables

Preface and Acknowledgements

This book is dedicated to the new profession of International Manager. It attempts to encapsulate the bundle of skills required. As far as this is possible in words, that is; obviously the demands of the profession go well beyond words into the instinct for handling delicate and complex situations.

Managers often remark that every company is unique; in the same way everyone is conscious that every person is unique. But there is another important sense in which every person is the same. Medicine and psychology are based on the resemblances between people; business studies and management sciences are based on the resemblances between companies. The poet emphasizes the uniqueness, the scientist the likeness. The reader's sympathy may be with the poet, his professional requirements probably lean towards the scientist. This book attempts to present the issues, problems, solutions and general patterns which emerge from the countless investigations of the subject which have been undertaken in recent years.

The book started with a proposal for a textbook which was to be largely a reader some years ago. Since then the proposal has gone through many changes as we have done our own market research and learnt more from our own teaching experience. Less than 10% of the original draft survives, and numerous people have contributed to the final result which is now 50% our own work and so no longer a reader. Assistance and encouragement was received from members of the Department of Management Sciences, University of Manchester Institute of Science and Technology, and especially from Peter L. Smith.

Acknowledgement is also due to all members of the International Business Unit there who have contributed suggestions, but especially to:

Mary Black, for research assistance.
Christopher Craggs, who read the manuscript and contributed to chapter 15.
Richard Ellison, who contributed to chapter 2.
Annie Hopley, for research assistance.
Paul Neville, who contributed to chapters 13 and 17.
Michael Ng, who contributed to chapter 12.
Jagdish Sachdev, who contributed to chapter 4.

Other contributors are:
David Rutenberg, who contributed to chapter 5.
Graham Buxton, who contributed to chapter 6.
Gunter Dufey, who wrote chapter 7.
Lars-Gunnar Mattson, who contributed to chapter 8.
Maurice McInnes, who contributed to chapter 10.
Warren Keegan, who contributed to chapter 11.
Duane Kujawa, who contributed to chapter 13.
Klaus Sahlgren, of the United Nations Information Centre on the Transnational Corporation for permission to use part of the Report of the Committee of Eminent Persons in chapter 15.
Hans Schöllhammer, who contributed appendix II.
Roderick Powrie and Peter Kirkaldy of BP gave valuable advice.

Details are given in the notes to each chapter.

Naturally the editors accept full responsibility for all the contents.

Martin Brooke helped to compile the index.

Numerous typists on both sides of the Atlantic worked on the manuscript and its various revisions, including:

Michael Brooke's secretary, Thelma Wright, who organized the typing of two books at once, and to her assistant Eileen Wheatley. Other typists in Manchester Beryl Heaton, Thelma Binnie, Pauline Lownsborough, Angela Mackenzie. In Columbia, South Carolina: Leslie Callender, Jean Moody.

1 International Business: The Body of Knowledge

The vital statistics of international companies, their contributions to the economic welfare of nations as well as the threats they pose, are reported on almost daily in the press. Already nearly a third of international trade is between two parts of the same organization; companies are accused of dominating markets and pre-empting money supplies. Labour unions complain that multinational business frustrates the attempt to improve the lot of workers by capriciously transferring production towards countries where there is cheap labour to exploit. Governments are concerned with businesses which avoid payment of taxes or thwart policies designed to improve the balance of payments. The multinationals have been accused of being the main culprit behind the massive transfer of money from weak to strong currencies thus provoking the periodic monetary crises which have occurred in the late 1960s and early 1970s. The companies have had their flatterers as well as their critics. They are credited with powerful improvements to the standard of living in countries where they operate, beneficial effects on the social and physical environment, the transfer of knowledge and wealth from the rich countries to the poor, and a contribution to international understanding and peace.

This book is intended to be a guide for the student and the practising manager to the burgeoning literature on international companies. Most chapters have a mixture of new material and excerpts. Despite scepticism in some quarters, a substantial body of knowledge on the operations of international business has developed over recent years. This knowledge has come from the wide range of skills and interests which have been concentrated on this subject. Among the skills those of economists, sociologists, psychologists, political scientists, accountants and many others are represented in this book. Naturally some of the studies have led into blind alleys, others have proved more fruitful. This is a selective survey which reflects the view and experience of the editors, confirmed by much discussion with other academics and with businessmen. This book is also designed to be used in connection with courses, and appendix I contains some suggested outlines for which this would be suitable as a course book. These syllabuses have been well tested and their validity proved. Appendix II is a survey of research, and should give some indications about where new discoveries in the subject are likely to arise.

All the contributors are established in their own fields and the range of their interests demonstrates just how much attention has been concentrated on this subject. This book is meant to provoke further thought and enquiry on the part of the reader. Hence it is mainly composed of short excerpts with introductions to point up the main considerations. It is not a do-it-yourself kit for the international manager, it is an aid for reflection and further thought on experience and knowledge so far gained. Nevertheless there is information as well as stimulus here, the thought is grounded in some of the hard facts of the situation and some of the complexities of actually managing and financing foreign operations. Most of the excerpts are from recent journal articles or conference papers. Guidance to readings from books is given in each chapter and there is a selected reading list in appendix III.

The book is divided into three parts: Strategy, Management and the Environment. Any arrangement of the subject is arbitrary, but the arrangement here is designed for learning purposes. A logical order would, no doubt, start from the environment; a management order would start with market research. We aim to develop an appreciation of the subject in an order which starts with the route abroad and developing strategies, then looks at the main decision areas and ends up with the environment within which all the activity takes place. The divisions are not always absolute. For instance an environmental issue like technology comes in a management chapter on communication, while a management issue like external relations comes in an environmental chapter (chapter 17).

There are, in this book, a number of cross-references to our other writings. We find ourselves in a dilemma here. If we try to make the work self-sufficient, we shall be told that we are repeating ourselves (in one book we attempted to bring up-to-date some previous writing, only to find ourselves faced with a reviewer who said we were repeating what we had said before) but other people will be irritated by too many cross-references. Hence we have taken the same line with our own work as with that of others: there are summaries where appropriate and cross-references where they seem more suitable.

With regard to definitions, wherever discussions of this subject are held they get bogged down with the word *multinational*. The editors must confess to a strong vested interest since they are much committed to this word in print already, but they are also ready to admit that it might have been better if the word had never been coined. At a recent count there were some 15 different definitions current, and more are coming in all the time. Additionally numerous other words have been coined in order to attempt to classify some real or supposed variations in the method of international operations. This passion for coining words does not seem to have contributed much to our knowledge, and perhaps it would be better if the word *international* was used for all circumstances. Particular situations could then be discussed as such without attempting to give them particular names. There does, however, seem to be a situation in which a company becomes especially subject to the pressures, opportunities, and problems of international business. This comes about when there is a substantial investment committed abroad and the company has hostages across frontiers. No one has produced any convincing evidence about the stage at which this occurs. A figure of 20% of net assets has been suggested but there is no evidence in support of this, the true figure no doubt is different for different industries.

The word multinational is used here for any company which has investment abroad in its major activity. The foreign subsidiaries of service industries are included, but small selling subsidiaries of manufacturing companies are excluded. It is not claimed that this is a satisfactory distinction, it leads to many an anomaly; but at least it identifies a company situation in which certain international patterns of business activity are likely to develop. The international firm is normally one that operates abroad without investment but the phrase is sometimes used more widely as in the title of this book. Among other definitions the country of origin of foreign investment is called the 'home' country, the foreign subsidiary is to be found in the 'host' country. The 'parent' company or head office is the originator of the business. These are generally accepted terms; other words will be defined as used. Inevitably in a book which contains excerpts from the work of others, there will be some words used in different senses.

The body of knowledge on international business is summarized in Fig. 1.1. This chart shows the five frameworks which represent the different management systems which develop in companies once the first steps abroad have been taken. In the rings at the bottom of the chart are the most significant pressures for change. The internal pressures—objectives, resources, control, communications and personality—apply to any company and are not represented by separate chapters in this book, apart from control and communications. Nevertheless the subjects themselves keep recurring.

Much time is spent in courses exhorting executives to clarify their objectives. Under some circumstances this clarification exposes the problems so clearly as to be demoralizing, for the goals of the different parts of the company and of other interested parties may be irreconcilable. There is a conflict of objectives which is an especially important problem of the international firm. The company attempts to solve this problem in the light of the assumed interests of the parent company but this may be unsatisfactory to the subsidiaries and will often be unsatisfactory to the governments in both the home and the host countries. Ultimately, a single-minded pursuit of the immediate interests of head office may not be to the advantage of the company itself. Hence, the planning and the other management processes must be much influenced by the objectives, however they are stated. In all the chapters on management, this subject is implicit.

The same is true of resources. In international planning the allocation of resources is a main concern, but there are difficulties in identifying and still more in quantifying all the available strengths of the international firm. Yet the firm's growth and profitability almost certainly depends on superior use of resources, that is, finance, technology, market knowledge, techniques, staff and the rest.

Another of the six influences is that of personality. The relationship of personality to business success and failure will be long debated. Some discussion appears to rest on the assumption that all progress depends on outstanding characters. This argument from what might be called the heroic character continues in spite of the number of heroes who have turned out to have clay feet in recent years. No doubt the outstanding personality does provide an impetus to a company, he may also do long-term damage by pitting his personality against necessary changes and losing enlightened managers in the process. The processes of international business, the forces pressing for change and the opportunities for development cannot be subject for long to personal influences, and this book examines a wide range of issues. But the international company can provide an opportunity for damage or benefit with its many points where abrasiveness is likely, where authority lines cross frontiers or where individual units are isolated but locked into global policies.

The lower ring on the figure lists the external pressures for change in the company. The economic factors are discussed in chapter 14. There is a complicated relationship between world trends in trade flows, exchange rates, movements of funds and company policies. The response of companies has proved harder to predict as older theories have been outdated by the effects of these policies. A significant part of the political and legal environment, outlined in chapter 15 has to do with government influences on economic factors. The international action has been partly directed towards a more orderly world system to counter the problems that have arisen as both individual companies and individual countries have pursued their own supposed advantages. Chapter 15 also outlines the moves towards an international economic order and the difficulties encountered.

The most elusive of all the subjects in this book is that of the cultural and educational environment, the subject of chapter 16. Cultural differences have been well-documented and analysed by generations of anthropologists, but the application of their work to business studies has

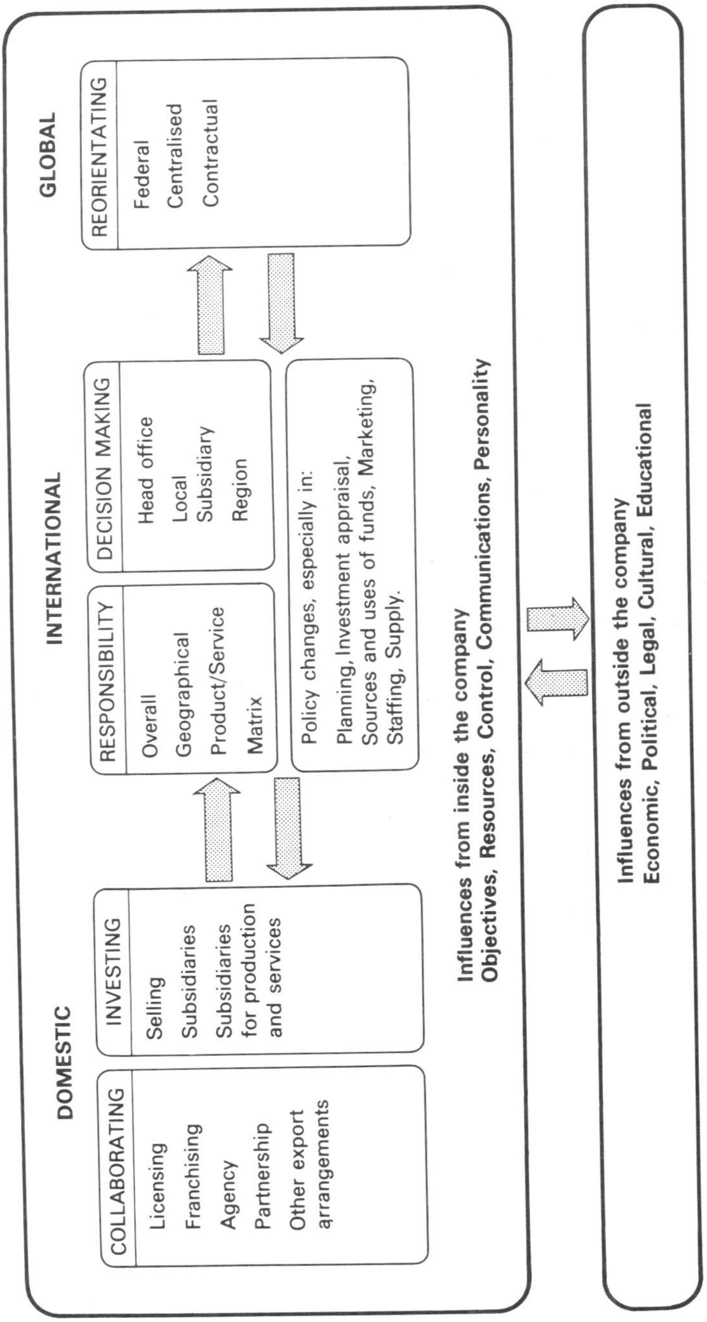

Fig. 1.1 The body of knowledge.

proved difficult. Nevertheless the importance of a better understanding of the nature of the differences that may be expected is clear both for general management and for marketing. Too often folklore and stereotypes of how other nations behave dominate the discussion rather than facts. In any case, as with the economic considerations, the activities of the companies are changing the facts, modifying the cultures of the countries in which they operate, and sometimes causing reactions which produce further and unexpected modifications.

The frameworks themselves, or units as they are called on Fig. 1.1, are not mutually exclusive. Companies may operate in more than one at the same time and they do not represent a one-way process of change. Too many facile statements about some alleged process of evolution in corporate policies, or internationalization as it has been called, have been made. The word unit is used to avoid such misunderstandings. The most advantageous business strategy will constantly vary in different markets and for different products. Hence the arrows point both ways. A suitable analogy would be that of the piano keyboard. Each of the five units can be regarded as a group of keys. All the keys on the board can be played in any combination, and the notes and chords will be constantly changing, but the right combination is vital as are the right sequences. To play the instrument correctly results partly from knowledge and partly from less definable skills, as does management. Some of the keys likely to be played are listed in each unit.

There the analogy ends, for each unit is a collection of concerns with an important priority. In the first two units the company's orientation is primarily domestic and the foreign business is not normally regarded as critical to its success and failure. The first is headed 'collaborating' because the main business activity abroad is selecting other firms through whom business will be done, and then arranging the terms and conditions for working together. The main problems are agreements made with unforseen consequences or unreliable partners, in particular it is common to make long-term arrangements for short-term business situations.

Thus an agent is found in one company, often after a brief search and with an inadequate appraisal. Then a long-term contract is signed, knowingly or unknowingly. The latter arises because of an inadequate knowledge of local commercial law which safeguards agents in ways that the foreign businessman, together with his legal advisor, often fails to suspect. Difficulties with agents are often found to cause such major problems that the company decides never to operate that way again. This decision, and it is taken with the other forms of collaborative strategy too, may well be a misreading of the difficulty; in any case the situation is constantly changing for each market and each product. So a slavish following of yesterday's experience can be a menace. The route into each market needs constant appraisal, as does the development of that market. Chapters 2 and 3 examine the various routes and give advice on how to explore them further. The accepted wisdom of the 1960s was that ultimately both the defence of a market and its growth would be limited if unsupported in this way. Mergers were justified by this alleged necessity. In some situations this may still be true, but in others the idea that investment will be required is misleading. This book attempts to explain the range of possible world strategies and the conditions under which any one may be viable.

Chapter 3 follows the chart into the second unit, where 'Investing' is the main heading, as the company is moving into the problems of committing capital abroad. The reverse process, the withdrawal from an established investment can be traumatic for a company—so much so that it has proved very difficult to collect evidence on this subject. Nevertheless, important decisions have to be taken in an increasing variety of companies, and more and more is being discovered about the groundrules for these decisions. After the discussion of this subject in chapter 4 the following chapter concerns corporate planning. After which part II covers the other issues raised in Fig. 1.1 in the context of the decision-making process. The means of taking the decisions change radically as a higher proportion of the company's business is committed abroad. Thus, in Fig. 1.1, units two and three are headed 'responsibility' and 'decision-making' because upheavals in fixing these and related matters between different units of the firm now dominate management considerations. Throughout the chart there is a network of arrows indicating constant change in both directions, sometimes at the same time in different parts of the same firm. A situation of constant change is being represented.

The final stage is headed 'reorientating' and lists three of the most likely systems of the future, which again may well occur at once in different parts of the same firm. One is called 'federal' and refers to a genuinely decentralized system with sophisticated management information retaining adequate links between companies otherwise independent except for complicated cross-shareholding arrangements. The word 'centralized' in this context means the reverse system, where an international group is run from one centre as much as if it was a domestic company as local laws allow. The third, 'contractual', refers to the increase of management abroad without investment. In connection with all these methods there may or may not be a global view of the company's resources and opportunities, but on principle there is. In practice the company may have very good reasons for taking such a view of some of its markets, and a more narrowly local one of others. In any case the *claim* by a company to be taking a global view has to be treated with more scepticism than is shown by many commentators who are ready to signal the emergence of a new phenomenon at the least excuse. It is all too easy to confuse the public relations with the reality.

The division of the subjects is necessarily arbitrary. Some would argue that the whole book is about international marketing and be surprised to find that that is the title of chapter 6. In that chapter attention is drawn to special issues which come on the horizon of the marketing manager in addition to those presented elsewhere. International cash management, the subject of the following chapter, is the most sought after skill at the time of writing. Interest rates, exchange rates, tax rates, all make the job of the finance manager especially skilled and his prestige is enhanced. Chapter 8 looks briefly at the often neglected subjects of international production and chapters 9 to 13 isolate some of the special skills which all international managers have to develop. The one most discussed is communications. There is the constant search for the elusive solution which will make the communications system fulfil its intended purposes. This search has never succeeded in a domestic company, and cannot be expected to do so in an international concern. What is clear is that success is to be found in tackling a number of diverse issues, many of them subtle and some of them contradictory, at one and the same time. These issues include confidentiality as well as communication, management style as well as regulations, personal contacts as well as mechanical links, the crossing of cultural barriers as well as the understanding of foreign languages. It is clear that specifically international issues like language, culture, distance, are no more significant than the other questions, but significantly add to existing problems.

One subject of increasing urgency to the manager is clumsily termed the 'government-company interface'. To avoid needless repetition, this subject has been discussed together with the external factors which give rise to it in chapter 15. The relations between companies and governments are not only concerned with restraints and incentives designed to reduce conflict between national economic policies and those of companies. This aspect of the subject naturally engages considerable attention, but of increasing importance is the direct involvement of the state as a promoter of international business. Official support for domestic companies that enter the international arena is one form of activity. Increasingly common is the appearance of state-owned companies both in trade and investment outside their own countries. A few years ago commentators were saying that one of the disadvantages of nationalization was that state-owned firms would be inhibited from activities outside their own countries, although these might be vital for their business. Now such firms both from Western and Eastern European countries are operating across frontiers; in some cases they are pioneering new ways of doing business. The other interesting development is the increase of Western business activity in Eastern Europe.

New patterns of licensing agreements, joint ventures and management contracts are emerging as this book goes to print.

The international company has considerable opportunities for rationalizing production and supply, but there are also powerful obstacles to taking advantage of these opportunities. Not only governments, but also trade unions are involved. Up to now the trade union response to the multinational has been mainly expressed in lobbying and other attempts to influence the actions of governments and international bodies. The gradual emergence of an international trade unionism is the theme of chapter 13. In the last chapter an attempt is made to sort out some of the signposts of the future. The body of knowledge traced out in this chapter and summarized in Fig. 1.1, is a means of interpreting what happens when business decision-making goes international. What patterns emerge, how problems can be analysed, how future moves can be predicted. The management systems themselves are the main focus of interest, but the response by other interested parties is also here. This body of knowledge provides a coherent framework within which further studies can be pursued.

How to use this book

Most chapters are partly text and partly excerpts from some other existing piece of work of direct relevance to the subject. With the consent of the authors, the excerpts have been edited to fit these pages. They are all from journal articles or from conference or other unpublished papers. There follows in each chapter suggestions for *Further Reading*. These include the most important books and a few other interesting writings on the particular subject.

At the end of each chapter there is a reading list. The books mentioned are carefully selected with a view to stimulating and assisting the reader. All the writings are graded.

(A) Introductory, ideal for the newcomer to the subject.
(B) More advanced.
(C) Specialist, but still suitable for the general reader.
(D) Specialist, for the reader with some background in the particular aspect of the subject.

International business has attracted a vast amount of literature, much of it repetitive or valueless and such writings have not been included. There is another caution, writings on some aspects of the subject soon become out-of-date. Regulations change, new ways of doing business emerge. The reader needs to be alert to changes. There are various agencies—government departments, libraries, universities and the rest—where facts can be updated. On the whole this book discusses general issues which are not subject to short-term change; but some of these cannot be realistically considered without reference to current, changeable regulations. This is particularly true in the matter of finance.

As a result of the changes that have taken place, most of the works listed have been written well within the last ten years. Older writings quoted deal with issues less subject to change. There is also a short list of general works in appendix III. To save repetition those works are mentioned in the text and footnotes by name of author and date. It cannot be over-emphasized that this book is meant to provide an introduction to further reading. As with any human activity, whether a job or a hobby, a few minutes of practice may be worth a few hours of study, and those with some practical experience will find even more meaning in the chapters which follow. Nevertheless unguided experience can be frustrating. This is particularly true in this subject where so much isolated experience is absorbed and not related to any body of knowledge. A soaking in the writings on international business is worth a shower of irrelevant or misinterpreted experience.

Each chapter also has its exercises and questions. In some chapters there are short incidents stating some problems which illustrate the text and give practical examples of points that have been raised in theory. When these incidents are used on courses it is suggested that students should be asked to prepare a presentation under five headings:

(1) Identify the problems to be solved, which are not necessarily the same as those suggested on the paper.

(2) Search out facts about the environment—economic, legal and social.

(3) Use their imagination and experience to propose operating figures for the company; market share and other facts needed to solve the problems realistically should also be determined.

(4) List out all the possible solutions, together with costings and cash flow projections.

(5) Select one preferred line of action and explain the reasons for the selection.

All the incidents are based on real situations but the companies have been carefully concealed.

Many chapters have references to case studies which can be used in connection with the subject of the chapter. The cases are meant to give comprehensive training in problem solving, and will usually cover many subjects apart from that of the chapter in which they are recommended. Each one is a substantial study of an actual situation. The entries are by title, date, source and reference, author (if known) and summary. Most of these cases can be obtained through the case clearing house in each country or through the issuing institution. If readers have any difficulties about this or any other question concerning the use of this book, they may write to: The Director, The International Business Unit, University of Manchester Institute of Science and Technology, Sackville Street, Manchester M60 1QD. This also applies to any of the papers mentioned which the reader may find inaccessible. Throughout the footnotes this organization, whose research forms the basis of a majority of the chapters, is referred to as 'The International Business Unit'.

In addition, each chapter has a list of questions which may be used for group discussion or for essay or exam subjects. This book can be used for courses at a variety of levels, so the questions are aimed at different courses. It is certainly intended as a textbook, but much more than a textbook, this work is dedicated to a new profession—the profession of international manager.

Thus each chapter has a similar framework, but this is not a straightjacket and there is considerable flexibility in the way each subject is handled. The differences partly depend on the amount of easily accessible material already available, and the questions for discussion derive from this as well as from material printed in these pages. The flexibility also extends to the level of study required. The book has been designed on the assumption that its readers will be a mixture of amateurs and professionals and that some will be knowledgeable in some aspects of the subject but be looking for a general introduction to others. The suggested readings in particular are suited to a range of users. The flexibility is also shown in the excerpts, some of which are think pieces and some are advisory.

Part I
Strategy

Attention is concentrated in this part on the strategic considerations which determine the decision-making of the international manager. In particular the main routes to foreign business are considered. This consideration was described in chapter 1 by the 'keyboard analogy'. The different routes were compared to notes on the piano. The analogy is useful in that it emphasizes the range of possibilities and combinations of possibilities that are available at any one time. The choices available are often overlooked when policies for foreign operations are developed in terms of one factor, market size or market presentation, and not in the light of a survey of the available strategies for each product in each market. But such a survey, if only conducted superficially, can be shown to have great advantages for a company. From this argument it follows that all the possible methods of operating abroad should be considered together, at one and the same time. This is clearly impossible, so in the following pages each route is considered separately and classified for further investigation. The classification used here is:

(1) Sales of goods and services abroad with minimum investment.
(2) Sales of knowledge abroad with minimum investment.
(3) Sales of goods, services and knowledge abroad with investment.

Minimum investment may include money put into agents or licensees and even sales subsidiaries or branch offices. Joint ventures and subsidiaries for manufacture or the provision of a service are counted as 'with investment'.

The object of the exercise, from the manager's point of view, is to make money abroad of which a reasonable proportion can be brought home. This very fact may help to determine the method used. In some cases it is easier to repatriate royalties, in others profits. But such facts change frequently, as do the tax considerations which also help to determine the appropriate method. The transfer of money, which will be considered in a later chapter, can also be viewed in terms of a range of choices the correct combination of which is important. This fact needs to condition the actual arrangements made for the foreign operations, a necessity which is often overlooked. The money has to be made in exploiting the company's strengths abroad and another initial activity is to appraise or reappraise where these strengths lie. The result of this discussion is a model which takes account of: company strength, product needs, market needs, company experience.

Too often only the last of those terms is considered. Conditions change so rapidly that a slavish following of yesterday's experience can be a menace. Experience can be a bad guide in other ways too, it can lead to the wrong lessons being learned. For instance, one company reported a major problem with a licensee in one market, and this led to instructions not to deal with licensees in future. Other forms of prejudice can also be a menace, one of which is that it is 'best to go it alone'. Collaborative arrangements are unpopular with many businessmen, who are strongly conditioned to keeping the decision-making in their own hands. It is with arrangements that are inescapably collaborative that the next chapter is concerned.

2 Foreign Business without Foreign Investment

2.1 A tale of two companies

Company A sends a bright young executive to France. He reports on the huge market, the weaknesses of the competition, the great opportunities for the company's products. He lists the many companies in that country anxious to be appointed agents or distributors. In the end it is decided that a full agency will serve the company's interests best in view of the considerable development that is possible. This, it was also believed, would reduce the pressure on the parent company, since the agent could be left to develop the business. A potential agent was named, investigated, and eventually signed up. But the results were disastrous. The competitors were not as weak as expected, the agent did not develop the market, the transport costs and delays killed the anticipated profits.

One of the reasons for the failure was that company B was sitting in the wings also observing the market. This company was based on a different country from company A. Its management considered that a longer-term view was needed, and a rather more complicated arrangement was made. A company in France was found where the proprietors were anxious to sell, and an arrangement was made for a temporary distributorship with considerable backing from the company B. The understanding was that the French subsidiary would be bought and used as the basis for the development of local manufacture if the parent company could satisfy itself and its probable financial backers that such an arrangement was viable. For most purposes the French company was treated as part of the organization from the start and the arrangement prospered.

In terms of the keyboard analogy used in the last chapter, company A pressed the wrong key but company B found the right chord. For company A there was a sequel. A bright, young executive (another one, of course) was sent out to Nigeria. There conditions were appropriate for an agency arrangement, and he produced convincing evidence of this. But his report was rejected at head office. Our experience is that agents are not suitable for our business, he was told. They cause a lot of difficulties, do not develop the business and you find you cannot extricate yourself from unsuitable arrangements. The company had played a wrong note once and other notes followed. This situation also re-emphasizes the difficulty of learning from experience. Organizational learning, as it has been called, can mean that the wrong lessons are deeply set into the decision-making process of the company, and cause further mistakes.[1]

This leads on to the more general considerations of this chapter. Most international business will always be done without substantial investment in the market and, to continue the analogy already used, half the keyboard will consist of the various non-investment methods. These may logically be divided between those that involve the sale of goods and services and those that involve the sale of knowhow. The choice between the two rests on a number of considerations:

(1) The resources available to the company. This will often be a determining factor, but if shortage of funds dictates the choice then it may be best to wait. There is much evidence that the cheapest routes may be the most wasteful in the end. This particularly applies to approaches to a market where there is not sufficient support and where failure produces disillusionment.

(2) The ability to make money out of the project. This includes not only the expected return on the resources put in and the likely growth that will result, but the ability to get the money back to the home country—exchange control regulations and withholding taxes are among the issues involved. Forecasts concerning the ability to get the money back to the parent company are frequently ignored.

(3) The suitability of the particular method to the particular market. Comments on this will be made throughout the text.

2.2 The sale of goods and services

To most practitioners, the first consideration in international business is the sale abroad of products developed at home. Both investment and knowhow arrangements come later. If all other things were equal, it is said, all the company's efforts would be concentrated on foreign sales. All other things turn out to be unequal, however, and there are many obstacles to straightforward export. Some of these are of the company's own making. The two problems that occur most often are concerned with the initial entry and with the choice of collaborator.

Companies of all sizes and with varying degrees of experience have these problems, but the particular difficulties of entry are confined to the less experienced concerns where a mistake can ensure that export is off the agenda for a long time. In any given year there are several thousand companies which either export spasmodically or enter export for the first time. They account for an insignificant proportion of British exports, but for a particular company the exercise may be very significant indeed; and it proves frustrating for the lack of a strategy and a systematic approach. There are a few much publicized examples of firms that push a few samples abroad and build up an export business that way. These are exceptions that mislead others with false hopes. The elements of a policy for the new starter or casual exporter include:

(1) Choice of likely markets.
(2) Market research.
(3) Decide market. Investigations show that this can be defined in many ways including geographical area or customer. The essential point is that the exercise shall be concentrated on one market however defined. One trap for the new starter is evidently the failure to concentrate the effort.
(4) Decide method of entry.

There are two problems that often arise at this point. One, again, shows up more commonly among the inexperienced. That is the tendency to assume that it is necessarily more profitable to go it alone. The other difficulty, that of the choice of collaborator, appears quite common even among experienced operators. It is not just that unsuitable agents or distributors are found, but that permanent arrangements are made with them for what may well be temporary business situations. A further consideration in the policy would then be:

(5) If the decision points to the sale of products or services should this be by direct sales or through a third party?

There are a limited number of goods for which direct sales are likely to be suitable; but it would seem that the criterion that most often produces correct results is the type of customer rather than the product as such. Thus a product that can be sold in substantial quantities to one buyer may be suitable for direct export. The buyer may be an executive of another manufacturer or of a store chain, so the range of products can be wide. Similarly service industries may go abroad on a few large orders; in their case these may well come from customers with whom they do business at home.

In the majority of cases where a third party is considered desirable[2] there then follow the difficulties of selection and of establishing a continuing relationship. This relationship cannot be legislated for, a fact that is often overlooked and that applies to all the collaborative arrangements. Great trouble is taken to draw up a contract which exactly stipulates what each party will do. As long as the collaborators are working together satisfactorily, the clauses will never even be invoked. Once they are called upon, that is an almost certain sign that the partnership is breaking up. So what is needed is a contract that makes specific provision for terminating the arrangement; other clauses are hardly required, but this is the very one which is so often missing. On some occasions when it is present, the divorce may be successfully challenged in the local courts, which shows that the wrong method was used in the first place.

Inappropriate measures have to be taken to end a collaboration which has ceased to fulfil its purposes because the foreign partner has legal rights which cannot be overcome. These measures can often be very expensive indeed; the differences in commercial law between countries make it difficult for a company entering an agency agreement to understand the problems that can arise. Some of the complications may be avoided by entering distributorship rather than agency agreements. The names and legal classifications vary but when the agent does get special treatment it is because he is assumed to have made a contribution to the development of the company in the given market, and in particular to have built up goodwill for which he is entitled to payment. He has acquired some rights in the company as a result. Numerous instances show that problems with agents are as likely to occur when the business is successful as when it fails. If the business grows, and the agent company is unable to grow with it, then the agency agreement proves most unsatisfactory.[3]

A further point about trade is that there are a number of points of transition such as:

(i) from general products to sophisticated components.
(ii) from manufacturing to service industries.
(iii) from exports to third parties to intracompany trading.

So:

(6) Another consideration is the appropriateness of the product in the light of the available strategies and of the need to generate income abroad.

Another important point in connection with the drive abroad is the necessity of reorganizing the management system at home to match the growth in the foreign business. There is plenty of evidence to show that the foreign business prospers to the extent that it has backing from home, and that this means the allocation of special responsibilities at head office. This is most important at the start of the exercise when it may be most difficult to allocate the necessary resources in products and production priorities as well as finance and manpower. The summary of the decision process may then continue:

(7) If the decision is to operate through a third party, there are numerous forms this can take from a simple distributorship to an elaborate agency agreement where the foreign partner is integrated into

the parent business. Many of the underlying issues are common to all such arrangements, but some guidelines are:

Appointment and support. Selection procedures are often haphazard. Selection procedures do not take sufficient account of the fact that the agent may need to fulfil a number of important requirements such as selling, servicing, information gathering, and so on. Growth potential may be too little considered. An agent needs qualities that complement those of the parent company. Permanent arrangements are unsuitable for what may well turn out to be a temporary business situation. A contract is needed mainly to ensure that there are arrangements for ending the agreement if the business situation changes.

Whatever the means of appointment, the agent will need support and stimulus. This will come from constant communication and frequent face to face meetings. Indeed the view of the most successful operators seems to be that the more nearly the agent is treated as part of the company organization, the more likely is the arrangement to be successful. Naturally this refers to the informal aspects of the treatment, and the relationship has to be handled with discretion. But the point would seem to apply to all aspects of handling foreign collaborators.

However delicate the management of agents has to be, what is certain is that an agent without adequate support will make money elsewhere.

Control and appraisal. Some companies have minimal control and lack of knowledge to increase it, however desirable.[4] Others have tight controls and demand detailed reporting from their agents. This latter approach is always linked to a carefully planned international marketing programme, and is usually more effective. Different patterns of management emerge for companies with tight control and those without. A whole group of activities from financial reporting to staff training is involved.

The control of agents certainly has to be handled with care. They are, after all, independent companies. Nevertheless, many of the most difficult problems actually arise where such controls are not exercised. Vague impressions that a particular agent is not performing satisfactorily may lead to the break up of a relationship which would have been known to be profitable after all if adequate controls had been operated. There is no substitute for continuous appraisal.

Multi-product companies operating in many countries. There is a need to co-ordinate the activities of the various product groups and agents and other outlets and to avoid duplication. Along with this goes the need to maintain the involvement of those units which have the appropriate knowledge and interest for any given project. A company with several product groups has to decide, at some stage, to which part of the company responsibility for exports is to be given. Carrying out this responsibility includes making decisions about whether each product group can handle its own products, whether there should be a central export department, or whether there should be a compromise between these two solutions. One company which tried to leave all relations with agents to product group managers found that these relations were badly neglected.

With sophisticated products and a small number of product groups, or a wide differentiation between the groups, the direct link between the division and the agent may be best even though there is the danger of neglect. Where a company also has foreign manufacture, then a subsidiary may be the most suitable agent for other divisions.

The implications for head office planning. The successful operation and integration of the activities of the agents involves effective control and planning systems. There is need to establish the correct head office organization. This has implications for recruiting and training policies as well as for a reconsideration of the management system at home.

In particular for most companies there is the need to build up a specialist department to keep up the pressure on the foreign operations.

This often goes against the grain. Senior executives take the view that all their managers should be export minded. A company changed its view when it was found that overseas opportunities were being neglected. An effective foreign trade specialist transformed the situation.

The other half of this chapter is devoted to the discussion of the various methods of selling knowledge. But there are a number of methods which fall between the two categories of selling goods and selling knowledge. These include turnkey operations, whereby a complete plant is installed and commissioned and then the operation is gradually handed over to the customer. Also included are various arrangements for a continuing relationship with a customer, from after sales service to technical aid agreements. Some of these arrangements prove expensive in the short-term, but refusal to take part in them proves much more costly in the longer term. The steady, inexorable increase of 'total package' business—where much more than just the sale of a product is involved—is more and more a feature of the export scene, as it is of the sales of knowledge.

2.3 The sale of knowledge

Every international company is, in a sense, exploiting its saleable knowhow in foreign countries. Normally this has been incorporated in the price of the goods; but there are circumstances where the knowhow alone may be saleable. Very few companies appear to work out the circumstances where this applies to their business. Most concerns treat the sale of knowledge as a last resort when others have failed. A number of reasons have been suggested for this. For instance, such sales may increase the return on investment without increasing growth significantly. In spite of protestations to the contrary, companies seem often more interested in the latter. But the figures show that knowhow agreements of one sort or another are increasing rapidly, albeit from a small base. These are of three main kinds, but the distinction is often blurred.

There is the sale of technical knowledge, usually known as licensing. In essence the company is selling its knowledge via the charging of royalties for the use of patents, but more may well be involved. The tactics of licensing involve long and searching enquiries to ensure that a collaborator can be found who will develop the business effectively. The strategy of licensing is as part of a global policy for obtaining maximum income from a saleable invention—an example of advanced technology, or just an ingenious idea. This strategy may be the complete foreign policy of a company; a small firm which has decided to put all its resources into new product development to exploit its technical advantages would be an example of this. More often, in keeping with what was said earlier, licensing will be part of a mixed strategy. It will be used for products or markets where some money can be made but where direct sales are unlikely, either because of local difficulties, or because the company lacks resources, or simply because such sales would be too expensive.

For all the potential advantages, licensing does not seem to be used nearly as much as it might. A likely, although unverifiable, reason for this is that by the time a company has grown to a size and developed a commercial expertise whereby licensing agreements can be readily handled, direct sales in more markets have become feasible. What is clear is that there is opposition to licensing where sales are possible, and that this opposition may not be based on adequate investigation and reasoning. What is also clear is that there are substantial problems in this method of doing business, as there are in all others.

The first set of problems concerns, as for agents, the selection and appraisal of the collaborator, in this case the licensee. This problem affects every company. Bad experiences caused by inadequate selection methods in the first place have been reported by many executives as a reason why a particular company did not go further with licensing arrangements although calculations suggested their profitability.

Another problem is that the licensee may develop into a competitor in markets where the company does maintain direct sales. Experience shows that the problem cannot be met by legal agreements which often prove unenforceable, it can only be met by establishing satisfactory relationships with the licensee. The same is true of quality control. This problem is more often expressed as a fear than as a fact. Nevertheless, where it is a fact this can be a disaster for the company concerned, the destruction by some licensee with low standards of a carefully established reputation for quality.

Another group of problems arises where the resources of the licensee are inadequate, and this inadequacy may occur in any of the functions. A lack of capital may make it necessary for the parent company to put much more money into the project than had been intended in order to protect the licensee, and this may wipe out the main expected advantages of this method. A lack of technical skill may force the parent company to second expensive technical staff to develop the operation, and thus again to commit resources which could be more profitably used elsewhere. The inadequacy most often mentioned, perhaps because least often anticipated, is that of marketing skills.[5] It has been said that one of the commonest causes of failure is the lack of marketing ability in the licensee.

Against the problems, there are many advantages in licensing. It enables the more rapid exploitation of new inventions in more markets at minimum expense and with the least risk from political and other hazards.[6] Problems with production and distribution abroad are eliminated, as is the over-extension of management.

Most of the same advantages and disadvantages apply to the second group of arrangements—that of franchising—except that here the parent company expects to put in the marketing expertise. On principle the difference between the two arrangements is that franchising is the exploitation of some marketing skill as opposed to the technical expertise which underlies the licensing arrangement. Most foreign franchising operations are relatively simple technically but a package of selling and promotion skills can be highly complex. Most existing franchising schemes are concerned with fast foods, hotels, car rental and soft drinks. This package may include the supply of materials, use of trade marks (often heavily advertised by the parent company), advice on financing, costing and selling, training programmes and much else. Often the franchiser has only to put in the equity, but many different arrangements are possible.

As with licensing, franchising has great advantages as a means of making the most possible money out of a saleable idea, but there are also similar problems. In particular quality control is even more difficult. A corollary of the high-powered advertising is that the reputation of the firm is even more easily sabotaged by the inadequate franchisee. A special problem of franchising is adaptability. The idea may be highly successful in some countries, but may not be so readily transferable to others. Similarly there may be legal difficulties. Perhaps it is no coincidence that most of the foreign income from franchising comes to a few firms with successful and well-established domestic bases. Without such a basis, there may well not be the resources to cope with the problems of adaptation however carefully the franchisee is selected.

The third method for selling knowledge abroad is the *management contract*. On principle this is the provision of a total management system for a foreign company. All aspects of managing a business are covered except the provision of equity, and there may be some of this. In practice this method may not be so very different from some licensing and franchising arrangements. All these ways of doing business contain varying combinations of expertise from the parent company. It can be said, however, that in licensing and franchising the parent company is concerned to stimulate the foreign collaborator; the money comes from royalties, which will usually depend on the successful drive of the collaborator. In the case of management contracts, the foreign collaborator may play a no more active part than providing the capital and a member of the Board. The parent company is effectively managing the contract company. This method may gain all the advantages of foreign investment without the necessity of raising the money or of accepting the risks involved. On the other hand the contract will be for a limited period and the parent company will need to keep well ahead of the field to ensure that it is retained. The following excerpt sets out the position clearly.

2.4 Management contracts[7]

'Perhaps the most important business development of the second half of our century may prove to be the rise of what I would call, for lack of a better term, 'corporate contract management'. Under this new concept, the corporation does not view itself as a direct mobilizer and allocator of capital but as a generator and seller of management capability in the broadest sense.'

The management contract is an arrangement under which a certain degree of responsibility for the operations of one enterprise is vested in another. The latter undertakes the usual management functions, makes available a whole range of skills and resources, and trains personnel. The contract covers payment to the company and the handing over of authority to the locals once trained. There is a similarity to other methods of operating overseas such as joint ventures, licensing and technical service agreements; but it is vital that the management contract is seen as being much wider in scope. Confusion with other methods can lead to quite inappropriate strategies being adopted.

A company may enter into a licensing agreement when the licensee does not possess a sufficient range of skills to cope with the new process and the company has to supplement these skills unexpectedly. On the other hand a company can enter into a management contract arrangement without fully understanding the nature of the commitment, the suitability of its particular products and skills, or the capability of the receiving enterprise. An important difference between the management contract and the other arrangements is that the latter must rely upon an already functioning enterprise, whilst the company using a management contract can build such an enterprise from scratch, relying not at all upon existing local experts.

It is necessary, then, to look at the nature of the resources and skills provided. These have been listed as follows:[8]

(i) human resources;
(ii) procedures, standards, processing;
(iii) corporate capabilities.

The first two categories are virtually self-explanatory and they are normally provided under the other contractual arrangements referred to previously. They remain a significant part of the management contract. It is important that a company should define the amount and nature of the resources it is willing or able to make available. Similarly, countries differ regarding the resources and skills needed. Particular management contracts can require anything from one or two key individuals up to several thousand for varying periods of time, raising implications for manpower planning, staffing, organization and other policies.

A careful specification of the nature of the procedures, standards and processes must also be made by the company. Many companies have not formalized these elements or have done so in a way necessary only for their own internal uses. Numerous questions are raised here, not the least of which is the suitability of the company's technology for a different environment. The basic requirement, however, is that the company must have a clear understanding of what, if anything, they have to sell.

Although a management contract would incorporate many features similar to some form of technical knowhow agreement together with commercial, administrative and management procedures, its unique quality lies in the provision of this 'corporate capability'. This is difficult to define but can include such easily understandable elements as the large company's access to funds, general reputation, and worldwide procurement capability. More important, there is a fundamental distinction between the skills, knowledge, and capabilities of individuals and of those same individuals working within some type of organization. A group develops, through working together over time, its own distinctive way of doing things. This has been referred to as the 'accumulation of inherited knowledge'. It is this almost indefinable skill which is such an important part of the management contract since the aim is to create a successful total enterprise.

There are examples of several companies co-operating together in order to operate a single management contract venture, and this opens up fresh opportunities. This can be done when, perhaps, the scale of the contract venture is too large or where one company does not possess the full range of skills or resources required and these can be complemented by those of a partner. It is more usual to have only one of the companies taking overall responsibility for the operation of the contract, certain aspects being sub-contracted to the second company. It is also possible to have joint ventures between companies to do this.

Reasons for using management contracts are:

(i) The management contract is the only method of involvement acceptable to a host government.
(ii) The company wishes to protect an equity investment.
(iii) The return from a direct investment is too low for the company.
(iv) The amount of capital required for a particular venture is too large for the company.
(v) The risk of investing is considered too high by the company.
(vi) To secure a market for the company's products.
(vii) To secure a source of raw materials for the company.
(viii) To support a joint venture.
(ix) To support a licensing or technical knowhow agreement.
(x) Where the company has a pool of under-used resources or has incurred high expenditure on R & D, the management contract can be a way of utilizing these resources or recovering costs.
(xi) As a complementary part of a company's overall international strategy, to obtain a substantial revenue from its stock of managerial skills and resources.

A distinction is apparent between 'offensive' and 'defensive' reasons. In some cases a company has taken a positive ('offensive') decision to use a management contract, for example to earn an income or to secure a market. Another company has adopted the arrangement because a host government has, say, acquired an interest in a subsidiary, or has prevented direct investment. This is a 'defensive' strategy and about half of the companies involved in the investigation could be placed in this category. Most of the other companies were operating management contracts for the reason outlined under (xi) above. This emphasizes the point made in the opening paragraphs about management contracts increasingly being used as an 'offensive' strategy in their own right.

Some critical problems

(i) *Types of contract.* There are obviously many different types of contract document which can be used depending upon the nature of the particular situation. An important distinction can be made between the *brief and general* contract document and the *detailed and legalistic.* The first type may be only three or four pages in length, in some cases there was no formal contract at all. The purpose of the relationship and the responsibilities of the two parties are outlined in general terms. The second type sometimes runs to several hundred pages and would specify in detail the parties' obligations, often going further and laying down how these are to be carried out. Circumstances may dictate otherwise, but the brief and general contract would seem to be preferable since in practice it leads to better relationships, disputes being settled in discussions regarding overall objectives rather than reference to contractual details. There would, however, seem to be a tendency towards the use of the legalistic contract resulting in part from the pressure of certain governments (especially in the Middle East), and of the often vivid imagination of the company's legal department. In most cases it would seem that such a contract neither protects a company from government action nor ensures in itself a company's effective performance.

(ii) *Remuneration.* The remuneration package for operating the management contract could be one, or a mixture, of the following:

Fixed fee.
Fee contingent on profits.
Fee contingent on sales.
Fee contingent on production.
Fees for the procurement of equipment or new materials.

The most common fee basis appears to be one related to sales. Although no definite rule can be given since circumstances differ so greatly, this would also seem to be the most advisable method. Fixed fees are obviously dangerous for a company in times of inflation and mistakes in calculating the amount or the cost of the resources provided can be disastrous. Many governments are now insisting on a fee fixed in advance but there are several instances of companies still securing contracts whilst refusing to accept this. A fee related to profits can cause serious problems if the consequent profit maximizing objectives of the company conflict with the social and political objectives of the host government. Official policies may often influence the operations and profitability of the management contract venture.

Two further questions arise. The first is whether the salaries and direct expenses of personnel seconded to the contract venture, as well as those paying occasional visits, should be met out of the fee or paid for separately by the local contract enterprise. Normally the latter alternative was adopted, although individual practices differ enormously. Secondly, on what basis is the fee to be charged? Only a few companies have established guidelines for this but there would seem to be scope for developing those based upon the treatment of the amounts expended by the company in operating such contracts as revenue expenditure or implicit capital commitment. The 'opportunity cost' of the resources provided could also be incorporated into such a formula. Again many companies fail to give serious consideration to the tax treatment of such fee payments. The tax position of the local enterprise can, in the long term, be as important as that of the company itself. Consideration has to be given for example to such factors as whether the fee payments are deductible as an expense in completing the tax liability of the local enterprise, or whether the company itself can incur a tax liability locally.

(iii) *Organization and manpower planning.* A company needs to adapt its organization structure, internal relationships and control procedures in order to deal effectively with management contract opportunities and operations. In fact few companies are organized specifically to deal with management contracts. There are examples of separate organization units being established with such responsibilities, in one case a company setting up a subsidiary which was represented on the parent board and was required to justify its existence by ensuring that the revenue it earned in fees was at least double the costs involved in providing its services.

In other cases responsibility was variously shared between main board directors and the product or geographical divisions of a company. Where the latter applied decisions were often unnecessarily pushed upwards to main board level. This was mainly where the resources required to operate the management contract had to be provided from more than one product division or from outside a particular geographical division. If internal mechanisms existed to determine the allocation of resources and their cost, then conflicts between different parts of the company would be minimized.

Manpower planning and staffing are often not as formidable problems as expected. Existing staff can be drafted in at short notice where the project has sufficient priority. Otherwise personnel can be employed on a short-term basis. But this requires a special expertise as far as the company is concerned. The problems of absorbing personnel back into the company after the completion of a contract, individual remuneration packages, and the like, are not essentially different from those faced by a company operating overseas subsidiaries.

Few of the companies involved in our investigations pointed to any serious problems at all in this general context. Indeed several times the management contract situation has been mentioned as an opportunity for management development, providing interesting positions of responsibility for those who were not quite ready for such senior posts within the parent company.

A major difficulty is that of justifying the secondment of senior key executives to a contract operation, not owned directly by the company. This has various implications. The fee charged would have to be worthwhile, which raises the issue, already mentioned, of the need to determine the bases for charging fees. The scarcity of key people would also lead the company to complete the contract as quickly as possible—rapid completion is the main factor in the success of a contract venture and the opening up for the company of further possibilities. Further the commitment of such scarce resources is vital to success in operating such management contracts. The use of only second-best resources can lead to a lack of performance so a company must, after ensuring that the remuneration is adequate, be prepared to commit fully its first-class people and resources if a decision is made to adopt the management contract as a strategy.

(iv) *The distribution of control.* The company does not own the local contract enterprise but would normally have as much operational or day-to-day control as if it did. Such operational control would often lead to control over matters of policy. The distribution of control between the company and the local partner would vary depending on various circumstances, such as the existence of any local expertise. The most serious problems often arise when a company is not prepared for the local government or other partner to assume control over certain policies such as pricing and personnel. It is therefore important for a company to understand the probable nature of the distribution of control before entering into the contract arrangement. Even though the company runs the contract enterprise in many ways as it would its own subsidiary it must be prepared to accept a limit on its authority. Many companies operating under management contracts as a second best alternative to investment, or for 'defensive' reasons after losing complete control of a wholly-owned subsidiary, find it difficult to accept these limits to its control. Similarly companies must be careful not to regard the arrangement as merely an extension to licensing or some similar technical transfer arrangement. The relationship is much closer and the company is expected to have greater responsibility for and authority over operations.

A final word: it has often been shown that the authority or control exercised by the company rarely depends on such factors as the wording of the contract, the proportion of equity held (if any), or representation on the board of the local venture. It is a far more subtle relationship dependent in many ways upon the reputation, image and success of the company, and the host government's perceptions of these.

(v) *Training and transfer*. In the vast majority of cases the reason for the management contract, as far as the local government is concerned, is that the company should train local personnel with a view to their assumption of complete responsibility in a short time. The most crucial problem of training is that company and government often differ as to their beliefs of how quickly this and the transfer of responsibility can take place. The most important determinant of the speed of this training would appear to be the attitude of the company towards the process, rather than the techniques used. This attitude seems to be a product of the company's reasons for entering into management contracts. Those having the 'defensive' reasons tended to see rapid training and transfer as an enormous problem and were involved in disputes with the government concerned. Companies which had entered into the agreement for 'offensive' reasons, accepting it as a short-term relationship, did not generally have such problems and were able in many cases to change from employing from between 50 and 200 expatriates to virtually complete local management in a period of two to five years.

Factors influencing success in management contracts:

(*a*) *Philosophy and attitude*. In order to operate successfully and without constant conflicts it is vital that a company accepts the short-term nature of the management contract, at the same time appreciating the longer-term opportunities which are often available. In many cases successful completion of one particular contract leads to further contracts being offered to the company, perhaps for a further expansion phase of the contract enterprise, a separate enterprise in the same country, or opportunities elsewhere in the world. Because there are relatively few companies experienced in operating management contracts their reputation becomes well known and success, albeit measured on the speed of contract completion, leads to further business. Companies established abroad for a long time often find it difficult to accept this philosophy; so there develops what could be described as a 'hanging-on' syndrome. There is a subconscious desire to retain complete control leading to a slower transfer of operations and conflicts with the local partner.

(*b*) *The holding of equity*. In most cases it has been shown that if a company holds a portion of the equity in the local contract enterprise this tends to lead to such severe conflicts in the relationship between the two partners that the management contract arrangement virtually breaks down. Naturally this depends on various circumstances such as the country of operation. It would almost invariably apply where the country concerned was, for example, one of the more nationalistic or left-wing African states. The main problem is the inherent conflict between the profit maximizing objectives of the company and the economic and social purposes of the local government. It may well not apply where the local partner was not a government body but a commercial undertaking since the basic objectives would tend to be similar. Hence, one of the most important questions to be considered when examining the advisability of equity participation is, apart from normal risk and return factors, the underlying objectives and likely policies of the other party contrasted with those of the company.

(*c*) *Remuneration.* This is very closely allied to the question of equity involvement by the company. The basic point, again put forward, is that, where certain circumstances apply which may lead to a conflict of objectives, a remuneration package which is linked to profitability by the company should be avoided.

(*d*) *The contract document.* Unless special circumstances dictate otherwise a company would in most cases be advised, as would a foreign partner, to base the formal arrangement on a contract document which is as brief and as general as possible. Further, the period of time for which the contract is to run should be as short as possible, between three and five years is the norm, with the possibility for renegotiation or mutual termination within the period built into it.

(*e*) *Authority and control.* Whilst a company must be prepared to accept a great deal of responsibility for operations and generally control the contract enterprise in many ways as if it were a subsidiary, it must also accept certain limits to its power. These limits will often depend upon the country of operation and may appear to interfere with efficiency. This is why a company must consider the implications of the distribution of authority on such factors as equity holdings, remuneration and performance measures.

(f) *Training and transfer of authority.* In most cases a company must accept this as a prime responsibility and recognize that the speed of the process is one of the main bases of success, at least in the eyes of the host government partner. It is all too easy for a company to point to the difficulties of training, the lack of qualified locals, and the conflict between training and operating, but comparisons between companies show that in practice the transfer of authority can take place completely in well under five years in the majority of instances.

2.5 Some interesting facts

In 1972 there were 10,495 US companies engaged in export. For Britain the figures are not complete, but over 85% of exports in 1973 were accounted for by 1568 firms (and this included all firms with over £1m worth of exports that year). The total value of British exports for that year was £11,500,000,000. Exactly half of this sum was made up by 82 firms. Only 2 of these firms were not part of groups with international investment and 30 were subsidiaries or affiliates of foreign concerns.[9]

Twenty-five % of all world trade is now between different units of a company, but the figure is considerably higher for the home countries of major foreign investments.

United States Franchising Outlets Abroad.[10]

	1972	1973
Total companies	175	208
Total outlets	6153	9509
In Canada	2758	4140
In Britain	—	1042
In the rest of Europe	—	1429
In Japan	525	862

In 1973 world exports and production by foreign subsidiaries of multinational companies each formed about 12.5% of gross world product.[11]

2.6 Suggestions for further reading

As in all the reading lists in this book, the intention is to give a selection which should provide a theoretical and practical approach to the subject. The readings listed are not intended to provide a *How to Do it Guide for the Export Office*. The rules differ for different countries and booklets are usually readily obtainable. To avoid duplication the name of some books are given by author and date. Full details of these are provided in appendix III.

General

(B) BROOKE & van BEUSEKOM (1979). Chapter 2. To be published.
(A) DANIELS, OGRAM & RADEBAUGH (1976). Chapters 18–20.
(B) GRUB & KASKIMIES (1971). pp. 165–178.
(B) MIRACLE, G. C. & ALBAUM, G. S. (1970). *International Marketing Management*, Irwin: Illinois, USA.
(A) NEILLANDS, S. R. & DESCHAMPNEUFS, H. (1969). *Exporting*, Pan: London.
(B) ROBINSON (1973). Chapter 1.
(B) TERPSTRA (1977).
(B) THORELLI (1973). Chapter 22–27.
(A) WHITEHEAD, G. (1976). *Elements of Overseas Trade*, Croner.

Agents and distributors

(C) BEETH, G. (1973). Distributors—Finding and keeping the good ones. pp. 273–279 in Thorelli 1973.
(C) McMILLAN, C. & PAULDEN, S. (1968). *Export Agents*, Gower.

Sale of knowledge arrangements

(C) DELAPIERRE, Michel (1975). La vente internationale de la technologie: l'optique de la firme. Centre de Développement de l'OCDE, July.
(C) GABRIEL, P. P. (1970). New concepts in overseas investment, chapter 9 in Mann, R. *The Arts of Top Management*, McGraw-Hill.
(C) GABRIEL, P. P. (1967). *The International Transfer of Corporate Skills: Management Contracts in Less Developed Countries*, Harvard.

Law and trade

(C) SCHMITTHOF, C. M. (1975). *The Export Trade* (6th edn), Sweet & Maxwell: London.

Trade with communist countries

(B) WOLF, T. A. (1973). New frontiers in east-west trade, *European Business*. Autumn.

2.7 Exercises for this chapter

Case studies

For a general note on the use of case studies throughout this book, see above page 10.

Pick & Wick (Cordage) Ltd., 1964. (Glasgow University BPI ICH 9–314–050) by Forbes, A. M.
An old established firm is forced to open a manufacturing facility in Chile in order to protect its Western South American market against the threat of prohibition of importation.

Centrifugal AB, 1968 (IFL, Instituet for Foretagsledring, ICH 9–374–740), by Engdahl, C. A. and Linder, S. G.
The process of internationalization of a typical Swedish industrial machinery company.

Terrapin Limited (A), 1964 (Cranfield Institute of Technology Mar –2, ICH 9–510–071), by Gowlland, R. A. and Wells, L. T.
This case presents the problem of whether Terrapin should try to sell overseas; if so, where and how, by export, licensing local manufacturers or establishment of overseas subsidiaries?

Baker Perkins Holdings Ltd., (A), 1964 (Cranfield Institute of Technology Mar –32, ICH 9–510–080), by Gowlland, R. A. and Taylor, C. S.
The export subsidiary Chairman considers replacing his French agents with a branch or subsidiary in France.

Incidents

For a general note on the use of incidents throughout this book, see above page 10.

The first incident is based on a problem that arose for a British firm operating in France before Britain joined the European Economic Community. Students should look up the legal background to agency arrangements for foreign firms in France. They may also need to determine whether these are affected by the Community regulations or not.

(1) The control of agents

R. O. Bury and Son Limited is a small family business manufacturing toys for young children. Mr Rob Bury, grandson of the founder, has been very successful at building up an export trade through many tours abroad. His goods are sold at toy shops, stationers and souvenir shops. So far Mr Bury has sold mainly to individual proprietors or small distributors. This has put enormous strains on his shipping office, and has proved expensive. The one exception to this method of distribution was France. Some two years earlier, on one of his travels, Mr Bury had met a Monsieur Vincent Oleur in a bar in Paris. Monsieur Oleur ran an import-export agency and in the course of conversation, he offered to promote Bury's goods in France. Mr Bury got his lawyer, who was a close friend and adviser who had no knowledge of French commercial law, to draft an agreement. This was done and Monsieur Oleur was granted exclusive rights for the sale of Bury's products in France and certain countries of North Africa. The result was extremely successful, and produced an immediate increase in orders. The success was maintained and France soon became the largest single market for the Bury products. Problems also began to emerge. Firstly, Monsieur Oleur began to demand an increased commission and Mr Bury then made some calculations which convinced him that sales in France were already so expensive as to make a negligible addition to his income. This was going to be an increasing problem if he had to increase his production capacity to meet these sales. In addition, Monsieur Oleur was selling goods manufactured by one of Bury's competitors, and this made the future uncertain; moreover he was complaining bitterly about irregularity of supplies, missed deadlines and lack of adequate information about new products.

While contemplating how he could reduce the problems without risking a loss of the market, Mr Bury learnt that one option was closed to him. Because of his lawyers lack of understanding about French law, the agreement could not be broken without paying Monsieur Oleur prohibitive compensation.

(2) A licensing agreement

FEC, S.A. was a French Engineering company with production in other European countries and in Latin America. It had no business in the Far East and had made a licensing agreement with a Singapore firm for manufacture in that country for export to other Far East countries. The royalty was based on a par product arrangement since the patents registered in Singapore were for components of other products which the licensee also manufactured. There was some provision for the royalty percentage to increase as the quantity increased. An elaborate agreement had been drawn up with the local licensee which defined the countries within which the products could be sold, details of quality control, protection of trademarks as well as patents. The management of FEC had now become dissatisfied with the arrangements. In spite of the agreement, the goods were being sold in other countries in competition with their own exports. They also suspected that other components were being used in some of the products, and thought that a breach of patent might be occurring.

The problem was to know what to do: legal action would be expensive and might turn out to be fruitless, besides their licensee in Singapore was technically competent in contrast to others they had used. They doubted whether they had the financial resources or the management expertise to set up their own subsidiary in the Far East. But was there any other option open to them if they were to build up a satisfactory business?

2.8 Questions for discussion

(1) Outline a strategy for foreign business for a company in advanced technology which has up to now made no sales abroad.
(2) Outline a strategy for foreign business for a highly successful restaurant chain with no experience abroad.
(3) Select some significant issues from which guidelines for dealing with foreign collaborators should be drafted.
(4) State and discuss some possible options for reorganizing head office to take advantage of foreign business opportunities.
(5) Discuss the advantages and disadvantages of management contracts and situations in which they might be used.
(6) Select and discuss some issues relevant to the decision whether or not to establish agents or distributors in West African countries. The company is British, in consumer goods, and has a group turnover of £20 m.
(7) Discuss the merits and demerits of manufacturing high Technology products abroad through licensees.

3 Foreign Investment

The Chief Executive returns home after a world tour. His main theme is the wonderful opportunities abroad for the company, and the neglect of the foreign associates by divisional managers at home. This is a common story and it has a number of reasons. One is that a hard pressed product group manager at home is reading some figures for his division:

Domestic Sales	£20 m a year
Foreign Sales	£1 m a year

He is thinking to himself that he can only spend 1/20th of his time on the foreign business. But even that is too great. For a problem in his home market is serious, it can shatter his business. A problem in any one of the scattered markets abroad will have little effect. He may also be reading some other figures that discourage him from worrying about what happens abroad even more. These show that the cost of the overseas sales are so high that less than 1/40th of his profits can be said to come that way.

The Chief Executive, on the other hand, is reading some rather different figures. These may read:

Domestic market share	60%
Average market share in other EEC countries	7%
Average market share in Latin America	4.5%

Another possibility is:

Total market growth (annual forecast for next five years by present trends)

UK	1%
EEC	4%
Latin America	7%

Yet a third possibility is:

	At present	Assuming sales quadruple (investment at home)	Assuming re-investment in largest foreign markets
Average profitability in UK	12%	12%	12%
Average profitability in EEC	9%	13.5%	15%
Average profitability in Latin America	3%	12%	18%

Instead of Latin America, the tables could read Middle East, Africa, the Far East or any other region.

These are hypothetical figures, although adapted from an actual case; but they do serve to explain strong differences of opinion at home, and why the company may need a specialist executive charged to oversee the foreign developments.

Yet another set of figures that may indicate the need for greater emphasis on the foreign side of the business could be found from an examination of the trade cycle which shows that the peaks and troughs that come in different economies at different times. There may be other facts which are weighing on the Chief Executive, such as the internationalization of customers and suppliers, the advantages of operating in different types of market. These may be industrialized markets for technological innovation, less industrialized markets for labour intensive machinery and so on. The result of these considerations is the gradual emergence of a complete international undertaking, using many options at the same time. Most of these options, it should be stressed again, shade into one another. An understanding of the reasons for corporate behaviour in taking decisions about foreign investment demands a theory and there are several available. But first a definition is required. The last chapter and this are concerned with a spectrum of possibilities which range from collaboration between two completely separate organizations to an integrated international organization. Figure 3.1 demonstrates the point.

As has been emphasized earlier there is no implication of evolutionary progress in this chart. The firm experienced in international investment will usually look for non-investment openings as well. Another distinction which has to be made is that the emphasis here is on direct investment, that is the management of overseas operations in which ownership is also involved. This contrasts with foreign portfolio investment in which there is ownership but usually no management, in other words the holding of shares in foreign companies. The distinction is made in Fig. 3.2.

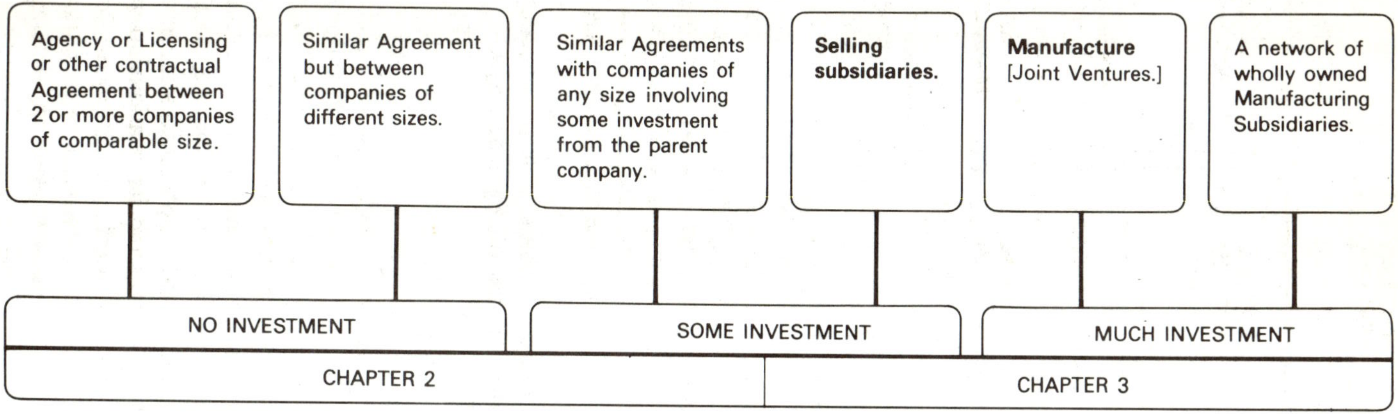

Fig. 3.1 The spectrum of foreign business activities. Any given company can be operating any combination of these activities at any one time.

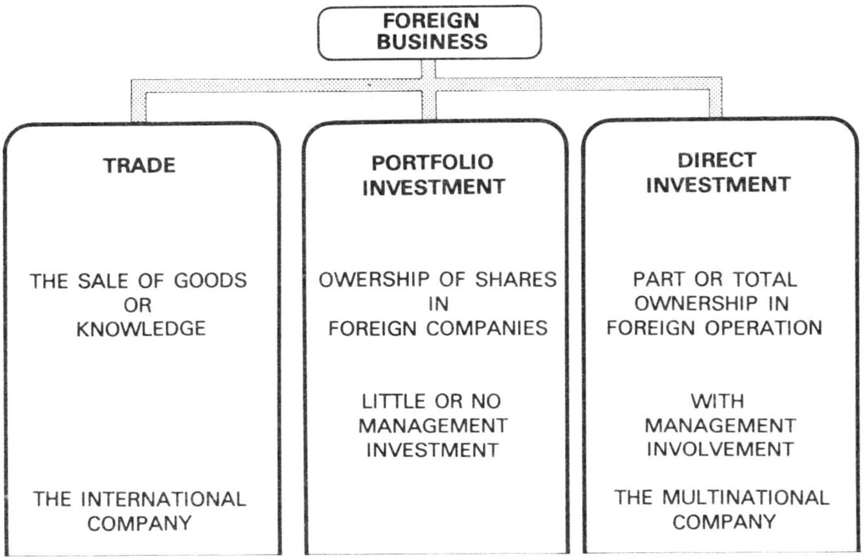

Fig. 3.2 Definition of the subject.

There is no further discussion of portfolio investment, as contrasted with portfolio theory, again, in this chapter; but that does not mean that it is not an important subject. Many of the advantages of a spread of income and of conserving resources can be obtained by portfolio investment across frontiers, although there are many difficulties involved. See below chapter 14.

So why do companies establish direct foreign investments? The question can be answered in a number of different ways.

3.1 The reasons for foreign investment

A theory of direct foreign investment can be constructed from a number of approaches. There is the economic approach which sees the changing pressures on the decision-making caused by changes in the environment which affect the pursuit of profit and the optimum use of resources. There is the socio-psychological approach which sees the incentives and constraints built into the organization and its relationship with the environment in a wider sense. There is the historical angle which looks at what has been happening over a period of time. There is the organization learning approach which bridges the gap between the economic and the socio-psychological. There is also the commercial approach which draws on all three, but which focuses attention on short-term needs and conflicts as well as the action of competitors. This approach surveys the actual decision-making process and analyses and interprets the results. The classification is set out in Fig. 3.3, the main characteristic of each approach is explained in the next paragraph.

The Approach	**Characteristic**	**Principal Concepts**
Economic	Motivation	Comparative Costs—Factor Involvement—Surplus Resources. The Product Cycle—Portfolio Theory.
Socio-psychological	Motivation	Power—Growth—Innovation—Conflict.
Historical	Motivation and process	Economic developments and power relationships in a historical perspective. Imperial and defensive considerations.
Organization learning	Process	Search—Bias.
Commercial	Process	Response—Organization—Defence.

Fig. 3.3 The reasons for going international

The economic and the socio-psychological approaches are concerned with identifying motives derived from the underlying pre-suppositions of the disciplines concerned. Thus the characteristic of these approaches is called *motivation*; the organization learning and the commercial generalize from the observation of companies in action and show the *process* by which the motivation translates into decisions. There is nothing necessarily incompatible between these approaches, however much some of their exponents seem to think there is, rather they form the different ingredients of a total view which is incomplete without the contributions of each.

An economic approach starts from a theory of comparative costs. These can be analysed in terms of the factor endowments and the demand conditions which produce relative advantages in different markets. Originally the flow of goods could be understood in these terms, but the understanding has to be extended to the flow of capital which in its turn would change the terms of trade. Thus a country with ample capital would tend to export capital intensive goods, and that with large resources of labour would manufacture goods which were labour intensive.[1] Advantages such as these would encourage investors to move to different parts of the world to suit their manufacturing process. This theory raised some questions. It was possible for manufacture to be performed by either labour or capital intensive methods; the companies had a choice. More serious was the result of investigations which showed that the exports of the United States, a country where capital was plentiful and wages (though not necessarily labour costs) high, included both capital and labour intensive goods. There are many suggested ways of explaining these problems—such as market distortions and imperfections and oligopolistic influences. The influence of organization learning and personal influences no doubt play their part; but three other economic explanations have emerged.

One derives from company strategy. The company becomes international by combining attempts to reduce costs with some form of integration.[2] This may be vertical, the purchase of suppliers or customers, or it may be horizontal, the expansion of the business into similar products internationally. The theory of logical diversification to protect the existing business or to use fresh resources is similar to that of the use of surplus resources.[3] The argument is that surplus resources in the company will be matched with scarce resources elsewhere. Thus a company with surplus funds will invest where there is suitable labour or to acquire market opportunities. This is likely to be into what has just been called logical diversification if the company also has usable knowledge and management skill. Indeed this skill may itself be an important surplus, whether it is in the technical or the marketing aspect. Some conglomerate diversification, which does not have the product logic described, may be due to an opportunity to use surplus financial resources and skills more effectively. Thus these theories can account for most forms of diversification, but their ability to predict is limited; a company has a wide range of choice as a surplus begins to appear and will not treat that surplus in isolation.

Portfolio theory is another way of interpreting corporate strategies for foreign expansion. This theory states that a spread of investment across different products and different countries can give the firm security against the risk inherent in growth and in over-exposure to single markets. The approach of the company in making its plans if analogous to that of the institutional investor surveying opportunities for the greatest possible return with the least risk.

Another economic theory is that of the product cycle.[4] This picks up the theory of comparative costs and explains one of its main limitations—the apparent contradiction of capital intensive products being produced in a labour surplus country and vice versa. The cycle is one that starts from an innovation; this is likely to be in a country with high research activity. Initial manufacture will be associated with research. Once established the new product will go into mass manufacture and will require expanding markets, this will take the company abroad. By this time there will also be competition and factor costs will have become important. Hence the company will be searching for foreign production, and siting will depend on which costs are most significant. In high technology products, where transport costs are not significant, proximity to the market may not be important once the problems of innovation have been overcome. An even greater choice of possible sites thus opens up. The product cycle theory is most convincing when explaining policies for advanced technologies.

The socio-psychological theories for their part, are concerned with different terms of reference from the economic; the objectives of the organization are seen as compounded of the aspirations of individuals and groups brought together in some form of uneasy coalition. The economic factors are regarded as powerful constituents in a continual series of conflicts between interlocking factions to whom considerations of power, status and personality are also important.[5] There are, in fact, two varieties of conflict inherent in any organization; one is a conflict of opinion as to how the aims of the organization are best met, the other is a conflict of interest between members of the organization. The two may be inextricably mixed. For instance, someone who sees the company's future in an expansion of the foreign operations may also see his future career in developing that side of the business. Appointments may often be made to ensure the coincidence of opinion and interest, and this may be the most effective way of ensuring developments abroad.

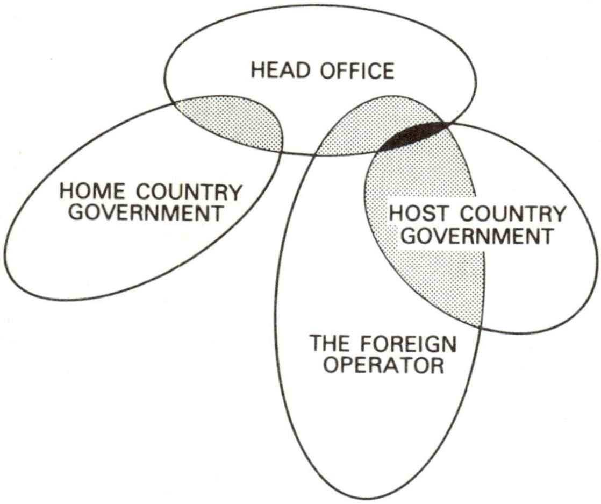

Fig. 3.4 The interlocking groups of conflicts and pressures that help to determine international business policies.

One way of analysing the behaviour and the particular problems of an international company is in terms of three groups of interlocking conflicts. This is to simplify a complex situation but is helpful in working out a framework for understanding. There is the internal discussion in head office about the commitment of resources abroad and their management; there is the relationship between head office and the foreign operation whether undertaken by other companies like agents or licensees or by a subsidiary; there is the relationship with the environment. This last comprises conflicts with numerous interests and individuals. In Fig. 3.4, however, attention is concentrated on the government-company interface discussed below in chapter 15. The figure sets out the position diagrammatically. This insight can be used not only to understand problems, but also to design organizations and procedures which will foster rather than impede international policies.

The exercise of power and authority within the complex organization is another subject on which the sociologist and psychologist have concentrated attention. That is the positive side of producing decision-making individuals and a decision-making process which can achieve the objectives which the economic insights and technological developments demonstrate to be possible. This point is made in this chapter, because for most companies it is the point when the company begins to invest abroad that radical changes gradually force themselves upon the structure and activities of the management.[6] It is the view of the authors of this book, already expressed, that the management system has to change to match any expansion abroad; but for most firms it is only after foreign investment has taken place, with its much larger potential for disaster as well as for profit, that changes actually happen. Power and authority are used to consider the way the new complexities of international management influence further changes within the system and with what are now becoming multiple environments. The results affect other issues like innovation, which can be either stimulated or frustrated by the organization and power structure. The behavioural approach is sometimes considered over-subtle for some of the issues it purports to settle. It acts as a corrective to over-concentration on the aims of economic man.

Between the economic and the socio-psychological approaches with their emphasis on motive and other approaches which concentrate on process is the historical. The emergence of international companies as a historical phenomenon is traced against the historical background. Technological, financial and commercial developments combine to produce such opportunities as large-scale production, international funding and above all diversification. These are seen to be translated into corporate strategies which produce growing and diversified international corporations.[7]

The next group of theories are those that have brought together the economic and the socio-psychological specifically for the specific purpose of studying the business concern. The phrase *The Behavioural Theory of the Firm*[8] is both the title of the best known book on the subject and an apt summary of this approach. The concentration is partly on the motivation, but primarily with observing the process whereby the motivation is translated into action. The connection between the economic factors on the one hand and the personal and group interests on the other is examined in terms of bias in the decision-making. In other words the responses of the organization to the economic factors are seen to be biased by the other considerations. Through the search process and through the accumulation of experience, itself interpreted in a biased way, a body of knowledge is built up in the light of which decisions are taken. Thus one impulse towards foreign investment arises from problems with other methods of doing business abroad rather than a clear knowledge of the potential of the investment. The search is problem centred, and the organization's concern with an issue is intense while it is seen to be a problem, but much less so when the urgency lessens. In other words policies arise rather from problems rather than from other stimulants.

This approach has the merit of taking seriously the theories which it incorporates, and does fit in with much experience. Indeed the fifth group of theories, here labelled the commercial, derive most of their value from the fact that they take the previous theories and rephrase them in the light of empirical research.[9] However it is pointed out that there are more immediate stimuli, which are usually seen to initiate action, and that most recorded examples of foreign investment in both the manufacturing and the service industries were essentially defensive in nature. That is to say they were undertaken to defend an existing market, not to attack a new one. While there are numerous exceptions to this, the evidence strongly supports what has been called an *incremental* view of foreign investment. Companies build up their foreign activities by non-investment means, support is then provided by a corporate presence in various parts of the world and finally a full manufacturing subsidiary is established. This incremental view fits in with the product life cycle theory and is borne out by numerous studies from different countries of origin.[10] A Swedish study, in particular, has traced the actual founding of foreign facilities in some Swedish multinational companies. As a company goes international it can develop an ever more subtle mixture of international strategies, but it is unlikely to establish foreign subsidiaries before other means have been tried.

The other principal reasons for developing investment are as a result of actions by competitors or customers. The only logic of concentrations of one type of business building up in one centre rather than another often seems to be keeping up with the competition. Once one company has moved, others say: 'We could not afford not to be there because our competitors were already in'. Other firms, including service industries like banks, went international in order to improve their service to their customers. This was another defensive reason, they had international competitors to whom the customer might turn. It will readily be seen that these commercial reasons are not inconsistent with the economic and socio-psychological. On the contrary, the terms of trade which produced the situations which caused the companies to take defensive action are explained by the economic reasons; and the way these situations touched off different reactions in different companies are further explained by the specific power structure and other characteristics of individual concerns. Different levels of causation are being examined; an adequate understanding of international investment is constructed by using all the approaches.

3.2 The appraisal of foreign investment

Once one of the situations discussed has signalled 'start', a systematic method of investment appraisal is needed which can say 'stop' or 'modify' or influence the process in some other way if necessary. The perceived reasons for undertaking the investment will clearly influence the way the appraisal is performed, and the calculations will need to take account of the overt objectives. But a few general points can be made; for instance, there are three appraisal processes to be gone through:

(*a*) The market;
(*b*) The money;
(*c*) Other policy considerations.

Most foreign direct investment is undertaken for market reasons, to develop or protect a company's sales. This elementary point is often overlooked. If a company goes abroad exclusively for financial reasons, it becomes a portfolio investor. The knowledge required to appraise a foreign market is discussed in almost every chapter of this book. It concerns judgments about the acceptability of products in other cultures and political systems as well as calculations about market potential and market share. One specifically international consideration has already been mentioned, the demographic. Most countries have numerous groups of people with varying degrees of affluence and different requirements within their boundaries. The structure of the population is likely to be quite different from that of the home country, and this is a trap in market appraisal. Calculations about market share and promotional allocations will follow once the structure of the local population has been understood. The costs of supplying and servicing the market will then be calculated and some point determined at which the marketing considerations dictate 'invest'.

At this point, financial considerations may still say 'No'. The capital may not be available, or not available on suitable terms or at a suitable price. The formal procedures for investment appraisal are not greatly different from those of domestic appraisal[11] except for the calculations that concern currency exchange, variable interest rates, and tax. These are considered in chapter 7.

3.3 The foreign selling subsidiary[12]

The inadequacy of existing arrangements stimulate the establishment of foreign selling subsidiaries. These inadequacies may be seen as a result of failures whereby the present methods are not gaining or retaining an adequate market share; the same result may come from successes which have strained the present resources or made the local market vulnerable. The arrangements may also have become inadequate because of changes among suppliers, competitors or customers. An accurate appraisal of this point will depend on:

(1) The supply of raw materials and components.
(2) Adequate knowledge of the market, its present as well as its potential size and structure.
(3) Assumptions about the strength of competitors and their likely reactions to the proposed move.

It is this last point that can be especially difficult in foreign business. Domestically, even if there is no collusion with competitors, much is known about their businesses and their staffs and the limits they have for manoeuvre; much less will be known about foreign competitors and the assumptions on which they base their business decisions.

A number of characteristics of the product make at least a selling subsidiary more likely; some of these also apply to manufacturing subsidiaries, but not all. For instance a local corporate presence, at least in a given industry, may make a selling subsidiary necessary in the capital goods industry where the products are of a 'one off' nature, or take the form of complete systems, or where the amount of capital involved is low. By low is meant in proportion to sales or as perceived by the supplier or the customer. Where the product is relatively simple to assemble, but has some highly sophisticated components, part manufacture locally is possible. These conditions alone are unlikely to persuade a company to invest locally, especially in heavy capital goods, unless some of the other conditions mentioned below are fulfilled.

Where product installation or after sales service or both are required, there is an incentive for establishing a local subsidiary whatever the industry group. Another range of incentives is provided by the need for close control in such matters as: the transfer of funds by whatever means, market penetration, information retrieval, sales and so on. A selling subsidiary is also likely to emerge where credibility is important. An example of this is in a company which sells dangerous chemicals for further manufacture. Yet another type of incentive is where a regional policy makes commercial sense in view of trading agreements, customs unions, cultural or political affinities. In this case, naturally, the local subsidiary needs a regional authority. In a consumer goods company a selling subsidiary is more likely to be a stage in the development of a manufacturing subsidiary as the market grows and the other considerations become important.

3.4 The manufacturing subsidiary

'We've got ourselves boxed into a situation where there's no room for manoeuvre.' This remark was made by a manager of a company which had established foreign manufacture in a small country with considerable government assistance by way of investment grants. The projected expansion had failed to take place and the subsidiary had been a persistent loss-maker. The circumstances of the original move, as well as the possible effect in other markets, made it hard to contemplate withdrawal. Most international executives regard a foreign investment as a permanent commitment. Withdrawal or rationalization is much more difficult than in the case of a domestic unit. The frustration is often compounded by the fact that the problems that actually arise are often unanticipated and are faced by managers who were not involved in the original decisions.

The motives for foreign manufacture have already been discussed as well as the precautions which have to be taken. The motives listed did not include companies which have to be foreign investors because of the nature of their business. This applies to most service industries like banking, transport, retailing, although not necessarily construction and consultancy services. Companies in extraction and plantation businesses also have been international in the past, although this is an area where disinvestment is taking place. Apart from these considerations, any examination of international investors demonstrates the large number of activities covered. Some assets, for example high technology, may be held to give the international investor particular advantages, but no industry group seems to be omitted and the search for business in different economic climates and the defence of markets may be sufficient reason for this.[13]

3.5 The ownership on the foreign subsidiary

Direct foreign investment includes any financial commitment abroad where there is management as well as ownership provided by the holder of the equity. This definition covers numerous different situations, and may even include an agent in a foreign country where the parent company inserts management expertise in return for some financial support. In the normal course of business examples of a proportion of ownership as low as 10% with some management control are not hard to find. Management contract arrangements go down to zero equity, of course, but different considerations apply. Companies which habitually invest abroad with minority holdings usually develop methods of retaining control over their essential inputs and of any business activities regarded as critical.

A subsidiary (as understood here, other words may be used such as affiliate or associate) can have any percentage of equity holding from the parent company. For purposes of analysis less than 50%, 50% or over 50% are the usual points of classification. Any arrangement of less than 100% can be with one or more other companies, or it can be reached by selling shares in the subsidiary on the local capital market. The joint venture, whether with other companies or with local shareholders, will have certain advantages. It can be established by buying a company which has existing facilities and its own market. The risk of the venture is reduced in proportion to the size of the local holding, and the ability of the company to invest in other markets is increased. The risk may be further reduced by the greater political acceptability of the joint venture and its more local appearance where this is important. In some cases local shareholding is enforced by law; the number of countries where this is so is increasing and there are almost certain to be competitive advantages for firms which can operate effectively without 100% ownership. Where other things are equal the management system which cannot accommodate local shareholders is unlikely to survive; but 'things' are not equal where advanced technology and other profitable knowledge is involved.

Companies have found substantial problems with joint ventures, as witnessed by the high casualty rate which many observers have noted.[14] Some of these difficulties go back to the choice of partner in the first place. Where the partners are of unequal size or have radically different objectives there is a special proneness to divorce. In particular entering a joint venture with an existing agent is often unsuccessful. There may be disagreements about responsibilities, and where more than one partner exercises control there may be the difficulty of putting together two incompatible management systems; nevertheless there are circumstances recorded where two supposedly 'incompatible' systems come together to make a very successful joint venture. The care which has to be taken is obvious to all parties in such a case, and the joint subsidiary may get the best of both worlds.

To the difficulties mentioned should be added another, that of ensuring a share of the profits commensurate with the effort put in. This is especially the case with a joint venture with a smaller firm. The original deal assumed that one company put in the technology, the other the marketing skills. This is a common recipe for trouble, especially where neither takes out management fees. The large foreign partner finds itself putting in marketing skills as well, and perhaps underpinning weak management. For this it is only taking out the share of the dividends that had been agreed on the assumption that it only put in technical skill. Any proposal to increase the share of the equity may be strongly resisted. Another problem is that certain policies of the parent company are constrained. These include the dividend policy which has to take account of the interests of the partner.

For all these problems, the joint venture is likely to increase and become the usual way of doing business in the future because of the political and commercial pressures.

3.6 The establishment of the foreign subsidiary

The successful act of foreign investment is usually preceded by a reappraisal of the resources available at head office and their deployment so as to derive the greatest possible benefit from the foreign developments and minimize any losses during the start-up period. This reappraisal includes a survey of: sources of finance available to the company, manpower and especially managers able to supervise the new operation both at home and abroad, the adequacy of the existing control systems, the strengths and weaknesses of the existing product range and marketing methods, existing legal and contractual arrangements which might affect the new project. These and other resources are going to be needed for the launch of the new operation, all of them probably in greater amounts than had been estimated.

Between the regulations of the home country and those of the host country, the choices of the financial structure will be limited. Fixed assets are likely to be financed by long-term funds from the parent company or from another subsidiary, while working capital will come from short-term loans raised locally with the parent company guarantee. The company will need to make adequate arrangements for bringing money home—by using the whole range of methods available.[15] These include dividends, fees, royalties and interest payments. Sometimes the use of any of these methods will depend upon prior agreement with the government of the host country; on the other hand the company will have made undertakings about repatriating profits as a condition of taking the money out of some countries.

Under the heading of manpower, the emphasis is on manpower both to control the foreign operations from the home base and to operate abroad. The subsidiary will have to be stimulated and controlled from head office as well as managed on the spot. This is done by an adequate control system as well as an adequate staff. Some of the most notable failures abroad have followed from an inadequate control system where the parent company did not get early enough warning of what was happening to take corrective action in time.[16]

On an appraisal of resources will depend the answer to another question that has to be asked—whether it is better to move into the new subsidiary by means of buying an existing company or by starting afresh. There are a number of possible advantages in buying on an existing company. Not all of them can necessarily be realized; but if a majority of them can be found in a purchasable firm then this may indicate the right route. The advantages may include: the existence of sound managers who made the company worth buying in the first place, skilled personnel, an existing sense of business purpose and morale, a valuable order book, an established market share, good relations with customers, useful sites, a satisfactory image, existing suppliers, political contacts, knowledge of the national environment and of the local market, links with local finance houses, understanding of national distribution methods and advertising channels, a low purchase price. The disadvantages of such a route to a subsidiary can include the reverse of any of those advantages. In addition local and political antagonisms may be generated. There may be trouble in integrating an established local firm into the management system of the international group. This difficulty can include control, structural, accounting and other problems. There can be difficulties with existing management, staff and trade unions. Finally the purchase may be prohibited by law.

The alternative is to start a new company. This also has advantages and disadvantages. It will be second best if a substantial number of the potential advantages of purchasing an existing company can be realized. Even so teething troubles can be expected in the subsidiary that has been bought. The new company can acquire fresh management without existing loyalties to corporate traditions. The recruitment is unrestricted, unlike the takeover situation. Indeed all decisions about the new venture can be taken in the light of relevant business considerations unimpeded by the status quo. There is less likelihood of political problems. This method will, in any case, be necessary if there is no suitable company to take over. The disadvantages of starting a new company include the lack of knowledge of the local market, the sources of finance, the culture and so on. The necessary knowledge can be acquired by hiring suitable local executives, but these may be scarce and it may be costly to lure them from competitors. The preference for buying an existing company applies to manufacturing and service subsidiaries; for the small specialized selling subsidiary a new company may be preferred unless it is possible to buy an existing agent or distributor. Where capital is in short supply, the market uncertain or political conditions dictate, a joint venture will be preferred. For all the methods timing is crucial—the stage of the trade cycle, the state of the market, the political condition of the country and other such factors affect the choice of method.

Whichever method is chosen, too, a number of requirements will need attention. One is the defining of the objectives to make maximum use of the resources of the new affiliate. This apparently commonplace statement covers one of the perplexing problem areas. Convincing definitions of objectives across frontiers depend on an understanding and rapport often difficult to achieve in a new operation. The second requirement is the provision of adequate resources. A subsidiary on a shoestring may prove a subsidiary heading for disaster. Further, adequate monitoring from the start is required. It has been found useful to insist that the subsidiary employ head office internal auditors. Clear lines of communication are needed at first between the top managers of the subsidiary and senior executives at the corporate headquarters. Informality and experimentation may come later.

Finally there needs to be a set of policies for writing off the new operation if it proves a failure. These policies may include insurance against loss of equity, placed with the home country government or a private institution where either of these is possible. If the investment is through a joint venture, some means for terminating this if the arrangement proves unworkable will be necessary. If the arrangement is 100% owned or with local shareholders, some outline of law to cope with failure will be needed. In the next chapter, disinvestment is discussed.

3.7 Suggestions for further reading

(B) BROOKE & REMMERS (1970). Chapter 9.
(A) DANIELS, OGRAM & RADEBAUGH (1976). Chapters 3 and 21.
(A) DYMSZA (1972). Chapter 8.
(C) EITEMAN & STONEHILL (1973). Chapter 10.
(B) ROBINSON (1973). Chapter 5.
(B) ROBOCK & SIMMONDS (1973). Chapter 2.
(B) SALERA (1969). Chapter 27.
(B) VERNON & WELLS (1976). Chapters 3 and 11.

For more specialized works, see the footnotes to this chapter and:

(D) ALIBER, R. Z. (1970). A theory of direct foreign investment in Kindleberger (1970).
(D) CAVES, R. E. (1971). International corporations: the industrial economics of foreign investment, *Economica*. **38.**
(C) DUNNING (1974). Chapters 2 and 3.
(D) MITCHELL, Daniel J. B. (1975). Recent changes in the labor content of US international trade, *Industrial and Labor Relations Review*, 28.3, April, pp. 355–375.
(D) HAWKINS, R. G. & WEBBINK, E. S. (undated). Theories of direct foreign investment. A survey of empirical evidence. Unpublished paper: New York University.
(D) HORST, T. (1972). The theory of the multinational firm: optimum behaviour under different tariff and tax rates, *Journal of Political Economy*, **79,** pp. 1050–1072.
(D) STOBAUGH, R. (1969). How to analyse foreign investment climates, *Harvard Business Review*, September/October.

For ownership policies and joint ventures, see:

(C) STOPFORD, J. M. & WELLS, L. T. (1972). *Managing the Multinational Enterprise*, Basic Books and Longman.

3.8 Exercises for this chapter

Case studies

Wilmot Breedon (Holdings) Ltd., 1964. (INSEAD) F–3135, ICH 9–210–117), by Bishop, J. R. A., Remmers, H. L., Smith, P. L. Overseas investment in subsidiary companies, raises general problem of a rapidly expanding organization subject to cyclical movements of the economy.

Allied Industries Corp., 1969. (INSEAD, ICH 9–213–038), by Remmers, H. L.
This case describes an opportunity for investment in a foreign country and raises the issues of financial structure, plant location, use of investment incentives, partner-choice for the venture and method of ownership control.

Zigzag Corp. USA, 1970. (California-Berkeley University, ICH 9–271–614) by Sethi, S. P.
This is a study concerning the investment feasibility for the establishment of a sewing machine operation in the UK and the Republic of Ireland.

Ransome and Marples Bearing Company Ltd., 1969. (Harvard, ICH 9–274–049), by Williams, C. M. and Ledd, E. H.
An effort is being made to rationalize the British-owned bearing industry by encouraging three companies in the industry to consolidate. The point at issue is the amount which should be offered for one company which has worked into a fine tactical position by developing another offer from a foreign competitor.

Rhodesian Selection Trust (undated). (IMEDE IB–12, ICH 9–307–136), by Brooke, P. L.
Describes position, economic growth and location of responsibility of a large industrial concern in a small underdeveloped country in Africa, 1961.

San Francisco Mines of Mexico Ltd., 1962. (IMEDE IB–19, ICH 9–307–171), by Goetschin, P. R. and Ehrenstrom, H. N.
This case of a joint venture in a developing country concerns a British company which is undergoing a process of 'Mexicanization' and is maintaining a 49% interest in its Mexican subsidiary.

Lesney Products Ltd., 1972. (Cranfield Institute of Technology, CCH 373–041–1), by Constable, C. J.
This case describes the development of the company's overseas operators from 1964 to 1972, and discusses specifically the performance of the US, Canadian and Australian subsidiaries.

YKK, 1934–73. (California State University-Hayward, ICH 9–374–823), by Moorman, N. M.
Examination of a variety of international policies developed in the Japanese multinational, Yoshida Kogyo Kabushikigaisha (YKK).

Incidents: (1) Foreign investment

VITAMORE S.A. is a Swiss Pharmaceutical company. Smaller than companies like Hoffman Laroche and Ciba Geigy, but growing rapidly thanks to the discovery of two powerful new antibiotics. Like their large competitors they now feel it is time to back their success as exporters with some foreign investment. However some major problems cause misgivings on the Board, and questions are asked as to how wise the policy is, and whether they can really achieve their objectives by foreign investment.

Some important considerations are:

(1) The company operates in three product groups:
Antibiotics, turnover $35 m
Analgaesics, turnover $45 m
Veterinary products, turnover $20 m.
Roughly 80% of the turnover in each product is export.

(2) For the more advanced products in each group, research and production were hard to separate as further developments were taking place all the time.

(3) There were numerous strong, and usually international competitors in all the product groups. Even the two new antibiotics were only expected to keep them ahead of competition for a limited period.

(4) Some of the products were manufactured in stages, which did not necessarily have to be manufactured in the same place. Some processes were simpler than others.

(5) The more sophisticated products were extremely demanding on skilled manpower, including chemical engineers and bio-chemists.

(6) A minimum viable cost in the home country for a complete plant system was $20 m, for a plant making the simpler ingredients it could be as little as $6 m.

In Switzerland there is an average turnover per worker of $35,000; but this is higher for the more sophisticated processes and much lower for the less so.

(7) The company considers that it has reached the limit of its expansion alongside powerful competitors also drawing on a limited manpower.

You are asked to draft a project plan for the 'internationalization' of VITAMORE, setting out what information you would require to make reliable proposals to the Board.

(2) The foreign selling subsidiary

Camford and Cross Ltd., manufactured machinery for the textile industry. They had a large and increasing market in the Far East. This market was serviced by travelling salesmen, led by members of the Board and divisional directors. These sold major plant installations. Routine sales of spare parts and servicing enquiries were attended to direct by the technical department at head office. The company was finding the going increasingly hard. Most of their competitors had a full-time presence in that part of the world. This enabled them to keep a closer watch on possible contracts, and to get quick feedback on developments in a region where rapid technical changes were taking place. They also had a number of separate and unco-ordinated projects subject to little control.

The situation led the Directors to consider establishing a selling subsidiary somewhere in the Far East, but there was strong opposition to this. It was said that to set up a subsidiary was an expensive and unnecessary complication for such a company. They should put all their resources into salesmen. Further, it was pointed out that their sales were in many countries, and in no one country often enough to support a local operation. It was also urged that what business there was was of two different sorts (the contracts and the sale of parts), and this fragmentation made a subsidiary even less worthwhile.

Eventually the Board agreed to seek advice, and especially the answers to the following questions:

(1) Would it make sense to establish a subsidiary in one country which would provide a sales and service centre for the region?

(2) If so, what would be a possible region? (e.g. should Australia and Japan be included?).

(3) What criteria should determine which country (or countries) is chosen?

3.9 Questions for discussion

(1) Discuss the general propositions which, in your view, make a theory of international investment.

(2) What are important reasons for the establishment of a foreign selling subsidiary?

(3) An international retailing company has asked your advice on the possibility of using its knowhow and business techniques in other countries of the EEC. Draft a memorandum on this subject as an outside adviser on international business.

(4) What are the advantages and disadvantages of 100% ownership of the foreign subsidiary? Discuss your answer in the light of possible options.

(5) Outline the major economic theories that purport to explain the causes of foreign investment and give a critical analysis of any one of them.

(6) How should elementary guidelines on the appraisal of large capital projects be modified to cover multinational operations and their uncertainties?

(7) What political considerations would you take into account when selecting between more or less similar, but alternative, capital investments located abroad?

(8) A machinery manufacturer with a turnover of £150 m is considering the future of its extensive operations abroad. Hitherto manufacturing subsidiaries have only been developed in industrialized countries where 100% ownership was possible. In the less industrialized countries there are licensing and agency agreements. The company has recently developed some new products considered to have great growth potential, but cash and other resources are limited. A number of ideas are being canvassed around the company—joint ventures, management contracts, rationalization and others. A member of the Chairman's staff has been asked to produce a memorandum for the Board advising on policies and the reasons for adopting them. Write the memorandum for him.

4 Disinvestment

4.1 The subject outlined

A commitment to an individual facility abroad may be harder to alter than a similar commitment at home, but the figures for disinvestment are increasing rapidly as the tables in this chapter show. Through the limited studies of this issue carried out so far it can be seen to be increasingly significant in international business. One of the reasons why it has proved a difficult subject to collect information on is that executives of companies are reluctant to discuss disinvestment which carries a strong suggestion of failure. Naturally some examples of disinvestment do result from failure, others are the result of hostile action by a foreign government and any discussion is politically sensitive. Much withdrawal is of neither of these types, it represents a change of strategy involving a partial or total withdrawal from one commitment in order to put more resources into another. Yet another reason may be the move to more foreign business without so much investment, like the licensing schemes or management contracts outlined in chapter 2. Whichever reason for withdrawal is considered, it can be undertaken in a planned way and lead to satisfactory results, or the reverse can happen.

The word 'disinvestment' is here taken to cover three different activities:

(1) *Rationalization.* That is the removal of facilities from one country to another in order to improve efficiency. This is not an easy operation within a country. It can be more difficult across frontiers. Equally it can be necessary as it is unlikely that the arrangements made when an investment is first undertaken will be permanently suitable; in particular multi-product companies have the chance of concentrating production in particular countries without overall disinvestment. Whichever method is adopted, steps have to be taken to ensure that the rationalization measures can be piloted through the various hurdles that are produced by exchange control regulations, local opposition and the operation of guarantees. On the other hand, some government demands may be easier to meet after the changes have taken place. These include the development of exports, but this exercise entails considerable planning.

(2) *Voluntary disinvestment.* This includes total or partial withdrawal

from a facility. If the withdrawal is total and not part of a rationalization measure, it will be because of unprofitability or because the money is required elsewhere. If the withdrawal is partial, it will be by the sale of shares in the local subsidiary to the local investor. One likely reason for this is, of course, to reduce the shareholding before such a move is made compulsory. Undoubtedly some companies have seen competitive advantages in selling shares ahead of government instructions to do so. Others have done this as part of a planned expansion. The sale of shares in a local subsidiary has strengthened their impact in the country concerned and the money repatriated has permitted development elsewhere.

(3) *Involuntary disinvestment.* This is the aspect of the subject which is most discussed. A number of countries have adopted measures of nationalization or localization which involve the takeover of foreign firms, and perhaps local ones as well. Certain sectors of the economy are likely to remain closed to the foreign investor in many countries, other sectors close and reopen as the country concerned passes through political or economic upheavals. Some companies have adopted a strategy of holding or until their position is no longer tenable; or they may retain any possible commercial links with the country concerned in order to demonstrate their readiness to reactivate the business if the situation changes. A number of countries in recent years have alternated between the expropriation and the encouragement of the foreign firm.

Some companies have met the threat or reality of compulsory takeover by moving to one of the other possible methods of doing business suggested in chapter 2. Management services contracts and other knowhow agreements, it has already been said, provide an acceptable means of doing business in many circumstances where investment is no longer permitted or is too risky.

Among those who have researched the subject in detail is Jagdish C. Sachdev and the following passage is an excerpt from his work. It is based on a small sample of British companies and indicates the most important issues that arise.

4.2 Disinvestment: a corporate failure or a strategic success?[1]

Today the trend towards disinvestment is becoming an increasingly important fact of life for multinational companies all over the world, and has wide implications for international business. Whether compelled by the attitudes and actions of host governments, or dictated by the parent company's own appraisal of its subsidiary's performance overseas, the multinational company is faced with a new challenge—how best to cope with the problems of disinvestment. Although the management of multinational companies may tend to consider their enterprises as 'eternal', recent findings reveal a natural running down process even in those areas where there has been an absence of any of the hostility which has recently characterized some host governments.

In the past, problems of disinvestment have not had to be faced by multinational companies on so vast a scale. Now this is proving to be a phenomenon which calls for new thinking and new attitudes on the part of corporate as well as subsidiary managements. Observers[2] have forecast that the 1970s promised to be the decade of divestitures at national as well as at international level. The first half of this decade has already proved some truth in the above statement. For example, as Fig. 4.1 shows, in 1971 there were 87 cases of British foreign disinvestments against 184 American.[3] Although it is difficult to put any definite financial figure on these cases due to lack of any published statistics, it is expected that they run into large sums. However, Fig. 4.2 gives a good indication of the sums involved in British foreign disinvestment.

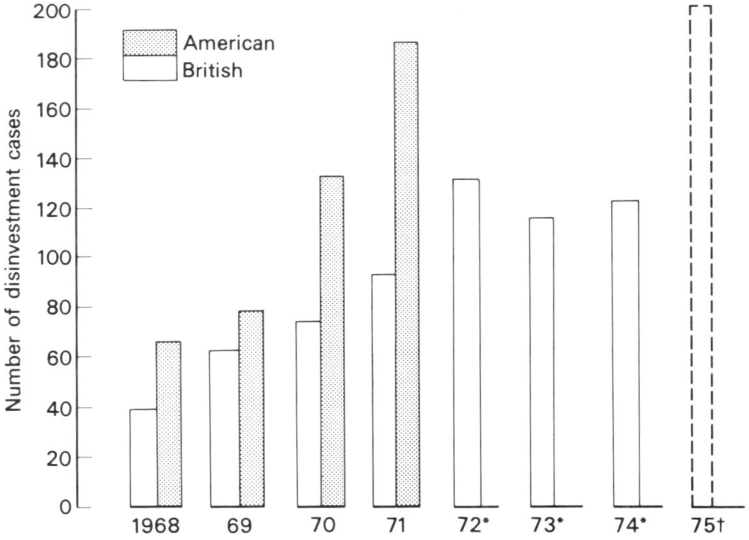

Fig. 4.1 British and American cases of foreign investment from 1968–75.

* American data after 1971 is not available.

† British data for 1975 is an estimation.

For present purposes disinvestment is defined as 'a reduction of ownership percentage in an active direct investment on a voluntary or involuntary basis'. Within this definition come those foreign operations which employ local citizens for the production of goods. Only those multinational companies which have tangible interests in the host countries are included. Covered are complete or partial sales or the liquidation of current operations as well as expropriation and nationalization.

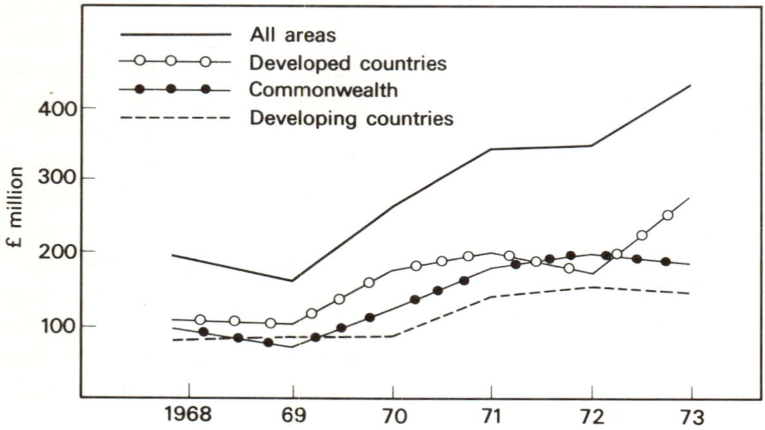

Fig. 4.2 British foreign investment. *Source*: Department of Trade and Industry UK.

There may be several factors which influence or force a multinational company to decide to disinvest. These factors can be categorized under two main headings:

Rationalization of resources—voluntary disinvestment

Briefly, this category encompasses all those cases of disinvestment partial or absolute, for which the company's own decisions are responsible. For example, a multinational may decide to disinvest a particular foreign operation on the basis of unsatisfactory profit performance or a lack of management and liquid resources. Failure in communications between the corporate management and the foreign subsidiary management may also be an important factor in persuading the company to disinvest. A further factor, rationalization of the company's resources, can play a vital role directly or indirectly in disinvestment. Also the sale of shares can be used to support high growth projects and low market share projects as well.

European and American and now Japanese multinationals have been expanding their foreign investment at a significant rate, in some cases as much as 10% a year. Against the background of such a record of foreign investment, some recent findings reveal that multinationals are entering upon a new era of consolidation with the prospect of decelerating growth rates in the years ahead.[4] Such findings are supported by several other studies[5] in the related fields of international trade which explicitly indicate that, following a decade of accelerated expansion abroad, United States based multinational companies are likely to undertake major structural regroupings and reorganizations. This trend in United States companies, also applicable to European multinationals, may call for a contraction of overseas operations. The governments of various host countries are expected to play a more powerful role through their policies on localization and nationalization, forcing the multinationals to adopt such actions.

The decision by a multinational company to eliminate a part or all of its ownership in a foreign country, on a voluntary basis, may affect many interest groups within the company and the host government. It may appear to present to potential shareholders that an unwise investment has been made by corporate management. And within corporate management the identification of any failure in a foreign venture, may result in an altered international expansion plan, or even the abandonment of future international projects.

Whatever the reason for disinvestment on a voluntary basis, a number of criteria may be used to identify a possible candidate. For example, the financial, organizational, technological, political or social aspects of a particular foreign operation may influence the company to consider disinvestment.

Involuntary disinvestment

Under this category come cases where the foreign investor has little choice other than being taken over by the host government through nationalization, expropriation or confiscation. Expropriation of foreign property is a modern phenomenon which has its roots in historical forces. These include Communism, Nationalism, land reform, and the results of economic development.[6] These four factors may be interlinked in some instances of expropriation, but independent in others.

From the host country's point of view, it may be said that in the last quarter of a century or so, most developing countries have seen their development plans as dependent upon outside assistance. This assistance has normally come from the governments of the developed countries in the form of foreign aid, and also from multinational companies in the form of foreign investment. Most developing countries have taken various forms of foreign aid for granted as a regular source of income, and thereby a majority of their plans are based on this. One may then question the consequences of the absence of such foreign aid. For example, in Sri Lanka in 1970 and Pakistan in 1971, net British investment was negative—that is, more funds were taken out than put in by British multinational companies;[7] this affected the national development plans seriously.

Developing countries that base their plans on foreign investment may not be inclined to sit and watch the foreign investment going out of their countries, or further foreign investment not coming in.[8] Two questions may arise in this context. Firstly, whether it is the host government policy or intention to encourage disinvestment and discourage investment? Secondly, if this is not the case, what measures are being taken by these governments to put a check on such matters? Studies carried out on this situation in respect of various countries show that generally nationalization of some sectors of industry is causing concern among foreign investors involved in other sectors of industry. This either puts some sort of a brake on further investment, or gives incentives for withdrawal of the existing foreign stakes.

It is not argued here that the host government should not consider the issue of nationalization of a particular sector of industry when foreign investment is involved. But that the effect on other sectors should be taken into consideration at the same time. In the present context only those cases of involuntary disinvestment are considered which are due to nationalization or expropriation resulting from ordinary political risks prevalent in host countries.

A host government may apply similar criteria to those used by the companies to identify suitable candidates for disinvestment and not necessarily through nationalization or expropriation. These criteria include the economic position along with the government's intentions to acquire control over ownership, management or technology of foreign owned business or social or political pressures.

Now if we turn to the present study in respect of British foreign disinvestment, it is clear from Fig. 4.3 that, although British gross and net foreign investments are on the increase, the gap between the two is also widening. This gap is termed the 'disinvestment gap'. For the purpose of analysis the range of factors responsible are considered very briefly in four groups.

It seems from the results that the companies are more concerned with the financial aspects of operations when deciding to carry out a particular disinvestment. Within the whole range of financial factors, the one which received the highest ranking score is low profitability and losses. The second and third in rank are commercial difficulties with restrictions on fund transfer by the host government followed by risks and uncertainties prevalent in that particular country. The position of other financial factors are shown in Fig. 4.4.

When analysing each factor individually on its importance to the company, it is observed that there are two distinct groups. Factors (a), (b), (c) and (d) appear in the high score group, and the rest in the low

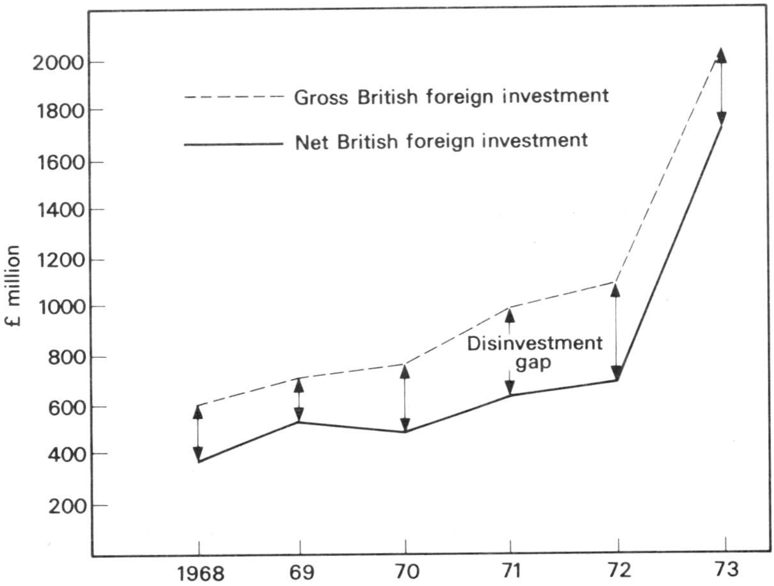

Fig. 4.3 The disinvestment gap. *Source*: Department of Trade and Industry, UK. The figures are slightly distorted by the repayment of loans.

score group. It is interesting to note that all the factors in the former group tend to be connected with the profitability of a particular investment. The factors belonging to the low score group, although they may affect profitability performance in general, represent various financial difficulties. The lowest ranking place is given to factor (l), withdrawal of incentives by the host government. The companies do take the effects of various incentives into account at the appraisal stage of a new investment or acquisition, but the withdrawal of such incentives does not give companies any substantial disadvantage causing that particular operation to be considered as a disinvestment case. Firstly, withdrawal of incentives does not affect the company in isolation, its competitors may be equally affected. Secondly, after a few years of operations, companies tend to incorporate the positive effects of these incentives into their general performance.

Organization. Irrespective of their profit performance more than one third of the companies interviewed were having organizational difficulties, prior to disinvestment, but these were not necessarily with the subsidiaries which they divested. The main constituents of these difficulties were failure in communication channels, and some disagreements in the general policies of the parent companies towards various foreign subsidiaries. Seven companies specifically reported that

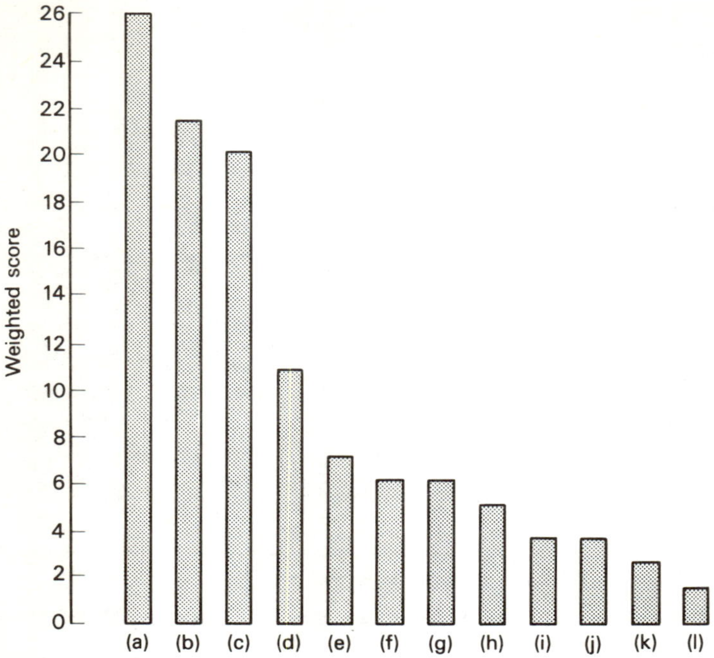

Fig. 4.4 Financial factors responsible for foreign disinvestment.

Key (a) Low profitability and losses; (b) Commercial difficulties; (c) Restriction in fund transfer; (d) Risks and uncertainties in the host country; (e) Licensing difficulties; (f) Better prospects elsewhere and fund raising; (g) Shortage of liquid resources; (h) Competition; (i) Other reasons; (j) Foreign exchange difficulties; (k) Production constraints; (l) Withdrawal of incentives.

in the pre-disinvestment period there were conflicts of varying nature and degree between the corporate management and foreign subsidiary management. The number of visits to that particular subsidiary by the person in charge at corporate headquarters increased many times in the pre-disinvestment period.

There have also been seven cases in which subsidiary managements were having some organizational difficulties with the host governments and two with local trade unions. The major elements with these difficulties are policies on staffing and expansion of operations. Three out of these seven cases specifically contributed in conjunction with financial aspects to bringing about disinvestment situations.

Technology. Only one case has emerged in this sample where the decision to disinvest was taken because the technology was becoming obsolete and the company was not allowed to bring in new technology. Actually the restriction upon new technology by the host government was used by the company as a main reason for disinvestment, but the company had been losing heavily in this particular foreign operation.

Factors for involuntary disinvestment

There were only two clear cases of involuntary disinvestment due to nationalization and localization in the selection studied. These were cases where the host government had to take such steps due to internal pressure by the general public demanding localization of foreign owned operations. An interesting feature of involuntary disinvestment is that seven other companies also reported that the host government's intentions encouraged the companies to think about disinvestment as did demands to dilute control by the foreign company over management, ownership and technology. If the companies were already suffering losses, with no better prospects in sight, they took the opportunity to bring their operations to an end. This happened in developing as well as developed countries.

The second area of the enquiry deals with the structure of the parent company, the state of industry in the host country, and the degree of integration and relationship between the parent company, the foreign subsidiary and the host government. It is again subdivided into different groups for the purpose of analysis:

The parent company

When looking into the organization structure of the companies it is observed that 13 out of 21 had some sort of geographical organization structure to run their overseas operations. This was either an overseas holding company, or an international division headed by a divisional manager or director. As a distinctive feature of this type of structure[9] a block in communications within the corporate management was observed during the investigation. Although this international division appeared to have a group of managers with skills and knowledge relevant to the overseas operations, there were also the formal relations between the corporate staff and the staff of the international division. This, in certain ways, hindered the possibility of using skills from each other. Figure 4.5 indicates the organizational structure of the remaining eight companies. However, it is interesting to see that the eight companies which said they did have special communication difficulties within head office used the geographical type structure.

Companies having a functional organization were either operating in one foreign country, or had only one more foreign manufacturing operation, or had no more foreign manufacturing activities left after this particular disinvestment.

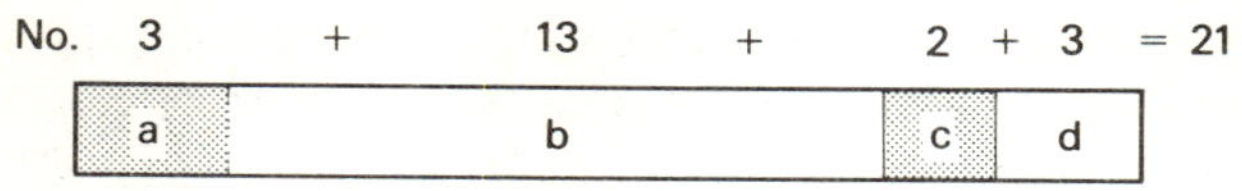

Fig. 4.5 Organization structure of parent companies.
Key (a) Functional; (b) Geographical; (c) Product-group; (d) Matrix.

Relationship

In general terms it may be appropriate to state at this stage that foreign operations involved 'strained' relations in most of the companies. As Fig. 4.6 indicates, six companies were reported to have 'strained' relations with the host governments, and eight with the local trade unions. These companies were asked by various ministries dealing with taxation, excise, development and planning, to prepare substantial documentation, in addition to the normal requirement from all foreign companies, for the purpose of special investigations. Until all such investigations were completed, which could take up to twenty-four months, all decisions by host government officials on other matters were held in abeyance. Similarly local trade unions put forward demands which were 'impractical' in the companies' opinion during the pre-disinvestment period, and were likely to work to rule until such demands were met.

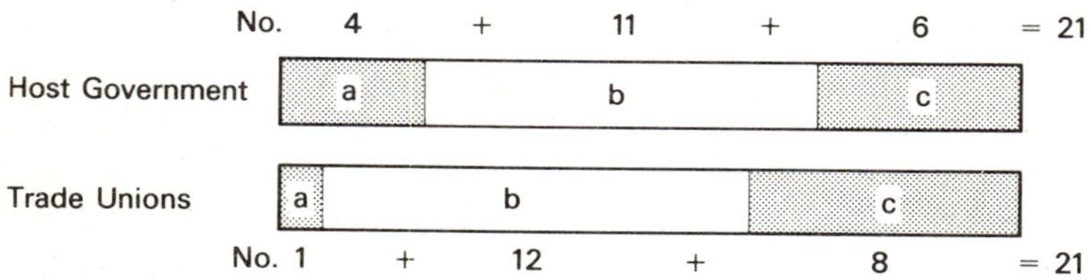

Fig. 4.6 Relationship with host government and trade unions.
Key (a) Pleasant; (b) Normal; (c) Strained.

It is difficult to get a clear picture of the relationships which these companies were having overseas, but it can be said strongly that the pre-disinvestment period of the operations in question is marked by industrial unrest and a high level of correspondence from the relevant department of the host government.

State of industry in the host country

The only results which are of any relevance in the present context are shown in Fig. 4.7, which indicates the stage of development of the industry in the host country in which these 21 companies were operating at the time of investment and disinvestment.

When the market share of these companies is analysed, it is interesting to see that six companies (nearly 29%) decided to disinvest their particular foreign operation even after having a virtual monopoly in the market. The whole sample is well spread in terms of market share. Eight companies had a market share less than 25%; six from 25–50% and seven from 51% to monopoly situations.

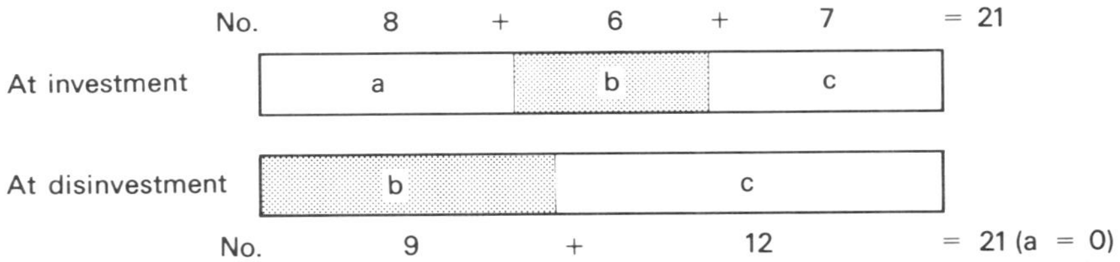

Fig. 4.7 State of industry in host countries.
Key (a) At infancy stage; (b) At intermediate stage; (c) At well developed stage.

The next sections deals with the policies adopted by multinational companies on the question of disinvestment, and also the resources available to deal with the situation both within and outside the companies. It also links into the implementation of such policies, if any, and the whole process of decision making.

Before considering policies and their implementation, it will be valuable to discuss briefly the pattern of ownership at the start of these particular foreign operations, and the subsequent pattern at the time of disinvestment. These are shown in Fig. 4.8. Eleven companies (53%) began foreign operations with wholly owned subsidiaries, while six (28%) and four (19%) companies began as majority and minority owners respectively. A quite different pattern emerged at the time of dis-

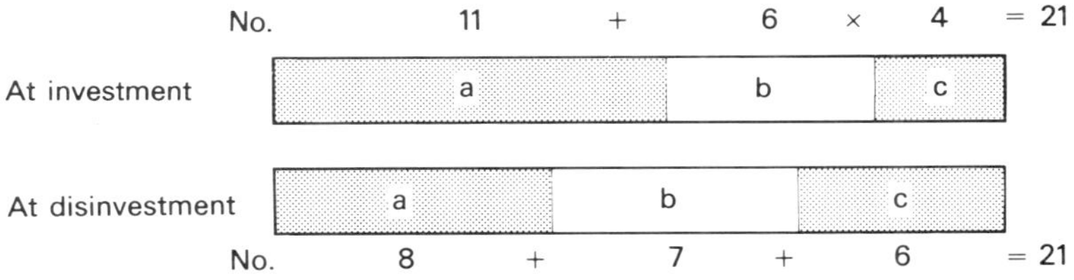

Fig. 4.8 Ownership pattern in host country.
Key (a) Wholly-owned, 95% or more; (b) Majority-owned, 50%–95%; (c) Minority-owned, less than 50%.

investment. For example the wholly owned fell from 53% to 38% while the majority as well as the minority owned increased by 6% and 9% respectively.

The drop in the wholly owned category arises from the pressures by the host government for the dilution of ownership and the hedging measures taken against risks and uncertainties prevalent in the host countries.

The policies themselves can be divided into five categories, of which those in our study came mainly into the first two. The five are:

(i) no disinvestment policy or experience;
(ii) no disinvestment policy, but some experience, with no constant pattern;
(iii) no policy, but management had experience with various types of disinvestment, and has developed a consistent pattern of action;
(iv) a formal overall corporate disinvestment policy has been developed, but has been ignored at some or all levels of the organization;
(v) a formal corporate disinvestment policy exists with corresponding divisional policies being implemented throughout the organization when and where necessary.

Although eight companies did report that they came into category (iv) if not (v), after critical questioning there is no doubt in the author's mind that these companies can be classed only between (ii) and (iii) because they had no formal policy on disinvestment, but did have some experience of voluntary disinvestment. Either no consistent pattern was recognizable from previous disinvestments or, more probably, the companies were not able to develop or perceive any consistent pattern. Most of these companies do not have policies specifically concerned with disinvestment. Only one company, after having three cases of voluntary disinvestment in 1974, started work on the formulation of definite policies for the future.

Eleven of the other 13 either had no policy or no previous experience of foreign disinvestment. In comparative terms these companies took less time in decision making, and also less time in implementation. The reasons for this appear to be threefold. Firstly these companies were in no position to sustain heavy losses from the operations in question, secondly these companies had limited resources, especially financial, and were keen to re-employ disinvested proceeds elsewhere in profitable projects; and thirdly, they were smaller in overseas activities and they did not want to let talk of withdrawal occupy the minds of shareholders, employees and management of other subsidiaries, and so were anxious to close the disinvestment chapter quickly. The lack of resources and capabilities in these companies is also reflected by their realization of compensation or selling price. Nine out of 13 reported that, in their opinion, the compensation or selling price paid to them was neither prompt, adequate or effective. They had to accept any concrete offer made to them.

Another feature of this section is the location of responsibility for taking the decision and its implementation. In the case of 17 (81%) companies the decision was taken by the chairman of the parent company. In the same number of cases its implementation was carried out by a person or team of persons from the parent company, appointed by the chairman, without any consultation with the management of the foreign operations. In one case only did foreign management take part in the decision making, and was mainly responsible for it. At the implementation stage only four companies involved the management of foreign operations in the process. In no case were outside consultants used. More than ten companies asked the author about the existence of any expertise in this area.

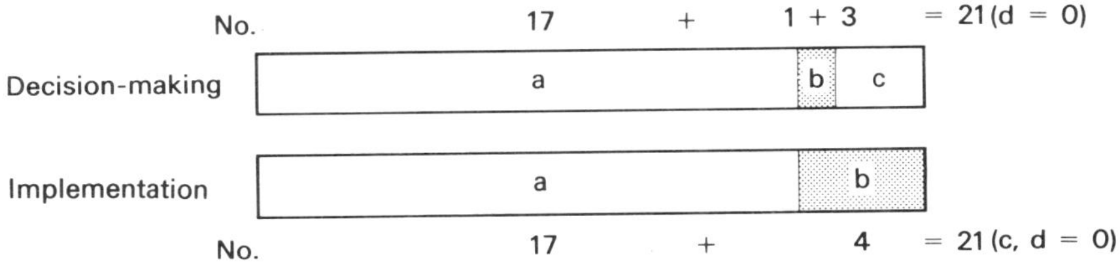

Fig. 4.9 Disinvestment decision-making and implementation.
Key (a) Parent company board; (b) Foreign management; (c) Outside consultant; (d) Host government.

This study suggests that as far as the management of the British multinationals is concerned, the whole process of corporate decision making for disinvestment appears to be at an embryonic stage of development. Their American counterparts are in no way better. One of the main reasons for this lack of progress is, perhaps, the 'closed' attitude of the management who consider disinvestment nothing but a failure. The whole secretive atmosphere in which decisions on disinvestment and their implementation are taken, along with the typical attitude of management, prevents the top as well as other managers lower down the line from learning from their and others' mistakes. Involvement of personalities throughout the life of a particular investment from its inception is another hindrance to rational consideration. This also strengthens the case within the company against using outside consultants. Among other reasons are: poor investment appraisal at the time of original investment or acquisition; too little involvement of management at lower levels in the organization and of the host and parent governments when making such important decisions.

Finally, it is concluded that multinationals in general and British multinationals in particular are ill-prepared and ill-equipped to deal with the problems of foreign disinvestment.

4.3 Suggestions for further reading

Most of the limited number of papers published on this subject are mentioned in the footnotes to which reference should be made. See especially KAPOOR & GRUB (1972), chapter 32–33. Reference should also be made to TORNEDEN, ROGER L. (1975). *Foreign Disinvestment by US Multinational Corporations*, Praeger. This book contains some case studies.

Case study

Expropriation of Alcan's Bauxite Mining Subsidiary, A–E, Harvard, ICH 9–375–661,2,3,4,5, by J. F. Truitt.
An account of the takeover of a foreign company in Guyana.

4.4 Questions for discussion

(1) What are the circumstances which signal to a company that a disinvestment needs to be considered? Discuss in some detail one of the circumstances in the light of economic or other social science theory.
(2) Outline a strategy for meeting a threat of expropriation in an important market for a company in an industry group of your own choice.
(3) Discuss some of the problems likely to be encountered in a rationalization programme across frontiers.
(4) Discuss disinvestment situations in various industry groups and foreign markets with respect to obsolete technology.
(5) You are asked to advise an electrical goods company with factories making similar products in seven different European countries. Write a memorandum on the possible opportunities for rationalization and the difficulties that may be expected.

5 International Corporate Planning

5.1 Planning for the large and small firm operating abroad

The title of this chapter conjures up a process of questioning, of exploration and at the same time of learning. Like other management processes, this is going on all the time whether those involved realize the fact or not. It is not uncommon to hear executives say that they started planning in their company at a specific time, say five years ago. A specific activity, a bundle of techniques, is meant; the formalizing of something that has always happened. An outline of the subject will make the point clear.

For many companies it does not make sense to separate the foreign from the domestic planning, but nor do other distinctions make any better sense and for the purposes of this book the specifically international activity is being identified. International corporate planning is here taken to include:

(1) The development of long-range plans and strategies for the company as a whole. This includes the development of a broad understanding of where the company is going in terms of products and markets.

(2) The search for special opportunities for realizing the objectives of the company outside its home country. Thus a company sets itself an objective of, say, 10% a year compound growth of sales. It soon becomes obvious that this is unobtainable in the domestic market, and so foreign operations are stimulated.

(3) A constant survey of present and possible foreign markets to ensure that the most satisfactory method of operation is used.

(4) A continuing survey of the operation abroad of the various functions of the company and the relationships with foreign collaborators and subsidiaries.

(5) A continuing survey of the resources available outside the home country and their most profitable allocation.

It will readily be seen that these activities constantly occur in a company; they are necessary for survival. The use of formal procedures is less common.

To carry out the planning function there are a number of requirements including:

(i) Some guidelines on the policies and objectives of the company.
(ii) Forecasting skills.
(iii) Establishing relationships with the other departments of the company, both at home and abroad.
(iv) Drawing up a list of guidelines for responding to opportunities that may be suggested to the company. Most international developments come as a result of the company responding to outside stimuli, and one frequent cause of failure is the lack of considered criteria for judging opportunities when they arise. This lack is a frequent source of problems.

International companies have been put together in different ways, and the position from which the company starts its formal planning procedures will vary according to the background. Let us examine briefly a few typical situations:

Company A is a small firm manufacturing specialized machinery components with some export, otherwise no foreign business. This company will not be able to engage in any elaborate forecasting. It can still develop an outline of the most likely markets which might be entered abroad and the most profitable routes to enter them. The company's international planning is not separate from the domestic, but one executive has been detailed to watch for opportunities abroad.

Company B is a larger firm but still middle-sized. The company developed abroad in a number of product groups put together by mergers. The domestic management of each product group managed its divisional affairs worldwide. The main priority of the international planning was some rationalization of facilities. The company is in process of establishing a separate corporate planning department at head office which will co-ordinate some of the currently independent international activities and search for new opportunities not strictly within the view of the present divisions.

Company C has grown the other way round, but is of similar size to Company B although most of the products are consumer goods rather than industrial as in both companies A and B. This company has always had a co-ordinated drive abroad and has established a number of subsidiaries. The main concern of international planning has become some form of rationalization across frontiers designed to improve the return on investment from the foreign operations.

Company D is a large, well-established international chemical firm, in both consumer and producer goods. This company has developed a large corporate planning department which is surveying world opportunities regularly. The principal interest is to look for new products, and to assess the relationship of the new products to established ones.

These companies have quite different objectives and purposes in any international planning they may undertake. Whether the steps taken are regarded as successful or not will depend upon the same criterion for all of them: are the company's resources being developed to the best advantage?

Answering this question is probably the most important activity of international corporate planning however conducted. The answer includes a concern that the various operations of the company shall fit together for the general good, and any new areas undertaken shall be judged by their synergistic relationship to those already there. This aspect is taken up in the excerpt in this chapter.

The answers to these first two questions—about the deployment of resources and the achievement of synergy with and between existing activities—are linked closely with a third about where the company shows the greatest ability at making profits. The answer will eventually be couched in terms of a set of criteria for judging opportunities. Almost every executive questioned agreed that the main activity in international planning is to formulate means of choosing between possibilities. In practice, whatever the literature may suggest, planning is usually a responsive activity. Once any contracts are made abroad, offers and proposals begin to come in. The company which has not developed a set of criteria will be accepting some opportunities which then prove incompatible with other developments. Of course this does not mean that the company will be entirely responsive, but that there is a great need for a sense of direction and an analysis of corporate strength so as to ensure that the future is not damaged for a short-term advantage which may well be more apparent than real.

The criteria can include stages for product as well as geographical diversification. The company may well want to increase its business in selected foreign markets to reduce its dependence on the trade cycle in any one country. This is a common policy, especially in companies which are most prone to movements in the local economy such as building and construction equipment. At the same time the search for new products will go on abroad as well as at home. A company, for instance, that is in a low margin type of business and in a particularly competitive environment may well look for higher profits in a different country.

In a small company this may be the limit of the ambitions of the international planner—criteria for limited geographical and product diversification together with an understanding of the best methods of doing the required business in the selected markets. For a large company there will be more detailed studies of potential markets and probable changes as well as an appreciation of where innovation is likely to come from and what will be its long-term effects on the firm.

Two other activities will exist in some degree in most firms. One is a means of judging risk in entering new countries. Here the small firm often has a dilemma. The certain competitive risks that arise from entering an industrialized market have to be set against the uncertain political risks of the less developed country. For new investment there will be the possibility of investment insurance. One of the arguments used for this type of insurance, which is promoted by government agencies in most industrialized countries, was that it would encourage small firms to invest in less competitive markets. Of course if the small firm has a specialized small niche in a domestic market that is otherwise dominated by a few giants, it may be able to find a similar situation abroad; but in this case careful investigation is needed, the similarity may be more apparent than real. The larger firm may well prefer to develop the richer industrialized markets as rapidly as possible. If it does go into developing countries with their future potential and their present high returns, it may prefer small investments in a number of countries to minimize the political risks. This is the sort of option less open to the small firm.

Another activity is the anticipation of what happens when the plans are carried out, the implications of the plans for the deployment of resources. The financing of the scheme, for example, is a crucial part of the scheme itself. The availability of finance at a reasonable rate may have been the final consideration which determined one country rather than another. There needs to be carefully thought out liaison with each department—finance, marketing, production, personnel—to ensure that the plans are put into effect.

The firm which is large enough to have its own planning departments will require special techniques for its international planning. These will include:

(*a*) *Forecasting techniques*, the ability to listen to what is happening in the environment. This activity proves most difficult in practice, and the discontinuities in the environment make forecasting even more suspect. Nevertheless, it is essential.

(*b*) *Management techniques*, the ability to listen to what is going on inside the company. This activity includes both the development of new techniques and the monitoring and co-ordinating of planning across departmental and divisional lines. Inside the firm it is an activity of a political nature and many of those concerned regard it as their principal task.

(*c*) *Global views and local initiatives*. This is a significant dilemma of all international planning, not just in companies where there is a specialized staff for the purpose. The relationship between taking a global view of the firm's opportunities and the individual foreign subsidiaries is bound to be difficult. To some extent the relationship will depend on the company's view of itself. A conglomerate will have a different relationship from a tightly integrated chemical company. But to a greater extent it has been found there are numerous centrifugal forces operating. These are discussed elsewhere in this book, but they are often activated by a central planning function.

(*d*) *Quantification of Proposals*. This is especially complicated, for international planners dealing in different currencies with their varying potential for devaluation or revaluation, inadequate local statistics, and other such problems. The figures have to be interpreted within the accuracies obtainable.

(*e*) *Monitoring development*. The control system is discussed later in chapter 10.

Another fruitful method of investigating and interpreting the problems and pressures within the organization is given in the article by David Rutenberg. He has produced several articles on this subject which have developed considerably our understanding of the structure of international companies and their likely future. The present excerpt summarizes succinctly his work on this subject, and links it to the crucial area of company planning.

5.2 Planning for a multinational synergy[1]

If the headquarters of a multinational company is to justify its existence, it must plan movements of products, ideas, money and people so that synergistic benefits of multinational co-ordination exceed the behavioural costs of intervening in the affairs of subsidiaries.

Planning in the corporate headquarters of a multinational company is more complex than in a domestic company in any one nation, so it appears sensible to use analytical tools developed in operations research and organization theory. The benefits from global movements can be estimated by formulating operations research models; these benefits provide standards against which to gauge the behavioural costs. That is to say, the base case for analysis is that of independent national subsidiaries with a passive holding company headquarters. It is a geographically diversified portfolio; there are no communication problems for nothing is communicated, neither are there control problems; the stigma of nationalism is minimized.

Many corporations became international by a process of creeping incrementalism, rather than by strategic choice. Unsolicited export orders were followed by commissioning agents abroad, establishing warehouses, then developing a sales force. The established market became a hostage as the host government threatened to withhold import permits unless an assembly plant was built. The corporation grew. Gradually it found itself subject to further pressure to increase the local manufactured content, and to train nationals for at least some of the managerial positions. Simultaneously, the corporation probably licensed technology and entered into joint ventures. Very rarely were these moves part of a comprehensive strategy. A quiltwork of *ad hoc* relationships became established. In fact, a comprehensive strategy may not have been possible, for in a few corporations the international operations were used as a depository for unpromotable deadwood. In the last decade the increasing percentage of assets abroad, and the recognition of foreign market growth potential, led many corporations to create an international division, this was responsible for all non-United States operations and was intended to absorb the uncertainty and confusion of dealing abroad. More recently many corporations have acknowledged that they cannot segregate US operations from the rest of the world and are moving towards some form of global, transnational, or truly multinational structure for decision-making.

Multinational marketing

Most aspects of marketing should be done locally, but a few may benefit from headquarters guidance. New product introduction follows a fairly standard sequence; consumer panel tests, test marketing, regional marketing, and national marketing. Each stage reduces the variance of the market forecast. Rather than test in each nation, it appears sensible to use national markets as test markets for other nations. The new product could be introduced simultaneously in all nations of the world, but it might be preferable to sequence the introductions; adapting to the revealed demand by advancing or delaying the date at which new plants come on stream and the dates on which the product is introduced into another nation. Production planning on a worldwide basis and the optimal sequencing of plants will be advantageous if there are economies of scale in plant construction, no alternate uses for capacity if sales collapse, and if experience gained on one plant can lead to improvements in the design of successor plants. The sequencing of nations will be advantageous if one expects a correlation between consumer tastes (rates of acceptance) in different nations so that a quick, low variance, estimate of worldwide demand results from introducing the product into a few key nations. This provides a better base on which to plan promotion and sales force expenditures in other nations. The sequence of national introductions appears influenced by advertising spill-over which is direct (US TV commercials are seen in Canada) and indirect (German tourists in Spain would like to buy products they saw advertised before they left home) and also by national differences in the costs of introducing a bad product. Pressure to shorten the introductory period arises from foregone sales.

It may be worthwhile to build a plant in a nation offering excellent commercial insurance for exports, even though the production costs may be higher than elsewhere, so as to assign to it all commercially risky orders. This practice requires a coherent pricing policy. In terms of operations research model profit, the company can do no better than be a discriminating monopolist for each item in its line in each nation in which it operates; that is the base case. Administratively more coherent policies would be to price an item the same in all nations, or set the price equal to a benchmark multiplied by a national weighting factor which applies to all items in the product line. In either of these two cases, one can compute the model profits, and subtract them from the base profit to get the cost of introducing administrative price coherence.

Product design must be scrutinized. Designs can be tailored to the unique specifications of each nation and, if the products are to be imported, with an eye to their customs classification and hence rate of duty. On the other hand, if there are few products the company achieves economies of scale from mass production, reductions in inventories, purchasing discounts, the reliability of having more than one plant producing an item and the flexibility of being able to divert product flows between nations with little paperwork and few erroneous shipments. A reconciliation lies in modular design, with many modules or sub-assemblies standard throughout the world, others standard to groups of nations, and yet others tailored to each different nation.

Multinational production

Production benefits from worldwide marketing standardization. It *is* possible to undertake worldwide production planning; the international oil companies have for over a decade. Multi-product, multi-destinational production can be allocated among various national plants by means of large (non) linear programmes. The constraint matrix is block diagonal[2] in the activities of each plant. Linking the block are transportation activities; their cost coefficients are the marginal cost of transportation plus import duty (unless import duty rebates are allowed for exports). The cost of transportation includes the freight rate plus the costs of inventory tied up on docks and in transit, plus the expected cost of emergency shipments.

Plant design engineers in a headquarters are human sacrifices who use off-the-shelf systems and design parameters, and perhaps even fear tailoring a unique plant to a nation lest they be sent to operate it. The benefits of having dissimilar plants may appear small in a static analysis, but appear larger where there is production smoothing to meet the fluctuating national demands. For example in France layoffs are expensive, but in Hong Kong they are not. Joint production smoothing (with reallocation of markets to plants) is done in practice and appears quite profitable.

A company may be able to reduce the vulnerability of its subsidiaries by dispersing sub-products over several independent nations. For example, a petroleum company might produce in Venezuela, refine in Curacao, and market elsewhere. Or a computer company might produce input devices in one nation, tape drives in another, processing units in a third, and printers in a fourth. The reduced probability of nationalization is a function of what the local government perceives to be the cost of filling the sub-product gaps. A dynamic analysis must be attempted, for simple products can be used to train workers to master more complex assignments in later years.

In summary there is pressure to build a great many plants which therefore will be smaller than might be desired. There will be greater trans-shipment of sub-assemblies than there would be if the world had one government. If the company has an adequate management information system, the rates of flow (even the patterns of flow) of these sub-assemblies can be varied in response to changing national market conditions. The analytical models are similar to those that would be used within the United States, but they must be richer for the opportunities are far more numerous.

Multinational finance

In 1962 the United States became the first nation to tax income earned abroad rather than waiting for it to be repatriated. It is difficult to manoeuvre liquid assets between subsidiaries, and the benefits clearly depend upon the cost of capital; this jumped as capital export controls were imposed in the USA in 1968. Liquid assets may be moved between pairs of subsidiaries as dividends, inter-subsidiary loans, managerial fees and royalties, and manipulated transfer prices. There are taxation and other costs on each of these four flows between each pair of subsidiaries as well as upper bounds on the flows. The problem is to find a minimum cost combination of routes by which to assure adequate liquid assets for each subsidiary in each year of planning horizon. It can be formulated as a network flow problem, so that 100 subsidiaries can be handled quite efficiently.

Clearly the world of a multinational company is not deterministic. Inflation rates differ among nations, so devaluations occur sporadically. For a price, the company can hedge (buy protection) against impending devaluation. The cost of hedging depends primarily on whether the central bank of the beleaguered currency is intervening in its forward market. The key problem is that of timing, for a conservative policy of continually hedging all exposed assets can become very expensive. Optimal hedging is a problem of decision theory in which sensitivity analysis can be performed on the subjective probability estimates so as to justify hiring more expert predictors. It should be noted that the exposure of a multinational company cannot be found from simple accounting rules. For example, a labour intensive company may benefit from devaluation, if its plant in the devaluing nation exports to subsidiaries in other nations. In fact it is the present value of marketing revenues which bear the full brunt of devaluation even though they do not appear on conventional balance sheets.

In each year in each nation the company makes profits or losses, and perhaps capital gains. These affect tax credits and charges for both this year and also for prior and future years. National tax jurisdictions overlap, and the definition and treatments are not consistent. So the tax implications of an acquisition or spin-off are not readily apparent. Only by synthesizing such a transaction with those which have occurred in recent years and which are planned for future years can the tax status of this transaction be understood. Simulations of worldwide tax status appear quite possible and very desirable.

When a company is raising capital the same theoretical concepts should apply whether it is sourcing dollars, Eurodollars, or Swiss francs. In practice, different simplified assumptions (necessary to get tractable models) have to be made. When the company is raising dollars, its treasurer can devote most of its attention to predicting interest rates to decide when to float.

In the USA the fixed costs of a flotation is of minor importance to all but very small companies. However, the fixed cost is very important when raising Eurodollars (or convertible debentures) because dozens of underwriting houses must, in effect, privately place the Eurobonds with individuals, yet no continuous secondary market has developed. When the company is raising dollars, its treasurer need not worry about the availability of the funds in the market. However, saturating the market is a distinct possibility if the issue is in Swiss francs. So when a multinational company has access to many national capital markets, it must supplement interest rate predictions with an analysis of timing flotations.

Organization of the multinational headquarters

Each subsidiary has its own organization structure. A passive headquarters, a holding company, requires almost no organization. If the headquarters is to engage in an international arbitrage of products, money and ideas as has been outlined in sections on marketing, production and finance, then the headquarters and its relationship with the subsidiaries must be organized. Cross cultural communication problems arise from differences in language, gestures and basic premises or world views.

Communication problems will probably become more acute in the future as it becomes more worthwhile to direct the affairs of subsidiaries and as governments apply more controls to resident foreign companies. One of the purest examples of communication (uncomplicated by legal and social control) occurs in licensing. The licensee is paying for the privilege of communication. The licensor can enforce territorial restraints (illegal under United States anti-trust laws) only by promising the licensee continued clear communication into the future. In comparison, problems of communication with a wholly-owned subsidiary abroad are easy.

Headquarters plans will be implemented only if headquarters has some control over the behaviour of the subsidiaries. Just as the purest example of communications occurs in licensing, so the purest example of behavioural control occurs in joint ventures. If a headquarters can control the behaviour of joint ventures over which it may have no legal control, then the same tactics will lead to comparatively easy control of wholly-owned subsidiaries. I feel that the study of licensing and joint ventures is justified by the insight they yield to the organization problems of multinational companies, so long as this study is accompanied by the warning that if a long-term strategy of the company is to become multinational, licensing and joint ventures may not be suitable transition states because of the large costs of breaking these relationships.

The ideal of a multinational company is to be rational on a global scale, with headquarters planning for flexible adaptations as national environments change. Organizational structures are required that combine flexibility with the synthesis of function, area, product, and planning time horizon into a four-dimensional grid structure. That is to say, each headquarters employee has four roles, is a member of four reference groups. The strategy of designing a formal organization must be to strengthen the dimension that is weakest, giving it authority to impose sanction. The strategy of managerial development and succession must be to help an individual develop in these four dimensions. For example, if a particular government permits subsidiaries in its nation to maintain only a very small number of resident foreigners, these opportunities should be allocated with care. Work in the subsidiary provides an opportunity to come to know the employees and their nation, and is vital for later behavioural control; so a steady turnover of resident foreigners may be sensible. Clearly the managers must themselves be multinational.

The relationships between a headquarters and its worldwide subsidiaries can be analysed in terms of the depths of understanding headquarters has of the subsidiaries, and that a subsidiary has of the headquarters (and hence of the global interactions). These two questions result in a typology of four archetypes,[3] each one of which implies different decision premises in formulating problems. Whenever headquarters personnel deeply understand the nation of the subsidiary, they can collaborate with subsidiary employees to predict host government actions, and the social and economic climate. Generally employees appear more likely to accept directions if they have helped set decision premises, and so the subsidiary employees should if they are ever to achieve a geocentric viewpoint. Thus it seems desirable that the concept of prediction as a solitary sport (to be played with a computerized crystal ball in a Manhattan aerie) be replaced by the practice of large group participatory prediction. Incidentally, it appears that the value of predictions is greater to a multinational company than to its domestic counterpart. In a domestic company in any one nation it may be difficult to adapt to a political or economic prediction, but in a multinational company the flows of products, money and men can be adjusted; hence the greater value of environmental predictions.

Conclusions

One can gain insight into an organization by comparing its performance with that of a market economy. That is to say, suppose the subsidiaries were autonomous local corporations, could they not wheel and deal together, moving capital around the world, and cross licensing technology? Just how necessary are multinational companies?

At present the question is either academic or revolutionary. Within a decade or so, we may expect that multinational companies will really have to justify their existence. From a viewpoint of a host government they are a partial invasion of sovereignty. Their operations may cement world peace if world peace exists, but may be used to escalate to war if it seems opportune to so interpret the incidents and provocations of commercial life. Multinational companies bring in much needed capital, but at a cost far greater than the government would be charged; they bring in technology, but almost as efficient technology is available as turnkey plants from specialized construction companies, or by licensing. They bring managerial skills which might not be appropriate to the nation.[4]

My personal belief is that a multinational company is something more than an instrument of superior bargaining power. Its profitability is the result of its ability to adapt quicker, and to communicate more clearly than independent national corporations could. For example, contracts between subsidiaries of the same company can be made and changed by telephone, without lengthy bargaining before shipments start. The justification for a multinational company, is to exploit the synergy of being multinational.

The moral of this somewhat sombre conclusion is that the headquarters of the multinational company might view itself as having a management service contract relationship with its subsidiaries. The opportunities for synergy justify the multinational company, and must be part of the inducements-contributions balance perceived by each subsidiary and each host government.

5.3 Suggestions for further reading

The literature on long-range planning is enormous and the subject rates a substantial journal to itself.[5] The writings on the specifically international aspects of the subject are much more limited. Most of them are of the 'this is how it has been done' variety. This approach is interesting and stimulating to the reader who can see how successfully international planning systems have developed; but this information can be misleading unless there is some attempt to work out the various conditions under which the different systems can be expected to succeed. Outstanding writers on long-range planning in general are:

(C) ACKOFF, R. L. (1970). *A Concept of Corporate Planning*, Wiley: London & New York.
(B) DRUCKER, P. F. (1955). *The Practice of Management,* Mercury Books, English edition. Heinemann: London.
(C) EWING, David W. (Ed.) (1964). *Long Range Planning for Management*, new edition, Harper & Row.
(C) STEINER, C. A. & CANNON, W. M. (1966). *Multinational Corporate Planning*, Collier-Macmillan: New York. Although somewhat dated, this book is still worth reading.

A companion volume seeks to discuss more thoroughly the issues raised here:

BROOKE, M. Z. & van BEUSEKOM, M. *Multinational Corporate Planning,* Pitman: London. To be published 1979.

See also:

(C) BROOKE, M. Z. & REMMERS, H. L. (1972). Where chapter 9 deals with international resource allocation.
(D) SETHI, S. Prakash & HOGLE, John T. (1973). A Conceptual and Operational Framework for Developing the Long-Range Planning Process, *Journal of International Business Studies*, pp. 31–49.
(D) GHYMN, Kyung-Il & BATES, Thomas H. (1975). Consequences of Strategic Planning: An Empirical Case Study. *Conference Papers*: Academy of International Business Conference, Dallas (Texas), December.

The amount of writing on international forecasting is limited. This is understandable in view of the hazards. The few books on the subject are quickly dated or too wide-ranging for inclusion here. Articles which readers will find stimulating include:

(C) CLIFFORD, D. K. *et al.* (1975). The game has changed. *The McKinsey Quarterly*, Autumn.
(C) JOHNSON, G. F. (1976). Putting forecasts to work in the corporate planning function, *Business Economics*, January.

See also:

(B) ROBOCK & SIMMONDS (1973). Chapter 16.

5.4 Exercises for this chapter

Case studies

Sama S.A., 1961. (IMEDE F. Z., ICH 9–207–030) by V. Jolivet.
A French manufacturer plans the construction of an assembly in Italy.

Capital International S.A., 1967. (IMEDE GM–172, ICH 9–313–280), by Uyterhoeven, H. E. R. & Massey, W. E.
Case focuses on the merger concept using the example of 4 small electronics companies from 4 different European countries; the expected synergistic and the possible future developments of the merger.

Fiat-Citroen Merger Talks, 1968. (Harvard University, ICH 9–370–121), by Davis, S. M. & De Choinit, J. F.
The problems of communication and co-operation in cross-border mergers—here, between France and Italy—and the development of a truly multinational enterprise.

The Fiat-Citroen Merger Proposals, 1968. (Cranfield Institute of Technology, CCH 373–032–1), by Constable, C. J. & Dodman, M.
The background to the 1969 merger of Fiat and Citroen in terms of ownership, management, output, sales turnover, manufacturing and marketing policies, competition and government influence; reactions of the Unions, political parties, competitors, suppliers and government to the proposed merger.

A. B. Thorsten, undated. (IMEDE C–131, ICH 9–414–035), by Shillinglaw, G. & Summer, C. E.
An investment proposal as made by the president of a Swedish company to the Belgian parent company. The two managements, evaluating the investment, dispute; financial and economic data, feelings, attitudes and politics of participants.

5.5 Questions for discussion

(1) List the main activities associated with international corporate planning, and discuss one of those listed in some depth.

(2) It is asserted in this chapter that forecasting for foreign markets is a particularly difficult activity. State whether you agree or disagree with this and give reasons for your answer.

(3) Write a briefing for an executive who has recently been appointed to promote international planning in his company. Select for yourself the size (by net assets) and industry group of the firm.

(4) What do you understand as a synergistic use of resources. Explain some possible difficulties.

(5) What are the main problems associated with planning across frontiers and how can they be solved?

(6) Discuss some consequences of size and industry sector in international corporate planning.

Part II
Management*

* This part discusses how the general strategies and tactics of the international firm translate into activities in the different functions of the firm: marketing, finance, production, communications and so on.

6 International Marketing Management

6.1 Marketing policies

A successful international firm is one that has effective international marketing. To many this is a self-evident statement. Suspicious researchers may cast doubt on it; no doubt there are many exceptions, a good invention can be a substitute for any amount of inefficiency and luck can help too. But it remains that, almost by definition, a world spread comes through good marketing. It is curious, therefore, to note a tendency that can be compared to pulling up the drawbridge. For an important debate in many companies is about the appropriateness of having an international marketing department. Central departments are abolished or slimmed down and the function is confined to the subsidiaries, and some international conferences are held to circulate experiences. Marketing, it is held, is essentially a national activity, with only certain policies such as pricing to be centrally determined. When a company takes this view, no doubt there are procedures with other labels for answering the specific international marketing questions; but it remains that many of the reorganizations noted by companies are not so much major restructuring along the lines to be discussed in chapter 9, but arrangements of the marketing function—the institution or abolition of a central or regional marketing department, the re-allocation of expertise in the group, or some other such change.

The specific concerns of international marketing depend on the answers to a number of questions. Routes abroad are discussed in chapters 2 and 3; of the remaining questions to be raised here two have just been proposed:

(1) What market skills are needed to ensure the development of this company abroad?
(2) Where should those skills be located?

Other questions include:

(3) What international standardization is either possible or desirable?
(4) What are the priorities in determining the foreign marketing strategies?
(5) What about pricing policies?

There are also a number of related questions about advertising, selling and market research. The answers to these will depend on how the earlier questions are answered; if such matters are to be left to the subsidiary's own judgment then they come outside the scope of the international marketing department for that particular company.

The question about standardization affects all the others and has been much discussed. Asked whether to standardize international marketing, most writers say yes and no. A satisfactory answer needs to go behind the question to the various activities included under the heading of marketing.[1] There is also the difference between the policy or formula and its application in practice. This can be seen especially in pricing policies. Obviously the actual price charged, even in intra-company transfers, will bear some relationship to local market conditions. Equally the way the price is determined, and especially for intra-company transfers, can be decided entirely at the centre. The local subsidiary does not have to have any discretion at all in the policy. The evidence is, though, that most subsidiaries do have some discretion except where that would be impossible. In such a case there may be a process of bargaining or there may be considerable central authority, where the decisions are taken by corporate management, and will be taken as much on financial as on strictly marketing grounds.

The local application of international price formulae may well encounter legal difficulties. Many countries have price controls and in some these can make life particularly difficult for the foreign firm. This may be because of overt discrimination against the alien, usually in the less developed countries, or it may be because there are a mixture of formal and informal controls which cause difficulties for everyone, but domestic companies are in a better position to negotiate the market. Indeed it is because of the need for negotiation that the subsidiary attempts to gain a greater control of the policy. In spite of this the advantages of corporate control of pricing policies are great, and most of the arguments against apply to consumer products; even these arguments in the end turn on practices rather than on policies.

One feature of pricing policies is that so many subtle issues are at stake, some of which are discussed in the next chapter. But product policies also stretch across functional boundaries and involve a mixture of international and national considerations. One that is straightforward is to assume that standard product policies internationally are required and examine the difficulties. There are a number of reasons for discussing the subject this way round. The starting point is the assumption that most companies make in practice, although they would not normally express it in that way; the examination of the problems that arise then follows.[2] The arguments in favour of standardization include economies of scale; this argument has to be carefully examined in each individual case. Failure to satisfy the customer is a diseconomy on any scale, and easily causes setbacks in an internationally standardized product.

Another argument supporting standardization is the importance of international advertising and the acquiring of an international reputation. This applies to many industrial and some consumer products. Perhaps the strongest argument of all is that, subject to the constraints listed below, changes of taste and economic conditions as well as advertising are making more products internationally saleable. The company may well be wasting money and missing opportunities by adaptations that are not required or are becoming out-of-date. Timing is of critical importance. Premature assumptions that a market is ready for a product may be disastrous whether or not the product is standardized worldwide.

Among the obvious difficulties of marketing identical products are differences of personal taste or national standards in matters of safety or in weights and measures. These must constrain standardization in some products, although the position is changing all the time. National standards may be negotiable, at least by a powerful supplier or trade association. More subtle difficulties include such matters as market segment. In consumer goods one of the arguments for standardization is the increase in international travel. But the other side of this is that the standardization must extend to market segment, for otherwise a reputation for high quality may be sabotaged in a particular country where the product is sold too cheaply. International executives often quote examples of this, where a local subsidiary has aimed at a different market segment to increase its sales. Avoiding this difficulty may be less easy than would appear; and markets where the demographic structure or patterns of trade make it difficult to adhere to the normal segment policy should perhaps be avoided. The foreign market segment is often determined for a long time ahead by the price at launching for consumer products, hence this price will be critical. The market position will go up or down with the price.

Sensitivity to cultural differences is another constraint on standardization. This subject is discussed in chapter 16, and includes all aspects of marketing especially product policies and advertising. The warning here is that the constraints are easily underestimated. Advertising folklore is full of examples of blunders in transferring successful advertisements across frontiers—tigers that got very much snarled up in tanks in French and sexy posters that discouraged people from buying a particular brand of cigarettes in Switzerland are examples. One book[3] tells of 'bodies' that become 'corpses' in motor car advertisements in Flemish, of 'Come alive with Pepsi' that somehow got mixed up with the resurrection in German, not to mention what happened to airline 'rendezvous lounges' in Portuguese.

The distinction between international policies and local practices fits other marketing activities. Market research is a subject where the pitfalls of using in one country methods that are successful in another can easily be demonstrated. Nevertheless all market research is an adapted transfer to other countries of both techniques and policies that were largely devised in highly competitive conditions in the United States. An attitude that makes sense is: this company decides centrally what is required of market research and under what conditions; the requirement itself is then handled locally by local methods. In research for some industrial goods, only local knowledge may be required and the product knowledge may be far more important. For other products the research may be conducted internationally.

Another important marketing policy is the organization of the foreign sales force. Here, too, examples abound of problems caused by ham-fisted attempts to introduce an internationally standard organization. The purchaser, or the person who determines the purchase, may vary enormously from country to country. In pharmaceuticals, to cite a particularly complicated example, the main influence on purchasing may be the pharmacist, the physician, the consultant or the medical school staff. Which it is will vary from country to country. The sales team must match up to the local buyer, understand him and probably have similar local qualifications. The computer salesman is in a similar position. The buyer of food or consumer durables may range from the wholesaler, the store buyer or the co-operative through many different types of organization to the small shopkeeper and the van salesman. There are so many arguments for the local organization of the sales force that these arguments themselves become powerful stimuli for the establishment of a local subsidiary. On the other hand techniques of training and motivation developed in one country are found to succeed, with necessary adaptations, in another. This does not, of course, support international standardization within a particular company. The central activity may be seen as advisory rather than compulsory. A powerful means of training as well as co-ordination is the international conference. This may happen at each level of the company from marketing managers to salesmen. This is the point at which standardization really enters rather than through rules and regulations.

The allocation of international sales areas, on the other hand, is a more delicate subject with implications that are becoming almost as explosive as transfer pricing. Indeed the two subjects may well be best considered together as closely related, although there is little evidence that they are considered together in practice. Increasingly countries are trying to force foreign investors to export, and these efforts make central determination of sales areas more and more difficult. One of the main reasons why companies wish to control sales areas is to gain the greatest possible advantages from pricing policies and pricing opportunities.

There are other motives, such as making the best use of production facilities and distribution arrangements. Even so a limited number of companies allow their foreign subsidiaries complete freedom in export decisions. These are mainly in consumer goods where inter-subsidiary competition may bring benefits, in contrast to industrial goods where it simply brings price-cutting.

There are a number of legal issues which come under the purview of the marketing manager. The protection of trademarks and patents varies from country to country. Regulations concerning price fixing and resale price maintenance are discussed in chapter 15. There are also laws on monopolistic practices and other restraints on trade which are burgeoning around the world. The marketing policy has to take account of all these factors as well as the tax and tariff position. There is also the question of risk. Most industrialized countries have official measures for insuring against the risks involved in financing exports. Unlike financial risks, marketing risks cannot be 'hedged'; on the contrary the most effective risk reduction is normally concentration, a common cause of failure is tackling too many markets at once. Companies, especially the smaller ones, find that there is no substitute for intimate knowledge of a market and of the informal 'rat runs' along which business is conducted in the particular country.

The following excerpt brings together a number of important considerations—the process of industrialization and current reactions, including the rise of environmental concern and consumerism, together with international segmentation. This is a different type of excerpt to that which accompanies other chapters in this book, it is intended to stimulate thought about aspects of the future for the international marketing manager.

6.2 'The role of the comparative analysis approach in societal marketing'[4]

The most commonly accepted definition of marketing is one which stresses the concepts of customer-orientation, corporate integration and profitability. The operation of the marketing process is seen as representing the satisfaction of the needs and wants of consumers by the co-ordinated and integrated efforts of a company which realize a measure of profit to the enterprise. Valuable though this definition is in enabling a company to appreciate its role in the exchange economy which characterizes many societies today, it fails completely to provide an indication of the role of marketing as a societal agent, that is, to what extent marketing is, or should be, a socially responsible activity. A number of factors have contributed to the importance currently being attached to this concept of 'social marketing',[5] most notably the increasing concern for mankind's human and social environment, the rise of consumerism, and the dominance of ever-larger trading corporations in today's market.

This state of affairs arises according to whether one treats marketing from a micro or a macro perspective. The micro viewpoint looks at marketing as a function of managerial activity, and emphasizes the relationship between marketing and other departmental responsibilities within a company. Drucker has stated that 'it is the first duty of a business to survive'. The guiding principle of business economics, in other words, is not the maximization of profits; it is the avoidance of loss.[6] While it is arguable how much emphasis should be placed on the survival motive rather than the profit motive, there is little doubt that the popular interpretation of marketing highlights its economic implications and consequences rather than its social ones. On the other hand, the macro approach to marketing looks beyond the frontier of individual firms, and attempts to analyse its contribution to the economic and social welfare of a nation, to the allocation of scarce resources, to an improvement in the standard of living and more fundamentally to an enhancement of the quality of life. Changes in marketing practices are recognized as contributing to changes in social relationships and cultural patterns, as much as arising from them. These two, often dissonant, levels of approach to the study of marketing provide an indication of why there has been no universal agreement as to the true aims of marketing. At the one extreme, the effectiveness of marketing is evaluated in terms of its contribution to company profitability, and at the other extreme in terms of its contribution to the realization of social and cultural ideals, even though these social goals may be beyond the tasks which marketing is able to perform.

The question has been raised whether social welfare is in fact consonant with the bilateral transfer characteristics of a market economy, and whether it can be realized only through the unilateral transfer of a grants economy.[7] However, management must look beyond the short-term gains to the longer-term social objective of improving the quality of living standards, for only by so doing can it be assured of a richer and more secure market. A more altruistic argument is that because marketing practices have the power to influence the environment within which we live, and often help to shape the way in which our personal relationships evolve, the marketing process has an important social responsibility in ensuring that it does not manipulate people against their wishes. Very few people would question that marketing shares in the problems and contributes to the goals of society, but the real difficulty arises in determining at what level the societal responsibilities of marketing should operate. It is in this area that an approach involving the comparative analysis of marketing systems can help us to understand more fully the relationship between marketing and the social problems and goals of the cultures and environment in which it takes place.

Comparative marketing defined

The term 'comparative marketing' can be defined as a type of analysis that describes and interprets the differences and similarities between varying marketing practices and systems in two or more different countries or societies. Systems of marketing are influenced primarily by the physical or geographical attributes of a nation, a multitude of economic factors, and the human or social elements which characterize a society. Some of these environmental elements are classified in Table 6.1.

Table 6.1
Environmental factors influencing marketing systems

Physical/geographical factors	Economic factors	Human/social factors
Climate	Size of GNP	Religion
Resource availability	Economic growth	Family structure
Transportation	Local costs	Local mores
Soil fertility	Income distribution	Social interaction
Topographical features	Taxation	Political maturity
Urbanization	Standard of living	Degree of literacy
Size of country	Economic stability	Language

A recent article proposes[8] a classification scheme of various bases for international market segmentation. Two types of bases are distinguished: general, or enduring, characteristics and situation specific characteristics. 'General characteristics do not vary across purchase situations, and include at customer level demographic, socio-economic and psychological (personality and life style) characteristics. Situation specific characteristics are those that vary with the individual purchase situation or particular product such as brand loyalty, frequency of purchase and attitude toward the given brand.'

Another authority[9] offers an alternative typology within a cultural anthropological framework, based on de facto, traditional, legal and marketing mix indicators, in order to satisfy the need for qualitative market evaluation. Whatever classification scheme is adopted, it should represent at least the most important factors which shape the practice and system of marketing within a society. For example, looking at some of the factors listed in Table 6.1: the type of transportation network, and its dispersion, will have an impact on the physical distribution activities which are carried out; the standard of living prevailing in a particular country will influence the types of products and services which are offered to consumers; local customs and the degree of literacy and education of the population will influence marketing communications; the degree of political control over business activities will affect a company's decision-making autonomy; resource availability will affect a country's import-export balance; and many other examples will readily come to mind.

The social, economic and socio-political environment will invariably change over time and, of course, certain features of the physical geographical infrastructure will also change, such as the degree of urbanization and the development of transportation routes. It is perhaps significant that the development of what is known as the civilized Western world was characterized by economic growth and development which occurred more or less in tandem with cultural, social and political progress, particularly when related to the present international scene. The parallel development of a nation's environmental elements was not severely disturbed. One may look at the experience of many of the emergent African and South American nations, where the political and economic independence in advance of a social environment able to cope with the new demands placed upon was accompanied by frequent coups and rebellions. The significance of this observation to the practical marketeer is that a social system is unlikely to absorb efficiently marketing techniques and concepts which are alien to its custom and human environment, particularly in the short term. A number of examples follow.

(1) In eastern Europe, selling is usually a very lengthy process. The bureaucratic buying system found in many countries is unlike anything found in western Europe, and conditions of purchase are often much more stringent. Patience in negotiations is therefore needed.

(2) Again, in eastern Europe, and in many of the less-developed countries, barter trading is accepted as a very convenient way to reduce cash payments (particularly if foreign currency is scarce). Western companies often have an instinctive distrust of barter without examining its possibilities.

(3) Communications in many parts of Africa are not yet good enough to alleviate problems of high transport costs and delivery delays. In many countries promotional communications must be approached in different ways, primarily because of different cultural standards, lower levels of literacy, poor education, unavailability of certain types of media.

(4) Shopping habits vary enormously, for example, the shopping behaviour of the population of a foreign country may prohibit the viable introduction of a type of distributive or retailing activity common in other countries.

The growth of international marketing

The growth of foreign trade, and the consequent need for both public and private sectors of business to understand the nature of international marketing, has occurred for a number of reasons. The most influential and enabling factor has undoubtedly been the phenomenal growth in communications and transportation. The trans-shipment of goods between nations has accelerated as a result of the availability of cheaper and speedier modes of transport across seas and by air. Also, as trade barriers are being broken down, more companies are discovering opportunities for expansion in previously inaccessible markets. The encouragement given by governments to increase exports as a result of balance of payments priorities has been a further incentive to companies to venture into the area of international marketing. However the problems faced by the international marketer are formidable. Essentially, they revolve around the difficulties associated with the task of comparing the marketing systems in those countries in which the company is interested, with the methods of marketing applicable in the home country, so that the relevant short-term and long-term marketing strategies and decisions are suitable to the environment.

'Paradoxical though it may seem, what we stand to gain most from comparative studies of domestic marketing systems is not what they tell us about others but what they force us to learn about ourselves in order to understand what we see abroad.'[10] This summarizes another advantage of comparative analysis. The environmental elements which shape the marketing system of a society are frequently taken for granted, and the relationships between these elements and the prevailing marketing concepts and techniques are not properly understood. It is only by analysing comparative marketing institutions that these relationships can be fully appreciated in the home country, and more fruitfully interpreted in foreign market situations. This point is taken up and developed later.

The studies which have been made of marketing systems prevailing in foreign countries have been more of a descriptive nature than a comparative one.[11] The emphasis has been on describing, rather than explaining, marketing practices: time and cost factors have been primarily responsible for this. Without any doubt, the costs involved in making depth studies of the relationship between marketing and its environment are enormous. Indeed, it is questionable whether the analytical tools necessary for determining, measuring and proving these relationships can be developed to an acceptable degree of accuracy in the near future. The most intractable problem would seem to be in the area of attaching values or weights to the relative influences of the environmental elements on the developments of a local marketing system. However, in many so-called comparative studies environmental elements are rarely given the consideration they deserve. The result is that much of the descriptive detail in a particular study may be equally applicable to other countries at more or less the same level of economic development. However, a perusal of the literature on marketing methods in foreign countries suggests that undue emphasis has been placed on the description of a marketing system in relation to its physical and geographical environment, with suggestions as to the probable pattern in the future within this narrow context. What is needed is a conceptual framework for a comparative analysis approach to marketing systems which enables the practical marketeer to devise marketing strategies pertinent to the national environment.

Such a framework should also assist our understanding of the social responsibilities of marketing: the social interpreting of marketing is a relatively new phenomenon since the beginnings of marketing thought in the early years of the twentieth century. It has now become apparent that 'there is a clear and present danger that marketing will lapse into the practice of normal science and shield itself from involvement in the issues most pertinent to the quality of man's life'.[12] It is to this problem that comparative marketing can address itself. In fact, the concept of the comparative analysis approach is a logical extension of the recognition that the marketing process transcends the boundaries of the activities of individual firms. Indeed, if the comparative marketing approach is able to contribute at all to the development of marketing theory, it seems proper that it should provide one with a better understanding of the relationship between marketing and the societal problems and goals of the culture and environment in which it operates.

It has been suggested[13] that differences in marketing systems which might be emphasized in simple comparisons may become similarities when related to an environmental frame of reference. The essence of this theory is that comparative study is not simply a description of either marketing or environmental differences, but rather a comparison of relationships between marketing and its environment in two or more countries. An analogy may perhaps be drawn from management accountancy. When comparing the profitability of one company with another, it is meaningless to look simply at profit figures: the statement that Company A returns a net profit before tax of £1 m and that Company B returns a net profit of £2 m does not enable one to conclude that Company B is more efficient than Company A, if profitability is a measure of efficiency. The accounting ratio of net profit to capital employed, however, is more significant: if Company A utilizes £10 m of capital, and Company B £50 m, then Company A shows a 10% return on capital employed, while Company B returns only 4% (whether return on capital employed is the most efficient measure of company profitability is, of course, another question). In other words, it is the relationships between net profit and total capital employed in two or more companies which enables one to make realistic comparative analyses about profitability. In marketing also, the theory suggests, it is the comparison of ratios or relationships which is significant. In Fig. 6.1 comparative analysis is suggested by the equation A : C = B : D, as A : B and C : D are merely descriptive studies of marketing systems, and A : C and B : D simply statements concerning the environment. An example, simplified for illustrative purposes, is shown in Fig. 6.2 and indicates the potential value of this approach. A contrast is drawn between specific methods of retailing and distribution in Sweden and Guatemala.

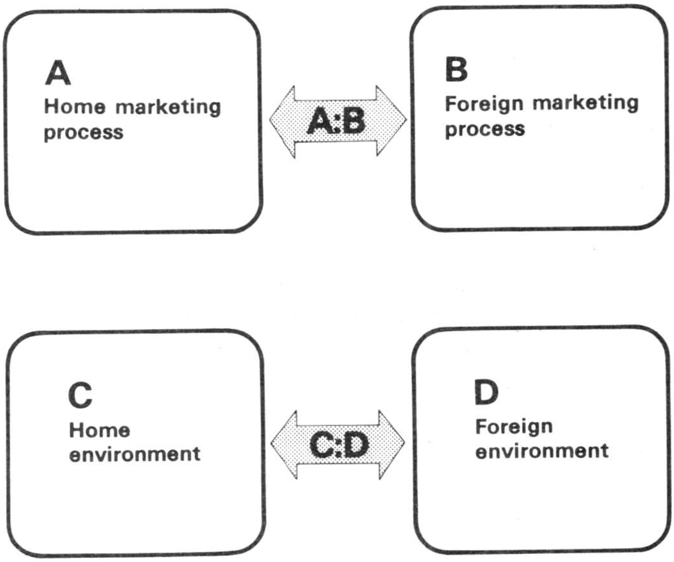

Fig. 6.1 Comparison of relationships between marketing and environment.

A : C = B : D requires one to compare the reasons why different retailing methods prevail. Are there any common factors? Perhaps there is a clue in the presence of non-economic factors which reinforce the continuation of market-place trading in Guatemala.[14] This may suggest that both types of shopping area are based on the need to cater for the social activities of shoppers. Does each, in its own way, represent a social en-

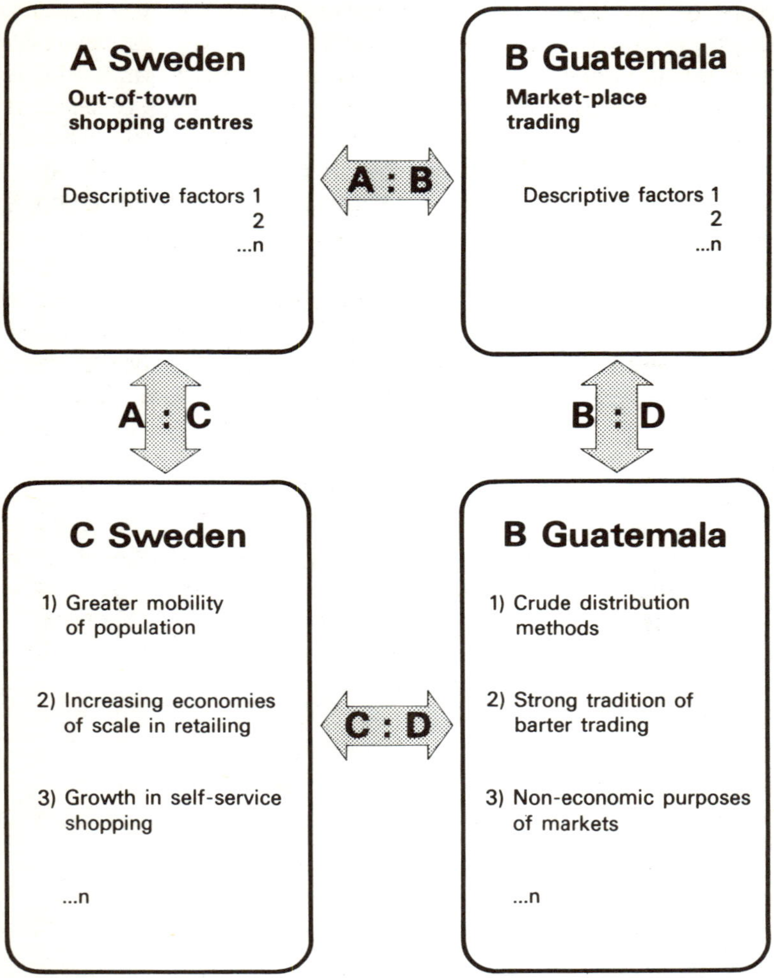

Fig. 6.2 Methods of retailing and distribution in unlike environments.

A:B represents a descriptive analysis of regional shopping centres and market-place trading.

C:D represents a statement of a number of relevant environmental factors in the two countries.

A:C and B:D represent explanatory statements of retailing methods, identifying factors which may have caused such methods to arise or be maintained.

vironment for shopping? It has been suggested that shopping *per se* is not much enjoyed as a social activity:[15] perhaps the successful growth of out-of-town shopping centres in Sweden will depend upon their ability to satisfy a range of non-economic purposes in addition to the need to purchase goods.

Figure 6.1 underlines the need to recognize and understand the relationship between a prevailing marketing system and the environmental elements surrounding it. A popular environmental approach has been to relate marketing practices to the level of economic development in the particular country, utilizing the concept of the five stages of economic growth: the traditional society, the preconditions for take-off, the take-off, the drive to maturity and the age of high mass consumption.[16] However, this approach is of limited value for two major reasons. Firstly, the growth in world communications and the influence, for better or for worse, of some nations on other societies has disturbed the harmony between the political, social, economic and cultural environments within a society susceptible to such influences. The experiences of the emergent nations of Africa and America, in particular, bear this out. Secondly, as has been pointed out,[17] the social aspects of marketing are the more sensitive to the societal environment, and one is at risk in concentrating on one type of environmental influence only.

Perhaps, then, as an authority quoted earlier[11] suggests 'a primarily marketing-oriented classification of nations rather than one dependent on the conditions of the economy as a whole, may be in order'. Six market groups have been identified[18] on the basis of middle-class development as a measure of achievement. It is argued that the consumer revolution is a revolution of the middle-class, since it is: 'the degree of development of a large middle-class which makes the difference between a backward and a modern country both economically and psychologically'. On this basis, the six market groups are as follows:

(i) the almost classless society, contented countries;
(ii) the affluent countries;
(iii) countries in transition;
(iv) revolutionary countries;
(v) primitive countries;
(vi) the new class society.

If we accept the implicit assumptions behind this classification, that the degree of middle-class development reflects the degree of marketing development, and that systems of marketing tend towards similarity within each of the six groups, it offers an environmental frame of reference for comparative marketing analysis. Comparative analysis between two or more countries within any one of the six groups becomes simpler, because environmental influences are, to an appreciable extent, equalized by reference to a common group. The two classifications between them reflect social and cultural progress, as well as economic.

Another approach[19] utilizes the concept of politico-economic organization as a basis of comparison. At one extreme there are the centrally-planned economies including the Soviet Union, eastern Europe,

South America. At the other extreme, there are the market-mechanism economies typical of the Western world. Such a basis of comparison is restrictive, since politico-economic organization encompasses a widely-varying range of social and cultural patterns.

Of the four contributions to comparative marketing analysis which have been discussed, the first is the most comprehensive and conceptually sound, but complex in its application. Of the other short-cut approaches, offering possible bases of comparison, the last is preferable because it implicitly recognizes environmental elements more closely related to the development of marketing systems. Whether middle-class development can be improved upon as a measure of marketing development is worthy of further study.

A framework for comparative analysis

From a practical viewpoint, the international marketer is not only concerned with the internal environment of foreign markets, he is also critically influenced by the external trading environment between nations. The degree of foreign appropriation of assets in the context of political discord between nations must be evaluated and foreign exchange regulations must also be considered. Such external elements are limiting factors on a company's operations in international markets. Furthermore, external trading situations may be an important influential factor in the structure of certain types of marketing sub-systems within a nation, this is an important point overlooked in the first theory. For example, the marketing of agricultural produce in the European Economic Community has been fundamentally different from the way it is carried out in Britain, because Common Market farmers are protected from cheap competition by import levies. In Britain, cheap imports have been allowed into the country, the farmer being protected under the guaranteed price system. The problems of change in this situation are now common knowledge.

The constraints of the international environment upon the marketer are recognized, but the first theory fails to indicate the possibility of a relationship between such an environment and a domestic marketing system. Theoretically, the conceptual framework is valid, except for this omission, but it suffers generally from the practical limitations of the time and cost needed to make comprehensive and exhaustive studies of a comparative nature, as well as the difficulties associated with explaining how the elements of the human and social environment interact with the prevailing marketing system. This latter problem can only be tackled within a multi-disciplinary framework: marketing must draw upon the contributions of sociology, psychology, anthropology, and other related disciplines, in order that these relationships can be adequately determined. Much has been written[20] which illustrates how the complementary approach of related disciplines can contribute to a greater understanding of the relationships between marketing and its social and cultural environment.

How, then, is the comparative analysis approach able to provide us with an understanding of the interaction between marketing and its many environments? A first step is to outline a structural framework within which such an analysis can be undertaken: in effect, a set of guidelines for comparative study. The following represents such a framework:

(1) The determination of the environmental elements within a society which shape the practice and system of marketing, and which themselves may be influenced by marketing. All elements will be present in a society, but will vary in importance and strength between societies. The classification scheme put forward in Table 6.2 is a useful starting point.[21]

(2) The description of a marketing system in each of the societies subject to the comparative study, in terms of both the mechanism of the marketing process (types of products, channel facilities, institutions, cost structures, pricing structures), and the human character of marketing (organization, roles, behaviour patterns).

(3) The determination of relationships between the pre-stated environmental elements and the mechanistic and behavioural concepts and techniques associated with the marketing process, with consideration being given to: the influence of external trading arrangements on the internal marketing system, the contributions which related disciplines can offer to an explanation of the presence within a marketing system of certain phenomena, the cause-and-effect nature of the interactions; the relative importance and strength of each of the environmental elements in their interaction with the system of marketing.

(4) The analysis and interpretation of the similarities and differences between each set of relationships and patterns of interaction, and the establishment of tentative generalizations on the basis of such an analysis.

Theoretically the conceptual framework outlined above is valid in the context of a comparative marketing study. The major obstacles to its adoption still remain. There is the difficulty of applying analytical techniques to the explanation of how different social systems affect the marketing structure of socially and culturally diverse nations, and vice versa. Other problems include the costs associated with gathering together all the data which would be required and the resistance which may be encountered in the undertaking of such a vast amount of work. Perhaps an international government-sponsored team of researchers could co-ordinate work which has already been completed in this field,

Table 6.2
A classification scheme of various bases for international market segmentation

	Enduring characteristics	Situation specific characteristics
Country	Geographic location	Economic and legal constraints
	Demographic and population characteristics	Market conditions
Characteristics	Socio-economic Cultural patterns	Product bound culture and life style characteristics
	Political factors	
Customer	Demographic characteristics: age, sex, life cycle	Consumption patterns Loyalty patterns
		Attitudes (perceptions and preferences)
Characteristics	Socio-economic	
	Personality and life-style characteristics	

and undertake full and detailed studies within the framework suggested above. But this could be difficult to organize. If the obstacles can be overcome, then the benefits which will accrue both to marketing practitioners and to those concerned about the role of marketing in society will be well worth the effort.

The basic premise running through this article is that an understanding of why certain marketing practices are not in evidence in some societies, or types of society, may provide an explanation of why they have appeared in others. This is not the place to be specific or make any value-judgments about certain aspects of marketing as socially undesirable or irritating, but it is reasonable to suggest that an analysis of the relationships between the existence of certain marketing phenomena and patterns of social, cultural and interpersonal behaviour may enable one to conclude that particular aspects of marketing can have adverse effects on society, and that it is perhaps in these areas that the role of marketing as a socially responsible activity should be emphasized. It has been observed that 'as the societal considerations of consumption become more intense, it is reasonable to expect a major increase in the influence of government on marketing decision-making'.[22] Indeed it is worth noting that, particularly in the highly developed economies, government is tending to demand a more influential role in free-enterprise marketing activities. However, 'markets were never intended to serve as an all-purpose institution, but in an industrial civilization it is easy to oversell business as the institution whose privacy goes unquestioned'.[23] The comparative analysis approach to marketing underlines this point, as it enables marketing to be studied and discussed, and its effectiveness evaluated, in relation to the other institutions within society. In this country social as distinct from societal marketing has a role to play in the deeper understanding of the way in which institutions relate to one another in society. Social marketing has been described as a 'bridging mechanism which links the behavioural scientist's knowledge of human behaviour with the socially useful implementation of what that knowledge allows';[24] societal marketing offers a parallel concern because of its ethical and moral dimensions. Effective comparative marketing analysis extends our knowledge of the interaction between human and business values, and offers the reward of a marketing concept which is more relevant to the social issues of the day.

6.3 Suggestions for further reading

Naturally much of what has been said in the previous chapter is also relevant to this, see especially pp. 79–80. See also chapter 16. There are a number of general books on International Marketing. A comprehensive coverage is provided by:

(B) KOTLER (1972).
(B) TERPSTRA (1972).

There are also some collections of articles:

(B) GRUB & KASKIMIES (1972).
(B) KAPOOR & GRUB (1972). Chapter 3.
(B) THORELLI (1973).

See also:

(A) DANIELS, OGRAM & RADEBAUGH (1976). Chapter 20.
(A) DYMSZA (1972). Chapter 5.
(B) ROBINSON (1973). Chapter 1.

Two specialist books on marketing in the European Community, each of which has lists of sources of information, are:

(C) BOLT, G. J. (1973). *Marketing and the EEC*, Kogan Page: London.
(B) DESCHAMPNEUFS, H. (1973). *Marketing in the Common Market*, Pan: London.

Many of the most interesting writings on this subject are to be found in articles dealing with specialized aspects.

For discussions of the advantages and disadvantages of standardization see:

(C) BUZZELL, R. D. (1968). Can you standardize International Marketing? (See note 1 to this chapter.)
(D) BRANDT, William K. & HULBERT, James M. (1975). Marketing Strategy in the Multinational Subsidiary: The Role of Headquarters. Paper presented at the American conference at Knoxville, Tennessee, April 20–22.
(C) SORENSEN, Ralph & WIECHMANN, Ulrich (1975). How Multinationals View Marketing Standardization, *Harvard Business Review*, **53.3,** pp. 38ff.

A discussion of other product strategies will be found in an article by Warren Keegan, see note 2 to this chapter.

For a discussion of pricing policies see:

(B) ROBINSON (1973), pp. 72–77.

Elsewhere in this book, issues concerned with the route abroad are discussed in chapters 2 and 3 with the decision-making in chapter 9 and with the environment in chapters 14, 15 and 16.

A discussion on advertising policies can be found in:

(D) MIRACLE, Gordon E. (1968). International Advertising Principles and Strategies, pp. 29–36. *MSU Business Topics 1968*, Michigan State University. Reprinted in KAPOOR & GRUB (1972), pp. 174–185.

For insurance against risks in financing Exports and other foreign operations, the reader should consult the appropriate government organization in the country concerned. In the United Kingdom this is the Export Credit Guarantee Department.

For the financing of export-import activities see:

(C) EITEMAN & STONEHILL (1978). Chapter 6. To be published.

6.4 Exercises for this chapter

Stone Plastics Ltd., Institute of Marketing (undated). A thorough survey of the considerations of a small British plastics firm in planning to extend its marketing in Europe.

Ing. C.D.O. Olivetti & Co., SPA, 1966 (Harvard University, ICH 9–313–139), by Guth, W. D. & Stevenson, H. H.
The world markets for Olivetti: free trade versus regional integration, entering Soviet market.

Fisher Price Toy Company, 1972 (Scottish Business School, CCH 373–045–1), by Diamond, S. L. & Milne, T. E.
Fisher Price linked up with Britoy Co. (disguised company name) and secured a European base. In 1972, the managing director has to devise a marketing strategy and create his first year's plan.

Gillette Industries Ltd. (Intro) and (A–F), 1962 (IMEDE M–145/150, ICH 9–509–009/15), by Leighton, D. S. & Keegan, W. J.
This series gives information in regard to problems of advertising policy, market research, pricing and product policy for introducing the same product into five different European markets.

Ample Marine Paint Co., undated (IMEDE M–164, ICH 9–510–026), by Thorelli, H. B. & Hempel, J. J.

This case focuses on international and entrepreneurial aspects of worldwide marketing and manufacturing operations in marine paints.

Polaroid France S.A., 1967 (INSEAD, ICH 9–513–119), by Buzzell, R. D.
This case presents the problems of developing a marketing programme in a multinational company; adaptation of US policies to French market.

Harbran AG (A), 1962 (IMEDE M–183, ICH 9–514–066), by Leighton, D. S. & Fry, J. N.
The switch to brand manager system in a large international drug company.

Noroco Ltd., 1972 (Institute of Marketing, CCH 572–009–1), by Rogers, L. A.
This case presents an oil refinery's examination of new markets for its products.

Kent Electrical Ltd., undated (Institute of Marketing, CCH 574–017–1), by Rogers, L. A.
The proposal to market a new consumer domestic appliance in Switzerland: marketability, appropriate forms of distribution and promotion.

Astra Pharmaceuticals, 1974 (IMEDE M–228, CCH 574–039–1), by Dunn, D. T.
The desire to place more emphasis on new product introduction into foreign markets raises the issues of changing the company's marketing organization, marketing planning and control systems.

6.5 Questions for discussion

(1) In what ways does Market Research in foreign markets differ from experience in domestic markets?
(2) At what stage in a company's phased growth would you advise its management to establish a permanent footing in the market, beginning with a sales office?
(3) Discuss some of the legal issues involved in entering a foreign market.
(4) What factors, in addition to those relating to a national market, would you consider investigating when attempting to develop a strategy for international marketing?
(5) What are the arguments for and against international product standardization?

(6) What steps can be taken to protect financial outlays in foreign sales?
(7) Discuss some aspects of international pricing policies.
(8) What are the conditions for and against international promotion campaigns and how can these conditions be identified?
(9) What are the particular legal problems with which an international marketing manager has to concern himself? Select one problem and discuss some of the issues at stake.

7 International Financial Management[1]

7.1 Introduction

Financial management in a firm is not just the responsibility of some specialized executives or a special department but it is concerned with the enterprise as a whole. However, its focus is quite specific; all activities in the firm are viewed in terms of flows of funds, and the variability of these flows in the face of uncertainty is used as a proxy for risk.

Finance can be broken down into two basic functions; (1) the acquisition of funds, and (2) the commitment of funds. The first function is concerned with the sources of funds, either internally through retention of profits, or from various external sources. This function also includes consideration of payments (interest and dividends) to those who provide funds. Frequently, this function is referred to as the *financing*, or *funding decision.*

The second function is concerned with managerial decisions such as (*a*) the total volume of funds to be committed to the enterprise, (*b*) the rate at which these funds will be committed over time, and (*c*) which specific assets an enterprise should acquire. This whole complex of issues is generally referred to as the *investment decision.*

It is important to recognize that the above holds true for companies that operate domestically or internationally, such as multinational corporations. Particularly the objectives of financial management are the same: to acquire funds at as low a cost as possible and make sure that they are invested in projects with the highest return compatible with the desired level of risk. However financial managers in such companies face particular problems which cause decision-making to be more complicated. The additional complications stem essentially from two sources. First, multinational enterprises by definition operate simultaneously in different financial markets. These markets are partially linked and partially separated. This fact causes complications not only for managers but also for those developing financial theory because it is always difficult to arrive at decision rules which apply to such grey areas. The second source of the basic difference is that funds flows are measured in national currencies, and as the value of such national currencies changes unpredictably, it gives rise to exchange risk with all its many ramifications.

Of course, these two basic factors can be broken down into various aspects and manifestations, and it is possible to establish a long list of special factors which make financial decision-making in international firms more complex. In the literature the following are most frequently enumerated:[2]

Differential rates of inflation
Differing degrees of uncertainty
Different cost of capital components
Different monetary systems with occasional changes of exchange rates
Different tax rates
Distribution of earnings in markets with different standards
Different legal requirements

Another way of summarizing the special challenge of international financial management is to view it in terms of a trade-off. When financial operations are conducted simultaneously in different financial environments, management has considerable opportunities to profit from arbitraging. At the same time, the very same differential conditions are also the source of added risk. To illustrate; changing exchange rates provide the firm with the opportunity to minimize the cost of funds by predicting appropriately movements in exchange rates. By the same token the uncertainty of international exchange rates also gives rise to unanticipated losses. Ultimately it is the job of management to maximize on the opportunities and to minimize the risks, and in order to do this, clear concepts and appropriate analytical tools are necessary. The remainder of this chapter reviews the state of the art in international financial management in respect to the (*a*) funding of foreign investments, (*b*) the management of exchange risk, and the (*c*) appraisal of foreign projects.

7.2 The funding decision

The financing decision (from which sources can the company raise funds in order to acquire productive assets in various countries?), must be made in view of a bewildering array of choices presenting to management opportunities but also sources of risk.

From the standpoint of the individual operating unit, say a foreign subsidiary, two basic alternatives present themselves. First, funds can be obtained from within the corporate family, either the parent or one of the sister affiliates or both. Secondly, the funds can be obtained in the form of one or more of various types of loans, or equity. Third, funds can be obtained from the group's own resources (retained earnings or the proceeds from the liquidation of assets), or from outside sources. Such outside funds can be acquired by the affiliate itself, or by the parent or another affiliate, either in form of loans or equity. In case the equity is sold by a foreign subsidiary, this makes it in essence a joint venture with all the implications for complex managerial and financial control patterns. Finally, with regard to outside sources, the parent and each affiliate must decide whether to obtain funds in their respective domestic market, the financial market of another country, or the external, or Euro-market, markets which have developed since the late 1950s.

From an analytical viewpoint the distinction between inside and outside funds has only very limited significance. First of all, it must be clearly recognized that ultimately all funds are outside funds in an opportunity cost sense. The alternative use for retained profits is always to repay loans or to increase dividends to stockholders. Thus the only difference between the cost of external and internal funds (capital) can be attributed to acquisition costs (issuing and underwriting fees) or tax-related costs. To illustrate, a number of countries, with Germany being a prominent example, have at various times applied a lower tax rate to distributed earnings than to funds retained within the corporation. In the absence of specific institutional costs or incentives, the cost of retained earnings in a multinational firm and its affiliates is equal to the weighted cost of capital for the group as a whole. The second point that needs to be emphasized is that funds obtained from sister companies or the parent are of a different nature than funds obtained from third parties, as long as the receiving affiliate is wholly owned.

This aspect is particularly important when financial structure decisions, dealing with leverage (or 'gearing'), must be made. To the extent that any priorities can be established among the complex, interrelated steps of a funding decision in a multinational company (see Fig. 7.1) such considerations probably take first place. The reason the debt equity ratio matters so much is that it determines the financial risk of the enterprise. Because of the contractually fixed nature of payments to debt holders, returns to the owners of equity will fluctuate more in response to a given, unanticipated fluctuation of operating returns, the higher the proportion of debt relative to equity.

This rationale also applies to multinational companies, but it is often mistakenly applied in the analysis of funding decisions involving individual, wholly-owned affiliates. What is usually overlooked is the fact that such affiliates have a distinct and separate debt equity ratio only if the parent is prepared to allow the affiliate in question to default on its debt without coming to its rescue. On the other hand, as long as the rest of the group has a legal (loan guarantees) or an effective moral obligation to prevent the affiliate from defaulting—even if this threatens the

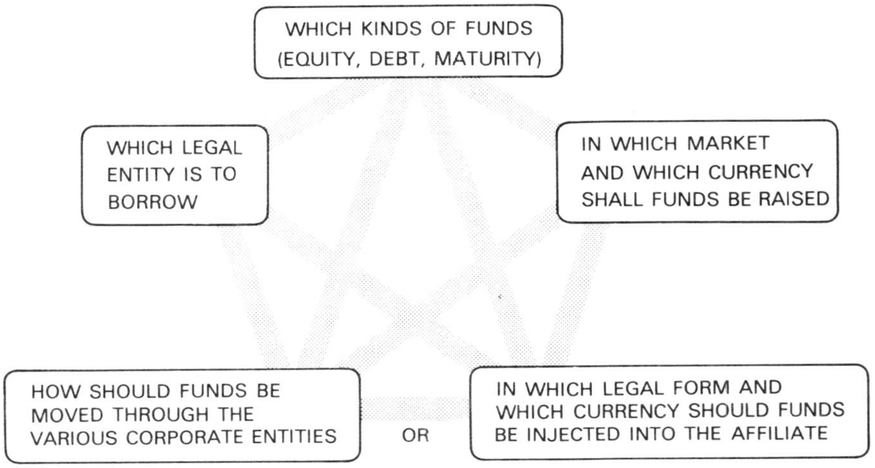

Fig. 7.1 Dimensions of the funding decision in multinational firms.

survival of the remainder of the group—the individual affiliate has no independent debt equity ratio. Its true leverage ratio is equal to that of the consolidated group.

Since virtually all multinational companies feel obliged to their wholly-owned (and sometimes even their partially-owned) affiliates, simply because they cannot afford to lose their financial respectability, the debt equity ratio of the affiliate is determined by purely institutional factors. Most prominent among such are (1) *statutory laws*, which prescribe a required minimum equity level in many countries; (2) *tax laws* which often treat interest payments differently than payments on equity (dividends); (3) *exchange control regulations*, which are usually less restrictive when interest payments are concerned; (4) *expropriation risk*, which may be lessened if the parent expects to default on its local debt in the specific case that the lending institutions have also been taken over by the government in question, or the lending institutions are state-owned in the first place already. Thus, the debt equity decision for foreign affiliates is either a purely legal one (as opposed to a financial decision), or it involves strategic questions of ownership to the extent that third party investors, local or otherwise, own a part of the affiliate's equity.

When it comes to making debt equity decisions for the parent, or rather the group as a whole, a very difficult issue arises: which market's standards will govern its 'acceptable' debt equity ratio? For domestic firms, the answer is usually quite clear. In different national capital markets, certain target debt equity ratios have been established for different kinds of firms. These acceptable debt equity ratios are determined by the nature of the firm. To illustrate banks and public utilities, whose operating risk is relatively low, are permitted to have a much higher proportion of debt before the market begins to penalize these enterprises by increasing the required rate of return on equity or the interest on their debt relative to, say, capital goods producers, whose return on assets is very much subject to the vagaries of the business cycle. The problem for the multinational firm is that different national markets differ quite a bit in terms of standards for acceptable debt equity ratios, and to the extent that companies sell their equity, or borrow funds, in many countries they must choose a reference market.

Theoretically this question is largely unsolved because financial theory is not sufficiently developed to answer the question precisely how financial assets are priced internationally. That is to say: Which is a more correct approximation of reality, that markets are separated or that they are integrated? In practice, most multinational companies do not have to face this problem head on because the great bulk of the equity is usually held by investors of one national market whose standards determine the applicable debt equity ratio. However as more and more companies make an effort to broaden their stockholder's base internationally by, for example, listing their stock on the exchanges of two or more countries, this issue will become more and more acute.

The problems encountered in the financial structure decision of multinational firm and its individual affiliates turn up again when broader questions of funding international operations are being considered. Multinational companies by their nature have complicated legal structures as is depicted schematically in Fig. 7.2.

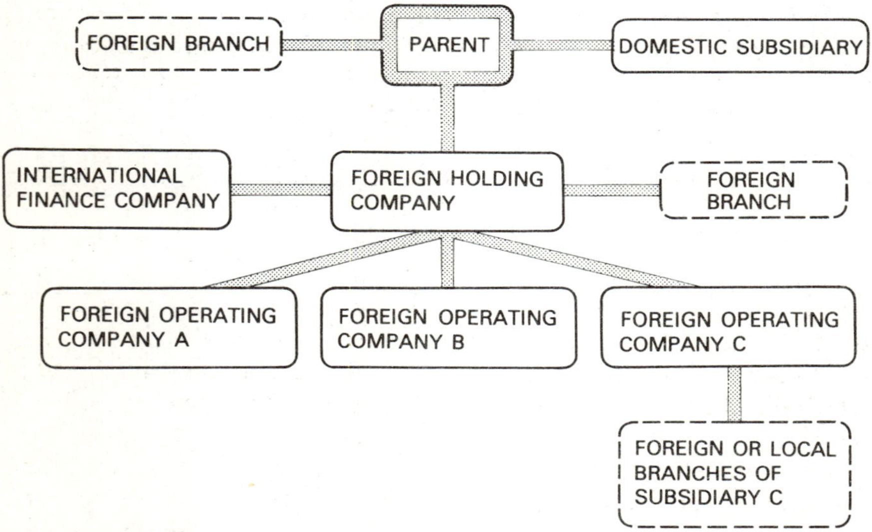

Fig. 7.2 Schematic presentation of the legal structure of a multinational corporation.

Of course, this is a schematic presentation only and in reality an almost infinite number of combinations is possible. For financial management, this raises the question as to which one of the entities should contract with providers of funds. In respect to equity this is almost invariably the parent company, especially if the firm has a policy of maintaining wholly-owned affiliates. With respect to debt, however, there are many possibilities. And unless the answer to the question is 'the same affiliate that needs the funds', another decision must be settled right away: how to move the funds through the various corporate entities to their final destination? In turn this decision is directly related to yet another question: in what legal form and in which currency should funds be injected in the affiliate that acquires productive assets?

Having affiliates in many financial markets provides the company with opportunities to minimize the cost of funds for the corporation by borrowing wherever the effective cost is least. In practice, however, there are serious constraints which limit these opportunities. After all it is *because* of the government restrictions, and to a certain extent institutional arrangements, that the cost of funds in various markets will not be equalized through direct arbitrage.

The only real advantage that the multinational company has in this respect is that it can somewhat more easily circumvent such restrictions, because of its particular structure of centrally co-ordinated, but legally separate entities. To illustrate, many countries have tight controls on direct lending to borrowers abroad. Theoretically, then, a multinational firm can get around this restriction by having its local affiliate borrow the funds and subsequently transfer them in some form to its parent or sister affiliates. Governments, of course, are aware of such operations, too, and they have usually issued all kinds of rules and regulations to prevent such international intra-corporate transfers of funds. However, if these regulations were written and administered too tightly, they would strangle international trade and investment. Thus, firms usually have some leeway in transferring funds although their flexibility is much more limited than is usually implied by critics of multinational firms.

In an integrated multinational company, where each affiliate has dealings with the other, transfers of funds can usually be effected because most are simply necessary to run the operation, regardless of the existence of restrictions. Thus, the question is not one of whether or not to shift funds among the company's affiliates, but how much and in which direction. This also highlights the fact that it is often impossible to determine the 'correct' arms length transaction, not only for the government but even for the corporate controller. To illustrate, economists and accountants still argue about correct cost allocation, transfer prices and interest charges in multidivision operations that are closely integrated. Interestingly, many financial executives in multinational firms point to the fact that their ability to move funds within the corporate family is severely restricted not only by government, but by the disadvantage of distorting their internal control system.

That multinational firms do have some freedom to move funds internationally is simply based on the fact that funds flows can be effected in very many ways:

Effecting payments on equity (dividends)
Effecting payments for services (management fees)
Effecting payments for technology (license fees, royalties)
Effecting payments for goods and components received (transfer prices)
Effecting payments for the use of productive assets (leasing)
Granting offshore term trade credit (lending and lagging)
Granting of direct intercompany loans
Receiving payments on equity (dividends)
Receiving payments for services (management fees)
Receiving payments for technology (license fees, royalties)
Receiving payments for goods and components delivered (transfer prices)
Receiving payments for the use of productive assets (leasing)
Accepting short-term trade credit (leading and lagging)
Accepting direct intercompany loans

Analytically, it is very important to generalize on a point that was made above in respect to the debt equity ratios; intra-company transfers of funds do not give rise to any change in the cost of funds or the risk of the multinational firm as such. These transfers have an impact only in terms of taxes, exchange controls and other regulatory aspects. The cost of funds and financial risk is affected only when there is a change in the kind or amount of *outside* sources of funds. Thus, the determinants of such inside transactions are to be found in tax and regulatory matters only. (See Fig. 7.3.)

While all this sounds very complex, and in reality it is complex because of all the environmental factors that impinge upon the decision (tax effects, exchange regulations, financial market regulations and practices, banking relations, etc.), the basic conceptual framework is quite simple and can be summarized as follows: If a multinational company requires additional funds, it can raise these funds directly or through any one of its affiliates. The conditions on which the funds are obtained from outside sources—debt versus equity, short-term versus long-term, currency of denomination, and restrictive covenants—will have an impact on the basic cost of funds and the financial risk faced by the group as a whole. And it is those relationships that determine the weighted average cost of funds that must be minimized.

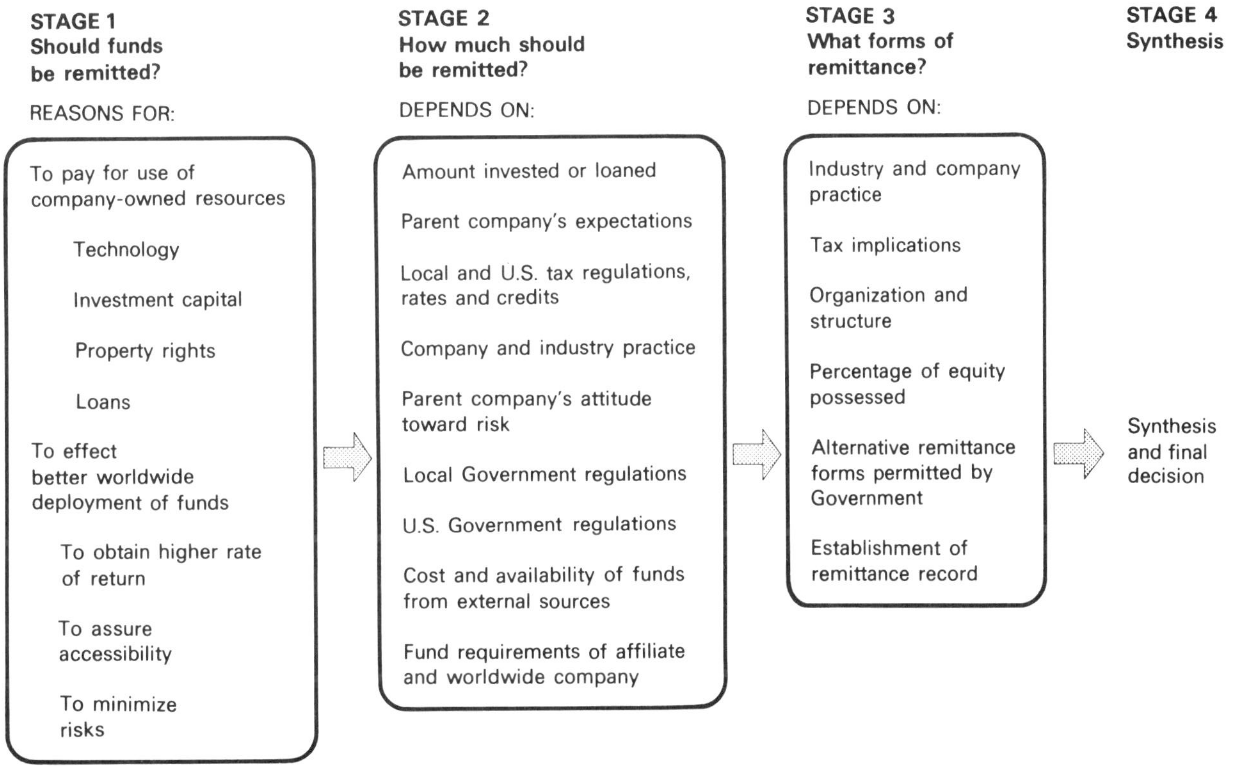

Fig. 7.3 Sequence of analysis and decision on movement of funds.
Source: ZENOFF, D. B. & ZWICK, J. (1969).
International financial management, p. 438, Prentice-Hall.

7.3 Managing exchange risk

So far, currency risk has been mentioned only in passing. For financial executives of internationally involved firms, as well as multinationals, exchange risk is probably the fundamental challenge. In the context of the funding decision discussed above, the effective cost of funds is determined by the interaction of interest rates and currency movements. To illustrate: assume two loans with a one-year maturity are being compared. One, is denominated in dollars at a cost of 8% per year, the other is a sterling loan at 14%. Which one is preferable?

One factor, of course, is *effective cost* which depends very much on the movement of the two exchange rates while the loan is outstanding. Thus, if sterling were to depreciate against the dollar by more than 6%, the sterling loan would cost less; but if sterling is expected to depreciate by less than 6%, it is cheaper for the firm to fund its operations in dollars. The same effects, of course, apply to investment returns. It is not surprising, therefore, that exchange rate forecasting has become a very important aspect of international financial management.

Right at the beginning of any discussion on exchange rate forecasting two issues must be clearly separated. The first is concerned with obtaining data external to the firm—future exchange rates and other data which are closely related, such as rates of inflation, interest rates, government policy and similar factors. The second concerns the question of how a given company will be affected by a range of (unknown) future exchange rates.

Turning to the problem of forecasting exchange rates, it must be recognized that the transition of the exchange rate regime from the post-war 'Bretton-Woods' system to one where major currencies float more or less freely has shed new light on the ability to forecast exchange rates. Under a 'fixed' exchange rate system monetary authorities endeavour to maintain exchange rates within small margins around a target rate, frequently referred to as par value. This par value is changed whenever a country's balance of payments moves into fundamental disequilibrium and when it becomes clear that various alternative policies such as internal deflation or controls are ineffective or politically not feasible. In respect to currencies that still follow that regime, forecasting consists essentially of a three-step procedure. First, from an examination of the country's balance of payments trends and other fundamentals, such as relative rates of inflation and trade flows, a measure of the pressure on a currency is derived. Second, changes in the level of foreign exchange reserves, including unused borrowing facilities available to the central bank, indicate when the situation will become critical. Finally, there is the crucial step of predicting which one of the rather limited policy options the economic decision makers of a nation will adopt in a crisis;

reinforced attempts at internal deflation, intervention and exchange controls, or devaluation of the currency.[3]

The success or failure of the forecasting game depends in these cases on the third step; as long as central banks and their governments play by the rule of that game, it is worthwhile for anyone dealing with foreign currencies to spend resources on analysing the economic fundamentals, as well as the power structure and the economic ideology of key policy makers.

For the past few years, the problem has been somewhat different in respect to major currencies. Central banks now hold much less firm rate objectives and their willingness, as well as their ability, to maintain rates has been reduced whenever private market participants have different opinions. As a consequence, foreign exchange markets have become much more like other speculative markets, such as those for commodities or organized securities markets. In such markets, prices are formed according to *anticipation* of supply and demand rather than on the basis of *present* supply and demand.

Those whose transactions affect foreign exchange rates invariably take future rates into consideration when making decisions that affect prices and foreign exchange markets directly or indirectly. Participants continually attempt to make profits by seeking and analysing new information that might allow them to predict price changes. Acting immediately on this new information, these decisions themselves produce frequent price changes. But new information useful for price prediction comes in an unpredictable fashion, otherwise it would be neither new nor useful. Hence price changes generated by the transactions of profit-seeking individuals are unpredictable, or random.

Loosely speaking, this argument constitutes the random walk hypothesis applied to foreign exchange markets. Generalized one can say that prices will fluctuate randomly where (*a*) prices are free to fluctuate; (*b*) no single trader has the ability to corner the market, monopolize information, or otherwise manipulate prices, and (*c*) present prices are strongly influenced by expected future prices.

The important implication for forecasting is that whenever such conditions prevail, one cannot expect to profit from forecasting because current prices reflect all that is known about the future. Future exchange rates, of course, are determined currently in the forward exchange market. Such forward rates then represent estimators of future spot exchange rates. And while the forward exchange rate is not a perfect predictor of the future spot rate, it is an *unbiased* predictor if the market reflects all currently available information, in short if it is 'efficient'. This means that forecasts made on the basis of forward rates may well turn out to be wrong, but it is unknown in which way the actual future spot rate will deviate from that predicted by today's forward rate.

As more and more currencies begin to float quite freely, it becomes more and more difficult for financial management to 'beat the market' because now the challenge is less to outguess the central banks, whose actions are governed by considerations other than profit maximizing objectives, but the traders and financial executives of other enterprises including those in financial institutions, who make their living by interpreting information concerning foreign exchange rates; unless the forecaster has superior information, which might be a superior forecasting model, he cannot be expected to do better than the market in the long run.

One important implication of all this is that the second task of forecasting, namely that of gauging the impact of a given foreign exchange rate change on the firm, becomes much more important. In any case forecasting exchange rates and forecasting the effect of changing exchange rates on the firm are quite different. If someone had the ability to forecast rates, he or she could profit from that ability alone through purely financial transactions; there is no need to engage in international production of goods and services, unless such activities serve as a conduit for the international movement of funds which might otherwise be more difficult, given exchange controls and related restrictions.

To forecast the impact of an exchange rate change on the firm is quite difficult and it is particularly confusing because several competing 'models' exist which purport to measure the effect of an exchange rate change on a corporation.

Empirical research on United States based multinationals has shown that the accounting model of exchange risk has a decisive influence on corporate finance policy.[4] Accordingly, exchange risk is defined as the possible loss or gain attributable to any change in the currently prevailing exchange rate that may show up in the company's published statements. The objective of foreign exchange risk management based on this model is to 'rearrange' balance sheet items in such a way that losses and gains offset each other, regardless of how the exchange rate may move in the future. This can be done by reducing (increasing) assets, or increasing (reducing) liabilities considered to be subject to a change in value when exchange rates move. Which assets and liabilities are 'exposed' is defined by translation rules (methods) which accountants apply to translate the books of the foreign affiliates into consolidated statements which are expressed in the parent's currency. One of the difficulties is that accountants cannot agree on the correct translation rule, and the effects of the devaluation of a given currency versus the currency of the parent can be quite different depending on the translation method used. (See Fig. 7.4.)

Thus, financial managers might pursue different policies in respect to

	Balance Sheet at Devaluation Date	Method of Adjustment: Monetary/ Nonmonetary	Current/ Noncurrent	Current Rate
Cash and current receivables	LC 800	LC 800	LC 800	LC 800
Inventory	900	—	900	900
Fixed assets (net of depreciation)	700	—	—	700
Total Assets	2400			
Current payables	LC (900)	(900)	(900)	(900)
Noncurrent debt	(500)	(500)	—	(500)
Net Worth	LC 1000			
Net position to be adjusted		LC (600)	LC 800	LC 1000
HC Equivalent —before devaluation (LC = 1 HC)		HC (600)	HC 800	HC 1000
HC Equivalent —after devaluation (LC = .80 HC)		(480)	640	800
Exchange Adjustment-Gain (Loss)		HC 120	HC (160)	HC (200)

Source: Financial Accounting Standards Board, *Discussion Memorandum on Foreign Currency Translation*, Stamford, Connecticut, 1974.

LC = Local currency.
HC = The currency of the country of the parent company.

Fig. 7.4 Accounts to be adjusted for exchange-rate change (20% depreciation of LC).

working capital positions and currency denomination of debt, depending on the translation rule that is used. It is not surprising, therefore, that thoughtful executives feel that they are really playing a 'paper game', and an intense search is on for the correct translation procedure.

The irony is that the results of all currently used translation rules are not in line with financial theory. Any rigid translation rule applied to assets and liabilities will yield a distorted picture of exchange rate changes on a given foreign operation as long as they are valued on the basis of historical cost. This is because exchange rate changes are very closely related to relative changes in both the price level and interest rates in the countries concerned. Indeed since relative price level changes and exchange rate movements have a tendency to offset each other in the long run, and since interest differences between countries tend to reflect expected price level adjustments and exchange rate changes, exchange risk stems from unexpected deviations from these equilibrium conditions.[5] Historical cost valuation cannot cope with such interrelationships. Particularly, current accounting practices do not distinguish between (*a*) *expected* exchange-rate changes which are already reflected in interest rate differentials and expected prices, such as quotes for goods and services to be delivered in the future, and (*b*) the impact of *un*expected movements of exchange rates.

In contrast, proper financial analysis focuses on the concept of *economic*-, or *cashflow exposure*. Accordingly, exchange risk analysis begins with the premise that the firm has committed resources in expectation of a positive net cash flow (discounted at the appropriate discount rate equal to the cost of capital for the firm) and this expected net cash flow must be protected from any (negative) impact of unexpected exchange rate changes.

To estimate this impact is quite complex. Thus, it is useful to break up the analysis into three manageable pieces: (1) operations, (2) funding, and (3) working capital adjustments.

The impact of an unexpected exchange rate change on the return on assets depends on its effect on projected revenue and cost streams expressed in local currency. For example, if the devaluation is greater than compensating price level changes, export-oriented operations can expect increased return on assets. Thus, a devaluation of the currency will have a positive effect on the value of that foreign affiliate in terms of the parent's currency, whenever the increase in the rate of return in local currency is greater than the percentage of the devaluation.

The analysis of cost and revenue streams must be undertaken for each firm individually, and no *a priori* judgments can be made. However, it is possible to specify the factors which determine the extent of the impact of a given exchange rate change:

(*a*) *pricing flexibility*, that is changes in profit margins to offset the exchange rate change;
(*b*) the *international diversification* of markets and sources of inputs; alternatively, the ability to shift markets and sources quickly;
(*c*) *volume effects* that might compensate for adverse changes in profit margins.

The impact of a given exchange rate change on the liability side of a foreign operation is somewhat different than the asset side, because the cost of debt (interest) is contractually fixed for the duration of its maturity. As shown in the example at the beginning of this section, a devaluation will affect the *effective cost* of funds, that is it will alter the outflow of funds necessary to service existing liabilities because the *nominal* rate is unchanged.

Foreign exchange management, based on the economic or cash flow model of exchange risk, uses the interaction between changes in the rate of return on assets and changes in the cost of servicing the liabilities to protect the expected net cash flows. This is done by structuring the currency denomination of the liabilities in such a way that any changes in operating returns, caused by a given deviation of the exchange rates from their expected rates, are offset by an increase (or decrease) in effective debt service costs.

The estimate of working capital adjustments caused by exchange rate changes is quite intricate in its details but the general principle is straightforward: to the extent that the exchange rate change causes additional (or fewer) net current assets to be required for ongoing operations, a one-time decrease (or increase) of remittable cash flow takes place. And this change in cash flow must be added to or subtracted from the change in operating cash flows in the planning period when it occurs in order to gauge the complete impact of the exchange rate change on the firm.

So far little has been said about traditional 'hedging' operations through forward exchange contracts, which are so prominently featured in the international finance literature. From the viewpoint of finance theory, two observations may put such operations in the appropriate context.

First the classical example of the exporter who hedges his foreign exchange rate by entering into a forward contract, selling each foreign currency receivable consecutively 'forward' for an assured amount of his home currency, is relevant only for what can be called the 'occasional' exporter. This is a firm which can easily find a different market for its product should the amount obtainable through the forward rate be below the minimum selling price. But how many firms have this choice, especially when they are multinational companies who have put considerable investment in place to service a foreign market through a stream of sales? They are not concerned with the gain or loss on an individual sale, but the change in cash flows caused by an exchange rate change. In such companies forward transactions must be viewed in the light of their effect on the currency denomination of debt. To illustrate: a foreign currency liability combined with a forward purchase of the foreign currency for the home currency results in a home currency liability for the duration of the contract; alternatively, home currency debt is 'converted' into foreign currency debt when a forward sale of foreign currency is contracted. Thus, forward contracts are tools to change the denomination of the company's liabilities (or financial assets).

The principles of *corporate* foreign exchange management can be summarized as follows:

(1) Rather than attempting to forecast exchange rates *per se* manage-

ment should predict the impact of unexpected exchange rate changes on operations and working capital positions.

(2) Such an assessment must take into account the interaction between exchange rate changes, prices, interest rates, and forward foreign exchange rates. In the long run, all these variables adjust—thus, exchange risk is relevant for the short-term or medium-term only; but firms are apt to make long-term commitments which are fixed and do not adjust.

(3) The corporation should structure its assets and liabilities in such a way that the impact of an exchange rate is minimized. The analysis must focus strictly on expected cash flows for the firm as a whole;[6] current values of assets and liabilities that do not reflect changes in cash flows lead to suboptimal decisions.

(4) This planning and forecasting process is so comprehensive that all functional departments of a company must be involved.[7]

7.4 The appraisal of foreign projects

The appraisal procedures of foreign projects are essentially the last link in a complex decision process that begins with such strategic considerations as to whether, where, and how a firm should undertake investment abroad.[8] Fundamentally management must decide whether future profitability is enhanced by further expansion at home, if necessary by changing its field of expertise or by exploiting its existing competitive advantage in a foreign environment. Simultaneously management must decide which foreign countries offer the best opportunities, and which method of penetration (exporting, licensing, or manufacturing abroad through a joint venture or wholly-owned affiliate) is best at a given time. All these decisions have to be undertaken first, because the data collection and investigation necessary for the appraisals of specific foreign projects is extremely time consuming and costly.

At the very beginning of any discussion of methods for foreign project evaluation it should be stressed that sound capital budgeting methods used for domestic projects are also appropriate for foreign projects. However, the special environmental conditions in which multinational companies operate must be carefully incorporated into the estimation of future cash flows, the specification of the cost of capital, and consideration of risk.

All capital budgeting texts emphasize that the relevant cash flows are additional, or incremental, flows that accrue to the enterprise as a whole because of the project under investigation. For integrated multinational companies such considerations are especially important, and often quite difficult to estimate if only because this analysis is performed by the operating subsidiary which is responsible for the project directly; but usually such projects have ramifications throughout the corporation. To illustrate,[9] the proposed manufacturing facility in a given foreign country may have negative effects on the exports of the parent or other affiliates. Revenues from licensing fees in the foreign, or even a third, market will be affected. Economies of scale will change and with them the cost structure throughout the enterprise; and these are just some of the changes that will occur. Other international elements such as tie-in sales, the contribution of used equipment and, last but not least, the complications of interacting effects of national tax systems can substantially increase the source of error of already difficult estimates of future cash flows.

A particularly vexing problem is posed by present and future remittance controls or repatriation requirements imposed by the various governments involved. This is often related to the question whether local or home currency cash flows are relevant. A little analysis will show, however, that the answer must be: 'remittable funds in home currency'. When putting this principle into practice a few caveats must be observed: (1) Not all remittance controls are effective; thus, there may be a limit on dividends, but few restrictions on royalties and management fees, for example; (2) the firm must actually anticipate to have funds to remit over the appropriate period. Most foreign ventures gobble up funds for several years and during that period even very severe remittance restrictions will not be terribly bothersome; (3) in case the firm does have 'blocked funds', usually some return can be obtained and often a portion thereof can be remitted, and this increases remittable cash flows. Because of all these complications decision-makers will usually find the Terminal Rate of Return or Net Terminal Value better suited than the usual Net Present Value, or Internal Rate of Return methods, for comparing competing projects; the terminal rate of return forces analysts to state explicitly re-investment assumptions, and this procedure is also helpful when dealing with different project lives.

Finally foreign exchange rate considerations can be built into cash flow analysis as outlined in the previous section. It must be stressed again that any such attempt must also take account of offsetting price effects. Indeed there is some evidence that, given a sufficiently long time horizon, price and cost effects compensate completely for exchange rate movements and vice versa. Consequently when long-term investment projects are analysed exchange rate effects can be neglected without adding greatly to the error of the estimates.

While the practical difficulties (and the cost) of arriving at reliable cash flow estimates for foreign projects is considerable, there are few theoretical problems involved. Unfortunately this is not true with respect to the cost of capital, especially with respect to the cost of capital for multinational companies. Because of a series of essentially unsolved issues in financial theory, it is possible, at best, to present what might be called a 'defensible approach' to the cost of capital estimation problem.[10]

One problem has to do with the interaction of the funding and the investment decision. Usually, it is useful and appropriate to regard these decisions as independent; the firm should first arrive at a liability structure that is optimal and use the resulting minimum overall cost of capital as the basic standard by which projects should be judged. But for multinationals a number of complications arise: (1) These companies consist of a parent company and a number of affiliates that are legally separate foreign entities. How can one take account of the environmental factors that may force the individual subsidiary to have a financial structure which has to be offset by the parent and other affiliates in order to achieve a structure that can be regarded optimal for the company as a whole? (2) How should one account properly for the cost, or the currency denomination, of financing that is 'tied' to a particular project?

Essentially all these questions boil down to one issue: Will better decisions be made if the company uses one 'worldwide' cost of capital, or should the cost of capital be estimated for each subsidiary as a whole? The use of the worldwide (marginal) cost of capital for new investment projects has the advantage that it is essentially consistent with the concept of the multinational, a corporation that seeks to employ its competitive advantage internationally through integrated operations.

It is only through the application of a common standard that the firm can establish investment priorities. Obviously, when estimating the worldwide cost of capital the result must reflect the firm's ability to obtain funds internationally, and funds obtained by foreign affiliates become part of the multinational company's total capital structure.

The standard established in this way should apply also to projects evaluated by individual affiliates. As was pointed out in a previous section of this chapter, foreign affiliates do not have an independent financial structure; they share the structure, and therefore the cost of capital, of the group as a whole. But foreign affiliates often consider projects which involve restricted funds. Government restrictions limit the uses of funds, and the cost of such funds is often higher or lower than equivalent funds obtainable by the company elsewhere. Such situations can be analysed in two ways: First, the marginal cost of capital can be adjusted for the project specific cost of funds. Alternatively the differences between the cost of specific sources of funds, including the effects of transfer restrictions, can be added to or subtracted from the project cash flow; one can view them like a cash subsidy or a special tax. Technically, either procedure will lead to the same results if properly applied. But the method of adjusting cash flows is a bit more elegant because it is easier to use with realistic re-investment assumptions, and errors in the estimation of the cost of capital number are minimized; and *that* figure is difficult enough to arrive at.

Finally, how shall foreign currency debt be included into the overall cost of capital equation? If the conditions for market efficiency hold reasonably well, the answer is relatively simple: the interest differentials among debt sources denominated in different currencies reflect expected exchange rate changes. Indeed interest rates differ because of different expectations about the relative value of various currencies. And in case markets are controlled, one can use the method suggested above to take account of the difference. To illustrate, if the cost of dollar-denominated debt is assumed to be 8% per year in the unregulated United States market, while equivalent sterling funds cost 14% in the unrestricted 'Euro' market but only 10% in the controlled domestic United Kingdom market, any project that a multinational can finance with domestic sterling receives a subsidy in the amount of about 4%, regardless whether the project is inside or outside the United Kingdom. This assumes, of course, that the firm's overall currency denomination of debt is not altered, that for the company as a whole it is a choice between domestic and Euro-sterling. If a trade-off has to be made between dollars and internal sterling, however, the company's overall net cash flow may be more subject to fluctuations in the dollar-sterling exchange rate, thus increasing risk.

If a foreign investment increases the riskiness of the multinational as a whole, either because of the change on the liability side, or because the new project alters its basic business risk, this may call for an adjustment in the cost of capital. Such adjustments are very difficult to effect in practice. Not only must the analysis deal with future values, but the theory of finance is still in a constant state of flux as far as the concept and measurement of risk is concerned. Still, some progress has been made, and some of the findings can be fruitfully applied to the special situation of appraising investment projects abroad.

The first challenge is to conceptualize risk. Any procedure must consider three requirements; (1) it must be theoretically defensible; (2) it must be cost efficient, the data requirements must be reasonable for operating managers to fulfil; (3) last but not least, it must be understandable to top management. The simplest procedure is to ask managers for their view of the best and worst 'reasonable' outcome of the project. Of course, these two cases are simply two points on a probability distribution of *all* possible outcomes. While few organizations will have managers trained to think in terms of probability distributions, the most useful approach would be to disaggregate the total incremental cash flow from a foreign project into those components that are decisive. This can be accomplished through sensitivity analysis. Subsequently, instead of using full-scale simulation, operating managers would supply a few points on a histogram for each variable to which a probability distribution could be fitted with the help of a computer. The computer would also combine the individual distributions to arrive at a joint distribution, or variance, for all cash flow elements that make up the total project.

The second challenge is to incorporate the risk measure into formal project appraisal. Technically, there are two methods available. One is the Risk Adjusted Discount Rate. The basic idea underlying this method is to adjust the marginal weighted cost of capital by a premium that accounts for the change in the overall risk profile of the company. The difficult task of choosing the proper adjustment factor can be approached by looking at the additional return required by shareholders for risky investments of this type in an efficient share market. In other words, an estimate of the market's price of risk relative to less risky investments can be used.

Since the adjustment of the cost of capital by a fixed coefficient involves assumptions about (*a*) the re-investment rate of cash throw-offs from the project, and (*b*) the constant increase (or decrease) or risk over time, which may be inappropriate, a second technique called 'certainty equivalent approach', is sometimes preferred. According to this method, project returns are brought back to their risk-free rate by comparing them to the risk-return trade-off. Again, this trade-off function may well be similar to that provided by shareholders in an efficient capital market.[11]

One can conclude with the observation that the unique aspect of financial management is represented by the special context in which multinational companies operate: Fluctuating currencies, different price level changes and interest rates, as well as the problem posed by operating in different regulatory environments, make international financial management a challenge for managers and financial theorists alike.

7.5 Suggestions for further reading

Books:

AHARONI, Yair (1966). *The Foreign Investment Decision Process*, Harvard.

ALIBER, R. Z. (1976). *The International Money Game*, Basic Books.

BAKER, J. C. & BATES, T. H. (1971). *Financing International Business Operations*, International Textbook Co.

BROOKE & REMMERS (1970, 1972).

BURSK, E. C. *et al.* (1971). *Financial Control of Multinational Operations*, The Research Foundation of the Financial Executives Institute.

CHOWN, J. F. (1974). *Taxation and the Multinational Enterprise*, Longman.

DUFEY, Gunter & FIELD, Judith J. (1971). *Financial Management in the International Corporation*, An annotated Bibliography, Michegan.

EITEMAN & STONEHILL (1978). To be published.

LEES, F. A. (1974). *International Banking and Finance*, Wiley: London & New York.

MANSER, W. A. F. (1973). *The Financial Role of Multinational Enterprises*, Associated Business Programmes.

MUELLER, Gerhard G. (1967). *International Accounting*, MacMillan.

NEHRT, L. C. (1972). *International Finance for Multinational Business*, 2nd Edition, International Textbook Co.

PRINDL, A. (1976). *Foreign Exchange Risk*, Wiley: London & New York.

ROBBINS & STOBAUGH (1973).

RODRIGUEZ, R. M. & CARTER, E. E. (1976). *International Financial Management*, Prentice Hall.

SINGHVI, Surendra S. (1972). *Corporate Financial Management in a Developing Economy*, University of Washington.

STONEHILL, A. I. (1970). *Readings in International Financial Management*, Goodyear Publishing.

WASSERMAN, M. S. *et al.* (1972). *International Money Management*, American Management Association.

ZENOFF, D. B. & ZWICK, J. (1969). *International Financial Management*, Prentice Hall.

Articles and papers:

See the notes to this chapter.

There is much in chapter 10 relevant to this chapter. See also chapters 5, 14 and 15.

7.6 Exercises for this chapter

Case studies

American Aluminium Corporation, 1975 (Harvard) by J. F. Truitt.

For a simulation model see Robbins & Stobaugh (1974).

Appendix B; the model was designed by M. Schydlowsky.

FORAD Simulation, 1977 (INSEAD 1977) by Remmers, H. L. *et al.* A foreign exchange simulation of multinational corporation currency management.

Sola Chemicals, 1976. Centralized versus decentralized management.

Marwick Home Products, 1976. Foreign exchange management.

These latter two cases are printed in Rodriguez & Carter (1976) see above, Suggestions for further reading.

Southport Minerals, 1975 (Harvard 4–274–110). Appraisal of Foreign Investments.

Cadbury-Schweppes (Harvard). Borrowing on the Euro-Currency Markets.

Machine Outil, S.A., 1976 (INSEAD). Foreign exchange risk.

For a large and thorough simulation exercise see:

THORELLI, H. B. & GRAVES, R. L. (1964). *International Operations Simulation.* There is a companion volume entitled: *INTOP International Operations Simulation Player's Manual.*

7.7 Questions for discussion

(1) Outline and discuss the main aspects of the work of the international finance manager.
(2) Identify and examine the most important techniques in the management of the currency exchange operations of the multinational firm.
(3) Establish a financial structure for a multinational corporation as a whole and for an individual subsidiary in a substantial market.
(4) How far should financing the foreign operations of an international company be a central function, and how far should local financing be delegated to the local subsidiary?
(5) What are the connections between inflation rates, interest rates, real and money terms, opportunity costs and cut-off rates? Describe the

considerations that must be applied to obtain uniform standards in the appraisal of capital projects at home and abroad.

(6) Discuss in some depth the opportunities, problems and choices faced by a company in moving funds around the world.

(7) Examine the problems of forecasting cash flow in an established subsidiary abroad and in a new project.

8 Production, Supply and Location

The least discussed aspect of international business is that which concerns the logistic and other problems of production, supply, distribution and the location of facilities.[1] Many relevant considerations are examined under other headings, such as the motives for foreign investment and the organization and communications structure of an international firm. Nevertheless the possibilities of an international production and supply system are increasingly being recognized as are the needs for a more rigorous examination of the issues.

8.1 International production

Many a company was driven into foreign investment to reduce the costs of production or to overcome logistic problems. The process has already been demonstrated, this chapter concerns itself with the policies for production that follow the move abroad. There can be a policy of mutual independence. Each subsidiary manufactures according to the techniques of its own country and the needs of its own market. If this happens there is likely to be at least advice from the centre. There can be a use of techniques worldwide, or there can be a highly integrated system whereby one factory supplies another across frontiers. This is one reason for looking at sourcing and manufacture together. The same options apply to both activities.

International manufacture develops in three ways. There is a conviction that some of the company's products will have to be manufactured abroad. The market defence mechanism is at work, and the question is—where? The pressures are on to invest in several places at once. Naturally the new plant will go to the country where the threat is greatest if other considerations are satisfied. Otherwise some planning framework is needed to decide between a bewildering selection of possibilities.[2] The second way is that of rationalization after a multiplicity of foreign units already exist. Operations have grown in different parts of the world, and there is a scope for concentrating them. This is a difficult exercise and may best be done in a company where there are sufficient products to negotiate exchanges of product between countries;

sometimes withdrawal from a country is necessary. At this stage decisions are taken about the reduction of manufacturing costs by varying the source of supply for different markets, the next way is when production for further manufacture within the group is planned.

Here manufacture develops through complex arrangements that involve both products and processes in many countries. This is found in some chemical companies, but mainly in branches of engineering like the automobile and agricultural machinery industries. The method is essentially a scheme for supply suitable for large companies. As such there have been both successes and problems. In particular more than one source of supply may be required in case a particular subsidiary gets into difficulties. The other form of integrated manufacture across frontiers is applicable to small as well as to large companies and is where partial manufacture takes place in one country for completion in another. This has happened in many industry groups. Often it has arisen as a result of government policies to and development in the country concerned by limiting the imports of finished products or charging higher duties on them. In many of the more industrialized of the less developed countries, the foreign company most willing to come to terms with stipulations about partial manufacture can find itself with both incentives and protection at the same time. Hence there is need of a strategy for determining at what exact point production may be divided or which parts of the final product are most profitably manufactured at home and which parts abroad. A variety of products, including light as well as heavy engineering and pharmaceuticals, lend themselves to the manufacture of the sophisticated part or ingredient in one centre of the world; the other parts can then be manufactured and the final product assembled in the local market. This is a possible route abroad for the smaller company with the capital available for foreign investment. For the larger company there is the further option of having a number of local subsidiaries feeding into assembly plants, so that no one assembly is dependent on one feeder. Decisions on these issues can be made centrally or by negotiation between the subsidiaries. Whichever is the method used, the result is an internationally organized production system. The options range from a centrally determined decision on the most suitable point of manufacture for each order to complete local autonomy. There are also a number of other issues, including production techniques, which come under the general heading of *international manufacture*.

Techniques. As with the other functions, there is the question of the international standardization of techniques. Naturally the international company has developed at the centre production techniques which are a part of its strength. It is usually believed that there is greater standardization in these techniques than in others. Foreign factories will be set up by technical teams from headquarters, and the language of production is assumed to be more intentional than that of marketing. But in fact this does not always turn out to be the case. For one thing production techniques have to be adapted to local labour. Both the differing customs and practices and the relative cost of labour and capital will affect the methods used. Even production planning, control and scheduling techniques are not so easily transplanted as is often suggested, although any form of international co-ordination will require this transplant to take place.

However the most significant problems come under the heading of *quality control*. One of the arguments used for establishing a manufacturing subsidiary is the difficulty of adequate quality control when foreign manufacture is undertaken by licencees. But the problem still exists with the subsidiary, and may become even more difficult when compounded by the question of market segment mentioned in an earlier chapter; the subsidiary may have a different market in mind altogether. But even without this extra incentive to different standards of control, the foreign subsidiary may not be able to use adequately the company's quality control techniques and may thus damage the reputation of trademarks and products. The difficulties of quality control alone may be strong incentives to keeping expatriate technical staff either stationed in one country or on tour.

Location. This will be determined by a detailed assessment of a number of factors. Some of these will weigh heavily in the decision, because they are connected with the reasons for seeking a foreign site in the first place. If, for instance, it is essential to reduce costs in line with those of competitors then clearly the proposed site must fulfil this objective and the one which fulfils it most effectively will be chosen if all other things are equal. But all other things are not equal and at this point there come into operation some factors which may disqualify or discourage. These are set out in Table 8.1. A look through the considerations will make the point clear.

One consideration is the availability and cost of capital. This is an important criterion of cost in any case, it becomes a disqualifying factor if the government of the chosen country will not give permission for the investment. Local capital becomes a discouraging factor if difficult terms are demanded.

Another issue is that of staffing. Companies have been known to establish a plant in an area where labour is plentiful and costs are low only to discover that vital skills are not available. This can happen in the home country as well as abroad. An even easier mistake to make abroad is to equate wages with labour costs. In some areas social security

Table 8.1
Pressures for and against integrated international production and supply

	Conditions favouring international integration	Conditions discouraging international integration	Conditions disqualifying international integration
Capital	Where cost is low Where availability is high	Where cost is high Where availability is low	Exchange control regulations in home or host country making movement of funds impossible
Labour	Where cost is low Where availability is high Where there are adequate education and training facilities	Where cost is high Where availability is low in required abilities or skills Where there are quality control problems abroad	Where some highly-trained or skilled occupations are non-existent
Transport	Where costs are high Where bottlenecks are common (Central control if not integration)	Where transport is no problem and so little is gained by global considerations	
Customers' Supplies	Where they themselves are international, especially where customers expect international service	Where they are fragmented or local	
Legal Taxation Tariff	Laws regarding: part manufacture locally high duties or taxes on finished goods high taxes on local profits or with-holding tax on transfers of funds	Where legal, customs or tax systems do not impede local decision-making	Prohibitions on specified imports

charges and fringe benefits may make the labour cost double that of the wages. Nevertheless in some labour-intensive industries, notably electrical components, these costs have been sufficiently low to make it worth a company's while to move and sometimes to export back to the home country. This applies to United States companies in Britain and German companies in Eire as well as companies from these and other countries in the Far East. Competitive conditions have sometimes made these moves essential for company survival. Whether the wage differentials between countries will remain permanently is still an open question.

Up to now statements that low wage countries will catch up as industry moves have not been justified in practice, although labour costs may run ahead of wages due to inefficiency or to social costs. In any case the amount of movement of production for this reason can easily be exaggerated.

Staffing does not end with what is usually called 'labour'. There are at least four groups required: managerial and supervisory, technical, skilled manual, semi-skilled and unskilled. The expenses of the expatriates needed to underpin local shortages both in the managerial and the technical categories can add to the costs of the exercise, as can the training of the necessary people in any of the groups. Indeed training costs should be added to the price of labour. International staffing is looked at more thoroughly in chapter 12.

Transport and the other problems of moving goods across frontiers are another important cost. Local manufacture obviously eliminates these difficulties altogether.

International production, in any form, depends on accurate forecasting and this can be difficult. Not only do markets change with the local economic cycle and for many other reasons, the competitors will be reading the same figures and will expand their production also. In an integrated international production system, as with all vertically integrated companies, the vulnerability of the company to market change is increased; this will be exacerbated where laws about laying off employees in one country act to encourage stockpiling in that country of components that may then not be required in another. The integrated company is also vulnerable to stoppages in one country which hold up production in another. The large firm, on the other hand, can insulate itself against these holdups by establishing sources of supply in more than one country, and this spread may also help in compensating for downturns in the economy.

8.2 International sourcing

Purchasing has traditionally enjoyed a low priority among the specialist functions of any company. Among international companies the rank of the purchasing official depends partly, as in all companies, on the business itself but partly on the degree of centralization of the organization. In a limited number of companies, there is a central or regional purchasing department which is masterminding the supply of materials to the units of the company within its authority. The determination of sources is based on: experience and other knowledge of supplier reliability, mathematical calculations to determine optimum pricing and transportation costs, other considerations such as legal and tariff.[3] Apart from the direct management of purchasing from the centre, with a liaison manager in the subsidiary or local unit, there are a number of arrangements for servicing. One is still centralized, but operated by a small central staff determining optimum routes which remain advisory to the local subsidiary. In this case, the local purchasing manager will have the recommendations in front of him, but may prefer his own judgment. Sometimes the company will require the subsidiary to produce evidence that the local initiative is not uneconomic.

Evidence has accumulated for supposing that there are some real savings to be made in international sourcing. Nevertheless most companies leave the decisions to the subsidiary, each affiliate does as it pleases. This does not, of course, apply to the vertically integrated company although even in this case there is a spectrum of regulations from the prohibition on buying outside the company to the consideration of the internal supplier as one option among many. Sourcing issues are further explored in the following excerpt in which the multinational buyer in industrial goods is discussed.

8.3 Buying: some characteristics of the multinational customer[4]

The paper by L. G. Mattsson contrasts the characteristics of the multinational as compared to those of the local buyer. The effects of these characteristics on buyer-seller communications will be analysed.

Localization of influence

The independent national firm makes its purchasing decisions autonomously. The subsidiary to a multinational firm can be more or less independent in its buying decisions but is always less autonomous than the independent firm. The degree of centralization can be different in different companies for a variety of reasons. Some of these are a matter of belief about which leadership style is the most efficient. Some reasons can be related to economic and technological variables. The latter alone will be discussed. It is assumed that the degree of centralization is affected by the following factors:

(1) The volume of the products that is needed for the whole company: if the volume is greater, then the economic significance is higher and it is more probable that the decisions are more centralized than if the volume is lower.

(2) The costs of sending input supplies across national boundaries: freight, tariffs, and other costs. If these are higher, then local suppliers have a greater competitive advantage and there is less advantage for the buyer to centralize buying. There is less opportunity for international competition on the supplier level and bridging the 'distance' between the local supplier and the MNC's headquarters is of relatively greater importance.

(3) The spread of the product over several subsidiaries: if the product is used by several subsidiaries, there is a greater likelihood that buying will be centralized, since there is more to gain from centralization than if one or very few subsidiaries use the product—that is gain with regard to buying power, costs of buying decision process, 'quality' of decisions made. Another way of putting this is to say that the interdependence between the subsidiaries' buying decisions are greater if many of them use the products and that the need and opportunity for co-ordination through centralized decision making is greater.

(4) Product category: input products can be classified in various ways. One criterion is its function in the buyer's production process, another is its interdependence with other products used in the process. A functional split-up can be made in the following categories: auxiliary material, raw material, machinery and parts of the end product. This list is not exhaustive. All other things being equal, it seems reasonable to assume that the more crucial the part played by the purchasers in the processes or end products of the buying firm the more are the buying procedures likely to run from headquarters. If raw materials are scarce or of a non-standardized character, then centralization becomes more probable for the raw materials.

The above reasoning is related to a product's 'degree of interdependence' with other products used in the process. Interdependence exists if decisions taken on one product have an influence on the decisions for others. The buying of parts probably carries a higher degree of interdependence than the buying of auxiliary materials. The choice of raw material is of course closely related to other decisions on the level of type of raw material but not necessarily so when it comes to choice of supplier. For machinery and related production and process equipment, the interdependence with other decisions is probably higher when the 'parcel' is larger. An example is the difference between buying a new process system to be installed in a new factory, compared with buying a tool fitting an on-going production line where there is not much room for the buyer to choose among very differentiated alternative products. The latter case is probably more decentralized.

A more general way of expressing the above is to say that there will be higher centralization when the buying involves a higher degree of uncertainty reduction and when the decision is more highly interdependent with other product acquisition decisions.[5]

(5) Centralization for other decision categories than buying: buying cannot be seen as an isolated activity. It has, of course, to be co-ordinated with decisions in other functional areas of the firm such as production, finance, marketing, Research and Development. If centralization is higher for these other activities, then centralization also is higher for buying. If, for instance, a multinational company makes decisions centrally about where production of specific products shall be located and with what kind of technological solution to the production problems, then also the buying of inputs is more likely to be centralized. One might argue that an important part of the buying decision is made as an investment decision or a product decision.

(6) The availability of suppliers and potential suppliers: centralization of buying probably has a diminishing effect on the total number of suppliers for a specific product. In the decentralized system there is less overlapping between suppliers to different subsidiaries. The greatest potential change as a result of centralization in the supplier structure can therefore be foreseen when the number of suppliers and potential suppliers is great. Therefore centralization is more likely to occur when the number of suppliers on the market is great. However one could also argue that if there are very few suppliers and, in a decentralized system, substantial overlapping between subsidiaries, it would be advantageous for the company to increase its bargaining power by centralizing buying.

The above analysis of some factors influencing the degree of central buying demonstrates that differences in influence on buying decisions between an independent firm and a subsidiary might be small or large. For the following I will assume that the multinational company goes in for central buying. In terms of variables of interest for the manufacturer that means:

(1) The bargaining power of the multinational company is higher because of its power to reduce uncertainty with regard to a larger amount of the sales volume of each supplier and, probably, for a larger number of suppliers. This power can be used to get lower buying prices or more favourable buying conditions in other respects.

(2) Higher competence on the buying side: the executives at headquarters that are involved in buying are probably more skillful and technologically competent than their counterparts at the local level.

(3) Contacts between buyer and supplier on more levels: central buying does not mean that contacts between the supplier and the subsidiary become insignificant. Since there is usually some discretionary power left with the subsidiary also in decentralized systems, since information from the subsidiary to the headquarters might influence the decisions, since contacts on the operational level for servicing and other

purposes have to be made and since important information about the customer's problems and the competitors' behaviour can be had on the subsidiary level, the suppliers' communications with the subsidiary are significant for his relations with the company.

(4) Information links between national markets: the multinational company's central buying department receives information from the various national markets through the subsidiaries or through contacts with geographically dispersed suppliers. The multinational company also transmits information to subsidiaries and suppliers concerning other national markets and where they are located.

(5) Larger quantities per supplier: this characteristic rests on the assumption that central buying implies more standardized input to the subsidiaries or more concentration to fewer subsidiaries of production in which a specific input is used or both. This leads to buying from fewer suppliers. The larger quantities might make some suppliers less satisfactory from the buyer's point of view since they might be too small.

(6) Change in criteria for buying decisions: whether multinational companies' headquarters use different criteria the independent company is debatable. It can be assumed that such companies are less nationalistic, have more reciprocal relations to other firms, have more clearly defined and more demanding requirements for buyer performance and are more inclined to change suppliers from one period to the other. They do not value stability as such as highly as does the local firm, all other things being equal.

Links with activities in other countries

The subsidiary's activities are more influenced by activities performed in other countries than are those of the local independent company. This statement rests upon the assumption that the multinational firm on a global level can choose which activities to perform in different countries and that the decisions for country A are dependent upon the decisions for country B. This interdependence may be small or great. If small, each subsidiary has a high degree of freedom to choose its product assortment which it sells only within its own national market, if great each subsidiary's production is carefully planned to fit a global production and marketing system. The interdependence can be related to:

(*a*) Horizontal specialization of production of finished products to the various subsidiaries with the products when marketed on several national markets, through selling subsidiaries.

(*b*) Vertical specialization of production, with more subsidiaries producing components for others within the context of a 'sourcing system'.

(*c*) Spread of technological knowhow and of new methods or

products within the company. This might take the form of sequential introduction of new processes or products on different markets. This internal diffusion process may take place also in decentralized systems.

In terms of buying characteristics the links with activities in other countries make the buying decisions in one subsidiary dependent on production decisions in other subsidiaries. In the case of horizontal specialization, where production of different products is concentrated in specific units, the interdependence with units of the same firm in other countries also comes through market conditions. A specific change in product attributes, for example, might be differently accepted by customers in different national markets or might have a different impact on the company's competitive position in different markets.

These interdependencies may or may not be associated with a high degree of centralization for the buying decisions. The co-ordination and the spread of innovations can take place through lateral relations between subsidiaries or centralized planning in a strict sense or centralized information links connecting subsidiaries.

For the individual supplier this means that he needs an understanding of how this interdependence affects the acceptability of his offers, and an understanding of which persons or units in the total corporate organization are his crucial communication partners. The greater interdependency between units located in other countries, if a foreign unit is compared to a local one, might be both a disadvantage and an assistance for a specific supplier. It is an assistance if:

(*a*) The supplier is accepted in another country, the use of his product might spread to this unit by the spread of technical knowledge as above.

(*b*) The supplier gets a competitive advantage over local suppliers in his international communication network with the multinational company.

(*c*) The interdependence is associated with buying centralization, if the supplier has a competitive advantage in the centralized case. The interdependence makes it harder for a new supplier trying to sell to a multinational firm since accepting the supplier might involve such changes in input product characteristics to this unit that changes become necessary in other units as well.

If we introduce the dynamic aspects of a change in the corporate strategy towards creating a higher degree of interdependency between the units, then this change probably has a considerable effect on supplier relations. The change in the company will probably involve changes in the degree of centralization, in localization of production, in standardization of inputs, processes and outputs as country-wide activities are concerned, in specification of the input products, and to a smaller number of suppliers to the whole corporate system for a specific product.

The relative position of buyer and seller are affected by the existence of alternatives. The buyer has a stronger position if potential suppliers exist that are offering almost as good conditions. The seller has a stronger position if there exist potential customers offering good conditions. The present supplier has also a better position if the cost of changing supplier is regarded as high by the buyer and vice versa. This reasoning leads to the hypothesis that the vertical market position in the multinational deteriorates more for standard product sellers, more for sellers with specialized production, more for sellers with low innovativeness, more for sellers belonging to mature industries. Thus the buyer is himself forcing changes on the suppliers.

Strategies for individual firms depend of course on many internal and external factors. The financial ability to grow and the profitability of increasing production capacity are not necessarily favourable enough to make such a growth strategy realistic and flexible even if it could help to improve the competitive position compared to the present one at the smaller firm size.

8.4 Suggestions for further reading

Much of chapter 5 is also relevant to this chapter, see especially pp. 80–1.

Production

(C) WEINSHALL, T. D. & TWISS, B. C. (1973). *Organisational Problems in European Manufacture,* Vol. 1, Part 1: Production In The Total System. Vol. 2, Part 2: Production In The Functional System; Part 3: Production In The Human Resources System. Longman.
This book discusses production techniques from several national backgrounds, the case studies are international in content.

See also:

(A) DYMSZA (1972). Chapter 6.
(C) STOBAUGH, R. B. (1969). Where in the world should we put that plant? *Harvard Business Review*, Jan.–Feb. (reprinted: Kapoor & Grub (1972), chapter 21).
(B) *Organizing for International Production* (1966). Business International Management Monograph no. 32 (reprinted: Kapoor & Grub (1972), chapter 22).

Sourcing

(C) FARMER, D. H. (1974). Corporate planning and management in multinational firms, *Journal of Purchasing Management*, **10.2,** May.
(C) DAVIS, H. C., EPPEN, G. D. & MATTSON, L. G. (1974). Critical Factors in Worldwide Purchasing, *Harvard Business Review*, November–December.

See also:

(B) ROBINSON (1973). Chapter 2.

8.5 Exercises for this chapter

Case studies

Massey-Ferguson Ltd., 1966, revised 1969. (Harvard ICH 9–313–12 3), prepared by Hofer, C. W.

An account of the development of international production in an agricultural equipment company.

Ing. I. C. Olivetti & Co., S.P.A., 1966. (Harvard, ICH 9–313–140), by Guth, W. D. & Hanna, R. G. C.
Production decentralization on a worldwide basis.

8.6 Questions for discussion

(1) Discuss the role of the supply function in the international firm.
(2) Discuss the conditions under which an integrated international production system might be recommended.
(3) Consider some techniques for determining optimum locations for manufacturing facilities.
(4) 'The manufacturing responsibility is possibly the least discussed aspect of international operations, often shunted aside in considerations of investment site selection, financing requirements, tax considerations, and market research and strategy. But the manufacturing sphere is probably the most complex facet of operations, and the one that offers the greatest possibilities for cost reductions and customer appeal in increasingly competitive world markets.'
(*Business International*). Comment.
(5) How would size be expected to affect corporate policies on each of these three subjects: production, location and supply?

9 Decision-making and Organization

9.1 Organization

The title of this chapter itself makes a point. Organization is seen as a means for facilitating and giving direction to the decision-making. The point at which decisions are to be taken, how they are to be vetted and how disseminated is one of the most crucial problems that faces the international manager. The tendency among companies over the years has been to regroup decision-making and authority away from functional subjects and towards product groups. Thus, in an electrical engineering company for instance, most of the accountants and engineers and sales managers will move into departments with names like domestic appliances, microcircuitry or lighting. Of course there will still be central finance, engineering and marketing departments; but these will be small and each division will have a complete range of functions. When the company goes international the decision-making becomes more complicated as a new dimension is added. Managers will be appointed whose responsibilities cut across the product groups and are concerned with countries or regions or the world outside the home country. Thus there is an inevitable conflict in the decision-making between the geographical and the product managers whose existence gives rise to upheavals in the organization. The various possible resolutions of this conflict provide a suitable means of classifying the organization into:[1]

(A) Foreign operations controlled by managers with *overall* functional responsibilities for the company as a whole.

(B) Foreign operations are controlled by managers with *geographical* responsibilities covering the whole or part of the world outside the home country.

(C) Foreign operations are controlled by managers with responsibilities inside the *product group* organization of the company.

(D) Foreign operations are controlled by product group and geographical managers at the same time forming a *matrix* organization.

Some companies do not fit neatly into the above categories usually because they are in a state of transition. Some have both a product group organization and an international division for some products. These are included in (C). The essential factor is that the decision-making process determines the classification.

The following is a summary of the main characteristics, problems and advantages of each of the different types.

Type A—overall

The foreign managers report to head office executives with *overall* company-wide responsibilities. The chief executive abroad normally reports to a main Board director in a British company, or to a member of the Executive Committee in an American. The most senior positions in the company are grouped around the specialist functions.

This structure is normally used:

(*a*) For small firms or for those whose business is in one main product group.

(*b*) For companies with over 70 per cent or under 15 per cent of their business abroad.

Some trend in the last year or two back towards this simple structure has been observed in large multi-product firms, at least with reorganizations to smaller numbers of large product groups even more completely self-contained. In this type there are short lines of communication and managers abroad have direct access to the top of the parent company.

Type B—geographical

Product group organizations at home with a *geographical* organization for the foreign operations.

In some countries there is an international division or some such management group with total world responsibilities. Other firms have *regional* organizations. In either case there may be managers with responsibilities for certain parts of the world who are located either in head office or in their own areas. The advantages of this type of company are that it is closely geared to the foreign operations, with whom satisfactory communications are more easily established. Foreign expertise is concentrated in the international division, whose managers are held responsible for the profitability of operations abroad.

This type of organization is better at avoiding political risks as it is more sensitive to local operations, where it stimulates growth. The difficulties of this geographical organization are usually found within the head office. It has been found hard to establish satisfactory communications between the product divisions and the foreign divisions. The passing of information and new technologies proves difficult. Just because the international expertise is concentrated in one part of the company, other parts may be too biased towards domestic operations. Extra difficulties are caused by the considerable emphasis placed in recent years on product group autonomy, and the appraisal by group management on the success of their part of the organization. It has also been found that companies with this structure grow more rapidly in size than they do in profits.

American companies often start with this type of organization and then turn to product group worldwide. Many European companies have moved in the opposite direction. Executives take the view that the world is one market, and all managers are international, until the emergence of problems abroad convinces them that some specialization in foreign business or in a particular region is required.

This type of organization may be preferred where:

(*a*) Product divisions are small.
(*b*) Geographical spread is large.
(*c*) The company is mainly in consumer products, or the products are closely related.
(*d*) Governments are customers, or the business is politically sensitive.

Type C—product group

Product group organization at home and abroad.

The advantages of this type are that all divisions are given responsibility for their foreign operations.

This avoids duplication and conflict in head office.

Type C companies may grow more slowly, but the growth in profits more closely matches the growth in investments.

The disadvantages of this type of company are that it has been found very difficult to establish satisfactory communications with the foreign subsidiaries.

The international expertise is thinly spread.

There may be duplication abroad, and the business methods of one product group may not be helpful to those of another.

This type of organization may be preferred where:

(*a*) There are a limited number of large product divisions (some companies have reduced the number of their divisions in recent years).
(*b*) Local expertise is of limited importance, and global strategies make particularly good sense.
(*c*) The company is mainly in industrial goods.

Type D—matrix

This is a type of organization with multiple reporting and responsibility lines. Foreign managers report both to those with product and those with geographical responsibilities at the same time. Occasionally they may report along functional routes as well. This type of organization has been adopted by fifteen to twenty of the world's largest companies. It is very complex but there is no reason why smaller companies should not adopt these methods, which produce a high morale, but depend upon the recruitment of particularly high calibre foreign executives. This type of organization is likely to become more common because it matches the facts of the decision-making process.

Regional policies

There has been a growth of *regional* policies, partly in response to economic and political agreements between countries and partly to produce more manageable geographical units. The following is a summary of the principle points that have emerged from investigations.

A *regional centre* can be associated with any of the organization types, but great care needs to be taken before superimposing such a centre on a C type (product group) organization.

The centre itself can be of different kinds:

(i) A national subsidiary with responsibilities outside its own country, including a brief to develop a market plan for the region of which the country is a part. This goes with an A type company.

(ii) A regional subsidiary will full line management responsibilities, consolidating the reports for the region and itself reporting to the Board of the company.

(iii) A regional subsidiary with staff responsibility only, to advise the national subsidiaries in the region and co-ordinate their activities.

(iv) A mixture of the last two options. The regional centre may, for instance, have staff responsibilities towards the more successful national subsidiaries and take over line management for those that are in trouble.

The regional centre may be physically situated in the region. This will often, but by no means always, mean in one of the smaller countries—Switzerland, Belgium, Singapore, Hong Kong; it may be at Head Office, or it may be divided between the two. So long as there is adequate communication within the regional centre, probably assisted by exchange of staff, this last possibility has much to recommend it, especially for type (iii)—the regional 'staff' centre. Most companies do not have regional centres, but there are increasing pressures towards establishing them. It is alleged that an organization nearer to the point of sale is required. Subsidiary managers often use this argument, especially in companies manufacturing consumer products or where governments are the principal customers.

When the centre is actually established, some managers react against it for two main reasons:

(*a*) They find it interposes an extra level between themselves and top management. It thus tends to demote the subsidiary managers, and to upset established lines of communication.

(*b*) It offers no particular additional expertise, and so the expense appears as an unnecessary and unwelcome addition to their budgets.

As a result efforts are made to bypass the centre.

These problems especially apply to type (iii). This is the most common type, indeed this is what most companies think of when regional centres are discussed. For the reasons just given, it often turns out to be a pointless expense; and the experience of this breeds disillusionment with any form of regional organization. When combined with the type C (product group worldwide) organization, the type (iii) centre is almost bound to fail.

A type (iii) regional centre, therefore, may be an expensive luxury, but it can fulfil certain functions. For instance:

it can negotiate with supranational bodies;

it can be an important part of the company's planning procedures;

it can be a training ground for international executives and organize some regional management development schemes;

it can provide expertise on a regional centre where this makes sense. If so, the expertise must be strictly restrained, otherwise regional centre managers tend to take on line responsibilities.

If these advantages are held to be sufficient to justify the cost, it may be best to allocate this to the head office budget and not just to the subsidiaries in the region.

Regional centres are likely to find a place:

(1) In companies, in most industry groups, where operations abroad are just beginning to expand, especially in small companies with limited resources.

(2) In larger companies in high technology or in heavy capital goods industries.

In both these situations a type (i) national subsidiary with regional responsibilities can be highly effective when combined with:

a type A overall organization for small companies and large single-product firms, a type B (geographical) company,

a type C (product group) company. In this case the subsidiary will service an individual product group.

(3) In large companies where regionally integrated supply, manufacture and distribution policies make sense.

(4) In companies heavily dependent on government contracts but with considerable activities in certain parts of the world.

In these situations, a type (ii) line management centre is possible. This would usually be in a type B organization, and the regional centre would replace the international division.

(5) In growing companies which are either conglomerates or in industrial goods industries with a medium or small cost per item, a type (iv) regional centre may have advantages. This will have little significance for well-established and profitable subsidiaries, but it will be vital as a fire-fighting force in emergencies, and may well form an important part of the company's planning procedures.

Some critical decisions have to be made, for instance: How much expertise is to be allocated to the centre and in what specialization, whether the centre will be a profit centre, the relationships between the centre and the local subsidiaries, the staffing of the centre.

9.2 The locus of decision-making

A small group of businessmen questioned about which was the most perplexing issue facing them on the international side of their business, placed the locus of decision-making first, slightly ahead of the sources of funds and planning fresh developments. To the social scientist the issue is of the greatest interest as demonstrating various facets of the complex organization.[2] But there are many pitfalls in investigating and generalizing about this subject. This section attempts a brief summary of current thinking.

The issue under discussion is the authority relationship between a company and its foreign subsidiaries. Nominally and in legal form this relationship is usually at 'arms length'. That is to say that the authority consists solely in the usual powers vested in a shareholder. The subsidiary can be called to account at a duly constituted meeting, the management can be changed, and binding resolutions can be passed. In practice much tighter controls are exercised, with the powers of the shareholder held in reserve as the ultimate sanction. The actual exercise of authority varies from company to company, and in some cases from subsidiary to subsidiary, across a spectrum that ranged from very little indeed up to constant supervision to the same extent as might be applied to a domestic unit where there is little delegation. Sometimes the situation arises by design, sometimes by accident. Where the company intends the degree of centralization that applies or attempts to justify it, four types of argument are used:

(1) That decisions are best left to the man on the spot, and that as much as possible is delegated.

(2) That there is no consistent policy, the degree of interference from head office varies from function to function with finance and production more centralized than marketing or personnel.

(3) That the degree of interference varies according to the nature of the subsidiary—its age, nationality or ownership.

(4) That the opportunities for global planning and the necessity of making the most effective use of the skills and resources of the company make for central decisions on most significant issues.

The argument most commonly used is some variant of the first—leave the maximum initiative to the subsidiary. Investigations have shown that the actual initiative is often less than that claimed. The reasoning in support of this argument is usually based on some theory of motivation, the subsidiary management is assumed to perform better if given independence. There are other arguments. Centralization makes communications more difficult and slower, while there are legal implications involved if the subsidiary is not left to itself. For the smaller company, centralized decision-making may be considered too expensive in terms of the staff required. As against those reasons, there are the commercial arguments stated above for the centralization. An international company is almost by definition a concern which has developed expertise which can be exploited abroad and often has surplus resources to back this expertise. Local decision-making can prove a waste of the resources and the subsidiary is seen to be behaving in a sub-optimal manner. Hence pressures build up for greater centralization.

There is evidence that this happens in all the functions, so the suggestion above that it varies according to the specialization must be modified. There are variations in most companies, but crucial decisions on marketing issues are taken internationally with the least possible modification that is needed to suit the local conditions. Some studies of this question are mentioned below. On the other hand the possession of international brands and trademarks, which might be thought to lead to some degree of centralization, do not necessarily do so. Clear evidence of this has been collected from a number of companies with widely advertised consumer goods. Companies manufacturing industrial goods are likely to be more centralized, although there are exceptions where governments are the main customer.

The view that the nature of the subsidiary determines the exercise of authority must also be modified. Some companies declare that they always try to own more than 50% of the equity of the foreign subsidiary in order to retain control. Others assert that this is not necessary and the evidence supports this latter opinion for subsidiaries with a minority holding are treated in many companies in exactly the same way as those that are wholly owned, although there is an assumption being made that this is not so; polite fiction might be more apt than assumption. The question of joint ventures and local participation has already been discussed in chapter 3. Other variations in the subsidiary relate to questions of size, age and nationality. Contradictory opinions are to be found where some companies maintain that large subsidiaries have more independence because they can more easily survive and are more substantial businesses in their own right. Others say the opposite, the large subsidiary can do the group more damage if it makes substantial losses. Some say that the long-established subsidiaries acquire greater independence, others that over a period problems are bound to arise in the subsidiary. These may not be its fault at all, but solely due to the fluctuations of the local economy. The response of most international group managers to problems whatever their cause is to tighten up the authority system; hence, so the argument goes, the long-established subsidiary will turn out to have less discretion than the new one. The influence of nationality is said to mean, among other things, that the subsidiary in the less developed country will have less autonomy than that in the industrialized one. But the argument of size is apt to apply here: the local company in the industrialized country is likely to be more important to the group and so will get more attention, and attention usually means centralization.

This maze of paradoxical and contradictory arguments has been penetrated by investigations which usually demonstrate a greater centralization than assumed at head office. Indeed there seems to be a process of creeping centralization going on in most companies, with an occasional conscious reorganization or other effort to reverse the process. There are a number of contexts in which this creeping centralization has been found at work. One is where there is delegation at head office. Functional specialists, and sometimes product group executives as well, exert pressures which effectively limit the discretion which the foreign managers are supposed to have. Another context is where the company has a central planning system strongly oriented towards 'top down' planning, and using sophisticated techniques which are unavailable to the subsidiaries. Such a system is compatible with a degree of decentralization because in name the subsidiary's acceptance may be voluntary. In practice this does not work out in numerous cases.

A similar and related example is that of a very detailed reporting system. In some instances this means decentralization. The parent company is satisfied that the feedback is sufficiently efficient to ensure that potential disasters will be quickly signalled. In some companies this has indeed been found to be the case, but usually the reverse has been true. The elaborate reporting system has been developed to feed the planning department rather than to make local decision-making possible. The effect of this on the subsidiary may be a considerable distortion of its business activity. It is forced to collect information on matters which may not be needed for the development of its own business.

These are some of the ways in which centralization develops contrary to the policies of the company. They depend on some action at head office which reduces, not necessarily intentionally, the limits of discretion and initiative in the subsidiary. A similar effect can result from action in the subsidiary, when local experts bypass routes of communications and authority in order to establish closer links with head office. The result is a gradual integration of operations which eventually reduce the autonomy of the subsidiary.

The trends to centralization are more easily traced out than are their consequences for business efficiency.[3] It is clear that there are powerful pressures operating both ways to ensure that few firms remain at the most extreme degree of centralization or the greatest local autonomy. It is also clear that there are tangible commercial reasons for reserving decisions to the centre, while there are less tangible or quantifiable but not necessarily less important reasons for greater delegation to the subsidiaries. This brief summary of a widely discussed subject can go little further than point out the situation and the issues to which it gives rise. One thing that is certain is that in terms of organization, a significant issue is the allocation of expertise. Whatever may be the intention, decisions are effectively taken at the point where the expertise is situated providing that that expertise is also backed by adequate communications. The next two chapters will discuss communications. Perhaps a fitting conclusion to this one is that the centre of expertise on any given subject should be as near to the operations as the scope of consideration, knowledge and communication requires. However the most significant indications coming out of current research are:

(1) Companies will be drawn into more centralized relationships with their foreign subsidiaries.

(2) This trend will need to be supplemented by greater foreign expertise and sensitivity at head office.

(3) A careful and regular appraisal of the commercial and financial considerations will be needed to identify clearly which are decisions profitably reserved to the centre and which are not. Resource decisions, including market areas, will be taken centrally; operating decisions will

be taken locally. Over-arching policies will only be promulgated where essential.

(4) These proposals will need to be pursued openly. Their implications include schemes for appraising subsidiary performances more realistically (in the light of the decisions and activities that are under subsidiary control), schemes for international management development to prevent executive frustration, and schemes for supplying information to local governments and other interested bodies.

9.3 Suggestions for further reading

Much of chapter 5 is relevant to this chapter, see especially pp. 82–4.

For further details of the points summarized here see: Brooke & Remmers (1970), chapters 2 and 3. There are innumerable other classifications of international company structure available. Most of them describe different organizations that have been observed without any relation to an analytical or explanatory system. A notable exception is the classification to be found in:

(C) STOPFORD & WELLS (1972). Chapters 2–6.

This derives from the well-known theory of organization change set out in:

(C) CHANDLER, A. D. (1962). *Strategy and Structure*, Massachusetts Institute of Technology.

Most of the general books on international business have chapters on this subject. See especially:

(A) DYMSZA (1972). Chapter 2.
(B) ROBOCK & SIMMONDS (1973). Chapter 18.
(B) SALERA (1969). Chapters 29–30.

The following papers are worth consulting:

PRAHALAD, C. K. (1975). The Strategic Process in a Multinational Corporation. Unpublished D.B.A. Thesis, Harvard University.
ZEIRA, Y. & HARAI, E. (1975). Planned Organizational Change in Multinational Corporations, *S.A.M. Advanced Management Journal*, **40,** pp. 31–39. Summer.
GHERTMAN, M. (1975). *The Strategy Formulation Process of the Foreign Subsidiary of a Selected French Based Multinational Corporation*, CESA Cahier de Recherche No. 30.

On the issues of centralization and decentralization in relation to foreign subsidiaries less has been written, although many of the general books listed above refer to this subject.

See also:

(C) JENNEGREN, L. Peter (1974). *Decentralization in Organizations*, Berlin: International Institute of Management.
(D) ABELL, Peter (1976). The Task Determinates of Decentralization between HQ and UK subsidiaries of International Corporations. Unpublished paper, Department of Sociology, University of Birmingham.

(C) BROOKE, M. Z. & BLACK, M. (1975). The Autonomy of the Foreign Subsidiary, *Conference Papers,* Academy of International Business Conference, Fontainebleau.

For some papers on decision-making in specific functions see chapters 6–8.

9.4 Exercises for this chapter

Case studies

An interesting discussion of the Matrix Organization is:

DAVIS, Stanley, *Matrix Organization*, ICH No. 9–474.
This is much more than a case study and should be read as an important text on the subject.

See also:

The Eaton Corporation, ICH 4–475–047(8) (9), compiled by Davis, Stanley.
A survey of the problems of a company expanding abroad.

'Corning Glass reshapes its international operations'. *International Management.* A form of Matrix organization.

Sola Chemical (Harvard ICH 9–371–338), R. Vernon.
This case describes the international finance function organization—issues of centralization against decentralization in control.

Galver Co., 1963–64 (Harvard ICH 9–313–180 and ICH 9–313–181), by Shapiro, E. & Adler, M.
Acquisitions of a French Electronics Company by a major US Electronics Manufacturer; the acquisition—negotiation and terms.

Brise Holdings A.G., 1975 (IMEDE GM218, CCH 375–019–1), by McDonald, Ph., Rotch, W. & Moeller-Racke, G.
The case discusses the improvement of performance of the Beaune France subsidiary of a large, multinational Swiss wine trading company.

Clark Equipment Co., 1969–70 (IMEDE OB 114, CCH 476–005–1), by Allen, S. A.
The move from a separate international division to a worldwide product group structure is presented as a prototypical change in the organization of a multinational company.

Incidents: (1) Corporate upheavals

The Board of Global Products Ltd., had been in almost continuous session for a week. A series of unexpected problems in their foreign subsidiaries now added up to a major crisis. These included:

16 May. Resignation of Chief Executive in Brazil (preceded by two other resignations earlier in the year).

29 May. Loss reported in French subsidiary. This had been totally unexpected as market conditions had appeared favourable in that country.

12 June. Australian subsidiary involved in serious problems over a major contract—numerous delays and customer complaints.

24 June. Advance warnings of losses in two other subsidiaries precipitated the present series of Board meetings.

It had indeed been a long, hard summer.

Twenty years ago the first foreign subsidiary had been founded in Canada. The market there for one of the company's richest products, an electrical component, had grown to the point where local manufacture would increase profitability and provide a defence against aggressive local competitors. As a result of the success of the first foreign ventures, a policy had been developed by which the company put as much new capital each year into operations abroad as at home. For some years this policy had appeared to pay off handsomely. The foreign subsidiaries had been profitable, and they had cushioned the firm against the ups and downs of the domestic economy.

During the growth of the international side of the business two major reorganizations had taken place. The first of these had been seven years ago with the formation of an international holding company, and the wholesale decentralization of the subsidiaries by country. Up to that time, most policy and many operating decisions were reserved to the head office. The foreign management reported to a liaison director on the main board, and his personal staff were the principal means of communication and decision-making. The subsidiaries had been set up with finance from the United Kingdom, and over all owned 100% by the parent company. They were manufacturing products to head office specifications and patents. No deviations were allowed, and any change needed the sanction of the liaison director. He and his staff kept up a steady stream of instructions that had to be followed.

Then the international holding company was formed, the intention was that a considerable measure of decentralization was to take place. The holding company managers were to fix details according to the experience and sophistication of each subsidiary. But, on principle, all operating decisions were to be taken by the subsidiary; and strict conformity to control policies was only required on major issues. These included the raising of long-term capital, the entry into a new market and a major change in a particular product. Board level appointments were also reserved to head office. The staff of the international holding company were to provide a close link with the subsidiaries. They were to ensure that reports came in regularly and were inspected. These were to be kept to a minimum and to consist of key monthly financial indicators, together with a few other figures like market share. The policy decided by the Board was to be a minimum of formal control together with a maximum of contact. The international staff were expected to visit the foreign companies regularly to discuss problems and opportunities on the spot. Mandatory orders, however disguised, were not to be used.

The transition to the new system was not altogether smooth in the foreign operations. There were some resignations, but nothing happened that could not be considered as a natural reaction to any change. However some problems did arise within head office, and the position of the international holding company was always a difficult one. This was generally assumed to be a result of the personality of the man in charge. He was always rubbing up his colleagues the wrong way. Further, no evidence came to light that the performance of the group or of the subsidiaries had improved. Eventually, some four years later, a further reorganization was decided. The international holding company was to be abolished, and the product group divisions were to take responsibility for their foreign operations. In some countries this meant splitting the local subsidiary, in others it simply meant that one product group acted as agent for others. Once the reorganization was completed the foreign companies were to be guaranteed the same degree of autonomy as before.

By the time of the Board meetings mentioned above, it had become clear that the autonomy of the foreign firms was much less than anticipated. Although the new system had now had plenty of time to settle down, decisions were being taken at head office which the rules reserved for the managers abroad. Further an ever-increasing amount of information was being demanded from the local managements. These latter were complaining that they were being tied to their desks by the pressures of a well-staffed headquarters which was making impossible demands on the small local organizations. Questioned about their allegations, head office managers were able to give completely convincing replies. The progress of the business depended on achieving at least the same level of sophistication as their competitors. Hence they needed to ensure that new products and new techniques were quickly adopted throughout the group. They also needed to ensure that there was adequate reporting for the planning system to function efficiently. No unnecessary interference with local autonomy was being tolerated.

Some of the questions raised at the Board meeting were:

Where, if anywhere, have we gone wrong?
Is it just a coincidence that these problems have arisen all at once?
Are our controls too loose or too tight?
Do local managers operate best when left to their own devices?
Why, above all, did some of the problems take them by surprise in spite of complaints that the reporting was already burdensome?

(2) Corporate expansion

A German food processing company with sales of DM. 400 m has manufacturing subsidiaries in eight different countries and agencies and marketing subsidiaries elsewhere. In those countries there are thirty factories which operate in five major products all closely related. At present each country has a national subsidiary reporting direct to a senior executive on the Committee of Management. In the home country, product group divisions have just been introduced. A consultant has been asked to advise on what, if any, changes should be made to the international organization of the company.

The first reaction of the corporate management had been to tell the subsidiaries that nothing would change as far as they were concerned. Effectively the chief executives of the foreign subsidiaries were to have the same status as the newly-appointed divisional heads. The consultant advised against this, but the committee of management said that any other arrangement would be unthinkable. With about a third of their sales and most of their future prospects abroad, the company could not afford to tamper with the foreign operations; these were all in industrialized countries and included a sophisticated company in the United States. They rejected the consultant's recommendation that the product group should have worldwide responsibilities and began to seek fresh advice.

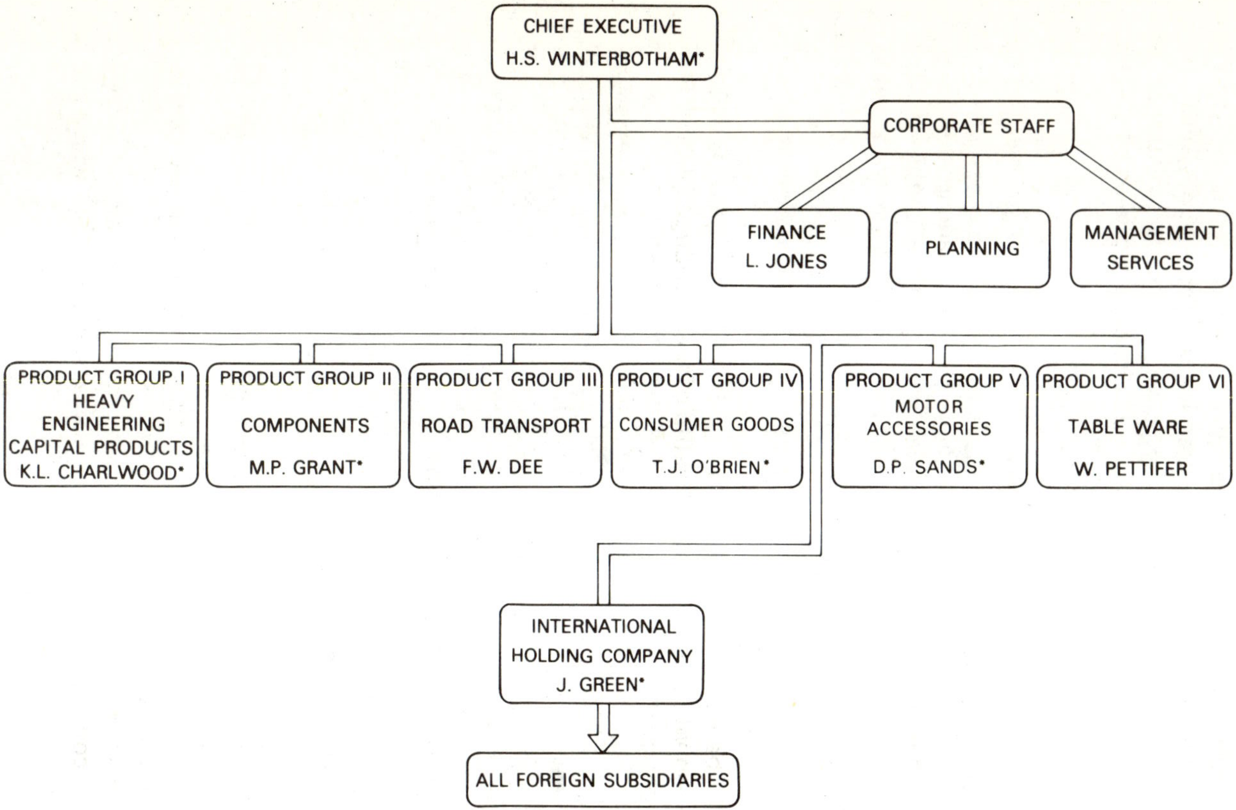

Exhibit I Global Products Limited: corporate structure after the formation of the international division.

* A member of the Main Board, together with four part-time directors: one banker, one customer of the heavy engineering group, one car manufacturer and one lawyer.

EXHIBIT II

6 September

CONFIDENTIAL

Circulation to
All Directors,
Executives, Managers.

GROUP REORGANIZATION

I have decided in the interests of group operating efficiency to make some changes to our organization.

As from the first of next month, the International Holding Company will cease to exist and its functions will be re-allocated between the product groups divisions. Mr J. Green, who has served the company well for over thirty years, will be retiring. I am glad to say that we shall continue to have the benefit of his assistance as a consultant. Other staff will be offered alternative employment in the next two weeks.

There may be some disturbance at first but I am confident that the whole group will be feeling the benefits of these changes within the next few months.

H. SEDLEY WINTERBOTTOM,
Chairman and Managing Director

9.5 Questions for discussion

(1) Comment critically on the classification of company organization contained in this chapter. In particular discuss the possibility of other ways of interpreting the trends in international company organization.
(2) What is the likely future for regional organizations? Give reasons for your answers.
(3) The Chief Executive of an international food preparing and canning company is worried about the slowness of communications which appears to be damaging the competitive position of the subsidiaries. He has commissioned a report by his personal assistant which concentrates on some problems in the decision-making process. Write the report. Do not hesitate to introduce imagined facts about the company where they are needed for the report.
(4) Explain where a product group organization would be preferred and the steps necessary to overcome likely problems.

(5) Under what circumstances would decentralization be particularly dangerous? Give reasons for your answer.

(6) One of the realities which complicates the work of the international manager is what has been called the 'three-dimensional decision-making—that is decision-making grouped around functional, product and geographical issues'. In the light of this complication discuss some possible plans for the management structure of an international company and the conditions under which particular plans might be preferred.

(7) Meanwell Plastics Ltd., is having trouble with its international division. This division controls plants in four European countries and five less developed countries in Africa and Asia; it also masterminds the company's marketing efforts in most other parts of the world. Growth has been fast, but profits are flagging. The main worry is about increasing friction at head office between international and the other divisions. Among other things, this has produced a dearth of technical information abroad.

Write a memo to the Managing Director advising on some measures that will improve the situation. Don't hesitate to tell him what further information you will need to make more confident recommendations in your role as outside adviser.

(8) Do you regard the degree of autonomy as a significant element in the development of a foreign subsidiary?

(9) Discuss the matrix organization in an international company. What future do you see for this type of organization?

10 Communications and Control

10.1 Outline

Few subjects are more discussed among managers than communications. It would seem that most executives take a resigned view of the difficulties. Problems with communications will arise and have to be lived with. This subject can be approached from many different angles—personal, structural and technical among others. Technical improvements have clearly improved communications between head office and the foreign subsidiary, but problems about making the best use of the available technology remain. In particular questions have to be asked about the amount of communication needed and the point at which any particular volume of information is required. This aspect of the subject will be not examined in any depth here. Nor will the personal side; on this it need only be said that any discussion needs to take account of the large amount of research done on inter-personal communications. The fact that the present chapter concentrates on the systems rather than the personalities should not be taken to underestimate the importance of the latter.

The communications system is always expected to be a greater problem in international companies. It also has to carry a wider range of items. In particular is the vexed question of the control system which is a major source of controversy in international firms. Passing references in earlier chapters of this book have already suggested some of the lines which this controversy may take. The parent company has the fear of inadequate information provided too late to enable disaster to be avoided. That this fear is not illusory has been demonstrated several times in recent years. Management also needs the information for planning purposes. On the other hand the subsidiary fears that its efforts may be wrecked rather than assisted by elaborate reporting systems.

The subject of international company control may be summarized thus:

(1) *Objectives*

To signal problems.

To feed planning.

To measure performance and potential—of the subsidiary as such

and of each individual manager.
To stimulate, educate and guide the foreign managers.

This last point needs some explanation, and is indeed the reason why changes in the control system need such careful examination. The foreign manager is likely to turn his attention to those matters which head office consider important enough to ask for reports. Similarly he may turn his attention away from those where reports are not demanded.

(2) *Needs*

A standard control system which can provide a universal language for universal application and which can absorb a wide variety of information into a scheme which allows comparison across frontiers.
A system which provides adequate feedback without being too tight or too loose.

(3) *Content*

Financial information.
Market information.
Production and technical information.
Personnel information.
Other key data that applies to the industry group or the particular firm.

The general reporting standards apply across many companies, but most have specific issues on which they collect information. These issues, referred to in the last point above, are often considered first when designing a reporting system. Examples might be safety in a chemical firm or advertising in a highly competitive consumer products concern.

(4) *Problems*

The facts are rooted in the past, and may not be relevant to the future. The system often find difficulty responding to changes in the environment, such as inflation.
The facts collected may be arbitrary.
The people involved often do not understand what they are doing.

The excerpt illustrates some of these points very clearly, although dealing exclusively with financial controls. The above considerations affect all the other activities on which the parent company requires information. These vary from organization, but the following are likely to be included:

(i) Market developments.
(ii) Market share.

(iii) Production and productivity figures.
(iv) Personnel-turnover, absenteeism, disputes.
(v) Other issues which are industry or company specific:

Most firms have a number of key issues on which they specifically require information. A firm which sells in a market segment where quality is very important will almost certainly require quality control and customer complaint figures from all its subsidiaries; even the companies where these are not so vital may require them. Chemical companies which manufacture explosive or inflammable substances often require safety reports worldwide. Companies which lease a significant proportion of their equipment will require reports on leasing activities. There are many other instances of subjects on which individual firms require reports.

10.2 Financial control systems for multinational operations: an empirical investigation[1]

Accounting

As a company expands its operations from a predominantly domestic base to a multinational base, it might be expected that its formal systems of reporting and control will undergo some fundamental changes. For example: 'Those responsible for foreign operations *need to create* management control systems tailored to the peculiar objectives, organization, and environment of their international operations, rather than simply exporting their domestic control systems.' But does this occur in practice? And, more important, should it occur?

These were the questions which motivated a recent study of the financial reporting and control procedures used by thirty American multinational manufacturing companies. The evidence obtained indicates that modifications to financial control systems caused by a multinational environment are not, as a rule, particularly extensive or fundamental; moreover, changes which could usefully be made to increase the effectiveness of financial control systems in a multinational context would, with the exception of the treatment of currencies, be equally applicable in a purely domestic context. In essence, the major influence of a multinational environment on a company's information flows was seen to be a curtailment of informal communication, as a result of which, shortcomings inherent in the design of formal systems are greatly emphasized.

The focus of the research was the design of financial reporting systems between corporate headquarters and foreign affiliates, and the use by corporate executives of reported financial data in the management procedures for its foreign operations. A company's reporting and control procedures for its foreign operations were compared with those which it uses domestically; in addition, a company's control procedures for individual foreign affiliates were compared.

Some of the research findings are presented below. The discussion is organized around three topics; accounting practices, the design of reporting systems, and the use of reported financial data in the evaluation of operations.

Accounting information is the basic input to a financial reporting system, and it is necessary, therefore, to examine the extent to which corporate managements supervise the accounting procedures used by their foreign affiliates. At this stage of the discussion, let us disregard complicating factors, such as the intrinsic variability in accounting data caused by inflation over time, and concentrate only on the mechanics of an accounting system and the policies governing its implementation.

A financial control system is, in many respects, a measurement system, but it can only measure in relative terms or, in other words, by comparison. In the case of a foreign subsidiary, three bases of comparison suggest themselves; reported results may be compared with other operating units, with historical results, or with a budget. More than one basis of comparison may be used by a company, and conceivably all three could be used.

For the first basis of comparison to be meaningful all of a company's subsidiaries must employ similar accounting systems and, in addition, similar accounting policies in implementing the systems. For the second and third bases to be meaningful, consistency of accounting practice over time is necessary or changes in practice must be brought to the attention of managers using accounting reports and an appraisal made of the effect of any change; it is not essential to these bases of comparison that all subsidiaries should follow the same accounting practices. But this may nevertheless be preferable. Even when accounting measures of performance are explicitly recognized as not being comparable, there is a tendency for operating managers still to behave as if they were. An example of this was provided by one company, although in a slightly different context, in which a belief had arisen that greater returns were available domestically than abroad. The belief arose from using a measure of 'return on net book value of assets'; foreign plant was, in aggregate, much newer than domestic plant.

A further aspect of comparability has to be considered—namely the detail involved in the comparison, regardless of the basis used. If the comparison is simply of absolute profit, or profit expressed as a percentage of sales or assets, then corporate management need concern itself only with consistency in those areas of accounting practice which influence the timing of reporting profits. If, on the other hand, the comparison includes a detailed examination of categories of revenue and expense, then corporate management has to be concerned with the consistent definition of accounting terms in relation to the transactions being accounted for.

Of the thirty companies in the research sample, eighteen or 60% have made some formal effort to standardize their accounting practices throughout the company. In a manufacturing enterprise, because of the wide variety of methods in common use for costing production, the *cost accounting system* is perhaps the area in which there exists most latitude for using different accounting practices. Moreover, the complexity of cost accounting reduces the visibility of differing practices, or a change in practice, and these may not show up at all in the format of accounting statements. The importance of cost accounting in the overall accounting system stems from the fact that the costing of production has substantial bearing on the timing of reporting profits; furthermore, managers of manufacturing companies tend to regard as significant the accounting measurement of manufacturing efficiency.

In addition to the question of evaluation by comparison, there are obviously several other advantages of having similar product costing among the affiliates of a multinational company. For example, if the same product is being made in a number of locations, corporate management, for numerous purposes, will require to know its cost of manufacture in each location. Fourteen (47%) of the companies in the sample indicated that they use a consistent cost accounting system worldwide. Twenty-four (80%) of the companies indicated that corporate approval is required by a subsidiary prior to making any significant change in its product costing. Eleven of the companies use an analysis of manufacturing efficiency as part of their regular evaluation of subsidiary operations. Of these, two do not use a consistent cost system worldwide, nor do they require corporate approval of changes in a subsidiary's costing of production. It is difficult, under these circumstances, to visualize any meaningful use of an analysis of production variances.

Suppose, as an example, that a subsidiary of one of these two companies uses a full standard cost system. A small change in the subsidiary's standards, or in its overhead rates, can readily go undetected in standard cost of sales, while having a disproportionate effect on reported manufacturing variances. The corresponding inventory revaluation would signal to corporate management what had occurred, but this could be concealed in 'other manufacturing costs', or some such category, thus distorting a comparison of profit over time. Alternatively, as is more likely, it might simply be postponed until year end and accounted for at that time as an inventory adjustment when valuing physical inventory.

One of the companies in the sample has initiated a project to develop uniform cost accounting throughout its operations. As yet this is still at an exploratory stage, but already it has been discovered that inter-company comparisons of product costs are meaningless, and production variances over time should be used only in a most general way as an indication of a plant's performance. The company's accountants have identified four important areas of cost accounting in which the foreign subsidiaries' practices differ from those of the domestic company. These are in the cost accounting systems themselves, in the policies used in implementing the systems (for example, in the degree of 'tightness' of standards), in the timing of recognizing variances (domestically, variances are recognized when incurred, whereas abroad they are for the most part recognized when a production order is closed), and in the amount of analysis of the reasons for reported variances. Despite these differences in the companies studied, corporate line managers generally accept reported variances at their face value as a measure of a plant's efficiency; in addition, decisions are commonly made on the basis of product cost information from the company's various manufacturing locations, such as whether to manufacture a part locally or to order it from another of the company's plants.

Accounting standardization. To the extent feasible, latitude for manipulating reported results should be eliminated to safeguard the integrity of reporting, and to reduce the incidence of misinterpretation in the use of financial reports. Corporate supervision of the accounting practices used by all of the company's operating units is one means which can help to accomplish this. Furthermore, the effectiveness of a financial reporting system as a management tool can obviously be increased by using uniform accounting procedures worldwide. For these reasons, it might be supposed that greater uniformity would be observed in multinational companies which have been operating abroad for a longer period of time. However, comparison of the responses from companies which established their foreign operations in the pre-war era with those which have gone abroad since the war gave no support to this postulate.

In the light of the fundamental importance of accounting to a financial reporting system, it is astonishing that only 60% of the companies in the sample have attempted to standardize their accounting procedures. It is sometimes suggested that local accounting practices, often legislatively required, cause difficulties in this respect. Corporate managers in the area of accounting, when questioned about this, all acknowledge they had experienced a certain amount of difficulty, but more at the level of an irritation rather than a fundamental problem. The tendency, moreover, was for corporate management to delegate problems in this area to local management. A typical comment of a corporate manager of a firm that attempts to standardize was as follows:

'We are sympathetic towards the problems which local accounting practices create for our foreign financial managers. Nevertheless, we insist on accounting reports to headquarters which conform to US accepted accounting practice.'

The task of developing uniform accounting practices throughout a multinational company is undoubtedly formidable, especially in terms of cost accounting, and once accomplished, it requires a continuing maintenance effort. The task is by no means overwhelming, but the inference drawn from interviews was that it is an area of reporting which tends to be neglected in favour of dealing with more visible problems. In the meantime, the usefulness of intercompany, or inter-plant, comparisons of financial performance is bound to be compromised in those companies which do not have uniform accounting.

Reporting

It is important to bear in mind that the functions of business are fundamentally similar in all countries. Regardless of the reasons for a foreign investment and its preference over a domestic investment, the factors important to its success are likely to be much the same as for a domestic investment. The information included in a financial reporting system, therefore, is likely to be basically the same whether the operations being reported are in the United States or abroad. A manager with responsibility for foreign operations, just as for domestic operations, requires certain basic information, such as what is being sold, where, and to whom: what assets are being used and where: and what costs are being incurred, what profit is being made, and what is the return on assets.

In practice, there tends to be a lag between the development of information systems and the development of the organization and its operations. As a consequence the manager's needs for information are usually pressing. Faced by such a situation, it is understandable that a corporate controller will install a management reporting system abroad which has been used and found effective domestically and is, at the same time, familiar to corporate operating management.

Twenty-seven (90%) of the sample companies use a standard reporting format from all their operating units, both foreign and domestic.

Conceivably the uniformity in reporting format may cause corporate managers to assume that the content of reports is equally uniform, an assumption which may be invalid in view of the observations with regard to accounting uniformity. Nevertheless, the uniformity of format is not surprising, because if a corporate management wishes to stipulate minimum reporting requirements from its operating units, by far the easiest way to communicate these requirements is by establishing a format. Furthermore, in the company's accounting and reporting procedures, this is perhaps the most practical starting point.

Table 10.1 tabulates the financial reports required on a regular basis by the sample companies from their foreign affiliates and domestic operating units. Nine (30%) responses to this question were identical for foreign and domestic operations. Among the rest, the main difference noted between reporting from foreign affiliates and domestic operating units is a tendency for fewer reports to be required from the former than from the latter. With the exception of reporting foreign exchange and local borrowing position, a report apparently is only required from foreign affiliates if it is also required for managing their own businesses.

Table 10.1
Regular financial reports to corporate management

	Foreign	Domestic
Balance sheet	28	30
Balance sheet supporting data	16	22
Inventory analysis	14	22
Receivables analysis	12	19
Income statement	30	30
Income statement supporting detail	22	26
Product line income statements	14	21
Margin trend analysis	6	9
Cash flow	10	18
Sales analysis	14	20
Order backlog analysis	18	23
Wage cost review	2	3
Value added analysis		1
Local borrowing position	21	19
Foreign exchange review	8	2
Capital asset schedule	3	3
Selling expense analysis	1	1
Balance of payments data (US)		2
Total	219	271
Average per company	7	9

Compared with the detail contained in reports of domestic operations, foreign reporting contains substantially less detail in the case of thirteen (44%) companies, approximately the same detail in the case of sixteen (53%) companies, and substantially more detail in the case of one company. The practice of this last company may appear somewhat surprising. However, when one considers the abundance of detail which is readily available about domestic operations simply by going to the journal vouchers, or even the source documents, it may be quite rational to require more detail in foreign reporting because the same acess to source data is not so readily attainable. This will particularly pertain if a large degree of decision-making authority is retained at headquarters, thereby necessitating a large amount of data in reports.

Concerning intercompany transactions of the twenty-seven companies which answered these particular questions, all but one make a clear identification of these in their reporting from foreign affiliates, and all but two make a similar identification in their reporting for domestic operations. This is to be expected, since a certain amount of data about intercompany transactions is necessary to consolidate financial statements. The point of interest, in respect to financial control, is how this information is used when measuring performance. In the companies in which interviews were carried out, substantial dissatisfaction was evidenced with the way intercompany business is handled in financial reports. A member of the controller's staff of one company commented:

'. . . some of our subsidiaries are very dependent on intercompany business, and their financial performance is influenced by it. Their reported performance, therefore, depends to a large degree on the performance of other organizational units over which they have little or no control.'

Regarding the currency of reporting, (17%) companies use only local currency in their reports from foreign affiliates, nine (30%) use only US dollars, fifteen (50%) use both local currency and US dollars, and one (3%) bases its practice on a consideration of the country involved. A conscious distinction was made in this question between reporting which is translated to dollars at the local level and reporting in local currency which is translated to dollars at headquarters.

Responses were examined for a correlation between a company's treatment of foreign currencies in its reporting and the incidence of major losses resulting from a currency devaluation. Twelve (40%) of the companies include a regular review of foreign currency position in their reporting systems, and among this group nine, or 75% of them, have operations in countries whose currencies have been devalued several times in the past five years. Of the eighteen companies which do not include a foreign currency review in their reporting system, ten, or 55%, have operations in countries with highly unstable currencies. Perhaps, then, there is some tendency for companies with investments in countries with unstable currencies to be more sensitive to currency problems, and for this to be reflected in their reporting systems. Four companies in the first group, or 33%, indicated they had sustained a major loss from currency devaluation, compared with nine companies, or 50%, in the second group. In neither group did the currency of reporting appear to influence this. Perhaps the inference may be drawn that increased sensitivity to currency problems lessens the likelihood of a major loss from currency devaluation. At any rate, the evidence, although not conclusive, at least points in the direction which would intuitively be expected.

Financial control

Table 10.2 tabulates the responses to a question asking what techniques of financial control the companies use on a reasonably continual basis for evaluating the operations of their foreign affiliates and domestic operating units.

Table 10.2
Financial control techniques used in evaluating operations

	Foreign	Domestic
Analysis of balance sheet ratios	17	17
Analysis of income statement ratios	24	24
Comparison with profit plan	26	26
Comparison with historical data	27	27
Comparison of costs with a budget	20	23
Return on investment	25	26
Analysis of manufacturing efficiency	11	17
Break-even analysis	5	8
Comparison with competition	1	2
Contribution analysis	1	1

The most striking thing about this data is the similarity between the range of techniques used for evaluating foreign affiliates and domestic operating units. Nineteen (63%) of the responses were identical. The ones which differed included more techniques for domestic operations than for foreign operations. In only two instances did companies indicate using a technique for evaluating foreign operations which they do not also use for evaluating domestic operations, and, in both cases, the technique is aimed at focusing attention on the degree of exposure to translation losses in the event of a currency devaluation.

The three techniques which are used more for domestic operations than for foreign operations are a comparison of costs with a budget, analysis of manufacturing efficiency, and break-even analysis. From interviews, it was evident that corporate managers tend to accord less significance to budgetary cost control for foreign operations than for domestic for several reasons, but primarily because of a lesser degree of involvement in compiling the budgets of foreign affiliates. Similarly, analysis of manufacturing efficiency is not specially meaningful unless there is considerable familiarity with day-to-day operations and with, as pointed out previously, the cost accounting system which is being used.

Finally, break-even techniques, to be meaningful, require a lot of careful research of the behaviour of costs and a large commitment to their implementation; perhaps few companies maintain sufficient financial staff in their subsidiaries to effect so sophisticated a technique of financial control. Despite this, break-even analysis recommends itself as a particularly powerful control technique for inclusion in a financial control system for multinational operations on three counts. First, it necessitates an identification of the cost structure peculiar to each individual subsidiary, a plea for which was common among corporate managers who were interviewed. Secondly, it facilitates the focusing of attention on the controllable items of a subsidiary's financial performance. And thirdly, since sales data is the most rapidly available in a financial reporting system, a knowledge of break-even volumes permits a rapid prediction to be made of the financial performance of an operating unit before the full financial statements are prepared; the system can therefore be used effectively on an 'exception' basis whereby a detailed analysis of a unit's results is made for management's attention only when actual is significantly different from predicted.[2]

Table 10.3 shows a partial tabulation of the responses to a question asking for the three control techniques which are found to be most useful, ranked in order of importance, for foreign affiliates and domestic operating units. A large number of techniques received mention, and only those with several mentions are tabulated. In addition, a number of non-financial measures were included in the responses, and these are not tabulated; in particular, market share and discussion of operating results were mentioned by several companies. The tabulation shows both the frequency of mention of each technique and a weighted frequency, ac-

Table 10.3
Most useful financial control techniques used in evaluating operations

	Foreign		Domestic	
	Frequency	Weighted	Frequency	Weighted
Return on investment	21	50	19	48
Comparison with plan	17	42	19	48
Comparison with history	11	20	10	17
Analysis of income statement	9	16	7	13
Analysis of balance sheet	—	—	5	6

cording first importance a value of three, second importance a value of two, and third importance a value of one.

Twenty-three (77%) of the responses were identical for foreign affiliates and domestic operating units. The differences which were noted tended towards a greater emphasis on purely financial techniques of analysis in the case of foreign affiliates, and more emphasis on techniques directed towards control of operations in the case of domestic units.

In foreign countries with a stable currency it makes little difference whether financial performance is appraised in local currency or in US dollars. But when a currency is unstable it can make a considerable difference which currency is used, and the complexity of the situation is compounded when an unstable currency is accompanied by a high rate of inflation.

Inflation and devaluation are often considered as one and the same problem, but in fact it is essential in the context of a financial control system to maintain a clear distinction between the two. Inflation is essentially an internal factor to a country, whereas currency valuation is essentially external. Unquestionably, changes in internal prices of a country are likely to reflect in its export prices resulting in a change to the country's terms of trade, and, perhaps as a consequence, in a change in its currency valuation. On the other hand, government controls can be used to shield export prices from the effects of internal price changes thus delaying, or obviating, the need for a change in currency valuation.

Rapid inflation presents a peculiar management problem. Essentially the problem centres around maintaining prices at an adequate level to cover the cost of replacing the assets consumed in the production process, while leaving a sufficient margin for satisfactory profits. The timing between acquisition of assets and collection of related revenues is critical, and, additionally, liquid assets, such as cash, must be rapidly reinvested in assets which maintain their value despite depreciation in the purchasing power of the currency.

Inflation is a feature of every country's environment, and has to be coped with by a manager of a purely domestic firm. The significant point in terms of multinational management is that the results of each of the operating units are affected by the inflation rates prevailing in their respective countries, and these rates can differ widely from one country to another. On the one hand, a manager of a subsidiary in a country with rapid inflation may have a formidable task in coping with the situation; but on the other hand, it has to be borne in mind that if he does cope successfully he has the advantage that his reported financial performance will show apparent improvements over time even if no underlying improvement, in terms of physical activities, has in fact been accomplished.

One means of dealing with the problem of inflation, both from the point of view of measurement of performance and of emphasizing the management problems involved, is to use price-level accounting. The difficulty of this solution lies in choosing an appropriate price-level index in each situation. Moreover, price-level accounting tends to be complicated, and not easily understood by operating managers. If one ignores small differences in rates of inflation, as experienced among the countries of North America and Western Europe for example, and is concerned only with the influence of a rapid inflation rate in a country, then by measuring performance in dollars rather than local currency an effect similar to price-level accounting may be achieved. This is true provided the devaluation of a local currency corresponds closely to its depreciation in purchasing power, which has in fact been the case in countries, like Brazil, which have experienced rapid inflation. The latter solution has the advantage over price-level accounting in that it does not require a restatement of the accounts of the subsidiary in order to make them consistent with those of the parent company for financial consolidation purposes.[3] One company studied uses price-level accounting in its Brazilian company for tax reporting, but reverses out the price-level adjustments for its management reporting.

When a currency devaluation is imposed on an inflationary situation measurement of performance becomes a matter of some difficulty. The devaluation of the currency of a country in which a company has investments can result in two kinds of loss: a translation loss, which arises from the conversion of a foreign affiliate's balance sheet from local currency to US dollars; and an exchange loss, which results from the purchase of hard currency with local currency after devaluation in order to settle an obligation in hard currency incurred prior to devaluation. Perhaps the only difference between these types of loss is in the timing of their affect on the company's resources. In an immediate sense, however, translation losses are not out-of-pocket whereas exchange losses are, and leave the enterprise poorer in resources than it was prior to devaluation.

As a result of currency losses common measures of financial performance, such as return on assets or sales, are likely to be different in magnitude when expressed in local currency as compared with US dollars, and their change from one period to the next may be in opposite directions. This raises the question of which currency should be used when evaluating financial performance. An American-based company is reporting the results of its operations to shareholders in dollars, and therefore the success of all its investments, foreign and domestic, has to be judged in terms of dollars. But the underlying competitive trend of a subsidiary's performance is likely to be more clearly reflected by measurement in local currency, especially from the standpoint of relating current performance with expectations of future performance. Therefore, it is likely that the evaluation of a foreign subsidiary as an investment is more meaningful in terms of dollars, while an appraisal of the effectiveness of its management is more meaningful in terms of local currency.

An additional question to be answered when choosing the currency in which to measure performance is the effect which the choice has in terms of taking steps to reduce exposure to currency losses in the event of a devaluation. The research findings identified a strong tendency for parent company managers to retain authority for substantially all decisions in this area, and to accord major attention to exchange losses with very little consideration to potential losses from translation. One corporate financial executive remarked, 'There is a real honest psychological problem to get a subsidiary manager to take action on the assumption that his currency is weak and may be devalued.'

In the sample of companies, twenty-three (77%) use US dollars in measuring the financial performance of their foreign affiliates, three (10%) use local currency, and four (13%) use both local currency and US dollars.

The controller of one of the companies which uses only a dollar measure of performance in its financial control system said there was less confidence among corporate managers in using financial reports from the company's Brazilian subsidiary than from, for example, its Canadian subsidiary. One of the reasons which he gave for this was a widespread feeling that profits currently reported by the Brazilian subsidiary were likely to be negated by future losses arising from a currency devaluation.

Apparently, from the research, most companies do not accord the peculiar risks of foreign investment much consideration in setting their financial targets of performance. One reason for this may be that these particular risks are at least offset by a smaller degree of commercial risk in foreign countries. For example, risks arising from the possible actions of well-established and sophisticated competitors may be less of a factor in many foreign markets than in America. And it may also be the case that most managements do not in fact incorporate risk as an explicit factor in the ongoing administration of the business. However, one must obviously be careful to distinguish between the treatment of risk in a financial control system and its treatment in capital investment decisions; in the evaluation of proposals for new investments abroad, risk is likely to be given careful consideration in a financial appraisal procedures.

Turning now to a consideration of the appraisal of management effectiveness, half of the companies in the sample, fewer than might be expected, make a distinction in their evaluation between the performance of an investment and the performance of the management responsible for it. Of the companies making the distinction, 60% formally recognize the differentiation by using two different financial targets. The most common procedure in this regard is to appraise management performance in terms of historical results or in terms of a comparison with budget, while retaining a longer-term target for evaluating the investment. Only two companies compare performance of subsidiary managers with that of local competitors.

Conclusions

The research findings give strong support to the view that there is very little fundamental difference in the design and use of financial reporting systems for foreign operations and domestic operations. Moreover, the similarity does not appear to be the result of an oversight, but instead results from a conscious choice on the part of managements. Even recognizing the restricted nature of the research sample, the data obtained seems to justify a general postulate to the effect that corporate managements of multinational companies have as one of their objectives the design and implementation of financial systems of reporting and control which are uniformly applicable to all the operating entities of the company regardless of geographic location. An essential proviso to this proposition, however, is that a company has broadly similar objectives for both its foreign and domestic operations.

The conclusion is not simply to suggest that a company exports to its operations abroad its domestic systems of reporting and control. The tendency to do this was quite evident from the research data and, not surprisingly therefore, differences were discernable between foreign and domestic operations in the functioning of financial control systems; furthermore, the disparities were more pronounced for operations in some countries than in others. The inescapable fact remains that a multinational environment is sufficiently different from a domestic environment to necessitate careful consideration of the factors involved before generally adopting procedures which have seemed adequate for domestic operations. These differences include the following:

(1) wide variations in rates of inflation encountered from country to country;
(2) changes in the valuation of the currency of a country of investment;
(3) the influence of intercompany transactions on the short-run performance of an operating unit; and
(4) wide differences in cost structures among affiliates in different countries.[4]

It should be realized that refinining a financial planning and reporting system to make specific identification of these factors is not such a major undertaking as it may appear at first sight. Indeed, it is likely that a large part of a company's current effort in the area of financial planning and reporting is largely wasted because of inadequate systems design. For example, one company with a subsidiary in Argentina uses only dollars in its budgeting and assumes that prevailing price levels will continue, except for clearly identifiable increases such as wage awards which have already been made. The budget of this subsidiary for 1968 included a substantial loss in the third quarter arising from a possible devaluation of the peso. The manager of the subsidiary explained the provision as follows:

'... All these factors tend to the assumption that a small adjustment of the peso would not be unreasonable. On the other hand if, as is possible, the peso stays pegged at 350, then rising peso costs will reflect as higher dollar costs than those forecast. The reserve then seems reasonable as a cushion against either eventuality.'

Since peso costs did rise steadily throughout the year but the peso was not devalued, monthly comparisons of actual against budget rapidly became meaningless. A lot of time was spent at headquarters trying to make sense of reported variances between actual and budget before the budget was finally discarded.

A system designed to provide a parent-company manager with the basic information which he requires to manage the business, and which clearly demonstrates the influence of the above four factors can go a long way towards achieving the postulated objective. But there are, in addition, other factors which hinder the uniform functioning of a control system in multinational context—factors which have their impact on the implementation of the system, as opposed to its design. The potentially greater distances and lesser accessibility of foreign affiliates from headquarters than in the case of domestic operations, and difficulties of verbal communication, are obvious factors which demand consideration when devising a total package of management control procedures. One manager, when reflecting on these aspects of control, commented, 'Perhaps the formal system has particular significance in the case of outlying subsidiaries, not just from the point of view of keeping headquarters informed, but more importantly as a means of giving subsidiary managers more feeling of being an integral part of (the company's) operations.'

10.3 Suggestions for further reading

This chapter considers straightforward control issues. For more subtle aspects see (B) BROOKE & REMMERS (1970), chapters 3 and 4. See also above chapter 7.

For an examination into how a control system is understood, or misunderstood, in practice see:

(D) BROOKE, M. Z. & DORRELL, M. (1976). The communication of control in an international company: methods of investigation, *Omega,* **4.2.**

See also:

(A) DANIELS, OGRAM & RADEBAUGH (1976). Chapter 25.
(A) DYMSZA, (1972). Chapter 10.
(C) EITEMAN & STONEHILL (1973). Chapter 14.
(C) ROBBINS & STOBAUGH (1973). Chapter 8.
(B) ROBINSON (1973). Chapter 8.
(B) SALERA (1969). Chapter 29.

An important paper is:

BRANDT, W. K. & HULBERT, J. M. (1976). Communications and Control in the Multinational Enterprise. Paper presented to the AMAM–MSI Multinational Product Management Workshop, Cambridge (Mass.) 18–20 January.

10.4 Exercises for this chapter

Case studies

NV Philips Gloeilampenfabrieken 1974, Harvard. ISCH 9–174–021. The Management Control System of a large international Electronics company.

Alfa-Laval NV, 1968, (IMEDE OB–79, ICH 9–413–087), by Summer, C. E. This study describes the management organisation and goal setting process in corporate headquarters, Alfa-Laval AB, Tumba, Sweden.

Incidents: (1) a control problem

Mr James Bevan was Financial Controller of the Eatwell Food Co. Ltd., a larger international food processing and distributing company. He was under considerable pressure to redesign the control system; but the pressure was coming from opposing sides. The headquarters corporate planning staff were constantly dissatisfied with the information they were getting. They had been charged to develop plans for new investments in different parts of the world; hence they needed a great deal of information on the progress of each of the company's products in all its markets.

Bevan himself was finding increasing difficulties in clearly allocating expenses and profits between products as the company expanded. Delays in supplying the information, and the fact that some of the subsidiaries had different accounting dates, was one of the problems. On the other hand, there was sustained pressure from abroad to relax the control system. There were constant reminders that most of the subsidiaries were small companies in intensely competitive markets. To them the time spent collecting and passing on the information the controller was demanding was expensive, frustrating and it diverted their attention from their business. The complaints of the foreign subsidiaries have been strongly put to the Board, and Bevan has either to change the system or justify current practices. Even stronger justification will be needed if he is to introduce the stricter control system both he and the planners want.

What are the criteria which he should be considering? What sort of information would justify each possible choice—keep the status quo, intensify the controls, relax the controls? (The participants could split into three groups, each representing one of the possible choices. Each group should plan its attitude beforehand, and then debate a solution with the others.)

(2) An insubordinate subsidiary

Megalith International Ltd. is a large diversified corporation with manufacture in nineteen countries and sales in over fifty. Each product division administers its own manufacturing units and has worldwide profit responsibility. One of the smaller product divisions has a subsidiary in Italy which has refused to declare a dividend for four years running. Each year senior divisional management has descended on the Italian subsidiary and instructed the local Board to declare a dividend but no money has been forthcoming.

The Chief Executive of the Italian subsidiary has relied on a clause in the articles of his company which states that the dividend shall be declared after necessary provisions have been allocated. Each year he affirms that the profits, admitted to be substantial, are not sufficient to pay for the necessary new investment and for a dividend. He has refused requests to resign and indicated that Italian law is likely to support his stand. The division has no other means of transferring funds from this subsidiary. There are no intracompany sales, and no arrangements for the payment of fees or royalties. The Italian Chief Executive has six years to go before reaching retiring age. In desperation the Board of the division are trying to discover every possible means of getting some return on their substantial investment.

10.5 Questions for discussion

(1) State briefly the objectives of an international company control system. Discuss in more detail the issues involved in realizing one of those objectives.
(2) What are the advantages and difficulties of an international standard accounting system in a company? Illustrate your answer with some examples.
(3) Discuss the most useful financial control techniques.
(4) A financial director of a company is dissatisfied with the control system in his company. Subsidiaries are constantly complaining about its burdensome nature, but at the same time required information is often unavailable. He has asked a consultant to write a report setting out the problems and probable solutions. Write the report, allowing your imagination to supply necessary details about the company's business.
(5) Outline the difficulties involved in appraising foreign subsidiary management in an international group.
(6) Write a memorandum on the issues involved in establishing a control system for a company's first foreign subsidiary.
(7) How would you expect the multinational company to motivate managers of national subsidiaries and managers of product lines so that their activities could be appraised as separate performances and as contributions to group performances? What accounting difficulties can you discern?
(8) A small multinational company (Turnover £10 m) has had great problems as a result of its inability to get accurate and up-to-date statements from its four foreign subsidiaries. It does not have the resources for establishing an elaborate control system. What would you advise?

11 Communication, Information and the Transfer of Knowledge

This subject is examined under three headings. First communication in general, then the transfer of knowledge and how this takes place especially with regard to technical knowledge, and finally the sources of information used by international companies. Financial information and control systems as such are omitted as they have been dealt with in the last chapter.

11.1 Communication in general

A Survey has shown that communications problems are just as likely to arise when the actual communications are thought to be good as when they are known to be bad.[1] This fact would seem to demonstrate two points. One is that for all the continual discussions that go on under this general heading, there is still widespread complacency about the effectiveness of communications systems. The other, more significant, point is that in the international company in particular there are tensions and conflicts which would distort the passing and receiving of messages however technically efficient the system. The position of the foreign manager, and even of the expatriate, is complicated by a different set of loyalties and perceptions of business interest than the head office staff with whom they are corresponding. Issues like the interests of the host country and its economy will be among those which will influence the views of the local management. These different commercial and national interests are bound to affect the interpretation of messages as well as the response to them. The interests of the whole are often not the sum of the interests of the parts. It is interesting that head office executives are often quick to point this out, but slow to realize that many of the communications difficulties which puzzle them result therefrom.

Personal interests will normally supplement commercial and national ones. That is to say the career prospects, time horizons and personal aspirations of the executives at each point in the chain will affect the communications. Sometimes there will be pressures against the commercial and national interests, such as those of a manager who sees himself having an international career path. Indeed the effects on the implementing of general company policies are an important consideration in developing the international career opportunities mentioned in the next chapter. In spite of which it can generally be said that a manager is conditioned by his position in a national subsidiary. Communications, it has often been pointed out, are culture-bound and this particularly applies to managerial aspirations and interpretations.

Another personal influence is the ability to ignore messages, the impossibility of not ignoring them it could be said when the extent of the flow is examined in some companies. Upward messages are lost because recipients are too busy or have lost the art of listening. Subsidiary managers, who think they spend a disproportionate amount of their time on reports, are often disillusioned to find how ill-informed are their visitors from head office. On the other hand foreign managers are known to complain that they have been kept in ignorance on subjects about which information has in fact been sent to them. In one case an actual investigation showed that nearly 90% of such complaints were unfounded.

Language is an expected problem, so much anticipated that it does not produce as many difficulties as is often thought. Apart from anecdotes about unfortunate mistranslations few companies can produce evidence of real problems from this cause although over-visiting from executives who cannot talk the language is often mentioned.[2] Sales conferences and other international meetings are more likely to be confused by those who pretend not to need an interpreter than by more insoluble problems. Along with the language question goes the issue of a common style of reporting, particularly financial, mentioned in the last chapter. Most subsidiaries have accommodated themselves to this although there may be more hidden expenses than sometimes imagined.

Problems in communications may, then, reflect commercial, national or cultural differences. Organizational arrangements may also cause difficulties. In the discussion on organization[3] in chapter 9 it was shown that the geographical type (B) is often associated with communications problems in head office, whereas in the product group type (C) the problems did not disappear but were moved to the links between head office and the foreign subsidiary. The required organization is selected on other grounds and the need to live with the problems has to be accepted. The mistake, so often made, is to change the organization in order to solve communications problems. There is no supportable evidence that this works.

The number of levels in the hierarchy is another organization issue which affects the information flow. Not only have researches shown the dangers of too many levels, but as the organization becomes more complex the senior foreign manager finds himself effectively demoted. His personal communications with the highest levels of the company are cut in fact, and often in name as well. Once again re-organizations precipitated when such matters come to light may do more harm than good. The unskilful abolition of managerial positions once established may lose much more in business than is gained in money saved on salaries. Another matter already discussed which affects communications is that of centralization and local autonomy. The jamming of communications routes through head office decision-making and endless consultation is a clear danger. Where, notably in finance, centralization is required special attention has to be given to the routes.

A pattern emerges of a number of specific points at which communications difficulties can be anticipated, overshadowed by major issues lurking in the background. To match this pattern there are some specific remedies along with a general need to anticipate problems and thus understand the implications of those that arise. Where there is an excess of messages being transmitted to such an extent that they are being ignored, indirect information may be more effective than direct. Thus the circulation of productivity figures (for both sales and production activities) has been found more effective in persuading subsidiaries to introduce new methods than the notices describing these methods. The control system can also be used to transmit the need for more advanced management techniques.

Investigations often show confusion as to what is being put into the system as well as what is coming out. Regular checks which isolate what is happening can make a considerable improvement. But the informal links should be emphasized. These are links which do not follow the lines laid down by regulations and organization charts. Some companies disapprove of any short-circuiting of official arrangements, and make efforts to stop them. Not only are these efforts themselves expensive, but the informal links may be more efficient even if they do cause inconvenience to some managers. Some companies assist the emergence of unofficial arrangements by management development programmes and regular international meetings of managers.

11.2 The transfer of knowledge

One aspect of the subject of international communications is the transfer of knowledge from one part of a company to another, usually the parent to the subsidiary. This covers every aspect of knowledge (technical knowhow, management techniques and so on) which is developed in one national unit and can be profitably used in another. Most, but by no means all, of the writing on the subject is about technical knowhow. The present section is biased towards the issues involved under this heading;

but similar considerations apply to any branch of knowledge that the business requires.

Two statements that are frequently made about international firms are:

(1) the multinational firm derives great benefit from its ability to transfer technology to its subsidiaries. This makes new products more profitable, extends the product life cycle and spreads the costs of expensive research;

(2) the host country derives benefit from the fact that the international firm brings advanced technologies to the country. If it did not do this the country would either not have them or have to import the products expensively. This brings new and valuable jobs and skills.

Empirical research has placed some question marks beside both those assertions. At the very least there are disadvantages as well which need to be examined. The first statement will be examined first.

The benefits to the company

The expectations are real enough, but the benefits are ones that often prove hard to realize in practice and this is notoriously a problem area. The difficulty applies both to the dissemination of the information and to the financial return. There are many reasons for this including the general problems of communication already mentioned. In particular technical information tends to be disseminated in an unimaginative way and the subsidiary just fails to get the message. There are also the special problems associated with the organization type since high technology firms tend to be organized by product group (Type C). The lack of specialized geographical managers makes for a lack of expertise in communicating with the foreign subsidiaries. Another problem in communicating technology has to do with the difficulty of getting the foreign managers to understand what is being offered. There is also the further difficulty of translating innovation into production, the difficulty of marketing if the new technology applies to the product itself, and the question of ironing out the problems that arise with any new product. This applies to teething troubles incurred at each stage: production, sales and aftersales. There are finally the implications of the widely held belief that the imitator does better than the innovator.

One research project unearthed some interesting facts on these points.[4] Table 11.1 shows the finding of a survey of twenty-five British companies selected for another purpose. When these were divided into the type of technology with which they were concerned, the other points followed. Technical effort was measured by the expenditure on research and development as a proportion of total expenditure.

Table 11.1
The relationship between the type of technology and other factors in an international company

Companies operating in:	New technologies	Traditional technologies
Technical effort	High	Medium
Organization type	C	B
Markets (contrasted with domestic)	More and Less	Less
Size (net investment)	Large	Medium

Another interesting difference was that the 'traditional' technology companies were inclined to place research facilities abroad, although these were more for development than research. At the time of the investigation the 'new' technology companies never placed research abroad. Instead they were beginning to establish technical liaison departments, which might be just one man, to keep more closely in touch with foreign manufacture. Since that research some companies have developed foreign research departments, in some cases out of the technical liaison.

Another study[5] divided companies into those that were research intensive and those that were not. The measure was again into the proportion of money spent on research and development. In this case the research intensive companies had 46.70% of the sales but 37.80% of the number of companies. This left those that were not research intensive with 53.30% of the sales and 62.20% of the companies. This confirms that the research intensive companies were larger, but denies the commonly held belief that it is technical innovation which is the main influence in taking a company abroad; for those that were not research intensive still took over half the business.

There are a number of means for the transfer of knowledge, and the judicious use of all the available ones may be most effective. These include products, people, printed materials, graphic materials and the mass media. However there are some important ingredients of any item of knowledge which cannot always be transferred. These include less tangible considerations like culture and goodwill. A skilful communications system takes account of this.

The benefits to the country

The second claim made on behalf of the transfer of technology in the international firm concerned the benefit to the host country. In this case also there is clearly much truth, but there are some reservations to be made as well. One of these reservations has to do with the way the company centralizes research. This may reduce career opportunities in the host country and have long-term effects on the educational system. Another problem is that the technology may still be very expensive, and the savings to the host country's balance of payments may be illusory if the company misuses its market power. It has also been pointed out[6] that the technology transferred may be inappropriate for the country concerned. In industrialized countries this may mean that scarce resources are deflected to uses which make commercial sense to the company but not economic sense to the country. National economic planning is made more difficult. In developing countries the new technologies may be too capital intensive or may replace the traditional too rapidly.

Just as a company can choose a strategy for selling abroad, so a country can adopt a policy for importing technical innovation. The necessary bargaining may be difficult, but not impossible. In both cases what is meant is really a collection of strategies or policies with certain priorities. Thus a country can: import direct, stimulate local invention, stimulate foreign investment, encourage foreign licensing. The bargaining process may well be coloured by the fact that countries will have different ideas from companies about relevant specializations to be encouraged. The attitude of governments is often complicated by their current difficulties. Some countries encourage licensing as leaving more of the local business in local hands, while watching carefully and sometimes taxing the money being made by the licensor. Other governments insist on direct investment because of the multiplier effect of this on the local economy.

Thus the multinational firm certainly stimulates the international transfer of technology; but it does so unselectively and perhaps expensively, and if this is to be controlled in the national interest vigilance on the part of governments will be required. Also, within the company the communications become difficult as a result of a number of intractable problems related to organization, financing and marketing. Special attention is needed to the transfer of knowledge together with the development of new techniques for the passing of information.

11.3 Information sources[7]

Method

For the present study, data were collected through personal interviews with respondents. The following request was made of each respondent:

'Please try to recall recent specific instances, within the past six months, where you personally obtained or received external information, that is, information which concerns events and circumstances outside your company, which was important to you in your job or important to the company. The information may have come from any source either inside or outside the company, and may concern any subject: marketing, economics, the competition, government regulations, technical developments, financial matters, and so on. If the subject matter or source of the information is confidential, feel free to use general rather than specific descriptions.'

Respondents were permitted to recall up to four instances. For each instance, respondents were asked to describe (1) the source of the information; (2) why they received the information; (3) how they received the information, specifically, via what medium; and (4) to whom they passed the information. To qualify for inclusion in the analysis, each instance had to involve external information, and to relate in whole or in part to international as opposed to purely domestic operations: instances of internal information or information relating only to domestic operations were excluded from the analysis.

The statistical data reported in this article are based upon the responses to the instance recall question. Respondents recalled an average of 2.78 instances, 139 in all. The research sample consisted of 50 executives located at the headquarters of 13 United States international corporations; 35 of these had full-time responsibility for some aspect of the organizations' international operations, and 15 were responsible for both domestic and foreign areas. Of this last group 14 were corporate executives and one was a product division executive.

Nine of the corporations, accounting for 44 of the respondents, were in the food industry; the four remaining corporations were in manufacturing. The international experience of the 13 corporations represented in the sample ranged from six to over 50 years. Other characteristics of the companies are shown in Table 11.2. Characteristics of the executives are summarized in Table 11.3.

In order to categorize the broad patterns, influences, and associations of respondents' source utilizations, a classification framework was developed (Table 11.4). Although for the organization as a whole external information comes originally from outside the company, for the individual executive much of his external information comes from sources inside his organization. All sources of external information utilized by respondents were grouped into three basic types: human, documentary, and physical phenomena, each of which included other categories as shown in Table 11.3.

Human sources were clearly more important than documentary and

Table 11.2
Sales and markets of corporations

Sales and markets	No. of corporations
Consolidated world-wide sales	
$50 to 199 million	4
$200 to 749 million	3
$750 million or more	6
Sales outside the US	
$6 to 49 million	5
$50 to 249 million	4
$250 million or more	4
Foreign sales relative to domestic	
Less than $\frac{1}{4}$ of domestic	6
One-fourth to $\frac{1}{2}$ of domestic sales	2
Almost equal to or greater than domestic	5
Markets served	
Consumer	4
Both consumer and industrial	7
Industrial only	2
Organization for international operations	
International division	8
Separate international company	2
Other	3

physical phenomena sources combined, accounting for 67% of all important external information reported by respondents, as is apparent from the following percentages:

Location of sources		Types of sources	
Inside organization	34%	Human	67%
Outside organization	66%	Documentary	27%
		Physical phenomena	6%

This finding corroborates the observations of other researchers who have studied the information acquisition.

One group, in their study of communications in the American political process, found that 'to a surprising degree, the American business communication system is oral or by memorandum'.[8] Another author, who used categories 'personal' and 'impersonal' roughly similar to our human and documentary categories respectively, found that 'personal sources (of external information) greatly exceed impersonal sources in importance'.[9] While yet another[10] found that, for engineers, customers

Table 11.3
Characteristics of respondents in sample

Characteristic	% of respondents N = 50
Travel	
Travelled outside US during preceding year	92
Travelled outside US for 10% of year or more	over 50
Education	
College completed	86
Masters of LL.B.	34
Doctorate degree	8
Experience in international operations (both full and part time)	
More than 10 years	46
Less than 2 years	18
Classifications	
Level 1—division heads, president and 1 company president	18
Level 2—department heads, executives responsible for specific programmes	68
Level 3—sub-department head	14
Functional specialization	
General management	32
Marketing	28
Finance	10
Planning	8
Other—mainly legal and personnel	22
Line and Staff	
Line—acting, deciding or doing	72
Staff—thinking, planning, advising	28

and vendors were the most used information source and literature the least; for scientists the literature was most used and vendors or customers were not a source at all. Businessmen clearly rely very much upon information that is not contained in the literature and must have, to be effective, a network of human or personal information sources.

Inside the organization a very important source of external information for respondents was a corporate executive outside the United States in the corporations' subsidiaries, affiliates, and branches. They are the source of 15% of all external information acquired by respondents, and of 23% of all information acquired from human sources (Table 11.5). The importance of executives abroad as a source of information about the world environment is one of the most striking features of the modern international corporation. When a headquarters executive in an inter-

Table 11.4
Classification or sources of external information

Location and types	Categories
Inside the organization	
Human[1]	International division executives based abroad
	Headquarters international executives
	Corporate executives and staff
	Product division executives
Documentary[2]	Information storage[3]
	Reports[4]
	Letters
Outside the organization	
Human[1]	Service-organizations staff[5]
	Competitors
	Distributors, consumers, suppliers
	Government officials and staff
	Other human sources
Documentary[2]	Publications
	Information service reports[6]
	Reports from external sources
Physical phenomena[7]	Objectives, events and circumstances

[1] All people inside or outside the company perceived by the person acquiring information as the source of the information.
[2] All documents perceived as the source of information by the person acquiring information. Included are inside documents such as letters, reports, and outside documents such as newspapers, publications, and information services.
[3] Any documentary, mechanical, or electrical storage of information, from a filing system to a computer data bank.
[4] Both regular and 'ad hoc' reports on specific subject areas.
[5] Staff members of organizations who sell services to manufacturing corporations: such as, bankers, lawyers, public accountants, etc.
[6] Regular reports from services which specialize in providing information covering specified subject areas.
[7] Information about any physical phenomena such as the size of a plant, the distance between two points, etc., which is directly perceived rather than obtained from a human or documentary source.

national corporation with operations abroad acquires external information, the most likely single source of this information is the corporation's own staff abroad. In interview discussions about information sources, executives emphasized the importance of their own staff overseas. The general view of headquarters executives was that company executives overseas were the people who knew best what was going on in their areas. For the most part, company executives abroad were in the same functional area as the headquarters executive acquiring information. The head of the international division tended to get information from the

Table 11.5
Relative importance of human sources

Sources	As percent of all sources N = 139	Human sources N = 93
Inside the organization	24	35
International division		
Executives abroad	15	23
International division		
Executives at headquarters	5	8
Corporate executives	2	3
Product executives	1	2
Outside the organization	43	65
Service-organization staff	14	22
Competitors	9	13
Distributors, consumers, suppliers	5	8
Governmental officials and staff	4	16
Other human	11	16

head of the operating companies abroad, the headquarters marketing executive from the overseas company's top marketing executive, and so on. There was a notable absence of information gained from lower-level employees such as salesmen whose work brought them into everyday contact with the environment. This pattern is not restricted to international operations. The author has analysed domestic business operations where there is little or no direct information flow from lower-level field sales people to headquarters marketing executives, product engineers, and so forth. The fact that the importance of the internal sources of external information was perceived to be greater than it was emphasizes the significance of giving more attention to the effect of organizational reporting relationships and functional specialization on information flows. The findings suggest that information moves principally in a functional specialization, across not more than one organizational level. While reporting relationships and functional specialization serve important functions in the modern organization, their effect on information flows should be more explicitly recognized by executives. Steps to open up flows of information across more than one organizational level (for example, an overseas salesman reporting directly to the subsidiary president or marketing vice-president in the international division) would greatly expand the scanning scope of higher-level executives.

The presence of an information network abroad, in the form of its corporate executives, is a great advantage to the international corporation;

but it may also, paradoxically, be a weakness in a corporation that has only partly extended the limits of its geographical operations, because organization sources abroad tend to scan only information about countries in which they are based, or at best the region.

Outside the organization service organizations are of almost equal importance as a source of information as the corporation's own executives abroad; these are principally bankers, lawyers, and public accountants, but also other specialists such as executives in advertising and public relations.

Respondents rely on the service organizations for three kinds of information. One is the monitoring of rulings, expected rulings, and decisions of various foreign and domestic public authorities, which control such things as foreign exchange rates, taxes, and the importing and exporting of both goods and capital. Financial executives particularly tend to rely upon bankers and accountants for this kind of monitoring—sometimes with regular reporting.

A second kind of information provided by service organizations is on the general investment climate for a country or area. Many banks have a worldwide network of personnel and officers visiting around the world. This makes their information on this subject especially valuable.

A third kind of information acquired from service organizations is competitive intelligence. One respondent, referring to advertising agencies said: 'Agency people talk about their client's experience and plans. They are not malicious, and certainly seek to do no harm to a company: They do just tend to talk more than company people.' Another said: 'My best information sources are advertising agencies and public relations people. Ad. agencies know a lot about their clients, and they are not so security conscious as company employees. Public relations people are good sources of competitive information because they hear so much. Even if they are not directly involved, they are on the grapevine.'

Another important human source of information for international executives are competitors, which accounted for 9% of all important external information acquired by the respondents, and for 13% of information acquired from human sources. There may be a much greater willingness and openness about exchanging information with competitors, particularly those representing other United States executives, than among executives within the United States. This may be due to the feeling among international executives that 'we are all in this boat together'. Overseas, American executives often face well-developed patterns of 'co-operation' among established national organizations.[11] At home, many international executives are still, or have until very recently been struggling to gain recognition, support, and understanding for international operations from corporate management. Finally, the perceived risk of antitrust problems is probably much lower abroad.

United States anti-trust laws are, in principle, extra-territorial in their application to American companies; Actions, anywhere in the world by American companies that diminish competition or restrain trade in this country are subject to the anti-trust laws. In practice, the application of the laws outside the United States appears to be less rigorous than inside.

All of these factors, plus of course the social factor of common experiences, languages, and attitudes in foreign environments may serve to create a climate of relatively free information exchange among United States international executives. Government officials and staff are important human sources and distributors, consumers, and suppliers almost as important. Other human sources include friends, acquaintances, and professional colleagues, which together are about half of this category, freelance university consultants, and various other people including a wife, and a candidate for employment.

The relative importance of the different categories of documentary information sources, which account for 27% of the important external information acquired by respondents, is shown in Table 11.6.

Table 11.6
Relative importance of documentary sources of information

Documentary sources	% of all sources N = 139	% of documentary sources N = 37
Outside the organization		
Publications	10	37
Information services	5	19
Reports	1	5
Inside the organization		
Letters	6	22
Reports	4	14
Information storage	1	3

Documents from outside the company were relatively more important than those from inside. Publications were the single most important category of documentary information. The most frequently mentioned publications were the *Wall Street Journal* and the *New York Times*, one or both of which were read regularly by almost all respondents. The second most important outside documentary source was information services. If these two outside documentary categories were combined, they were mentioned as often as international division executives abroad as sources of important external information. Inside the company letters and reports, mainly from executives abroad, were the most important documentary sources of information.

Information storage, which was taken to be broadly inclusive of any kind of documentary, mechanical, or electrical storage of information outside of the human mind, was found only once as a source of external information in the entire sample. In this instance, a respondent who had recently accepted a position with an organization gained information from his organization files, which he was reading as the first stage of a personal project to reorganize the files in his office. This finding underlines the difficulties of storage and transfer of external information outside of the human memory. This finding is also a reminder that the comprehensive computer-based information systems in many organizations are almost exclusively concerned with internal information. It also suggests that even an extensive library and clipping service is only a small part of a company's information system.

In the interviews, it was clear that to the respondents, the information explosion is essentially a publications explosion. Many respondents expressed frustration at the difficulty in trying to keep up with the outpouring of publications. A few of the companies in the sample relied upon an internal routing arrangement for publications, which permitted readers to note articles of particular interest for subsequent readers. Based upon respondent reports, these formal routing systems were of little significance as a scanning aid. Respondents felt that informal systems of co-operative scanning of publications were much more valuable. Executives passed documents on to other executives whom they felt might be interested. These arrangements were reciprocal when executives were at the same level. In superior-subordinate co-operative scanning, however, the flow was mainly upward.

None of the management groups in the sample used a formal system for monitoring published information, a somewhat surprising finding in light of the size of the larger companies in the sample. When questioned, executives were divided between those who expressed some interest in the possibilities of such a system, and those who felt that an expenditure on such an effort would not be worth the gain.

The lack of a formal system for scanning documentary information has resulted in duplication in many of the organizations in the sample. For example, in three companies, the executives reading information services were all reading the same service. If one executive in each of these organizations read a different service, the scope of the information service scanning in each organization would be considerably extended.

Physical phenomena

Physical Phenomena were the source of 6% of the information acquired by respondents, and eight of the nine instances occurred while respondents were travelling abroad; so that a major independent variable in utilization of this source by the respondents was travel. The instances cited were of two types:

(1) Where the information gained by the respondent was easily available from other sources but which required sensory perception of the actual phenomena to register the information in the respondent's mind, and

(2) where the information gained was not readily available from other sources.

An example of the first type was a respondent's astonishment when he realized that his flight from Australia to New Zealand had taken three hours, so that the distance was much greater than he had thought (based upon looking at maps and globes). He had suggested that New Zealand be placed under the operating control of the Australian manager, but the direct perception led him to recommend that authority for New Zealand be transferred from Australia to New Zealand. This example illustrates the crucial importance of first-hand observation in providing information that becomes the basis for informed judgement and decisions within the organization.

An example of the second type was corporation A's information that a corporation B was constructing a plant capable of producing a directly competitive product. Corporation B had announced that it was to produce a noncompetitive product. Local executives of corporation A had accepted this announcement; they drove past the new plant every day on their way to their offices, unaware of its potential for producing the competitive product. The executive from headquarters in corporation A realized immediately as he was driven by the new plant that it was potentially capable of producing the competing product. His technical knowledge enabled him to perceive information in a physical object, the plant, which his local executives, lacking this knowledge, were unable to perceive.

For the overall sample, 22% of the important external information acquired came from sources located outside the respondent's organization. This overall reliance upon outside sources is one of the surprising findings of this study and runs counter to the widespread view that executives rely principally upon company sources of information for information about the environment. For example, Peter Drucker, after emphasizing that the executive is within an organization, stated that: 'What goes on outside is usually not even known first hand. It is received through an organizational filter of reports: that is, in an already predigested and highly abstract form that imposes organizational criteria of relevance on the outside reality.'[12]

When instances of information acquired from overseas sources were examined separately, the importance of sources inside the organization was greater than that of sources outside (52% versus 48%). This difference reflects an understandable response to the constraints upon the headquarters executive travelling abroad. His time in each country visited is limited and his personal acquaintanceships, with the exception of those in countries where he has lived or worked, do not generally extend beyond his organization. The little reading time he has available is devoted largely or exclusively, to material from inside the organization. The reasons for this behaviour are understandable, but the executive who relies heavily upon inside sources runs the risk of source distortion, which may be biased in support of the reporter's special interests. In another analysis, a comparison of the inside sources of information utilized by respondents located in their organization's international division and in other divisions, the overwhelming proportion (97%) of important information acquired by respondent in international divisions came from sources within their own divisions. This reflected the extent to which the international executive was focused upon the kind of information available internally from other international executives. However, in interviews, there was evidence of a desire by some executives for a greater interdivisional flow of external information.

This desire was particularly evident for executives, often called product co-ordinators, who were responsible for stimulating a flow of product information within their organization. These executives, found with increasing frequency in the international divisions of major corporations, were responsible for generating and maintaining a flow of information about product experience and product ideas from one part of their organization's worldwide system to the other. One of their major potential sources of product information was frequently a domestic product division. The international division product co-ordinator often had an extremely difficult time in keeping information flowing from a domestic product division over a sustained period, because of the tendency for the volume of information to flow one way from the domestic product division to the international division. It then became difficult for the international executive to continue to obtain information, because they did not have information to exchange.

This type of problem underlines the extent of barriers to internal information flow presented by organizational boundaries. Whenever there is a need for information exchange between groups it is greatly facilitated by placing the groups in the same organizational structure. Other researchers have measured the patterns of organizational change in multinational organizations and have noted the pressure to abandon the international division for a more integrated global structure.[13]

Relation of sources and functional specialization

Table 11.7 is a profile of the importance of different sources for different functional specializations. The extremely high relative utilization (88%) of outside sources by financial executives is notable, and is largely attributable to the excellent external information services of major city banks, particularly prescriptive information, an area which is intensively scanned by financial executives.

Table 11.7
Relative importance of sources for executives in different functional specializations (in per cent)

	Functional specialization			
	General management N = 45	Marketing N = 40	Finance N = 16	Other N = 30
Location				
Inside	31	40	12	40
Outside	69	60	88	60
Total	100	100	100	100
Type				
Human	71	65	40	74
Documentary	18	30	60	21
Physical phenomena	11	5	—	5
Total	100	100	100	100

The relatively greater importance of documentary sources for financial executives and of human sources for general managers is related to their functions. The financial executive intensively scans prescriptive information which applies equally to all firms and is the kind of information which can be transmitted in writing. The general manager, on the other hand, is more concerned with strategic factors that tend to be specific to his own company. His information is more particularized, and is therefore more likely to come from other people directly.

The findings of this empirical study suggest that executives in large business organizations rely much more on external sources for information about their business environment than is commonly believed.

Secondly, the study emphasizes how little the systematic methods of information scanning have become a part of the way in which executives learn about their business environment. Computer-based systems were not found in this study, and even traditional manual systems of information retrieval were hardly significant as factors in day-to-day information gathering.

Thirdly, the study underlines the importance of organizational boundaries on intracompany information flows. Divisional boundaries, functional specialization, and level are significant barriers to the flow of information, therefore, these are important in designing the organization.

Overall, respondents acquired external information mainly from sources outside their own companies. However, abroad they relied mainly upon sources inside their companies. The importance of inside sources abroad explains one of the major strengths of a multinational company—it is a worldwide intelligence gathering and processing system. The subject of scanning, therefore, deserves more attention by both researchers and executives.

11.4 Suggestions for further reading

Some important articles:

(C) PENROSE, E. (1973). International patenting and the less developed countries, *Economic Journal*, Sept.

(D) COOPER, Charles (1970). The Mechanisms for the Transfer of Technology from Advanced to Developing Countries. Paper prepared at the Science Policy Research Unit at Sussex for the Secretariats of ACAST and UNCTAD.

(C) Thomas, M. J. (1975). Location of research and development in the international corporation, pp. 35–41, *Management International Review*.

(C) PIGANIOC, P. (1968). International competition and R and D, *European Business*, Jan. Reprinted in Kapoor & Grub, 1972.

(C) PAVITT, Keith, The multinational enterprise and the transfer of technology, Dunning (1971), chapter 3.

This article is a careful study of the issues, and shows advantages to industrialized countries of the way technology is transferred and the probable disadvantages to less industrialized countries.

See also:

(C) CHORAFAS, Dimitris, N. (1969). *The Communications Barrier in International Management*, American Management Association.

11.5 Exercises for this chapter

Case studies

Northern Star Electronic A.B. (1973), Harvard, ICH 9–174–135–127. Issues of centralization and decentralization in the management of information systems in a large international group.

Incidents

The AZED Corporation is a United States Electronics Company with a turnover of $850 m. It is selling high technology products worldwide, but manufacture outside the United States has only developed in the last 3–4 years. From the first there were problems of quality control in the subsidiaries, and engineers from the parent company were sent out to assume managerial positions. Owing to the shortage of suitably qualified staff, the American engineers were withdrawn as soon as possible. In some cases the withdrawal proved too soon, and when they returned they had great difficulty in establishing their authority. More recently the problem of quality control had been overtaken by the wider problem of persuading the subsidiaries to update their products and the manufacturing processes as new ideas poured out from headquarters. Many of these, and some that were expected to be most profitable, were ignored by subsidiary executives who, at the same time, complained that they did not get adequate information about new developments.

At present the company relies on the expatriate engineers where they exist, occasional visits from head office engineers, and a constant stream of circulars from central research and development. New methods of disseminating information and ensuring its use were eagerly sought.

11.6 Questions for discussion

(1) Identify some problems of communication in an international business, discuss solutions.

(2) What are the advantages to a company of the ability to transfer technical knowledge to its foreign subsidiaries, and how can it minimize the risks?

(3) Discuss information sources required to keep an international business competitive.

(4) The chief executive of an international electronics company manufacturing advanced control systems is worried about the lack of response in some of the subsidiaries to new products and to new processes. The company operates in Germany, the United States, Brazil, Nigeria, India and Australia. Present a brief outline of points that should be considered in relation to the general problem in each of those countries.

(5) Discuss national reactions to claims that foreign companies bring new technologies in a beneficial form.

(6) Write a memorandum to the Director of Research and Development of a large international pharmaceutical company advising him on the more effective dissemination of information on the product and the production process around the whole company. Assume that you are an adviser on international communications whom he has called in for the purpose.

(7) 'Communications in an international firm are often discussed but seldom improved'. Set out some reasons for the difficulties, together with possible solutions.

12 Staffing the Multinational Firm

12.1 The international executive

The terms of the discussion on the employment of managers in foreign subsidiaries have been changing. At one time it was assumed that senior posts abroad were filled by executives from the home country. For instance companies that followed the imperial route, in the various European countries that had colonies, developed over the years some well understood procedures for moving men around the world. Then the discussion shifted to the promotion of local nationals and the conditions required for that promotion. The terms of the discussion have moved again, now towards international management development. Not all experienced multinational firms accept this third stage, but, it is important to emphasize that there is available a three phase programme; it is equally true that all three can be going on at the same time in a given firm.

The first stage is the appointment of head office executives to senior posts abroad. Although the colonial route was mentioned in the last paragraph, this stage applies to investments in industrialized as well as less developed countries. Indeed nowadays it is often easier to make expatriate appointments in the former than the latter. For an inexperienced multinational there may be advantages in such appointments. The manager and the company learn this way. The expatriate can ensure that the skills of the parent company are properly disseminated and that advance warnings of problems are understood even before head office has a well-established international controller's department. Indeed there may well be a problem if the expatriates are withdrawn too soon. Experienced foreign investors have also commented that the premature withdrawal of head office nationals from the foreign subsidiary produce a number of unexpected side effects.

It may be easier to place an expatriate in an industrialized country simply because the negotiations required to get the necessary permits are less stringent. Nevertheless there may not be suitable people available in the less developed country. The hardest bargaining takes place in the more advanced of these countries, notably in Latin America. Here there are more qualified people available, but there is usually more legal protection for the local manager once appointed. So companies may well be fearful of premature promotion and strive to keep the expatriates until they are confident about the stability of the subsidiary and the quality of the managerial succession.

The problems of promoting local nationals are now only new to companies that have come recently into the foreign field. But the methods used to build up integrated international organizations when one of the elements of cohesion has been taken away are still controversial. The need, as companies see it, is not just to provide some general management training to their foreign managers, but to turn them into company men, to devise arrangements whereby they will acquire the same understanding of how the company works as did their predecessors. This attempt has a number of pitfalls, not the least of which is the feeling increasingly produced in host countries that the local culture and the local nationalism is being overridden by the pervasive corporate organization. More serious is that many efforts just do not work and companies are increasingly led to formalistic and expensive systems of communication to make up for the lost natural processes.[1]

Where, however, a company has a successful scheme for developing local nationals, there follows a demand for international promotion. Some companies have taken this in their stride, others have been totally unprepared for it and find the consequences too expensive and too beset with legal problems to undertake. There is the third stage, where a company works out a management development scheme on a corporate basis with promotion available as far as possible to any position and from any position.[2] This stage three policy may be particularly important in a centralized company. If the view is taken that centralization causes personal problems, such as lack of incentive, then global promotion opportunities can compensate. Another advantage hoped for is to have the right skill available where it is needed in the group. There are also a number of problems that have to be overcome including salary and fringe benefits, return home conditions, acceptability abroad. In the excerpt which follows (in 12.3) the policies here described are examined in more depth under four headings: expatriate, local national, third country nationals, international grade; but first a brief note on personnel policies in general.

12.2 Personnel policies in international companies

In addition to executive staffing issues just examined and labour relations to be considered in the next chapter, there is the question of how the multinational company copes with other personnel problems. Many companies claim advanced policies in host as well as home countries, particularly in incentive schemes, productivity deals and training methods. Some evidence has been assembled to support them, although the claim to innovation in personnel practices may well be hard to reconcile with the assertion that head office does not interfere in the personnel policies of affiliates.[3] The process of influence is a subtle one. The company establishes its foreign subsidiaries with certain standards for personnel practices, the subsidiary is left to approximate to these standards and to reconcile them with local custom and host government requirements. Where there are important financial implications for the future a greater degree of consultation will be required than where there are not. Thus wages policies are left to the subsidiary as long as it is known to keep roughly in line with local practices; but pension schemes are more closely scrutinized since the parent company may find itself committed by local initiatives. One study suggests that the subsidiaries of multinational firms have a significantly higher number of disputes over the employment or discharge of workers than domestic firms. This does support the view that multinationals of American origin are anxious to guard the right to hire and fire.[4]

The control of the personnel function is not usually very tight, although there are exceptions to this. Where the company does have personnel staff internationally, their expertise is usually in payment systems or training methods rather than industrial relations. Reports, when required, will normally be in general terms although labour turnover figures may be collected. In chemical companies reports on safety internationally are sometimes required. Details of training and figures concerning disputes are less frequently asked for. As in the other functions, there are informal as well as formal controls at works ensuring at least some move to uniformity throughout an international group.

12.3 Staffing the multinational[5]

Managers in international enterprises are confronted with a different and more complex set of managerial problems than their domestic counterparts. The distinguishing characteristics of these problems are closely related to the external factors (economic, social, political, cultural, legal) to be found in the various environments in which the company operates. The managers who staff international operations are expected to cope with all the problems of operating away from the parent company: the problems of communication, control, decision-making and working towards a common corporate goal from the diverse environments.

Management development: a systematic approach

Most international firms have hitherto adopted a haphazard approach to the management of personnel in international operations. International policies are based upon domestic policies or extensions of these rather than on rational choice. Personnel practices are more *ad hoc* and short-term. In short there is a lack of a more systematic approach to the personnel management function in international firms. When the multinational enterprise sets out to have an effective international management team and to be able to utilize its human resources to the best advantage, the need of this systematic approach becomes apparent.

Owing to the diversity of the environments in which multinational enterprises operate, staffing is subjected to a variety of influencing factors both internal and external to the firm. These influencing factors affect the choice of an effective management development policy and the subsequent implementation of the chosen policy. Thus in effect we have a simple three stage model as in Fig. 12.1.

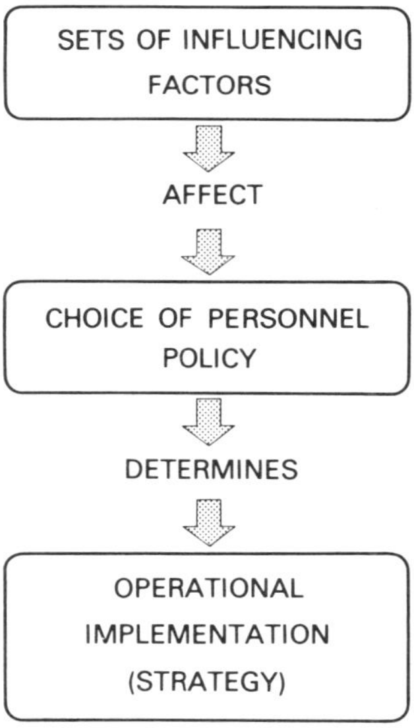

Fig. 12.1 Management development policy.

Sets of influencing factors. About thirty of these have been identified of which some relate to the characteristics of the company itself, some to the individual and some to the host country.

Company characteristics that influence staffing policies are:

(1) Ownership of foreign subsidiaries; a different policy, and indeed a different kind of person, will be required according to whether the invest-

ment is short or long term. The investment which is expected to be short term can be used either as a training place or a final posting for those about to retire. The latter policy would overcome the problems of re-integration. Similar considerations may apply where minority holdings are concerned; but in many joint ventures considerable powers of diplomacy and knowledge of the company may be required. Longer term management policies are appropriate where the parent company has majority or total ownership. Many companies use skilled international staff in all situations mentioned in this paragraph.

(2) Industry group; policies will vary at least between manufacturing and service industries. The latter may depend more on intangible knowledge from headquarters and so are likely to continue to employ expatriates, although this does not necessarily apply to banks who employ local nationals for their knowledge of local business conditions.

(3) Technology; the level of the technology in terms of sophistication, together with the amount of the research effort needed to sustain it, will affect the policies of both the technical and the marketing departments; this will apply particularly when the transfer of knowledge virtually requires the transfer of staff. There is some evidence, too, that companies operating in high level technologies are more likely to transfer other personnel policies.

(4) Market influences; if the market for the product is purely local and the techniques employed are well within the capacity of local management, expatriates or third country nationals are much less likely to have a part to play than where global techniques are applicable in worldwide markets.

(5) Age of Investment; the older foreign subsidiaries are likely to have established means of staffing which are hard to change unless problems arise.

(6) Organization structures (see chapter 9); companies with product group worldwide structures are likely to have more expatriates; those with matrix organizations are almost certain to have some international management development schemes.

(7) Commitment to International business; a company that does not have a substantial part of its business abroad would not consider the more elaborate schemes for international promotion.

(8) Cost factors; these are debatable and there is no formula for working out the costs and benefits of the possible programmes. The costs of expatriates of all types, especially third country nationals, are increasing rapidly; but the benefits have also been shown to be so great as to make their employment almost certain under some conditions.

(9) The communication and co-ordination system; this may affect staffing policies in many ways. One is the use of international transfers, meetings and educational programmes to facilitate the development of

more efficient international communications.

(10) Style of management; companies will settle for a distinctive style which suits their business or their personalities. This style is likely to be culture bound, however, and may cause difficulties.[6]

In addition to company factors, the policies are also influenced by the characteristics of individuals who may be available. These include their life style, their expectations, their ambitions and can be listed as follows:

(i) Qualifications and experience.

(ii) Record of previous performance.

(iii) Commitment to international business, including aspirations to international promotion.

(iv) Suitability for international business, including ability to adapt to new environments and to show sensitivity to new situations. Family commitments.

Finally there are the host country characteristics:

(1) Level of economic development. This naturally affects the ability of the company to recruit in a given country either for local or for international posts. On the other hand there will be pressure on the company to assist the development process by the establishment of educational programmes to facilitate rapid promotion. Applications for permits for foreign residents, wherever they come from, are likely to be scrutinized even more carefully in those countries which yet have most need of foreign management. The industrialized countries place less obstacles to the movement of managers across frontiers.

(2) Political stability and nationalist sentiments, including the propensity to nationalize or expropriate. Similar considerations apply, but skilled and experienced management may be required to maintain a presence or get the best possible terms for a withdrawal.

(3) Control of foreign investment and immigration policies. The control of ownership and the issue of work permits are usually the subject of negotiation, even where there are laws on the subject. If the company has international policies, however flexibly they have to be operated in practice, these will aid negotiations.

(4) Availability of qualified and experienced managers, the need to develop and promote local managers and technical staff. These considerations apply in the same way as those already listed.

(5) Socio-cultural setting. There are clearly problems of adjustment across boundaries of culture, race, language and religion. There are, equally clearly, some boundaries that cannot be crossed; these are mainly political and sometimes prove impermanent. In general these problems are the subject of many myths which are dispelled in practice. Some of the most difficult cultural boundaries are crossed successfully,

and the myths are dispelled after brief examination. On the whole, if other considerations require that a manager move between two incompatible countries, then selection and training can minimize the problems to the point where they become tolerable.

(6) Geographical location. As with the socio-cultural setting, the location is obviously an important consideration, but does not make for impossible difficulties for actions that are otherwise desirable.

These lists of influencing factors are by no means exhaustive. They do include some of the more important factors affecting the rational choice of an international management policy. Within each set, variables themselves are interdependent. That is to say, a number of influencing factors within the host country may interact to affect strongly the choice of one particular policy rather than another. Also each set of influencing variables interact with one another. In choosing a personnel policy one set may be weighed by itself and in comparison with the others, especially with a view to reconciling differences between the three parties involved: the company, the individual and the host country.

The choice of policies. The most commonly used policies are:

(1) Employment of home country personnel from the parent company or headquarters for foreign operations. This will be called the employment of expatriates.

(2) Employment of host country nationals for managing the subsidiaries within that country. This will be called the employment of local nationals.

(3) Employment of third country nationals. Third country nationals can best be described as nationals of country A working in country B for a company whose origin is in country C. That is to say, a third country national is neither a national of the home nor host countries.

(4) Employment of an international grade of executive or international cadre. The international grade executives are a group of various nationalities who are deployed all over the world. This policy is usually complementary to any of the above three policies and has only emerged within the last few years.

The employment of expatriates

It has been a tradition of multinational companies to staff foreign subsidiaries with expatriates at least at the onset of the investment abroad, and in later stages especially in higher-level positions. Some of the reasons given by companies for the adoption of this policy are lack of qualified, experienced and competent local nationals to fill the managerial positions, familiarity with parent company's management techniques and methods as well as the technology and product development, the need for expatriates to train and develop local managers, the need for expatriates to maintain communications channels with head office, the need for expatriates to facilitate control and ensure that the subsidiary's operation is attuned to the general overall global policy.

The expatriates are employed in two basic roles. The first seems to be a temporary one in which they are expected to train and develop local nationals for higher level positions and subsequently replace themselves. The second is a role of more permanence and greater authority. The expatriate is at the foreign subsidiary to keep an eye on the situation. Although some companies have openly stated this as a reason for the employment of expatriates, this view is often not made explicit though the practice is evident. If the company employs expatriates temporarily to groom local nationals to take over key positions, then it is obvious that the company is planning to adopt the second policy: that of employing local nationals at some time in the future. In this case the expatriates may be expected to identify themselves with the local environment and community so as to gain acceptance for themselves and hence facilitate their roles as trainers. However, if the expatriates are employed for the second role, identification with the local community and environment may not be in line with the purpose of employing them as they may then be tempted to allow more independence to the subsidiary.

Employment of expatriates also gives rise to some problems. The most notable are:

(i) Unfamiliarity with local languages, customs and ways of doing business and therefore lack of sensitivity to the local environment.

As a consequence, expatriates are often conspicuous characters and give a very foreign image to the firm which may not be in the best interests of the company especially if local nationalist sentiments are strong.

(ii) There are adaptation problems, including the effect of the so called culture shock. These adaptation problems may affect settling quickly into the job on hand and may even impair job performance.

(iii) Expatriates are expensive to employ. They are paid their home salaries plus substantial allowances for overseas assignments in the form of premiums. The compensation and remuneration of expatriates are extremely costly for the company and for this reason alone, many companies prefer, where possible, to employ local nationals.

(iv) Once away from the parent company, the expatriate can be somewhat out of line with the progress at home and his very absence from the centre of power is a threat to his own promotion prospects as it may be difficult to return him to a suitable job when he completes his assignment abroad. The repatriation problem is one which affects both the individual and the company.

The employment of local nationals

Most companies nowadays adopt a policy of employing local nationals to manage their foreign subsidiaries as far as possible. This policy is favoured because of its many advantages. Some of these are:

(i) Local nationals are familiar with local culture and customs and local ways of doing business. There are no language problems and together with their understanding of the local environment, the company can save on the costs of training expatriates in language proficiency and in time taken to adapting to the environment.

(ii) Local nationals are assumed to have an intimate knowledge of the local business situation. This is vital in establishing good relationships with customers and clients especially in marketing services and with governments.

(iii) Having local nationals in management positions especially at higher levels, reduces the 'foreign image' of the firm. This is especially advantageous in countries with strong nationalistic sentiments.

(iv) Having local nationals in management positions at the top level may also enhance the morale of other local nationals—the feeling of working for a boss from the same country.

(v) The costs of employing local nationals are less than for employing expatriates even if the company pays a salary above local scales in order to attract more capable people and to retain them.

(vi) For the local nationals themselves the multinational company, because of its seize and prestige, provides better employment opportunities.

However, there are a few drawbacks to a policy of employing local nationals only. These are:

(i) Unfamiliarity with the parent company's management techniques and operating systems. The education as well as the experience in business and the environment, to which the local nationals have been exposed may not have prepared them to understand the concept of a multinational enterprise or attuned them to global corporate goals rather than local ones. (However a new breed of international manager may be emerging with loyalty to company rather than country. The local national may be less sympathetic to national ambitions than the expatriate.[7])

(ii) Owing to differences in attitudes and values the former may also be reluctant to delegate authority or to adopt more aggressive approaches to business deals.

(iii) Where the local national is identified with his country this may give rise to conflicts of loyalty between the company and the country. This is especially so in the repatriation of profits—the local national may feel that to arrange for the remission of profits to the parent company may not be in the best interests of his own government's policy although it is important for the company's survival. In such situations, he may be put in a difficult position because of the pressures from his own government. Local nationals in more senior positions may have to pass on to their subordinates information which may cause resentment. Here again they are torn between fighting for their own colleagues or preserving their livelihood.

(iv) In most cases, a policy for the employment of local nationals only creates an inbuilt immobility in that once one reaches the top of the management hierarchy in the subsidiary he is stuck unless there are avenues for promotion beyond. Owing to this ceiling on promotion an aspiring local national may resign to join another company or government employment. His value has risen considerably as a result of experience gained in the local subsidiary.

(v) The ceiling to which he can go tends moreover to block the promotion of other aspiring local nationals. This has the overall effect of damping the morale of high-flyers and at times gives rise to a high turnover of local personnel.

The employment of third country nationals

A third personnel policy which has become more apparent over the last few years is that of employing third country nationals. This goes some of the way to meeting the problems of the local nationals but has similar advantages and disadvantages to those of using expatriates. Indeed some companies and subsidiaries tend to regard third country nationals as expatriates in the strictest sense of the word in that they are not local nationals and they serve outside their own home country. However there are a few notable differences that should be brought to light. Third country nationals form a third source of recruitment for the companies in the staffing of overseas operations. This source is especially advantageous and important in cases where the shortage of competent and qualified local nationals is critical and is further aggravated by the lack of home country nationals able or willing to serve abroad. The second advantage is cost saving. In most cases, the costs of maintaining third country nationals are less than the costs of maintaining expatriates abroad. For instance, if the salary of the executive is tied to that of his home base, and if the level of remuneration of that particular base is lower than that of the home country, a substantial saving of salary costs can be achieved. Savings from differential payments of fringe benefits and other compensations are also significant, though it is likely that in time to come the difference in remuneration and compensation between expatriates and third country nationals will narrow. There may also be savings in the transfer of executives from other countries than that of head office.

Besides costs savings, there may be a greater cultural flexibility and ease of adjustment. For instance having an Argentinian in the Venezuelan subsidiary of a British multinational enterprise would not only enable savings in terms of remuneration and relocation costs but also in the intangible costs of being able to eliminate language problems to some extent. United States firms operating in Latin America have recognized this advantage and have used third country nationals effectively in Latin American countries. The common language, coupled with similarities in cultural backgrounds would in effect mean less difficulties of adaptation and settling in faster on the job.

It is apparent then that some of the disadvantages of using expatriates in foreign operations can in fact be overcome through the use of third country nationals. However, there are also drawbacks as this remains an expensive policy compared to that of using local nationals. Remuneration and compensation are still higher. This in itself tends to create tenuous relationships even though, if the cultural background of the foreigners are similar to those of the locals, the local nationals may still feel that they are being discriminated against.

In extreme cases, moreover, third country nationals may be rejected by local nationals rather than be more acceptable because local nationals may tend to perceive them as outsiders not even directly linked to headquarters as in the case of expatriates. For example local nationals may feel that at least with managers from the home office, they can perceive a more direct relationship to their presence in that they are looking after the interests of the group. Whereas the third country nationals, even though they are employed by the parent company, produce a hostile feeling among local nationals. The attitude is 'if you can't send an expatriate from head office you really ought to employ a local man'. Further it is not always possible to use third country nationals because of political constraints.

The employment of international grade executives

An even more recent development in international staffing policies is the emergence of the 'international grade of executives'. In principle, this policy allows almost unrestricted movement of executives of any nationality to anywhere within the group's operations. Obviously in practice there are limitations, but the advantages include:

(i) The international grade positions are usually opened to senior international managers with some experience in international operations and these managers in effect form an international fire brigade to service the firm's worldwide operations. They are, in effect, trouble shooters. They are constantly on the international circuit and not necessarily tied to one particular home-base.

(ii) The international grade is an avenue of promotion for local nationals beyond the host country operation. With an international grade the local ceiling placed on the promotion of local nationals is lifted. As a consequence of this opening, the morale of local nationals is enhanced with the subsequence lowering of turnover rates.

(iii) Because the international grade consists of career international managers, the company in effect has a ready reservoir of expertise to draw on for assignments anywhere in the world. This gives the company the flexibility and competitive advantage using its human resources effectively.

(iv) As an international reservoir of expertise, the international grade manager complements the other sources of management within the multinational group. Expertise is provided where it cannot be found amongst local nationals or is not available from the head office.

(iv) The international grade is in itself a big step towards the internationalization of the company, it reduces parochialism and gives the firm a more international image.

Obviously the objectives of the international grade, now only in a nascent experimental stage in a few of the more adventurous multinational enterprises, are not easily met. The practical implementation of this policy has met with some difficulties including:

(i) The cost factors which are once again major obstacles. The international grade executives are expected to be remunerated and compensated according to an international salary scale regardless of their assignment locations. Such a scale of salary is certainly expensive to administer. It is expensive also in that it requires elaborate recruitment and selection schemes and also investment in linguistic training, cultural orientation programmes and most of all the constant relocation costs.[8]

(ii) Owing to the constant up-rooting expected of international grade executives, the pressures on families and the executive himself can be distressing and hence impair his performance. The international grade manager's long absence from his home base may leave him out of line for even higher level positions in the home country should he wish to return home.

(iii) To ensure that the international grade works effectively a central manpower plan monitoring requests for managerial assistance and expertise from the company's worldwide subsidiaries is necessary—

again such a co-ordinating centre is not only expensive but difficult to operate.

(iv) Though the international grade provides an avenue for promotions beyond the local subsidiaries, some host country governments may feel that it runs counter to their policy of having locals to head foreign subsidiaries they may also complain that foreign firms are causing a brain drain, when their own nationals are promoted.

The choice of policy. As mentioned earlier, the three sets of influencing factors interact with each other and the interactions exerts influence on the national choice of a suitable staffing policy for multinational companies. For instance, within the company itself the foreign investment is wholly owned and the technology for production and manufacturing is complex. If the investment is at the start-up phase, then obviously all these factors point towards a greater use of expatriates from the home country than any of the other three options. If the company weighs the influencing factors of the individual and the host country in which the investment is made and finds that the level of economic development is low and there is a shortage of competent managers and technical personnel, then the likelihood that the company would employ expatriates would be all the stronger. For the individuals concerned the company must consider the structure of the jobs it offers. Will the job descriptions attract capable managers? Would the potential managers have room to move up the hierarchy and to develop their own interests? How would the personalities of the available staff fit in with the requirements of the job? Will the constant up rooting put undue stress on the individual and his family? Perhaps the most vital question is whether the individual managers would be able to reconcile effectively the complex influences and to do so in the context of insuring the survival, growth and profitability of the company? Thus, by considering these influencing variables from the three parties, the company itself would minimize its risks in international staffing; it is also important to note that the company can have difficulty in choosing one single staffing policy for its international operations.

This systematic approach to the staffing of international operations allows for flexibility. A company can choose one policy and supplement it with other options. In fact most firms prefer to follow a policy of employing local nationals as far as possible, but to retain a few key positions in overseas subsidiaries for expatriates and in some cases third country nationals. It is not rare to find swings of policies in staffing as a result of some crisis or other. For instance, the company may over-react to management problems in the subsidiaries and send in more expatriates to try to resolve the situation. On the other end increasing turnover of capable local managers may be a symptom of dissatisfaction arising from blocked promotions, and the company may be tempted to withdraw expatriates quickly and promote local nationals in an effort to stabilize the situation. Third country nationals may be brought in when expatriates themselves fail on the job and have to be repatriated, but a suitable local man cannot be found to fill his place. At times the too rapid withdrawal of expatriates so as to have local managers in positions of higher level management as far as possible has resulted in over-promotion and expatriates may have to be used again.

In theory it is often perceived that, as international operations expand, the firms move from the use of expatriates to the use of local and third country nationals and eventually the development of an international grade. In practice, however, whichever staffing policy a firm adopts there is always a mixture of nationalities involved; to some extent the proportion of other nationalities, apart from those from the home country, in the management of subsidiaries overseas often provides a good measure of the extent to which the company is internationalizing its executives.

The implementation. The next step is to put the selected policy into operation. This is perhaps one of the more difficult parts of the international staffing operation. Owing to the difficulties in the environment in which the company operates, carrying out any international staffing policy is heavily constrained by the factor that influenced the choice of the policy.

One issue is the method of recruitment. Expatriates, naturally, are recruited from the home country. They are also usually recruited from inside the company, and if the appointment is a senior one almost invariably so.[9] One of the reasons for their existence is to take the corporate presence abroad, and this is difficult for an outsider. The local national on the other hand, is selected within his own country, but appointed by some central or regional authority if the position is sufficiently senior. For levels below the board or executive committee abroad, the decisions are normally taken locally. But in both cases the recruitment may be from people educated in the firm's home country. United States companies, in particular, are liable to look for men trained in American Universities. Third country nationals may be recruited from a wide variety of sources; but, like senior expatriates, the international grade executive is almost certain to come from within the firm. Some companies are using worldwide internal job advertising.

Another issue is that of selection, especially the criteria for selection. For expatriates previous international experience is usually a prerequisite; for others the track record is vital. One study revealed that the selectors usually select candidates that they personally know or have at some time or other worked with.[10] The use of psychological tests is an almost outmoded approach insofar as international selection is concerned, especially for higher level positions. The value of these tests is usually questionable in cross frontier selection as most of them suffer from cultural bias. However some attitudinal measure as to the sensitivity to differing cultural environments may at least give an indication of the adaptability of the person to his new environment. Prolonged interviews, often with wives too, are used to filter out candidates who may be especially prone to fail abroad.[11]

At the international executive level training is principally concerned with understanding different operating environments, although promotion may be involved as well. Management development programmes take place at national, regional and corporate level and the executive is finding his way around the organization. This process is carried further by international company meetings and cross-visiting; there may also be some form of job rotation.

Generally there are two sorts of assignment, the long term and the short term. Either of these may be to replace scarce skills, to aid expansion, to facilitate communication and control, to develop talent, to promote greater flexibility in the deployment of resources or to foster the internationalization of the company. One common problem is what happens when the assignment ends. The ability, or frequently the inability, of the company to absorb the returned expatriate is a test of an effective international management development scheme.[12]

International salary scales also cause many difficulties. Companies report that they have suffered from inept arrangements which effectively contradict other staffing policies. People may be discouraged from going where they are needed. But in the conditions of varying rates and varying expectations in different countries, suitable schemes can be hard to find. The local national's position appears relatively simple; he will be paid according to the standards of his country. But the reality is less simple. If there is no chance of promotion beyond the frontiers of his own country, then the company may resort to higher salaries to keep the able managers who might otherwise leave for senior posts with local competitors where there is no permanent subordination. The presence of highly paid expatriates, especially if they are in junior positions, will also enhance salaries. If payment goes well above local standards, for whatever reason, the company may find itself in trouble with other employers and perhaps even with the host country government.

There are a number of schemes of payment for expatriates and third country nationals; some are more sophisticated than others but most are related in some way, to the home base as are the pension schemes. The international grade by definition, implies a special international salary scale of its own; but it will still be related to the home country of the company and cannot be free from all anomalies and inconsistences. Finally nine varieties of allowance complete the available international salary package: overseas premium or position allowance, international adjustment allowance, allowances for going into unstable situations, as well as allowances for housing, cost of living, education, travel, medical attention and tax equalization.

A final list of issues includes the problem of appraisal of the international manager, his identification and the ensuring of succession. In each case there is a problem of how to do it, but also one of by whom it is done. The case of appraisal is as difficult as the appraisal of the subsidiary discussed under the heading of control in chapter 10. The other two issues may be looked after in a management development or an administration department. But the problem of co-ordinating information on managers may be as great as that of co-ordinating the activities of the managers themselves.

12.4 Interesting facts—executive earnings compared[13]

	Gross pay $	Net after tax $	What that buys $
Switzerland	51,253	34,661	34,661
	Other countries		
Brazil	49,919	33,590	47,986
Netherlands	49,491	23,828	29,785
W. Germany	47,921	29,804	32,396
Belgium	46,759	27,328	34,592
France	46,069	36,655	43,637
USA	43,769	27,049	42,264
Sweden	41,573	16,011	15,697
Spain	35,401	26,678	41,684
Singapore	32,974	22,300	32,319
Australia	29,493	18,365	25,866
S. Africa	26,458	17,719	33,432
UK	18,000	11,520	20,945

Source: Employment Conditions Abroad Ltd.
The figures in the left-hand column show the average salaries for a similar grade in each country.

12.5 Suggestions for further reading

See the articles mentioned in the notes to this chapter, and:

(C) ALPANDER, Guvenc (1975). Who Manages the Overseas Operations of the US Multinational Corporations, *Conference Papers*, Academy of International Business Annual Conference, Dallas.

This article is interesting as showing a relationship between the employment of expatriates in middle management and product group worldwide organization type.

(C) EDSTROM, Anders (1974). Beliefs about International Transfers and their Implications for Transfer Policy. CESA Seminar, Sept.

(C) MILLER, E. (1973). The international selection decision: a study of some dimensions of managerial behavior in the selection decision process. *Academy of Management Journal* **16**, no. 2.

This is just one example of the work of Professor Miller who has done extensive research in depth on the assignment of American managers abroad. For the other side of the picture, how managers determine who is to be selected, see *Michigan Business Review*, May 1972, pp. 12–19.

(C) PATRIC, S. & KNOWLES, D. (1974). How to pay multinationally, *Management Today*, August.

(B) *Profile of a Chief International Officer* (1975). HEIDRICH & STRUGGLES.

This is a short booklet giving the typical organizations of American international companies and how they are led, together with numerous details outlining the typical executive who has responsibility for foreign operations.

(D) STONAR, J. A. F. *et al.* (1972). Factors associated with effective performance in overseas work assignments, *Personnel Psychology*, no. 25, pp. 303–318.

(C) SCHOLLHAMER, H. (1969). The compensation of International Executives, *MSU Business Topics*, Winter, reprinted in Kapoor & Grub (1972). Chapter 9.

See also:

DANIELS, OGRAM & RADEBAUGH (1976). Chapter 23.
ROBINSON (1973). Chapter 3.
ROBOCK & SIMMONDS (1973). Chapter 21.

12.6 Exercises for this chapter

Case Studies

The Tug of War Rope Co. Ltd., 1960, (Institution of Works Managers no. 29), by Kent, R. CCH 365–045–1.
Managing director sends his London works manager to Sweden, where the company had extended operations. Good progress was reported in London and Sweden for several years, until production ceased in the Swedish factory, and the director then had to decide on a course of action regarding his London works manager.

General Foods Corporation—International Division, 1964, (Harvard, ICH 9–313–218), by Carey, E. R., Newton, D. A., Hawkins, D. F. Discusses the problems in executive manpower: domestic personnel policies, evaluation, incentive plan. American nationals abroad and the training of overseas managers.

General Foods Corporation—International Division, 1964 (Harvard ICH 9–313–219) by Corey, E. R., Newton, D. A., Hawkins, D. F.
Personnel policies in three subsidiaries: England, Mexico and Brazil: the role of headquarters in management development abroad.

Construction Equipment International A.G., undated, (IMEDE OB–75, ICH 9–413–083), by Summer, C. E.
This case describes business operations and the evolving of a big subsidiary in Zurich (CEIAG) of an American company in Detroit (RMA—Road Machinery of America); management attitudes and practices.

Incidents: (1) a staffing problem

Signore Juan Alamos was the Chief Executive of a Latin American subsidiary of the British international conglomerate Gigantic Holdings Ltd. His reports to the Board in London had persistently complained of the interference of the local government. For some time the group Board had had a high opinion of him, and he was often praised as an outstanding manager who had turned in reasonable results in spite of severe difficulties caused by an unreasonable government. Now the Board were receiving some disturbing reports, and these were confirmed when two members visited the country. It appeared that Signor Alamos was running a private vendetta against the government, that the restrictions against which he was campaigning were quite normal and acceptable, and that he was making many enemies in the country concerned through his unreasonable attitude. He was using his position in the company to influence local politics, totally contrary to group policy.

As soon as the Directors realized this they asked him to resign, which he refused to do. Then they dismissed him. The next move was his reinstatement by order of a court and a summons against the company for illegal dismissal. It appeared that the law of the land did not allow a foreign company to dismiss local nationals in managerial positions. The Directors were caught between an employee who was discrediting the company, the industry group and foreign firms in general in his country, and the fact that the government of that country still afforded him protection. Not unnaturally the Board wondered what to do next.

(2) Staffing an international company

Powerful Engineering Ltd. is the name of a large international company in heavy engineering. It is London-based, and has subsidiaries in the United States, Venezuela, Brazil, France, Germany, Sweden, Iran, India, Kenya and Australia. Apart from the appointment of the chief executive in each country, members of the group board have not considered staffing or personnel problems for their foreign subsidiaries for many years. Indeed they are proud of the fact that between 1955–1965 they successfully went over to local national control in all their foreign companies. Apart from general world conditions, this change was stimulated by the loss of able local managers particularly in their two Latin American subsidiaries. Now they have only local national executives overseas, apart from some British staff men (Mainly engineers) abroad on short-term assignments.

In order to achieve the complete nationalization of their foreign appointments and retain some elements of the personal control that existed in the days of expatriate managers, the firm instituted a regular training course in England. Carefully selected managers in each of the ten countries in which the firm has manufacturing subsidiaries are brought to England for a year. During this time they get to know their way around head office thoroughly, become personal friends of many of the executives with whom they will later correspond, and do limited projects to familiarize themselves further with the way the company works. After returning to their own countries they are rapidly promoted to senior posts, providing their performance is satisfactory. Apart from their own personal involvement in this programme, members of the Board had had no worries about the scheme which had worked well for ten years. Now they have in front of them a report from the Group Personnel Officer which raised some puzzling questions about the foreign staffing policy. Some points from this report were:

(1) Once again the turnover rate among foreign executives was becoming alarming. Indeed it was worse now than it was around 1960 when it was taken to signal the need for local managers. But what was being signalled this time?

(2) The training scheme was not in fact building up the informal network that had been intended. The foreign managers kept in a group to themselves, and formed limited contact with the British staff members. These latter often failed to find the time to see them, and were sometimes away in any case.

(3) Managers in some of the countries are showing great sensitivity to the way the control system is working, and are failing to send in their reports regularly. Other communication problems are mentioned.

(4) Able personnel in the group, and especially those with much needed skills, always seem to exist in the countries where their talents cannot immediately be used and not where they are urgently needed.

The Board are wondering if the situation demands the development of some new policies on staffing.

12.7 Questions for discussion

(1) How are the parts of an International Company held together? Sketch out the personal influences involved, and discuss the qualities required of staff with international responsibilities.

(2) 'The international manager faces rapid change in all the countries in which he operates, but with a bewildering variety of speed and direction in each.' Comment.

(3) What external criteria influence the choice of staff in an international business? What practical considerations limit a company's freedom in placing staff in overseas locations? Discuss possible answers to these questions.

(4) Comment critically on the statement in this chapter that: 'The ability, or frequently the inability, of the company to absorb the returned expatriate is a test of an effective international management development scheme.'

(5) Discuss the advantages and disadvantages of international personnel policies:

  (*a*) To the company
  (*b*) To the foreign employees.
  (*c*) To the host country governments.

13 International Industrial Relations and Trade Unions

'In Western Europe some 25 major companies belong to the exclusive 'multinationals' club. The only control over the big multinationals are national boundaries, but they leap these virtually without hindrance. So one of the most important requirements of national and international social democracy is the creation of a 'multinational'—or better, an international—forum of public opinion which could work as a corrective to this particular power development . . .'[1]

While some managers may be surprised to learn that they leap 'virtually without hindrance' over national frontiers, 'this particular power development' has considerable consequences for the trade unions. There has been a change in the balance of power. Just at the moment when the unions have built up strong positions in a number of industrialized countries, and seen a legal framework of labour protection established, companies seem to them to have found a way out.

The companies can develop fresh investment in other countries to avoid union pressures in a country where they are currently operating. Negotiations can be confused by statements that the decision-makers are in another country. The companies can play off one union against another. The union response has been partly to try themselves to develop international operations, but this has proved weak and ineffectual for a number of reasons. Hence labour organizations have turned increasingly to political action and attempts to influence the law, nationally and internationally. Some of the consequences of these attempts are shown below in chapters 17 and 18. Meanwhile, on the other side, some companies have attempted to initiate international negotiation especially where some form of international rationalization is being attempted. The major issues in international industrial relations are listed below.

13.1 Issues in international industrial relations

The way any particular union sees the effect on its members of a company's international moves will depend on a number of factors. A different collection of interests arises and they are influenced at different points. For one thing the unions themselves represent different groups of workers in different countries: a well-known distinction is between unions that represent workers with a specific skill and those that represent employees in a particular industry group. Another is that there may be a direct conflict of interest between workers in the same industry in two different countries. This arises when a company chooses a new site or tries to rationalize its facilities. Rationalization can be a complicated and controversial issue inside a country, internationally it produces problems which find the unions at their weakest.

It has been pointed out[2] that a number of changes in the domestic situation of unions will affect their international posture. Changes in many countries include the shift of power within the unions and the increasing importance of the white collar worker. Another element is greater centralization nationally that follows the increasing role of trade unions, together with employers organizations, in the processes of government. At the same time there are increasing demands for plant agreements and for employee participation in the decision-making of the firm.

In the protracted discussions towards the emergence of the European Company registered with the European Economic Community, the unions have made demands. If these are not met they will oppose the scheme altogether. Included as a minimum is representation on the supervisory board. This could be only a third, if another third goes to representatives of the public interest. Otherwise a higher proportion will be demanded. Another demand is for European works councils, yet another is that one member of the board of management should have special responsibility for manpower and social policy questions. The satisfaction of these demands now seems probable, but the unions do not seem to have developed a relevant organization to accept the responsibilities they will acquire if their demands are met. Nevertheless it is being said that international trade unionism is likely to develop in the European Economic Community and to spread from there.

No one doubts that at present management is much more international than the unions, and that for a number of reasons this is likely to remain so. For the foreseeable future the unions are bound to put most of their resources into domestic activities, and the expense of attempting to match the international expertise of the companies would be prohibitive. Further the usual sanctions used by the unions would in many industries, hardly be assisted by international action. Railway workers, bus drivers and coalminers are just three groups of workers for whom an international strike is hardly likely to be more effective than a national one. As against the industrial weakness of the unions internationally, they have some political strengths; this point is well realized when trade union statements on multinational firms are made. For one thing most industrial democracies have a party which is at least strongly supported by the unions and therefore responsive to their views. In Europe it is common for ex-trade union officials to be members of governments. Hence the unions can influence the activities of governments and of intergovernmental bodies. Of course the companies also have official support.

Most multinational firms recognize unions, like most other firms. There have been some hard battles for recognition, usually with American companies. But it would seem, at least in the industrialized countries, that failure to unionize is as often a result of apathy on the part of employees working for a generous company as it is actual opposition to their organization. As an exception to this, white collar unions have had particular difficulty with American companies which do not have to deal with them at home. Another difficulty is that of information. Employers say that they cannot afford the wages demanded; incidentally they may also blame the unions for unreasonable demands when the information on which these statements could be checked is not available. In most countries the subsidiaries of foreign companies do not have to publish accounts separately and so it is impossible for the unions to judge of their success.

The unions are also much concerned about where decisions are taken. Companies often turn out to be more centralized than is supposed, but industrial relations are usually left to the local subsidiary.[3] One reason for this is the lack of interest in industrial relations on the part of most senior managers as well as the local nature of the subject and the wide diversity of laws and practices. Whatever may be the reason, however, there is no doubt that union negotiators are confused and expect a clearer definition of authority when dealing with highly organized concerns. It is difficult to know whether statements about the need to refer decisions to the parent company are true or are a camouflage to influence negotiations.

If the argument about centralization is largely an argument about the relative well-being of the whole and the parts, this also is a subject that affects the unions as well. There is often no clear division of responsibility, but indeed tension between the centre and the locality in the unions. This makes the credibility of any international moves hard to establish. Finally there is the point that the large, powerful and capital intensive international firm can gain advantages of opting out of the whole system of industrial relations in a country and simply giving the workers a better deal than they can find elsewhere.

To meet the changing situation with which the multinational faces them, the unions are gradually beginning to produce some international activities themselves. These operate within the constraints already suggested and are outlined briefly.

13.2 The structure and strategies of international trade unionism

There have been optimistic statements to the contrary, but a fact of international trade union organization is that it is in a very rudimentary condition.[4] There are three types of body: loose-knit international federations like the International Confederation of Free Trade Unions and the World Federation of Trade Unions,[5] advisory councils like the Trade Union Advisory Committee to the Organization for Economic Co-operation and Development and the European Trade Union Confederation, International Trade Secretariats like the International Metalworkers' Federation. Each of these bodies has their own particular work to do mainly as lobby and pressure groups and in the collection and exchange of information. They can facilitate meetings between trade unions in different countries to sort out problems that have international implications and to co-ordinate any policies decided. They are subject to all the problems outlined earlier in this chapter, in particular the difficulty of co-ordination given the different union structures in the different countries.

A fourth type of trade union organization should really be added, that of *ad hoc* groups set up between trade union bodies in different countries. These groups may be called together by an organization of one of the types already listed, or they may result from informal contacts. Much of the current development of international trade unionism is taking place gradually through this sort of activity.

The union strategies that are merging can themselves be seen in terms of three types. For reasons that have already been explained the strategy that is thought to be most effective at the moment is pressing for legal regulation. This is also extended to the development of codes of conduct which may have no legal support, but which have public opinion behind them. The reliance on political action can be especially seen in the efforts to reverse the trend evident since the war towards the greater liberalization of capital movements. The moment when fresh investment is being undertaken provides an opportunity for the local government to impose conditions like union recognition and the granting of bargaining rights; hence the unions are pressing for these conditions.

The second strategy is the use of the strengths available to certain groups of workers to co-ordinate international action. Dockers and seamen have been mentioned although there have been few clear signs of success hitherto. The third strategy is rather an accumulating bundle of small strategies designed to bring some opinion to bear at specific points and gradually to construct stronger international links between labour organizations. These include: exchanges of information, consultations, demonstrations of solidarity, agreements on objectives and the presentation of demands, the beginnings of international bargaining.

13.3 Transnational industrial relations and the multinational enterprise[6]

In the United States, government intervention has mostly been confined to regulating the framework of collective bargaining; the determination of substantive issues has been left in great part to management and labour through collective agreement.

In Europe the situation is different. Government's role is greater. The party-union character of European labour movements, as well as the older tradition of state intervention in economic life, has produced an industrial relations system in which legislation is regarded as the 'normal' means of determining wages and working conditions.[7]

Clearly, very different fundamental relationships can exist among the parties, labour–management–government, a fact affecting any comparison among different industrial relations systems. Thus the starting point for this transnational inquiry cannot be the parties and their relationships, since these vary considerably from system to system. A reference point common to all systems, however, is the content of the output.

Outputs can be categorized into two groups; one relating to benefits the parties receive; the other defining specific relationships among the parties. 'Benefits' (limited only to those received by *employees*) include direct wages, job classifications, wage supplements, vacations, holidays, and severance benefits. 'Relationships' cover grievance procedures, employee (or employer) representation units, and limitations on the use of strikes and lockouts. While there are other relevant outputs, this inquiry will be limited to these nine, since they cover the more significant interests of the parties involved, and the conclusions reached in a more detailed, expanded study were not substantively different.

'Industrial relations' then, may be defined as the process wherein these outputs are determined. 'Transnational' industrial relations occur when two of the parties—labour and management—interact on a multinational level to determine simultaneously outputs applicable to one or several (previously) nationally-contained systems. Within this conceptual framework, governments' interests are impressed on the system as management and labour accommodate them in their own interactions. The assumption here is that governments predominate since they determine the legal environments within which industrial relations operates and which cannot be compromised by any international collective bargaining agreement.

Any positive model portraying transnational industrial relations must first consider the influence of different national laws on the nature of the outputs of such a system. While other important influences, such as local labour market conditions, institutional impediments on the labour side, and differing cultural contexts are also certainly important, they are not as consistent in either fact or effect as is the law.

Likewise, the model must be timely and efficient in its application, covering those countries or situations where transnational industrial relations are most probable. National systems, where labour is not only organized but also *desirous* of handling employer relations on a transnational basis, appear the most appropriate for analysis. Such desire would apparently arise wherever workers in two or more national systems feel threatened by a common adversary. Such threats would likely be borne more logically in manufacturing, as opposed to agriculture or mining and other extractive industries, and in countries where Multinational Enterprises have concentrated their operations.[8]

Industrial relations in the United Kingdom have traditionally been characterized by the relative absence of legal constraints. Unions by and large refused to register under the 1971 Industrial Relations Act (replaced by the 1974 Trade Union and Labour Relations Act) and ignored its provisions on collective bargaining. This is not to say, however, that government has no influence. Wages and job classifications are usually determined free of any government participation. Recently, however, negotiated wage settlements have required government approval before becoming effective. During the latter 1960s the Department of Employment and Productivity approved increases above the 'norm' only if justified in terms of offsetting productivity increases. Wage increases had to relate to employment conditions *at the plant level.* In mid-1975, the Labour Government was being strongly advised to apply severe ceilings on all wage increases.

The structure of bargaining in the UK also mitigates against substantive transnational determination of wages and job content. Federated bargaining, as in the engineering industry, had traditionally resulted in determination of wages and other conditions on a national or district level by multi-employer, multi-union groups. However fewer issues are today subject to bargaining at these levels. At first glance, this narrowing of the jurisdiction of federated bargaining would appear to favour transnational bargaining, since negotiating plant or company level agreements can be more open to transnational, company-specific influences. However, even at enterprise levels there frequently exist diverse, and often mutually antagonistic, worker representatives.[9]

'Britain (has) . . . not one but two industrial relations systems . . . often in conflict . . . (one) . . . based on industry-wide collective agreements; the (other) . . . derived from understandings on the factory floor between management and individual work-place groups. . . . This conflict expresses itself in a gap between contract and effective wages, in chaotic forms of grievance handling, and in a disturbing number of "unofficial strikes".'[10]

This same type of conflict can occur within the context of enterprise bargaining where the factory floor-level system functions concurrently with multi-union negotiating committees—as illustrated in the long Ford strike in 1969. This institutional problem still exists because '. . . there is no organic link between shop stewards' committees and the negotiating committees of the federations of unions which conduct negotiations . . .'[9] Stewards focus on a workplace unit and enforce unit-level negotiations. Since they counter even company-level bargaining with unions, the possibility of transnational bargaining affecting issues viewed as within their purview is certainly questionable.

Shift premiums, overtime pay and other wage supplements are frequently defined in agreements negotiated at one or several different levels and may appear suitable for transnational bargaining. However, as discussed later, other important influences render such bargaining on these matters unlikely.

National agreements usually include provisions on holidays and vacations including six statutory holidays. Where such agreements are not applicable, the Minister of Labour, under the authority of the Wages Councils Act of 1945 and 1959, can issue a Wages Council Order mandating that certain vacations be given. Where federated agreements, laws or administrative 'orders' establish holidays and vacations, an individual multinational cannot counter such provisions. There may, however, be individual cases where holidays and vacations in excess of those otherwise provided are granted.

Unlike the situation in the US, severance (redundancy) payments are mandated in the UK in accordance with the requirements and provisions of the Redundancy payment Act of 1965. Prior to this law, severance payments were not obligatory. Collective agreements can define levels of (redundancy) payments so long as these levels are as favourable as those formulated in the 1965 Act, but '. . . managements and unions have been generally content to depend on the statutory provisions'.[11] British labour apparently prefers legislative channels, rather than collective bargaining, for securing severance payments.

Most agreements contain procedures for handling complaints (grievances) arising under their provisions. There is no uniform grievance procedure established by law in the United Kingdom. Thus the system defined in any international agreement for resolving complaints germane to the application of a specific contract would be acceptable, but would apply only to issues arising out of the application of the international agreement.

As already noted, employer and employee representation units are several and quite varied. At the national and regional (or district) levels in metalworking, for example, federated bargaining is carried on between the Engineering Employers' Federation and the Confederation of Shipbuilding and Engineering Unions (CSEU). There is no direct CSEU affiliation with the International Confederation of Free Trade Union's (ICFTU's) International Trade Secretariat for this industry, the International Metalworkers' Federation (IMF)—the organizational vehicle spearheading the trade unions' international labour activities as against the multinationals. Unions belonging to the CSEU may, and do, also belong to the IMF but, the commonality of membership is far from complete. Co-ordination of action between the two could result in the dereliction of responsibilities towards members not in both. More importantly, the two have vastly differing objectives.

Divergence of interest and conflicting jurisdictions over members and issues alike, between trade unions and stewards at the works levels, also support the expectation of a similar fragmentation which is not conducive to transnational bargaining, or the resolution of disputes arising under any international agreement. This leads, incidentally, to the curious observation that from a union worker perspective, a transnational agreement on British wages or other benefits would be acceptable only if it negotiated up to levels found in other countries. Such upwards negotiations would compromise the credibility and usefulness of the lower levels, and could lead to opposition to international bargaining. Stewards might resist wages higher than those received by other workers at nearby plants in favour of some other concession of a more localized character and significance, the 'winning' of which is more directly traceable to stewards' actions.

There are virtually no limitations on the right to strike in the UK. Frequently, as workers' and unions' interests shift, or perceptions on the interpretation of rights under an agreement vary, negotiations are reopened and a new agreement negotiated. This situation obviously lends itself to an international 'coincidence' on termination dates of different domestic agreements and the use of the strike to support transnational bargaining demands. However, the Labour Government's current statutory incomes policy prohibits collective labour agreements of less than twelve months duration, and has frustrated the efforts of the Transport and General Workers' Union in moving to agreements with expiration dates co-terminus with agreements in other countries. Thus, unions are more constrained today on this issue. Many in the labour movement regard co-terminus contract expiration dates as an essential first step in the evolution of transnational collective bargaining. This begs the important question of workers' willingness to strike in one country to benefit workers in other countries, a point discussed later.

The influence of law in *West Germany* is much more evident and extensive. Also, collective bargaining, which is concerned with the major conditions of employment, usually occurs on national and regional levels by industry, while secondary conditions are settled at the plant or company levels. Under German law,

'Collective agreements are binding contracts, and not mere gentlemen's agreements. They create legal obligations concerning the mutual relations between unions and employer association.'[12]

Regarding the plant or company levels, the Works Constitution Act of 1952 is the basic law establishing the authority, jurisdiction, and structure of the worker representation unit (the 'works council') and management's responsibilities to that unit.

Several agreements, usually with varying termination dates, frequently define the major conditions. For example, in the metalworking sector there are four such contracts:

(1) The general employment conditions contract—covering vacation periods and pay, overtime premium, working time, personal leave, short-time work, and dismissal rules.

(2) The wage and salary structure agreements—defining wage and salary grades and the percentage differential between grades, remuneration systems, and special allowances.

(3) The tariff agreements—stipulating wage and salary rates (on a minimum basis).

(4) The agreement on the protection of employees against consequences of rationalization—providing for special compensation, retraining allowances, and redundancy payments (in case of dismissals) for workers whose jobs are eliminated or affected by technological change.[13]

These are negotiated between the association of the employers for the area and, in this case, the union, Industriegewerschaft Metall, representing both salaried and hourly workers, and the Deutsche Angestellten Gewerkschaft, representing only salaried employees. They legally bind only the firms which are association members; however firms not in the association commonly apply the terms of collective agreements in their own establishments. As noted, tariff agreements stipulate only minimum wages. Actual wages are set by employers applying the percentage increases negotiated for the minimum rate on their previous actual wages, a different percentage increase may result from labour market conditions or worker pressures.

With regards to transnational harmonization of major conditions of employment, the conclusion seems clear. Minimum wages, wage and salary classifications and important wage supplements are set at federated bargaining and enforceable in court. Granted that pressures may be put on individual firms to upgrade benefit and pay levels negotiated by the unions and employer associations, such pressures at the international level are not anticipated because demands on individual firms cannot be supported with strike action when a tariff agreement is already in effect. Tariff agreements only cover minimum wages; above-tariff increments are established separately. A non-enjoinable strike can thus only be called to support negotiations for minimums and not increments such as might result from transnational bargaining. In the absence of union or labour market pressures there would be no compelling reason for a company to pay an 'international increment' on top of the basic wage and the 'German increment'.

Holidays in Germany are designated by law by the States and range from ten to fourteen days per year. Collective agreements do not add holidays to those legally required. Evidence of this can be found in the 1971 survey report of the International Metalworkers' Federation on employment conditions at Ford, General Motors, Volkswagen, Daimler-Benz, and BMW plants in Germany. While conceivably additional holidays could be negotiated in company-wide transnational bargaining, the likelihood of such appears extremely remote.

Severance or redundancy benefits paid directly by firms are not required by law in Germany. However, public unemployment compensation is provided for by the 1927 Act for Job Placement and Unemployment Insurance, as revised. The probability of transnational determination of severance benefits is low. They are not negotiated domestically in terms of any generalized programme and, in the case of 'technological unemployment', at least in metalworking they are provided for in a national agreement. Indeed, this latter point suggests that bargaining on severance or other benefits on jobs lost because of multinationals rationalizing production internationally is also most probably at the national industry-wide level.

The Works Constitution Act of 1952 gives company and plant-level, employee-elected works councils the right to negotiate over work rules and to handle employee grievances, but grievances may also be taken to the Labour Court by individual employees. Collective agreements rarely contain any formal provisions for handling grievances. Transnational action on grievance procedures seems remote since, by law, these are handled by works councils or the judiciary—neither of which is institutionally evident at an international level.

The idea, however, of a German union negotiating at the international level cannot necessarily be dismissed out of hand. Collective bargaining between a company and a union is not totally absent in Germany. For example, *The Wall Street Journal* (6 March 1974) reported that Volkswagen negotiated directly with IG-Metall over wages and other important matters. But, if necessary, what sort of *pressure* could a German union bring to bear in support of these negotiations? Of course, maximum pressure is applied via the strike threat. Can a German union deliver here? This leads to yet another question: Is any strike in support of transnational bargaining prohibitable by law in Germany? The legal status of the 'transnational strike' would seemingly turn on a series of issues such as the objectives of the strike, alternate means for achieving these objectives, and the importance of the objectives to German workers and to the German union in terms of institutional strength and survival. It would be expected that these and other questions would be placed before the German judiciary if a strike were called by a German union in support of transnational bargaining.

A union-sponsored strike in Germany can be legally called only at the expiration of an agreement and over an issue not resolved by another agreement already in force. Since a variety of agreements usually cover different issues and have different expiration dates, for a German union to call a legal strike in support of transnational negotiations, the issue would have to be one covered in a collective agreement negotiated at the German level, most likely on a federated basis, with a termination date coincidental with the international bargaining. This is not a probable occurrence, and the moving of termination dates on regional or national agreements to suit the unions' needs appears equally improbable. If the union does call for, or otherwise support, a transnational strike over an issue covered in an existing agreement, it is legally liable to remedy the damages suffered by the firm, and other employers in the same association may lockout any or all of their employees in support. The threat of strike action by German unions in support of transnational bargaining demands would ring quite hollow under the present circumstances.

In *France*: '. . . law and administrative action determine many fringe benefits, although collective agreements have provided either for supplements to the legal arrangements—as in the case of old age pensions (1957)—or added social benefits (agreements on employment and vocational education, 1969–70) . . . collective bargaining itself takes place at rather high levels—sometimes covering the entire nation, sometime covering a region. Government representatives take part . . . A further remarkable feature of the system is the fact that many supplementary social benefits were the result of agreements concluded by the union confederations—that is, above the industry level . . . Unilateral determination of wages and working conditions is still fairly widespread because unions are fairly weak, but undoubtedly they exert some direct influence, partly by the 'extension' of agreements by administrative action and partly by the "sympathetic" influence of the terms of collective agreements.'[14]

Collective bargaining has its legal roots in the Act of 11 February 1950. Under this law, collective agreements, normally industry-wide, are negotiated by employers' associations and union delegations of 'most representative societies', unions acknowledged as meeting certain specified conditions by the French Minister of Labour.[15]

Minimum wages and job classifications are defined in industry-wide collective agreements. Wages above the minimum are unilaterally set by employers in response to local labour market conditions in the great majority of instances. Bargaining on wage increases is usually conducted within the context of a mixed commission of employer association and union representatives, convened by the Minister of Labour. Negotiated increases on minimum result in similar increases in actual wages. Agreements reached in mixed commissions can be extended to cover all local firms in the industry by the Minister of Labour. Thus the active role played by the French Government in wage determination is evident and calls into question the efficacy of transnational bargaining on wages or other matters usually within the jurisdiction of these commissions. Plant-level bargaining would provide a medium for avoiding direct government involvement and such does occur, but it is frequently concerned with very specific points, like profit sharing, or 'merely repeat(s) industry-wide settlement ... adapting them to local conditions'.[16] Thus it appears that bargaining on wages is largely within the jurisdiction of the mixed commission and thereby subject to government interest and influence.

Wage supplements are determined in a variety of ways. Overtime, holiday pay, shift premiums and length-of-service supplements are frequently fixed by collective agreements. Family supplements, not found in Great Britain or West Germany, and housing allowances are legally required and financed by a tax on employers. Agreements on profit-sharing, a statutory obligation, are negotiated with works councils. So transnational determination or harmonization of wage supplements would be difficult given the structural barriers involved; the federated bargaining with government participation, statutory requirements, and the lack of works council representation at the international level. Also some supplements are uniquely French and have low transnational transfer appeal.

In France, vacations and holidays are statutory obligations, but frequently augmented by collective agreements. For example, except for Labour Day, the law specifies other holidays which may be worked by adult males without premium pay and collective agreements provide for paid unworked holidays. As already noted, French collective bargaining is not judged favourable to the elevation of bargaining issues to transnational determination.

Unemployment benefits are provided for both by law and collective agreements in France. Unemployment benefits were expanded considerably in a 1974 national agreement between the French Employers' Association and the French unions and now workers dismissed for economic reasons are assured of 90% of their gross salaries for a 12-month period. Regarding technological unemployment, government funding of in-plant vocational and technical training helps to keep technologically obsolete workers in the plant until they acquire new skills. Clearly, the situation regarding unemployment programmes and benefits is not conducive to transnational determination and harmonization.

Grievance handling is done by shop delegates elected directly by the plant employees who are legally responsible for relating to employers both individual and collective labour demands which are not satisfied specifically in collective agreements, other labour claims, and the enforcement of the Labour Code. Transnational determination of grievance procedures could be viewed as an usurpation of the role and authority of the delegates, and possibly challenged by any delegate not affiliated with the union or unions party to the agreement.

Given that there are just a few large national unions in France, the elevation of union interest to an international perspective would seem quite easily achieved. Conversely, with an attenuated influence at company-levels, transnational bargaining would probably be beyond French unions' interest and potential. Also, since several unions usually represent workers at the plant level, international bargaining would have to include these same unions. But these unions frequently profess divergent political and social values. They are not characterized domestically as mutually reinforcing and co-operative. Why should they be so at the international level? Finally, collective bargaining done via employer's associations and the tripartite, employer–union–government, composition of the 'mixed commissions' are similar structural impediments.

A strike in France in support of transnational bargaining is a questionable prospect. Workers generally strike only over a major issue. Major issues invariably involve the mixed commissions.

Thus, from the onset, a strike is impressed with a formal government interest and direct involvement. Should a major issue arise as a possible strike issue during transnational negotiations, the French government would probably act quickly to re-establish its effective jurisdiction. Also, French workers would be unlikely to strike over transnational wage harmonization (upwards), for example, when their perspectives and aspirations on such matters have always related to regional (or national) levels and differentials among different industries.

A great variety of circumstances, including the legal and structural, peculiar to each country appear to support the contention that meaningful transnational bargaining, resulting in the determination of substantive issues, is just not to be expected. This point is well established in the preceding country reviews. In addition to these country-specific variables, there are also cross-country variables which would equally affect the conduct of transnational bargaining. Finally still other variables exist which have their roots in the difficulties inherent in harmonization across national boundaries.

International wage harmonization is an announced objective of transnational collective bargaining, but this involves more myth than reality. Real wages are mainly a function of market conditions, which encompass the labour supply, both in terms of quantity and quality, supply of other productive factors available, the level of productive technology available, and the value of the production to consumers. These conditions sometimes vary considerably among and within countries.

International wage harmonization is also an unrealistic expectation for yet another reason. Harmonization of monetary wage rates on an inter-country basis requires translation of wages at certain rates of exchange among the currencies of the countries involved. So long as labour productivity varies among countries, average money wages cannot be equalized via the exchange market except in the very short run. Specific money wages can admittedly be equalized in isolated industrial sectors. However, as the incidence of such equalization spreads across other sectors, or if the isolated sector becomes important in external trade, there will be pressures on the exchange rates to change, since product unit prices will differ by country given the productivity differences. The direction and extent of the movement of the rates will re-establish the productivity differentials as measured in local monetary terms. Thus, international harmonization of wages can be neither a *generalized* nor a *permanent* condition because of differences in productivity between countries.

Similarly wage supplements, since they are really only a part of the total wage package, are not amenable to international harmonization. Further some are valued in one country but not in another because of cultural or traditional differences. Finally incompatibility of different payments systems among various countries can make the equalization of supplements impractical. For example in the United Kingdom overtime and some other premium payments are frequently based upon consolidated or district time rates, but in the US upon an individual's standard of rate of pay.

Regarding all the above outputs and the question of harmonization of 'bargaining up', there is a behavioural dimension to collective bargaining which influences both the desire and the expectation that the 'best of all worlds' will be contained in an agreement. Unions do not expect to be able to take different 'plums' from other contracts and expect to get them all in their own agreements. Trade-offs are made among a variety of 'plums' reflecting specific priorities, and *complete* agreements are either accepted or rejected. It would be a poor bargaining strategy indeed, for internal union purposes, to push blindly for the ultimate across the board, and such a strategy would be exploited thoroughly by the employer side.

This leads to the question of worker solidarity in support of transnational strikes. Would a worker in the United Kingdom, for example, strike in support of demands benefiting French or German workers? Empirical evidence here is rather thin; however an opinion survey[17] of Canadian Auto Workers (Chrysler), found that while 52% were willing to strike in support of fellow Chrysler employees in the United States, only 13% and 12% were willing to do so for fellow employees in the United Kingdom and Mexico respectively. While the United Kingdom and Mexico figures are obviously low, even the United States is significantly low in the light of the circumstances. The Canadian workers polled are in the UAW. Workers in both the United States and Canada are members of the same union! Blake also found that when the action was not so costly, respondents were much more willing to support workers in other countries. For example, 70% would give 'moral support' to their United Kingdom, and 62% to their Mexican, counterparts. Apparently international solidarity in terms of actual strike support is low indeed. This conclusion is further supported by the less-than-substantive, sometimes vague, forms of international solidarity reported thus far.

'... in 1970 strikers at May and Baker, a British subsidiary of Rhone-Poulenc, won a 16% pay raise "largely due to large-scale international intervention" at the company's French headquarters ... (and) Puegot workers in Founee threatened a 15 minute stoppage in 1968 to back 1000 workers suspended in an Argentinian subsidiary ...'[18]

Conditions in the automotive industry—as evidenced by the experiences of Chrysler, Ford, and General Motors—support the conclusion that transnational collective bargaining has yet to occur, and are consistent with the inferences identified by the 'positive model' described earlier.[19]

This leads to the interesting question: if transnational collective bargaining is not the anticipated mode of substantive interaction between labour and multinational enterprise, then what, if any, alternate form might a substantive interaction take?

It is possible that international collective bargaining would develop first within the European Economic Community. It would however, have to be preceded by a European Economic Community statute of incorporation and considerable legislation on the harmonization of social policy within the European Economic Community. The first of these is less topical today than it was a year or two ago. Also, there is no effective move at present to harmonize social security laws among European Economic Community members.

There should be some movement in the social policy area, however, relative to multinational enterprises. In the United States, for example, the AFL-CIO-sponsored programme to impose some social controls on multinationals, or to redress undesired effects of multinationals' operations, might meet with some success—especially regarding taxation and adjustment assistance. More national policies supportive of organized labour's interests can be expected, resulting in more controls upon multinational enterprises.

There is a certain vulnerability developing too as multinationals increasingly integrate manufacturing operations across national borders, giving unions in individual countries tremendous leverage. However, unions which use leverage to secure gains inconsistent with the competitive aspects of the resource markets cannot expect expanding employment opportunities in the long run. Multinationals will locate new investments in the less threatening union environments, where a larger or more stable return on capital can be realized. Thus, for the unions, short-term gain may involve a long-term loss.

Another more positive factor strengthening the power and influence of unions at the domestic level is the movement in Europe to expand co-determination rights of workers. With a greater voice in top management decision-making, the influence of workers and unions in such matters as new investments will definitely be strengthened. For example worker representation on the Board of Supervisors was undoubtedly an important factor in Volkswagen's recent decision to hold off on a final determination to build a major production facility in the United States.[20] Political pressure is intensifying for expanded co-determination in Germany and the Netherlands and even in the United Kingdom and France. If successful, this will strengthen the unions at national levels vis-à-vis the multinational enterprise, especially where parent company operations are domiciled in these countries. Where the parent is located in a different country, this influence may be circumvented as subsidiaries would not usually, at least legally, be concerned with decisions involving investments in foreign countries.

Developments within the international union organizations favour increased emphasis on a country-level focus. The significance and importance of United States-based unions are surely declining as Western European unions gain more economic power, political influence, and a heightened interest in multinational enterprise-related problems. The

United States unions are bargaining-oriented, with transnational bargaining the most logical response to transnational business operations. European unions are more politically attuned and their actions centre more strongly on political entities and social policy actions.

To conclude, the overall expectation is for more effective collective bargaining and supportive social policy at national levels. Also in most market-oriented, industrialized economies there is a definite movement towards company-level bargaining. When this is accomplished, which may be many years off in France, for instance, the balance of power can then be more equalized between multinational enterprises and the unions with which they deal. In the interim the principal issue facing labour in dealing with a multinational is its ability to prevent a centralized management from playing workers in one nation off against those elsewhere. This requires standardization neither of agreements nor of conditions within agreements. Some level of co-ordination or harmonization would suffice. This may occur, at least as far as industrial societies are concerned, sooner than institutional arrangements to bargain transnationally, or to have workers in different countries share common goals.

13.4 Suggestions for further reading

(C) GUNTER, Hans (1972). *Transnational Industrial Relations*, MacMillan: London.

(C) KUJAWA, D. (1971). *International Labor Relations Management in the Automotive Industry: A Comparative Study of Chrysler, Ford and General Motors,* Praeger: London.

(C) KUJAWA, D. Ed. (1975). *International Labor and the Multinational Enterprise*, Praeger: New York.

(C) LEVINSON, Charles (1972). *International Trade Unionism*, Allen & Unwin: London.

(C) VALL, Mark van den (1970). *Labour Organizations*, Cambridge University Press. Points out some notable differences between United States and European systems of industrial relations. In the United States neither managers nor trade unions are anxious to set up a system of joint consultation on European lines because their existing methods are flexible enough to include this. In Europe, he asserts, co-operation leads to apathy, but in the United States conflict produces participation.

The Trade Union response to the multinational is well exemplified in:

(D) *TUAC Document on Multinational Corporations* (1975). Paris: Trade Union Advisory Committee to the Organisation for Economic Cooperation and Development.

See also:

(C) WARNER, M. & TURNER, L. (1972). Trade unions and the multinational firm, *Journal of Industrial Relations*, June.

13.5 Exercises for this chapter

Case Studies

Hoffman Circulators, 1972, (IMEDE, ICH 9–373–905), by Baden, C. Southern Ireland meets most of a German Manufacturer's need for cheap labour; the case describes the company background, the incentives offered by Ireland and the businessman's impression of the country.

Labour Relations in Europe, undated, (Graduate School of Business Administration, University of Virginia, ICH 9–474–647), by Grayson, L. E., Heiser, J. M.
This case points out that the multinational corporation must be aware of the labour relations' principles peculiar to Western Europe in operating its European subsidiaries.

13.6 Questions for discussion

(1) Outline the problems which the development of the multinationals poses for the labour organizations.
(2) Imagine yourself being asked to advise a union of skilled workers in an industrial country who see their job disappearing to less developed countries. Recommend any action you think might be taken, giving reasons for your suggestions.
(3) Explain why the emergence of multinational unions has not occurred.
(4) What are the main procedures for international collaboration already existing? List and discuss.
(5) Discuss the advantages and disadvantages for managers of dealing with international trade union bodies.
(6) Explain how the trade unions are reacting to the multinational company and what further developments are likely.
(7) Discuss the view that trade unions are structured in such a way as to make the task of protecting employees in multinational corporations extremely difficult.
(8) An American businessman has spoken recently about an 'underlying identity of interest' between governments, companies and trade unions. Do you agree with him? Give reasons for your answer in terms of the cross-frontier operations of companies.
(9) Discuss the view that multinational business as a phenomenon highlights the inherent inequality between capital and labour.

Part III
The Environment and the Future

The last part of this book looks at the environment within which the decision-making process takes place, with its stimulants and constraints. That no discussion of management can ignore the environment is evidenced by the fact that many of the points covered by the following chapter headings have already been discussed. The subject is considered under four headings: the economic, the political, the cultural and the climate of opinion. This last is considered separately because the consciousness of managers is so much affected by the controversial atmosphere in which they now live. Indeed common to all the questions discussed in the next four chapters is the fact that the international manager is profoundly influencing the environment in which he is working. His management skills are changing the terms of trade, his financial abilities are determining investment flows and currency exchange rates, his marketing effort is changing local culture; and all these successes are producing reactions and causing changes in the law and in public opinion which are constraining the operations and the established means of using the skills and abilities. A final chapter discusses briefly some of the landmarks of the future.

14 The Economic Environment

14.1 Significant issues

A number of features of the world economic scene condition the activities of the international firm. One such feature is summarized by the phrase *patterns of trade*. Trade flows have traditionally been analysed into a number of factors concerned with the comparative advantage of operating in one particular product-market rather than another. The advantage may be concerned with production costs or it may be concerned with political conditions. The route may be an established one, an international grouping like COMECON or the Commonwealth, or one that has been altered by tariff barriers or other impediments to trade or their removal. Nowadays the patterns of trade are being changed by the companies themselves, with increasingly large amounts of goods being transferred between units of an international firm. This means that the point of advantage is being shifted from the possession of abilities to supply a market to more complex considerations which are concerned with the firm's perception of its overall advantage which is broken down into individual considerations. Thus some countries may provide suitable manufacturing centres without providing a substantial market; others may have advantages as finance centres, for the holding or raising of funds, without being suitable locations either for production or sales. A company may raise funds in one country, for manufacture in another country, which will be servicing further manufacture in a third country with the final market in yet other countries; all the decisions may have been taken in the light of company-wide advantages and produce flows of goods which are novel.

The location of financial facilities brings up the second element in the environment: the availability of investment funds and their movement across frontiers, together with the cost of finance in different countries. Some of the main centres of funds for international operations, like Switzerland, are traditional and continue. There are two new factors in addition to the operations of the companies themselves. One is the influence of changing exchange and interest rates which alter the advantages of different centres and different currencies, together with complex exchange control regulations. The other influence is the emergence of international investment currencies such as Eurodollars which have been popular with both governments and companies, at least until inflation pushed up interest rates. The exchange rates themselves form a third element in the economic environment. These three are considered in the context of investment in developing countries in the excerpt which follows later in this chapter. Their effects on management decision-making have been considered earlier in this book, while the next chapter looks at national and international regulation.

Another important element of the economic environment is that of the financial institutions which finance trade and investment. The major banks in industrialized countries have themselves been developing internationally, and this is a significant change in the environment. Even those banks which already provided international services and had branches abroad have been re-organizing to offer more comprehensive banking services to international customers. The change has partly come about at a time when banks are diversifying into new products both through their own investment and through consortium arrangements. These latter may vary from what may be called 'industrial goods', the financing of substantial new investments which are being built by international contractors, to consumer goods like credit cards.[1] For small firms embarking on international investment the increasing complexity of the international monetary system has been partly offset by the greater possibility of getting skilled advice from the bank. To such firms, however, credit ratings and currency available at reasonable interest rates are critical. The larger firm may find that advantage can be taken of greater competition between the banks. For many of the banks themselves, the first steps towards a range of services abroad has been the establishment of offices in other countries where information can be collected and advice given without providing other facilities. Apart from the banking system, there are the numerous official and semi-official sources of funds mentioned in the next chapter.

Another feature of international finance is portfolio investment. This, foreign investment without management involvement or with that involvement at a minimum, has declined in relative importance but is still significant. There has also been a change of character. International portfolio investment used to be concentrated on collecting savings in advanced industrialized countries to place them in countries where there were industries considered likely to expand in reasonable safety. Nowadays the trend is still towards countries where expansion is expected but other considerations like taxation, currency exchange and the relative attractiveness of different industry sectors have changed. So have ideas about what constitutes safety. Hence there is a move towards portfolio investment in the most advanced industrial countries within constraints fixed by such factors as interest rates and exchange controls.

International portfolio investment may be in equities; in the United

Kingdom this takes place nowadays through unit trusts as well as private investors and more traditional institutional investors like insurance companies. The other form of portfolio investment is in fixed interest loans and debentures. These have less attraction except as short-term placings for funds that are anyway mobile, including moneys held by international companies. This leads to another recent development, the Eurocurrency market. The emergence of the Eurodollar and other international sources of finance has been well charted in a number of writings.[2] This development, in its turn, has facilitated the spread of international business although international currencies have been used for domestic business as well.

Another source of funds is the government. National assistance to the international firm may take a number of forms. These include incentives to foreign companies to operate in the country which are not available to domestic companies. These are mainly loans and tax reliefs. Most inventives are also available to domestic companies, and may be for the general encouragement of new investment as such or for the siting of new investment in areas of unemployment in a country. On the whole the less industrialized countries are encouraging investment in industry sectors considered appropriate, whereas the industrialized countries (which include state governments or regional authorities as well as national governments) are likely to encourage investment which aids regional needs. There is also the growing tendency to a mixture of incentive and constraint which is discussed in the next chapter. Alongside government assistance, there are aid funds. In order to take advantage of the aid or loan schemes provided by one country for another, the company may need subsidiaries in both countries. An important source of finance for projects in the less developed countries is the World Bank, which channels funds from the rich to the poor countries. These funds are used 'in such sectors as agriculture and rural development, education, electric power, industry, population, planning, telecommunications, tourism, transportation, urban development, and water supply'.[3] There are also regional development banks set up under United Nations auspices and some privately organized funds as well.

Among constraints in the international financial environment, the most complicated is the tax system which varies from country to country and which is always changing. Many decisions may carry tax advantages or tax penalties. Those taxes which fall specifically on the subsidiary as a company registered in its country of operation may be distinguished from those taxes which affect the remittance of moneys across frontiers. But even this distinction is not entirely valid. For national tax systems will obviously help to determining siting, the allocation of resources and pricing policies. Further they will exercise this influence on an increasing number of companies and hence affect competition, the availability of funds and so on. The main difference between national taxation systems is between the proportion of direct taxes on profits or income and indirect taxes on sales. Both, clearly, affect business and there may be intermediate taxes like those on machinery which are not imposed on sales or profits. With regard to taxes on remittances, these used to be mainly levied on dividends or interest. Hence it was possible to say that other forms of payment like fees or royalties were advantageous. This is less true now, and there may well be substantial taxes on all forms of remittance. These vary according to the type of payments and, in some countries, the industry sector. Taxes on payments abroad are used to foster foreign investment in sectors considered desirable and to discourage it from others.[4]

Other government constraints, like credit control, also help to determine the economic environment. Other means by which government and inter-governmental actions affect the environment are discussed in the next chapter. Thus the economic environment can be said to consist of trading patterns, currency exchange, investment flows, sources of finances, together with official and private incentives and constraints which together form a pattern. Some implications of this, particularly with regard to the Less Developed Countries, are explored in the following excerpt.

14.2 Manufactured exports from less-developed countries and multinational firms[5]

International trade theory has been going through some difficult times lately, at least as far as those who still consider that theories should bear some relationship to measurable realities are concerned. Following the shock created by Leontief's paradoxical results in his test of the factor proportions explanation of international trade, trade theory has been groping its way towards new sets of explanations based either upon the introduction of 'non-traditional' factors of production like skill and research and development, or upon wholly new conceptions of the interrelationship between international trade and operations of large firms, or both. Scale economies, technological gaps, product and marketing cycles and trade intermediate inputs are the stock in trade of the latter explanations.[6]

At the same time that these new directions are being plotted for international trade theory and empirical testing of the resulting propositions continues there is a minor revolution also occurring in the theory of direct investment. No longer can direct investment be analysed in the classical manner as a flow of extra capital into a country within which all else is held constant with the static effects evaluated according to the tenets of orthodox marginal productivity analysis. The new approach applies the theory of industrial organization to the activities of large oligopolistic firms who happen to straddle international boundaries.[7] Tariffs, other trade barriers and incentives or disencentives to international capital flows are analogous, in this approach, to transport costs within national-level analysis of such firms' behaviour. Since investment and production abroad is quickly seen to be an alternative to selling abroad the produce of one's home plant, overseas investment becomes only a special case in the general economics of location.

There are obviously close links between the new theory of direct investment and the new theory of international trade. How close these links are in practice as well is indicated by the data showing the remarkably high proportion of international trade in manufactured goods which takes place within multinational firms.

These new approaches have direct application to the problems of industrialization and trade in the less-developed countries. In the earlier literature of development economics there was considerable emphasis upon the export bias imparted to the economy by the development, usually by foreign investors, of raw material exporting sectors. The latter sectors, it was argued, tended to absorb domestic capital and skill which could otherwise have been directed into different activities from which long-term growth might more reasonably have been expected. In particular, the industrial sector was generally believed to have been neglected, if not indeed actively discouraged. At least partly in response to this interpretation of their economic history many less-developed countries, as soon as they were free to do so, went to considerable lengths to stimulate the development of import-substituting manufacturing industries, although much of the resulting industrial activity remained heavily dependent upon foreign capital, technology and expertise. In the 1960s there was growing recognition that manufacturing sectors in the less-developed countries have been employing too capital-intensive a technology, operating on too small a scale, and earning their countries too little in terms of income, foreign exchange or employment.[8] In consequence, there has recently emerged a new orthodoxy to the effect that (labour-intensive) manufactured exports, able to benefit from scale economies derived from sales to world markets, which were under-emphasized in the past, must now be encouraged with at least the same vigour with which import-substituting industry was encouraged in the past. Incentives for this purpose are to be offered both by the less-developed countries and by the industrial nations to which they aspire to sell. If the World Bank's aspirations are to be fulfilled, the less-developed countries must achieve a 15% *per annum* increase in the value of their manufactured exports to the developed world during the 1970s.[9]

In the colonial era private foreign businesses profitably invested considerable sums in raw material extraction (mining and plantations), trading and banking in the overseas colonies. With development, and in particular after the coming of independence in former colonies and as improved incentives were offered, foreign businesses added profitable import-substituting industrial investments to their portfolios in the less-developed countries. In the last two decades manufacturing replaced mining and other primary production as the major outlet for United States (and other) overseas private investment.[10] At the same time international business was confronted with a much greater variety of host country regimes with which to deal, and a much richer collection of conditions and demands both in the field of primary production and in manufacturing. Yet the flexibility and pragmatism of the international business community has enabled it to deal profitably with them all. If the developing countries, and the major aid donors, are now convinced that what should be emphasized in the immediate future is labour-intensive industrial exports, and adequate *incentives* for them are offered, one can be confident that the international business community will be quick to respond. On the face of it, the fact that the exports in question are 'industrial' meets one of the objections offered in the early literature to primary product export-biased development; at the same time the fact that the activities in question are labour-intensive and not, apparently, subject to heavy domestic protection appears to meet some of the major objections of those who have criticized both the policies of host governments and the activities of foreign investors in previous industrialization efforts.

Manufactured exports

Manufacturing for export can be developed by a large developing country, in which balanced industrial growth is occurring, either in a relatively few highly export-dependent industries (with new ones added one by one) or in a wider variety of less export-dependent industries. These options are not open, however, to the small developing country, and most of the poor countries are small in terms of their market size. Since the opportunity for efficient import-substituting industrialization is exhausted relatively quickly, the possibility of establishing a fairly wide variety of industries, none of which is overtly export-dependent, on the European model does not really exist. A small country *must* have its individual exporting industries quite heavily dependent upon their exporting activities because its domestic markets are too small to sustain a wide range of industries or to sustain sufficient growth in those industries. The question is which industries to create in the knowledge that they will each be overwhelmingly export-dependent.

While it is undoubtedly possible to formulate more detailed classifications, the following four broad avenues for the development of manufactured exports can be considered.

Local raw material processing

The value added in further processing of local raw materials is frequently not a very high proportion of the value of the material itself; there may, nevertheless, be substantial aggregate value added realizable through this form of manufacturing for export. Some processing activities, however, particularly in the minerals industries, are quite capital-intensive and perhaps skill-intensive as well and may not therefore be the most suitable for location in a low-income country. The heavy effective protection offered by the tariff structure to the processing industries in the developed world is a further significant obstacle to the development of processed manufactured exports of this type. Particularly this is so in those instances where raw material extraction is not under the control of the same firms as the processing. At least in the latter case the firms may respond to bargaining demands or incentives and are, in principle, indifferent as to the location of their various plants so long as they are profitable to their total operations. In that it reduces the measured value added which results from processing in the less-developed countries, the heavy protection of developed country processors offers an obvious rationale for the use of offsetting export duties or other devices to lower the price of material imputs to export processing. Even the use of such indirect policy instruments can be sufficient, however, to generate retaliatory action on the part of importing states with powerful processors' lobbies, as was demonstrated in the case of Brazilian instant coffee exports to the United States.

Conversion of import-substituting industry to exporting

The heavy protection which has been required to enable most import-substituting manufacturing establishments in the poor nations today to survive augurs poorly for the possibility of their sustained entry into competitive world markets. It would, in principle, be possible to offer sufficient subsidies, direct or indirect, to encourage exports by existing plants, at least in those cases where the agreements with foreign investors do not specifically prohibit them; but their cost, in view of the present levels of efficiency, may not be justified by the social benefits.

Some manufactured exports from developing countries which are apparently of this type do at present take place, but they are usually in the nature of 'overspill' from domestic production, reflecting over-capacity which is itself the product either of bad planning or of conscious expectations of future domestic market expansion; in neither case is it a basis for *continued* export development. The fact that such exports are likely, perforce, to be priced below the domestic protected price renders them vulnerable to anti-dumping duties, and therefore markets are uncertain. It may be possible to maintain growth in exports of this type by continually 'turning over' the individual industries so involved. Significant volumes of such 'dumped' exports in any one industry, however, cannot realistically be planned for.

Further progress in the creation of customs unions and complementarity agreements among less-developed countries could generate increase in manufactured exports to one another. The argument that trade in the manufactures is most likely to be found among nations with similar *per capita* incomes is relevant to the poor countries as well as to the rich to which it has customarily been applied; it acquires its full significance in this context if manufactured products really do cater for the peculiar characteristics of demand in the less-developed countries rather than merely replicating the products of the developed world.

It is noteworthy that multinational firms are firm supporters of common markets, customs unions and free trade areas in the developing countries since these enable them better to rationalize their production planning in these areas. The development of manufactured exports from already existing foreign-owned manufacturing plants, which is occurring in Latin America, is thus to a considerable extent 'internal to the firm'. In Tanzania, foreign-controlled firms have resisted attempts by the Government to provide them with transfer tax (internal import duty) protection against Kenyan competition, which was permitted under the terms of the East African Common Market, where Kenyan production was controlled by the same foreign firms.[11]

Foreign firms are both better able and more willing to move into exports not only to other developing countries which may be partners in a customs agreement but also to the home markets of the investors in the developed countries themselves.[12] It is striking that, although US controlled manufacturing subsidiaries produced in 1966–68 less than 10% of Latin American gross manufacturing value added, they accounted for over 40% of Latin American manufactured exports. These overseas exports of manufactures emerged in industries with relatively high barriers to entry and relatively sophisticated and controlled marketing; they are most likely in those cases where the firm's strategy is built not upon national marketing and product differentiation but on international production and cross-hauling.

New labour-intensive final product exports

Most earlier discussions of the prospects for manufactured exports from less-developed countries have emphasized the possibility of their selling unskilled-labour-intensive final products, in which poor countries can be expected to possess a comparative advantage. These products are typically at present produced inefficiently under heavy protection in the industrial countries themselves. Lists of suitable manufactures for low-income countries to export usually include such products as textiles, sporting equipment, shoes, toys. It is indeed along this path that the most rapid strides have been taken in recent years. The resistance to further developments of this sort is obvious, however, in the growing list of quota arrangements, voluntary restraints, and other non-tariff barriers which are being added to an already highly discouraging tariff structure.

There may exist unexploited opportunities for small countries to enter these markets in what, for the world market, is a modest way but for them may be a quite significant degree. It is obviously worth exploring these well-known possibilities further. The recommendation to one small country is, however, subject to the fallacy of composition; if all small countries adopt such policies on the assumption that their individual impact upon the world market for labour-intensive manufactures will be small, the total impact may nevertheless be large and may generate the market barriers which each alone could successfully have avoided.

Only where there are powerful interests from the developed countries involved in this type of exporting is there likely to be much relief from the heavy protection now found in the markets of Europe and North America. Multi-product international firms may choose to locate the production of particular new final products or product lines, presumably those most intensive in the use of unskilled labour or, perhaps, those most liable to pollution legislation, in less-developed countries. Of more immediate importance, however, is the emergence of large trading houses with the capacity and the initiative to search the world for low-cost sources of the products they sell. Several large American retailing firms already have permanent representatives in South-East Asia contracting with local firms to supply garments to quite precise quality and fashion specifications. the large Japanese trading houses undertake similar functions. With such contractual arrangements the producers in the less-developed countries are relieved of the (skill-intensive) marketing functions which normally must precede production. This 'commercial subcontracting' may be the best prospect for truly international subcontracting—that which involves indigenous enterprises in the less-developed countries rather than merely subsidiaries of foreign firms. Whether these firms together with consumer groups have the influence and power to gain reductions in trade barriers is questionable. The facts that the protected industries are not usually dominated by large international firms, and tend to be located in depressed areas and to employ the least affluent workers of the rich countries produce wide political backing for the joint pleas of labour and capital in these industries for defence against foreign low-wage products.

Labour-intensive processes and component specialization within vertically integrated international industries

In the second half of the 1960s there rapidly emerged a fourth path along which poor nations seeking to initiate or accelerate their industrial export growth can travel: the development of specialized labour-intensive activities or processes within vertically integrated international manufacturing industries.[13]

The variety of activities now being performed for export on this basis in the less-developed countries is already very large. It may be worth listing some examples in order to show the flavour of these developments. Semi-conductors, valves, tuners and other components are manufactured or assembled for a large number of Japanese and American electronic firms in Hong Kong, Singapore, South Korea, Taiwan and Mexico. The electronics industry is by far the most important industry in this field. Garments, gloves, leather luggage and baseballs are sewn together in the West Indies, South-east Asia and Mexico for American and Japanese firms. In the case of the baseballs, the leather covers, cotton yarn, thread, latex and cement are all imported from the United States. Automobile parts are manufactured for British, American and Japanese firms in a wide variety of countries: for example, radio antennae in Taiwan, piston rings and cylinder linings in South Korea and Taiwan, automobile lamps in Mexico, braking equipment in India, batteries and springs in Thailand. Data are flown to South-east Asia and the West Indies for punching upon tape by low-wage key punch operators, following which the tapes are flown back again. Swiss watchmakers send jewels to Mauritius for precision drilling. The United States army sends loose ammunition to Mexico for loading into magazines by local labour.[14]

Among other industries already engaged in these activities in less-developed countries are those producing electrical appliances (including television and radio, sewing machines, calculators and other office equipment), electrical machinery, power tools, machine tools and parts, motorcycle and bicycle parts, typewriters, cameras, optical equipment, watches, brass valves, aircraft parts, telecommunications equipment, chemicals and synthetic fibres, and musical instruments.

While this is not a totally new phenomenon the speed with which it is developing is unprecedented. Imports into the United States from less-developed countries under items 806.30 and 807.00 of the US Tariff Schedules, which permit import duties to be levied only upon value added abroad where imputs originated in the United States rose from $61 million to $539 million between 1966 and 1970, or from 4% to over 14% of total US imports of manufactures from less-developed countries. Imports under these items accounted for about 27% of the increase in the total of such US imports in the 1966–69 period, despite their start from a very small base. Declared value added abroad in these activities increased by a factor of seven between 1966 and 1970. The steady succession of announcements of further such developments in the business press is perhaps the best guide to the recent pace of events.

This development is at variance with the usual thesis that foreign investors have a bias towards capital-intensive techniques.[15] The much discussed difficulties of training and organising a labour force of another culture, the risks of strikes and disruptions, the purported inefficiency and resulting low quality output, and the consequent advantages of 'machine-pacing' are not apparently so overwhelming that they cannot be overcome. The international firm is thus emerging as a major supplier of *unskilled-labour-intensive* technology as well as capital-intensive technology; and the real problem of technology, its ownership and the price to be paid for it, is more starkly revealed.

The future of exports in vertically integrated industry

There are firm reasons for believing that this is the beginning of an inevitable and important trend in the evolution of international trade and investment. Large multinational firms will move increasingly into the internationalization of their production and marketing, knitting the less-developed countries into their international activities as suppliers not merely of raw materials but also of particular manufactured products and processes. If one likes historical approaches, one can depict this development as the next logical step for international investors following the two previous major stages of resource exploitation and import-substituting manufacturing. Manufacturing for export is the 'new frontier' for international business in the less-developed world, and process and component specialization is likely to become the chief, or at any rate the easiest, avenue for less-developed countries seeking to expand their manufactured exports.

Why is this particular type of manufacturing for export going to spread and accelerate?

The opportunities for alternative foreign exchange earning activities in a majority of less-developed countries are severely constrained by the well-known problems of international commodity markets and the trade barriers of the industrial countries. Even if the prospects for commodity markets were somehow to improve, most developing countries would still aspire to the development of industry and the generation of industrial jobs. Incentives are therefore going to be offered in the less-developed countries for the development of industrial exports; one can also expect incentives favouring labour-intensive activities increasingly to be introduced.

At the same time, however, the tariffs and trade barriers of the industrial countries are not neutral in their impact upon various types of industrial exports which less-developed countries may seek to expand. While the generalized system of preferences sponsored by the United Nations Council for Trade and Development and the European association schemes may partially mitigate the existing structure of industrial effective protection, there is every reason to expect that success with manufactured exports of the 'traditional' final product type (such as textiles, leather goods, toys, shoes) will in the future as in the past be met with tariff increases, quotas and retaliation.

While expansion of these types of manufactured exports will face 'traditional' barriers to markets, the export of labour-intensive components and processes or even final product lines within internationally integrated industries is likely to be relatively easy. Items 806.30 and 807.00 of the US tariff are the harbinger of further such tariff provisions in other countries. Japan has already negotiated similar such provisions for value added tariffs bilaterally with South Korea, and is likely to introduce more. There will be increasing demands for the introduction or liberalization of such clauses, demands actively supported by powerful lobbies in the form of the multinational firms who stand to benefit from them. Even when effective protection is not modified by such provisions, these lobbies can be expected to prevent the introduction of non-tariff barriers and high tariff rates of unreasonable proportions. Just as in the past the tariff structures of rich nations and poor combined to favour the development of capital-intensive import-substituting manufacturing in the less-developed countries, so they are likely in the future increasingly to favour the development of labour-intensive manufacturing activities, particularly those at *intermediate* levels, geared to export markets controlled closely by multinational firms.

While pressure increases for the introduction of more labour-intensive techniques in the less-developed countries, research and development expenditures upon them minuscule in size; existing research in this area in the developing countries is neither well financed, nor well staffed, nor well co-ordinated. On the other hand the direction of a small part of the research and development activities of the large multinational manufacturing firms merely to the *identification* of labour-intensive activities which are potentially transferable to low-wage countries can be of relatively very great significance to total research and development in this area. They do not, in the first instance, even need to develop any new technology; it is merely a matter of locating existing activities suitable for relocation abroad.

The example of the electronics industry has already made a considerable impression upon the business community; the business literature of the past few years is full of the possibilities for combining profit with a solution to the world development problem.[16]

At the same time the international agencies have become interested in the possibilities of sub-contracting and the relocation of manufacturing activities, through the multinational firms, in the less-developed countries. in the short to medium run this identification of labour-intensive activities for transfer will out-distance all other sources of research and development in the field of labour-intensive manufacturing; the choice of labour-intensive technology will therefore be much more a matter of product or activity selection than of altering techniques in existing production.

When new labour-intensive technologies are *developed*, rather than merely being identified in existing activities, they too are likely to be developed where the skills are; for research and development, even if conducted on the subject of unskilled-labour-intensive technology, is itself a skill-intensive activity, just as the production of capital goods can itself be labour-intensive. As soon as restructured incentive systems make them profitable, they will be developed and therefore owned by the same large multinational firms which at present possess the available labour-intensive technologies. Thus, even in the longer run the role of the multinational firms in the development of labour-intensive manufacturing, whether for export or not, is likely to be important.

Multinational firms are already international in their outlook. The rationalization and internationalization of their world-wide activities, including the location of their plants and suppliers, is the next logical step in their evolution. A new generation of international managers, with new emphasis and training in 'international business', is emerging from the United States business schools,[17] and by all accounts from the Japanese system as well. 'Intensified multinationalization' can be expected among European firms as well as American ones.[18]

The speed with which the innovation can be expected to spread will be great. The shifting of unskilled-labour-intensive activities to low-wage countries by private firms is an innovation like any other—one in the field of processes rather than products. High rewards accrue to the first in the field,[19] but there cannot be much room for a long technological lag or for continuing monopoly profits from the knowledge of this particular cost-reducing process.

The innovation will quickly be copied as it was in the case of the electronics industry. There is probably something akin to 'herd psychology' in this sphere, particularly if the innovator is a major participant in the relevant industry. Moreover, as will be seen below, risk aversion will lead firms already engaged in these activities to seek a wider dispersion of locations overseas.

One must consider the possibility of collusion, particularly in those industries characterized by a high degree of concentration, to suppress this type of innovation, perhaps with the assistance of tariff and other trade policies designed 'in the national interest'.[20] Even then, however, there are likely to be possibilities for small and more competitive component suppliers and subcontractors outside the large multinationals themselves to relocate their production in low-wage countries; such relocations may even be prodded or assisted at the outset by their multinational buyers.

The incentives for the relocation of labour-intensive manufacturing activities in low-wage countries will *increase* with time, whatever the policy measures introduced by governments or the technologies emerging. There is by now general agreement that the absolute *per capita* income gap between rich nations and poor is going to widen during the next few decades; the international wage differential for unskilled and semi-skilled labour can therefore safely be expected to widen as well. Absolute improvements in education, nutrition and health in the poor countries are likely at the same time to narrow any existing international differentials in labour quality and efficiency. In addition, the costs of air and ocean transport can be expected to fall with the development of containerization and jet transport facilities. The discriminatory freight rates at present discouraging the shipment of manufactured products from less-developed countries can also be expected to be reduced. Perhaps even more important are the reductions in the costs of telecommunications, and the contributions of computer technology to the processing and distribution of information, which are certain to reduce greatly the influence of 'distance' in international business decisions.

The only major obstacles in the developed countries to the rapid emergence of this form of manufacturing for export by the less-developed countries are the trade unions and, though this is less likely, the small businesses affected by the transfer of their sub-contracts overseas. American trade unions have already launched a crusade for protection against 'runaway plants', and more opposition can be expected from this quarter. Two recent studies have sought to demonstrate that the tariff provisions against which their attack has been launched have actually saved more jobs in the United States than they have cost in that they have prevented the *complete* migration overseas of the industries concerned;[21] but labour in a labour-scarce economy can be expected to continue to press for protection in its own interest. The likelihood that trade unions can succeed in raising protection when their employers are opposed (or at best indifferent) to it, however, seems small.

Identifying the processes and the industries

Considering all these factors, can one offer any generalizations concerning the industries in which this type of manufactured export from less-developed countries will be likely to develop? One of the consequences of the development of process and component specialization is the difficulty of employing the usual industrial classifications at all. As large firms locate activities within single industries all round the world, the usefulness of existing classification schemes is called into question. A far more detailed classification of industrial activities seems necessary. The theory of effective protection has already been leading us in that direction. Industrial statistics are nevertheless still collected on the basis of standard industrial categories. Within which of these categories would one expect to find those activities which are likely to be transferred to low-wage countries?

One could certainly hypothesize that industries characterized by *overall* unskilled labour intensity are most likely to have blocks of activities or components within them which are suitable for transfer to low-wage locations. There has been extensive use of item 807.00[22] in the textile trade (particularly in body-supporting garments and women's and children's clothing), toys and gloves, all of which are quite labour-intensive. There has, however, been much greater resort to it in various metal products industries in which multinational firms are predominant, and which are not so obvious in their labour-intensive characteristics—office machines, television receivers, radio apparatus, semiconductors and electronic memories. The rapid growth in exports of machinery and transport equipment from such countries as Taiwan, South Korea, Hong Kong and Mexico, to the industrial countries also indicates that 'moderately' and 'marginally' labour-intensive industries are among the most active participants in overseas component manufacture, processing and assembly.

Another source of clues as to the possibilities for manufacturing for export in the less-developed countries is the structure of industrial production, purchasing and subcontracting within the developed countries. In the US machine tool industry, for instance, there are scores of highly specialized and fairly small plants each producing only one tool; a detailed study of multi-plant firms and industries could undoubtedly reveal opportunities for overseas low-wage suppliers. Labour-intensive spare parts, components and processes now sub-contracted for by large firms in the industrial countries are further obvious candidates for sub-contracting where wages are much lower. Many of the manufacturing plants in other developed countries which now benefit from item 807.00 of the US tariff (including those producing motor vehicles and parts, some types of engines, electrical hand tools, household sewing machines, tractors, air conditioning machines, compressors and parts, electric hairsetters, and hearing aids) might also be suitable for transfer to less-developed countries.

The influence of transport costs upon the selection of industries is obvious; high value or low bulk products are the best candidates for activities necessitating international transport. As has been seen, machinery parts and components clearly fit into the 'suitable' category in this respect.

Do scale economies matter? A large firm contemplating relocation of some of its production facilities abroad may face scale diseconomies therefrom, particularly if risk considerations require it also to disperse them geographically to a greater extent than before. There may therefore be a presumption that multinational firms will be more likely to transfer abroad activities which do not benefit from scale economies. A high proportion of Japanese manufacturing investments in lower-wage countries is undertaken by small and medium-scale firms for whom the diseconomies of scaling down are not so great. On the other hand, a prospective independent component manufacturer in a less-developed country may be able to avail himself of scale economies not available to the producing unit within a single firm by selling the same item to a number of independent firms; thus the presence of scale economies where components are standardized for the industry as a whole, can be a factor contributing to the success of an independent venture.

One variant of the theory of the product cycle states that it is in 'mature' industries, in which products and production processes have become fairly standardized, skill requirements lessened, and lengths of runs increased that the industrial comparative advantage of the less-developed countries lies. A related suggestion, in this context, is that United States firms are more likely to experiment with new production processes where they think of their market positions as dependent mainly upon cost and price considerations rather than on quality, and where production costs make up a large proportion of the total sales price. But the electronics industry, within which the development of overseas labour-intensive (component) manufacturing and assembly for export has been most spectacular, is certainly a 'new' and quality-conscious industry. Managers within this industry have even argued that it is its very speed of technological change and new product development which makes it difficult for them to automate their assembly activities, and requires them to retain highly labour-intensive techniques.

The introduction of the possibility of overseas component manufacture and middle-stage processing within international industries rather knocks the bottom out of *any* stage theory of the development of industrialization and trade which focuses upon final products. While it may be usual for a final product manufacturing firm to sell first to its home market, there is no reason for it not to locate some of its component production overseas, if it is more efficient to do so, even at the earliest stages of the industry's development. It has been acknowledged that: 'By 1970, the product cycle model was beginning in some respects to be inadequate as a way of looking at the US-controlled multi-national enterprise.'[23] The 'global scanning capacity' of the modern multinational enterprise is making any particular sequence such as that model describes obsolete.

Conclusions

The multinational manufacturing firm is likely to play a major role in the future development of manufactured exports from the less-developed countries, whatever the avenue these countries choose to encourage. In the next decade or two processing, assembly and component manufacture for export within vertically integrated international industries is bound to become an increasingly important element in this development. The less-developed countries must now begin to calculate the potential gains from entry into this new form of manufacturing for export as against those realizable from other types of export, other forms of industrialization, and other sources of income and employment. In these calculations, account must be taken of the potential for linkage and learning effects, neither of which are in this case likely to be large, and other 'dynamic' influences, both positive and negative. It is quite possible for a country, particularly one at a relative disadvantage with respect to labour and transport costs, to build infrastructure to offer subsidies to attract this particularly 'footloose' type of manufacturing activity, even on occasions when the social opportunity cost of these outlays exceeds the apparent income gains from the new activity; in such cases, the country is better off without it. Where these calculations do demonstrate the potential for income gains, there may still be legitimate concern about the degree of independence or structural imbalance which too much development of this enclavistic sort may create for the host country.

There are undoubtedly elements of strategy and tactics through which potential host countries can seek to increase the gains from this form of manufacturing for export, when once they have decided to proceed with it. They will normally have some powers to influence what happens and they may be able to use these to impose conditions on the foreign companies which will bring other benefits besides immediate employment opportunities on simple, repetitive work. Among the major questions they must consider are the selection of appropriate activities, the potential for institutional alternatives to the wholly-owned subsidiary, the potential for diversification with respect to firms, industries and markets, and the creation of suitable and internationally co-ordinated incentive schemes.

14.3 Suggestions for further reading

(D) ADLER, F. M. & STEVENS, G. (1974). The trade effects of direct investment', *Journal of Finance*, May.

(C) BALDWIN, R. E. & KAY, D. A. (1975). International trade and international relations, *International Organization*, **28.1,** Winter.

(B) DUNNING, J. H. (1971). *The Multinational Enterprise*, Allen & Unwin: London.

(C) DUNNING, J. H. (1974). *Economic Analysis and the Multinational Enterprise*, Allen & Unwin: London.

(C) GABRIEL, P. P. (1973). The multinational corporation and the world economy, *Conference Papers,* Conference on Industrial Relations and the World Economy, Chicago.

(D) HIRSH Seev (1976). An international trade and investment theory of the firm, *Oxford Economic Papers*, **28.2,** July. This short article sets up an economic model to determine the conditions of foreign direct investment and of post-investment strategy. There are numerous references.

(C) KEOHANE, R. O. & OOMS, Van Doorn (1975). The multinational firm and international regulation, *International Organization*, **29.1,** Winter.

(C) KOLDE, E. J. (1968). *International Business Enterprise*, Prentice-Hall: London & New York.

(D) KOPITS, G. F. (1976). 'Intra-firm royalties crossing frontiers and transfer-pricing behaviour', *Economic Journal*, December.

TUGENDHAT, C. (1971), *The Multinationals*, Eyre and Spottiswoode and Penguin.

(B) WELLS, L. T. (1968). A product life cycle for international trade?, *Journal of Marketing,* **32,** pp. 1–6 (reprinted in Thorelli (1973). chapter 16).

Credit control is a subject not mentioned in this chapter, but is an important feature of the environment as most countries take some measures to restrict credit. These will be intensified at times of economic crisis. An example of work on this subject is:

(D) Credit control in Latin America (1973), *Journal of International Business Studies,* Spring, pp. 31–41.

14.4 Exercises for this chapter

Case studies

European Stock Exchanges: An Introduction (undated). Harvard, ICH

9–174–057. A survey of the main European Stock Exchanges.

Bank Credit Card in Europe, 1972 (IMEDE, ICH 9–373–883), by Baden, C.
The report describes the internal workings of an American Bank credit card plan, for the use of European bankers who might consider initiating bank credit card plans in their own countries.

European Motor Industry, 1965–71 (Cranfield Institute of Technology, CCH 373–030–1), by Constable, C. J. & Dodman, M.
A note on the trends of the European vehicle industry in terms of market growth, product characteristics and movement of trade up to the early 1970s. France, Germany, Italy and the UK are considered in particular.

14.5 Questions for discussion

(1) Name the main subjects evoked when mention is made of the 'economic environment' of international business. Discuss one of the subjects in some depth.
(2) What is a reserve currency? How can such a function embarrass a national economy?
(3) '. . . trade theory has been groping its way to new sets of explanations . . .' (Helleiner). Comment.
(4) Discuss the development of financial insitutions internationally and their part in the development of new patterns of business.
(5) Examine the trends of international portfolio investment.
(6) Outline the main sources of government funding for foreign companies.

15 The Political and Legal Environment

'Threats to National Sovereignty', 'Purveyors of national prosperity', phrases like these summarize the opposite poles of a wide range of views about the relationship between the company and the nation state. A later chapter (17) examines the climate of opinion generally, while the present chapter thinks in terms of law and national policy: the national response to the development of the international firm, and more briefly the corporate attitude to the role of the state. The purpose of the first section is to identify some of the legal changes that are taking place and that affect business in foreign countries.

Perhaps the most important point to be made is that there are numerous different political environments, and as many different sets of legal and political problems. Usually the sets are divided into three: the industrialized, the less developed and the communist countries. This simple classification is both followed and discussed in the second section.

A high proportion of the rapidly increasing literature on the multinational company in recent years has concerned itself with the relationships between the company and the nation state and other national institutions. We have pointed out several times[1] that public discussion has been stimulated by an unlikely coincidence of the interests of capital and labour. Financial interests in countries which have been at the receiving end of foreign investment have become increasingly worried at the amount of foreign control that is exercised in the most important and fast developing sectors of the national economy. Since foreign subsidiaries are usually wholly owned this has meant that attractive investment opportunities are being taken out of the local money markets. The opportunity to buy shares in the parent company may be a poor substitute and is often impractical anyway. For organized labour, there has been the problem of the company which can switch production and jobs across frontiers and thus evade trade union pressures. But there have been other problems which have brought the multinational company to public attention. There is the more general problem of decisions made in a foreign country which vitally affect the interests of the country concerned. Increasing evidence of these decisions is becoming available, and some examples are given in this book. One thing that is obvious is that some of the issues are more elusive than others. Elusiveness does not make an issue less important, on the contrary the reverse may be the case. One of the unfortunate consequences of the never-the-less important search for more precise and quantifiable means of studying business decision-making has been the tendency to relegate the highly significant, but less precise, issue to a secondary place.

15.1 The changing environment

A number of trends can be isolated which are happening in several countries at once, but in different ways and at different speeds. One of these is the transition from the negotiated to the competitive environment.[2] In the United States there have long existed laws to prevent actions in restraint of competition between companies. These include the prohibition of price-fixing and the restraints on monopoly or other forms of undue power in a market. Under these measures famous companies have been broken up, like Standard Oil, or forced to disinvest substantial holdings like Dupont. Action has also been taken against price-fixing agreements and this has, occasionally, even led to the imprisonment of senior executives. No such severe legal actions have been taken against European firms, but the legislation has gradually developed in recent years.

One of the difficulties of the legislation is that intense competition may itself lead to near monopoly power. This difficulty has been found in the United States, where companies prosecuted for price-fixing have pleaded that without it they would knock out their weaker competitors and thus find themselves prosecuted under another measure. In smaller European countries, this is much more likely to happen especially in high technology industries where larger companies have a broader base from which to meet research and development expenses. There is the further problem in smaller industrialized countries that a company which is large in relation to its national industry may still be small when faced with international competitors outside its own frontiers. This fact alone has encouraged governments to foster mergers even though a near monopoly may be created at home. With all these reservations the trend remains. Indeed it is almost certain to become more important because competition legislation is increasingly seen to be the alternative to increased state control or outright state ownership. The coming of the European Economic Community has stimulated competition policies, because these policies can now be taken out of the national arena and considered at a community level where competitive influences can be more satisfactorily appraised. An extra trend which has now become apparent is that non-European companies are likely to be treated differently from European.

Outside Europe and North America the negotiated environment remains the rule and in some of the less industrialized countries once a substantial company emerges it will be protected from external competition. In all countries the degree and nature of the negotiations with political authorities and with competitors will vary by industry sector. Contracts for local authorities may well go to local firms even without any collusion between companies. There may be understandings which are never tested in the courts but which are as strong as any industry sector agreements.

The transition to a more competitive environment stems, we have seen, from the United States and is moving to Europe. The transition from free enterprise to state intervention, sometimes including state ownership, is a move in a different direction. A company penetrating other countries may find the state or a state-owned industry either as customer, competitor or supplier. The forms of direct state regulation of business also vary from country to country and affect a whole range of issues from capital structures to employment policies. United States executives coming to Europe often remark on the greater degree of state intervention there than they are accustomed to; but the trend exists in America as well as others. It was recently remarked that, during a fifteen year period, the Federal Government had passed over 100 laws in just one aspect of the Company–Government interface—the relations between companies and their employees. These laws covered conditions of work, safety, equal opportunities and many other matters; they are mainly regulatory measures inspired by some perceived abuse. Apart from the Tennessee Valley Authority[3] and local transportation systems there is not much public ownership in the States.

In other parts of the world the public and the private company are working side by side and anyone ignorant of the shareholdings might be hard put to it to know the difference. Nevertheless there is a difference. The tendency to increased competition, mentioned earlier, is reversed in certain specific cases where state ownership of an entire industry group eliminates all effective competition, as with tobacco in France or steel in Britain. This changes the customer supplier relationship. Where the state enterprise is not a monopoly, as with cars in Italy or France or food processing in Italy, different guidelines for investment may apply. The State enterprise may be more influenced by social and political considerations than private firms: but this statement should not be taken for granted, however often made.

Other elements of state intervention besides competition policies and nationalization include laws that regulate imports and that concern product safety and quality. Another aspect is state intervention in company planning, as in Sweden and France.

Another notable change, that from the individual proprietor to the professional manager, will be mentioned in chapter 16. But there is the further trend to the involvement of interest groups like workers and consumers. These various trends are influencing the political environment within which the international firm has to operate. The company–government interface can be examined in terms of a number of 'packages' which will be presented in the next section.

15.2 The political environment: some approaches

The approach of the home country can be seen in terms of the problems and benefits. The problems can be summed up in three phrases: balance of payments, export of jobs and tax avoidance. Reports in both the United States and Britain commissioned during the 1960s[4] showed, in considerable detail, the effect of outward investment on the domestic economy. The general conclusion from both reports was that timing was all-important. While the long-term income could be beneficial to the economy, the short-term problems caused by substantial outflows at a time when the currency was in difficulties could outweigh likely benefits. The extra measures the government would have to take to support the economy would damage the domestic economy and the effects of the cutbacks in terms of reduced income would not be compensated by the income from abroad. To minimize the difficulties the governments and central banks in countries of outward investment have developed controls and agreements with companies. Typically these will try to limit the export of capital, to encourage local borrowings and to ensure repatriation of profits.

The export of jobs has also been studied, but without the thoroughness or objectivity of the export of capital.[5] Indeed the problem of determining what are relevant facts makes objectivity difficult. Take the expansion of the foreign labour force. In a successful and expanding company this need not at all be at the expense of the domestic employees. The extra jobs might not arise at all if the company had not invested abroad. The foreign expansion may well lead to expansion at home which would not otherwise take place. But if counting the number of jobs abroad, and showing that they have increased, does not necessarily mean that jobs at home are being reduced, the opposite argument may be equally untenable. This argument is used to rebut critics by counting the jobs at home. The well-being of the company cannot be so easily parcelled up into domestic and foreign prosperity. Success is all of a piece, and the only convincing evidence for the movement of jobs would be a severe phasing out of domestic production at a time when the economy was improving; while evidence that a company does not move would require a clear refusal to accept foreign opportunities on the grounds that this might endanger the domestic labour force. Even if these arguments could be substantiated and the company's well-being abroad somehow divorced from that at home, there are other factors to consider. The home countries of foreign investors are highly industrialized as a rule and depend on expanding markets abroad. Foreign direct investment may benefit the home industry, at least indirectly, by helping to expand those markets. There do still remain, however, some examples of companies with substantial exports to their home countries from foreign subsidiaries. These examples may be considered evidence of damage to the home economy, although they exist in a limited number of industry groups and may be regarded by the firm as a *quid pro quo* for exports from the home country; their trade with the host country may well have been negotiated on these terms.

From the home country's point of view there is clearer evidence that the international company is using its opportunities of tax avoidance, although it may not look like that to the company. At least the evidence is clear enough for the United States authorities, for instance, to nullify the benefits of tax havens by taxing foreign companies on profits that are not repatriated. Even so a tax officer in that country said recently that the companies are able to take measures, especially with regard to transfer pricing, which the authorities have not the resources to trace. In addition to tax evasion, companies operating abroad have special opportunities of evading national economic policies by moving money to subsidiaries.

There is also a positive side to the relationship between the company and its own government. There may be encouragement in more or less tangible form for companies that immerse themselves in international competition, and use all necessary means to compete effectively. Among the most tangible forms is the provision of government insurance to cover the risks of losing money invested abroad. Most industrialized countries provide this insurance. Among the arguments used to promote such a scheme originally were the advantages to small companies of investing in less developed countries where the risks of loss were high but where the less competitive environment was more favourable to the small investor. In the event, the schemes have been widely used by large firms too although they can hedge their risks in other ways. It seems that large companies have been better able to make use of the benefits that were intended for the small.

The approach of the industrialized host country can be described as positive with some negative aspects. Such a country is usually also the home government of international investors, and some form of reciprocity of treatment is probable. The country has hostages who may come under attack elsewhere if unduly restrictive measures are taken.

Nevertheless there is the worry about how far international companies can damage economic policies. Domestic companies can of course do this too; indeed it has been argued that international companies are under greater difficulties because they are more conspicuous and more subject to government pressure. On the other hand, there are opportunities, whether fully used or not, for foreign firms to have more influence on national policies than local ones. The ability of multinational firms to move money around by various means is greater, since their funds are more mobile anyway. There is also a greater ability to raise funds by using the power of their financial assets, and in particular the parent company guarantees, against loans in the host country. This allows the company to use national assets for purposes which may not be in line with national policies.

The two other main worries have both been discussed already: the question of labour relations in chapter 13 and of the transfer of technical knowledge and its effects on science policy in chapter 11. The assistance that foreign companies can bring by the local manufacture of new technologies means that this latter subject also appears on the credit side. But the strongest point in favour of the foreign firm is the need for investment, and in particular a form of investment which fits with regional policies. Here the foreign firm is found in practice to have advantages over the domestic one. In country after country national or local bodies charged with finding jobs for areas of high unemployment have turned to foreign companies after failing to attract the local. In some cases national governments, like that of Eire, and in other cases state governments including most of the Southern United States are conducting sustained campaigns to encourage the investor from abroad.

Another form of government intervention is that of sponsorship for high technology projects which are both international and inter-company. Apart from some well-known civilian examples, like Concorde, most of these projects are for military equipment. Their success has been mixed, but there seems little doubt that such activities will expand all the same. Experience may be gained and more effective guidelines developed to overcome the problems.

On the whole industrialized countries do not insist on local participation in foreign companies, but this may well change.

The Socialist Bloc countries have increased their trade both with one another and with the rest of the world. A number of their enterprises operate in the west, and at least one important joint venture made up of state enterprises in a number of East European countries is selling advanced technology in Western Europe. It has been alleged that one of the reasons why Russia has been comparatively lenient in international discussion on the control of multinationals is because of an intention to develop her own.[6] Although the figures as proportions of world trade are small, the facts are significant as the communist countries seek for new ways of doing business abroad, and western companies are looking for new ways of expanding their trade with them. The emphasis has been on innovation for political reasons, but the innovation has importance in other contexts, too. There are two main areas of change. One is from direct trade, including barter, as practically the only means of doing business. A whole battery of joint ventures, licensing, management contract and other arrangements make up the second.

The less-developed countries are in a different position altogether with regard to the multinational firms. The main headings may be the same (the need for investment as against the problems that investment brings with it, the transfer of technology, the effect on national economic policies and so on) but the discussion under these headings is different. It is not just that the balance of power may be different, the balance of need may be different also. The power of the country lies in refixing the foreign investor or in hedging him round with conditions which may lead to withdrawal anyway. The country may well be inhibited from taking such actions by the urgent need for the products that the foreign investor brings. At the same time, the country may be persuaded to forego some of the benefits by paying incentives, both in the form of positive measures to encourage the company to come in and of protective measures to encourage it to stay. For the foreign firm itself the benefits may be much less obvious. The business with an individual less developed country can be a small part of the firm's total business and the costs can be out of all proportion to the income even if the return on investment is high. To stay may be harder to justify to shareholders than to withdraw, especially if the expectations of a rapidly increasing market are not fulfilled. The fact that countries do get benefits, in spite of the problems, is attested by another feature of the environment: the fact that some countries which at one time discouraged or even expropriated foreign firms are now once more encouraging them.

The ability of the international firm to play off one country against another is one of the reasons for strong support among the less developed countries for some form of code of conduct. But the arguments used above do not apply to all the countries equally. Some provide more attractive markets than others either because of their size or their wealth. India, for instance, is a poor country if measured by averaging gross national product; but it has been estimated that about 5% of the population is affluent and that the 5% amounts to nearly 30 million people—a larger number than the total population of many industrialized countries and a substantial market by any standards.[7] The oil rich countries, like Iran, have markets that are increasing so rapidly as to be attractive. Thus some countries are in a strong bargaining position and these have managed to develop elaborate batteries of controls and incentives to ensure that companies do assist the national development effort rather than impeding it. The controls may not always work as intended, but at least the framework of a new style of involvement on the company-government interface is being constructed.

The elements of the framework are: the limitation of imports by insisting on part local manufacture, the insistence on local participation in the local subsidiary, restrictions on remittance of funds to the parent company which vary according to the industry in order to ensure that activities that are seen to aid national development are more worth while than those that are not, encouragement of exports by similar means, careful scrutinizing of work permits for expatriates, and so on.

The company and the nation state is a subject which merits further comment. Some writers and some company spokesmen have been vigorously forecasting the demise of the nation state. This has not happened; indeed the growing strength of nationalism has been one of the constant features of recent years hardly affected by the more chequered growth of international institutions and internationalized personnel. It is, indeed, unlikely that a writer in 1980 will describe nation states as 'petty, independent, quarrelling human groups' as did one in 1966.[8] Nevertheless there is a strong feeling, often expressed, that national frontiers are not relevant to business, that these boundaries act as brakes on progress, and that means should be found to overcome them.[9] Ancient boundaries, the argument goes, formed as a result of compromises after wars have no connection with contemporary commercial realities. This realistic pressure of business acquires an idealistic expression as well when statements are made about the internationalism of the modern executive. Indeed a corps of executives is being created with some sort of international outlook, but the pressures on the company are now the other way, and companies are more likely to speak about good citizenship than world citizenship. Statements or generalizations about international business which suggest that there is some special virtue in a supranational orientation are out of fashion. Nevertheless the problem remains that business could operate more efficiently if some of the national barriers could be reduced, and that most of the citizens of the states would benefit from this. So far the significant moves in this direction have been the regional common markets and free trade areas. At the time of writing no arrangements for supranational corporate registration have actually been achieved although there have been a number of measures to facilitate freer trade.

15.3 The company—government interface: the important issues

Some of the following issues have already been mentioned, they are repeated here as a summary.[10] Under each heading the advantages and disadvantages of the international firm from the country's point of view are identified.

Competition

Outside the United States, companies are encountering a more competitive environment than previously. The companies themselves have powers which could be used to limit competition, and some of them have considerable market dominance. Nevertheless a company becomes international often because it thrives on competition and its power is often used in practice to raise the standards of the industry and to stimulate the market.

Consumers

The international companies may limit choice and standardize in undesirable ways. They may also take advantage of their market dominance to raise prices. On the other hand many of the companies expand by innovation and may be able to make otherwise expensive goods available at popular prices. The companies may also be more responsive to complaints, partly because of greater marketing skills.

Education

The tendency to centralized research means that a company may lose its facilities; as a result a sector of research and of higher education in the host country may be damaged and able people lost. As against this some international companies do give limited assistance to education in countries where they operate. The demands of the multinational are a powerful stimulus to management education in a country, and the need for more skilled and educated manpower may help indirectly to raise the general educational standards of the country.

Environment

The effect on the physical environment is also two-way. Some firms have been seeking sites in countries where the pollution laws are comparatively lenient, while others have been developing and marketing internationally equipment for pollution control.

Information

Some multinational firms are secretive and use the opportunities provided by their spread of investment across a number of legal systems to conceal important facts about their existence. Most companies do not make public some details about their operations which policy-makers would like to know. But there are some companies which have pioneered new ways of presenting facts about themselves, an expensive process and one that it is often hard to make meaningful anyway. Indeed, the costs involved may make serious problems for small firms. Hence the demand for more information may be a way of aiding the big against the small, often the reverse of the intention of those who make the demands.

Labour

Companies have the ability to move facilities in order to avoid labour troubles, and some pursue anti-trade union policies. On the other hand multinationals innovate in personnel as they do in other policies and they show more willingness than domestic companies to locate in areas of unemployment. Work is also provided, often in desirable jobs in advanced technologies. It remains to be seen whether the emergence of co-determination in some countries is held to threaten the powers of the parent company. In some cases these powers may be guaranteed by treaty.

Management

The problem under this heading is identified as restricted opportunities in highly centralized firms which yet control key sectors of the economy. For the mobile manager there may well be much wider international career prospects than he would have in a domestic concern. There is also the advantage of working for a company that is developing new management techniques.

National income

The movement of money out of a country may be damaging especially at a time of currency difficulties. Under some conditions the movement of money into a country may be damaging. In both cases the problems are increased by the unpredictable nature of the movements. Some multinationals, also, restrict exports from their foreign subsidiaries. The manipulation of the financial policies of the subsidiary in the interests of the parent company is, in any case, normal. On the positive side the foreign investor stimulates the local economy at the time the investment is made, and the stimulus is often in growth areas of that economy.

Many multinationals establish plants to serve a regional market, hence they have good export records from the host country to the other countries in the region.

Regional development

In contrast with the last point, this refers to regions within a country. Competition between countries for investment in areas of high unemployment can lead to the offer of concessions which cause unanticipated problems. For instance a country may give a firm a tax holiday for ten years. At the end of that time the country may depend on the company and thus be forced to extend the concession for a further period. But countries are more often assisted by foreign firms who prove more responsive to attempts to direct them to development areas; they are less wedded to traditional business areas. At the time of entry, in any case governments can direct them to designated regions.

Resources

There is the possibility of companies moving resources into countries where they might not be most required, and the further possibility that some companies can exert undue control over limited supplies. As against this is the attempt by companies to distribute available resources as equitably as possible.

Sovereignty

A frequent accusation that is made is that the powerful international company is a threat to national sovereignty. This is not technically true, as companies are quick to point out. Sovereignty is a legal concept and business concerns are always subject to the law. What is meant is some phrase like national aspirations. There is certainly evidence, discussed elsewhere in this chapter, that companies are impatient of the restraints imposed by the nation state; but with the positive desire of the state for enrichment they are certainly not out of sympathy. The only reason for their existence is to provide goods and employment which between them raise living standards. Naturally there is scope for legitimate differences of opinion as to whether in practice they raise living standards in any particular country or whether a particular company's products are appropriate for that country. Without deliberately setting out to impoverish their market, the companies may well be pursuing policies that effectively do this. As a result there may be strong disagreement between companies and governments as to the most suitable means of achieving the objectives. The companies indeed express opinions on these matters and lobby decision makers. Evidence of actual interference in national politics is limited to a few cases which appear to be exceptional, like Chile, whereas evidence of the lengths to which companies have gone to accommodate themselves to policies they dislike is considerable.

Stability

Prices, inflation and the balance of payments. On the negative side companies can move money around to avoid what they see as threats to their business; in doing so they may damage the economies of both home and host countries. Pricing policies are determined in accordance with central corporate interests. On the positive side, multinational companies make a contribution to the control of inflation by their efficiency.

Standards

Many international companies contribute to the improvement of the work environment by the introduction of new techniques and by their general receptiveness to new ideas. Other companies have developed their facilities in countries where labour, health and safety laws are lenient to the companies, and labour costs can be kept down.

Taxation

As frequently repeated on these pages, corporate policies are biased to head office and to the shareholders in the home country. Pricing, credit and intra-company loan policies, among others, will be biased to central corporate requirements. On the other hand, the prosperity of the large company makes it a significant contributor to the national exchequer, and its wealth makes it less likely to come to the state for assistance in any of its countries of operation.

Technology

Some companies buy up foreign research facilities and close them down, transferring the research effort back to the home country. On the other hand new and much needed technologies are often brought to the host country. This question has been fully discussed in chapter 11.

15.4 The international framework

A number of treaties and treaty organizations determine the context within which international business is conducted. The most important of these regulate trade, currency exchange, commodities and investment. However international agencies are being called on to operate in different directions. In the past the pressures have been for international action to negotiate freer movements of goods and funds over frontiers where governments were increasingly establishing barriers. This continues with regard to tariffs; at the same time the demand is to reverse the liberalization of investment flows and use international bodies to strengthen the resolve of governments to attach conditions to the movement of capital, and to ensure that companies cannot play one country off against another. So this section deals with the four elements in the international framework: trade, currency exchange, investment and commodity agreements.

The General Agreement for Tarriffs and Trade is the instrument which attempts to regulate trade barriers.[11] This grew out of a treaty signed in Geneva in 1947, which in its turn was based on an earlier conference in 1944. Legally speaking the General Agreement, usually known as GATT, was a set of principles regulating trade; however it became, in practice, an organization to maintain the principles. The original agreement covered four subjects:

(1) The most-favoured nation principle whereby any favour that one member showed to another should be extended to all. Exceptions to this included customs unions and free trade areas.

(2) Countries reduce tariff barriers on a basis of general agreement, and can raise them again so long as they make some reciprocal concessions. The reductions are known as 'rounds' of which there have been seven since the agreement was first made; the latest was the Tokyo Round. The conclusion to this round was long-delayed because of disagreements on agricultural goods, the safeguards against excessive imports, the question of whether or not there should be a differential reduction of duty on manufactured goods and a number of other matters.

(3) Non tariff barriers to be abolished as soon as possible.

(4) Arrangements for membership and resignation, and dealing with infringements.

The United Nations Conference on Trade and Development was established as a department of the United Nations in 1964. UNCTAD operates through four committees—commodities, manufactured goods, invisible trade and finance, and shipping. Major decisions are taken at conferences, the last one was UNCTAD IV at Nairobi in 1976. At this conference there was a direct confrontation between the industrialized countries and the Third World. There were few agreements apart from one on commodity price stabilization. Among some general resolutions passed was one calling for greater control on multinational companies.

The Organization for Economic Co-operation and Development was set up to improve trade and investment flows between member countries. Since the development of GATT it has taken on a mainly consultative role, with an expert staff producing reports on a wide range of economic and commercial matters for members.

In addition to the bodies specifically charged with facilitating trade among member countries, there are the regional groupings with customs unions or mutual free trade. The difference is that a customs union, like the European Economic Community negotiates a common tariff between its members and the rest of the world as well as other measures to facilitate commerce between its members; a free trade area, like the European Free Trade Area, only abolishes duties between its members. Besides the two mentioned other regional groupings include: the Caribbean Free Trade Area, the Central African Customs Union, the Latin America Free Trade Area. Trade within Eastern Europe is regulated by COMECON.

The regulation of currency exchange, the second element in the international framework, was organized for the post-war world at the Bretton Woods agreement of 1944 which founded the International Monetary Fund among other institutions. For a number of years the Fund helped to maintain some order in currency exchange. Among its achievements was the establishment of Special Drawing Rights, designed eventually to replace gold as an international basis for currency values. During the 1960s the speculative pressures on the reserve currencies, those against which the parties of the rest were fixed, grew greater until the devaluation of the dollar in 1971. This brought about the final collapse of the international monetary system devised at Bretton Woods, and attempts at revival were frustrated by the oil crisis two years later. There are now three types of currency arrangement:

(1) Currencies floating in isolation.
(2) Currencies floating in regional parity groups.
(3) Currencies pegged to the dollar, sterling or special drawing rights.

The International Monetary Fund still acts as the main source of borrowing for short and medium term balance of trade deficit finance. With its 128 member countries it also provides a forum for the discussion of monetary problems. Drawing on the fund is through a series of *tranches* representing different sums, the conditions become more severe with each tranche. Fig. 15.1 shows how the system works.

Other elements in the internation framework for currency exchange include regional groups like the European Economic Community, the Organization for Economic Co-operation and Development and numerous bilateral financial aid agreements.

Fig. 15.1

A poor country's guide to the IMF

	Type of facility[1]	per cent of quota available	Cumulative per cent of quota available
A country may have a	Gold Tranche of without conditions	25	25
or a	first credit tranche of	25	50
provided it presents a	programme representing a reasonable effort to overcome balance of payments difficulties; performance criteria and instalments are not used.		
But when you need	higher credit tranches of	75	125
you must develop a	programme giving substantial justification of member's efforts to overcome balance of payments difficulties; resources normally provided in the form of stand-by arrangements which include performance criteria and drawings in instalments.		
When in real trouble you may enquire about the	extended facility of	140	190[2]
but have on hand a	medium-term programme for up to 3 years to overcome structural balance of payments maladjustments; detailed statement of policies and measures for first and subsequent 12-month periods; resources provided in the form of extended arrangements which include performance criteria and drawings of instalments.		
Anyone can run into a spot of trouble; if so there is a	compensatory financing facility	75[3]	265
You can ask for terms when the exchequer shows the	existence of a temporary shortfall for reasons beyond the member's control; member co-operates with Fund in an effort to find appropriate solutions for any balance of payments difficulties.		

Having difficulty building up buffer stocks in your commodities?	Buffer stock financing facility[4] Existence of an international buffer stock accepted as suitable by Fund; member expected to co-operate with Fund as in the case of compensatory financing.	50	315
Feeling the pinch of the oil crisis? Then you may take advantage of the	oil facility 1974	75	—[5]
or the	oil facility 1975 for 1975: As under purchases in the first credit tranche, member expected to follow trade and payments policies consistent with the Rome communique of the Committee of 20.	125	—[5]

Fig. 15.1 *(contd.)*

[1] Members are not expected, and may not qualify, to use all of the available facilities at the same time. In addition, use of maximum available resources under a particular facility, namely tranche policies, is usually made in a period of years and not in one year.

[2] The combined use of the extended facility and the regular tranches may not be above 165% of quota. Adding the use of the gold tranche raises the maximum to 190%.

[3] Normally not more than 50% of quota in any 12-month period.

[4] Until the proposed Second Amendment enters into effect, a member with gold tranche drawing rights who purchases under the buffer stock financing facility would lose his gold tranche drawing rights.

[5] The oil facility was set up on a temporary basis for 1974 and 1975 only.

Source: IMF Survey. Reproduced from *The Banker's Magazine,* Oct. 1976, with permission.

The Commodity Markets are another subject which is part of the international framework. These are important for their effect on world prices; they are vital to the economies of many countries, especially the poorest. The most discussed is oil, where the main oil producing countries have since 1973 been determining world prices. After many years as a bargaining force the Organization for Petroleum Exporting Countries (OPEC) has come to exercise considerable power in the world through a commodity that can be turned on and off at will, but is more difficult to store in significant quantities. Other commodities cannot be controlled so easily and efforts have been concentrated on the establishment of buffer stocks and import–export controls to cushion the producers against severe swings in price and demand. The main method of control has been by world agreements, but increasing efforts are being made to strengthen organizations of exporting countries although this has proved more difficult than with the oil countries.

The final element of the emerging international framework is the development of controls on investment. The object is usually to ensure that companies comply with certain minimum standards of behaviour in the host country and do not play one country off against another. To this end increasingly codes of conduct are being produced which will apply to trade as well as to investment. The European Economic Community, the Organization for Economic Co-operation and Development and the United Nations all have codes of conduct in preparation, as do other inter-governmental bodies. The United Nations has published a series of documents on the subject, one of which is quoted in this chapter. One of the most advanced codes is that of the Organization for Economic Co-operation and Development.[12] The codes reverse the trend since the Organization's foundation towards the liberalization of capital movements; but this is only true to a limited extent. Most countries have special conditions that attach to government contracts both as to their trading arrangement and labour relations. Similar conditions apply in the codes which it is intended shall become mandatory on companies as they are incorporated in national legislation.

No doubt there will always be countries which do not accede to the proposals, and companies will be able to register with them, as ships register under flags of convenience. Registration is itself another aspect of foreign investment, with the possibility of companies registering with an inter-governmental body. The European Economic Community first put forward a statute for the European Company in 1970. In those days companies were keen on the grounds that this would release them from national restrictions and from any liabilities that the political or economic position of their home country might give them in their host countries. Although an international form of registration may yet come about, the drive towards it has lessened. Companies have been finding that international bodies are less sympathetic to their aspirations than they expected; it is also suspected that for the foreseeable future any form of international registration will only add an extra set of rules and will not release the company from any. So there seems little to be gained, from the company's point of view, in a move which now seems designed to increase the controls. The attempt is frequently to provide a comparatively sophisticated mixture of encouragement and constraint aimed at giving the greatest possible stimulus to the local economies. The Andeen Pact countries have devised a set of rules with this intention.[13]

The main issues in the political and legal environment of the company have been outlined in this chapter. It has been seen that governments, especially in the less developed countries, are finding the need for an international framework for investment as has already developed for trade and currency exchange. The cure for this, and its implications were most clearly set out in the report from which the following excerpt is taken.

15.5 The multinational corporation: the United Nations Report[14]

Multinational corporations are important actors on the world stage. The report entitled, Multinational Corporations in World Development,[15] aptly describes their current significance and recent trends. The total value of international production controlled by such corporations now exceeds that of international trade. Their spread and growth has been one of the outstanding phenomena of the last two decades, and in many countries, outside the centrally planned economies, they have significantly increased their share of national output.

Most countries have recognized the potential of multinational corporations and have encouraged the expansion of their activities in one form or another within their national borders. The role of foreign private investment in development is indeed acknowledged in the International Development Strategy for the Second United Nations Development Decade.[16] At the same time, certain practices and effects of multinational corporations have given rise to widespread concern and anxiety in many quarters and a strong feeling has emerged that the present modus vivendi should be reviewed at the international level.

Home countries are concerned about the undesirable effects that foreign investment by multinational corporations may have on domestic employment and the balance of payments, and about the capacity of such corporations to alter the normal play of competition. Host countries are concerned about the ownership and control of key economic sectors by foreign enterprises, the excessive cost to the domestic economy which their operations may entail, the extent to which they may encroach upon political sovereignty and their possible adverse influence on socio-cultural values. Labour interests are concerned about the impact of multinational corporations on employment and workers' welfare and on the bargaining strength of trade unions. Consumer interests are concerned about the appropriateness, quality and price of goods produced by multinational corporations. The multinational corporations themselves are concerned about the possible nationalization or expropriation of their assets without adequate compensation and about restrictive, unclear and frequently changing government policies.

From all these expressions of concern, one conclusion emerges: fundamental new problems have arisen as a direct result of the growing internationalization of production as carried out by multinational corporations. We believe that these problems must be tackled without delay, so that tensions are eased and the benefits which can be derived from multinational corporations are fully realized.

Although international, intergovernmental and governmental bodies have been devoting themselves to the issue for some time, most efforts concentrate on the problem as seen in certain countries or groups of countries, or with respect to particular subjects, rather than taking up the total international implication of multinational corporations. It is in this context that the present involvement of the United Nations acquires particular significance and leads the way for pioneering work within the Organization.

There are frequently alternative ways which should be actively explored of obtaining the benefits provided by multinational corporations. These enterprises are not the only vehicles for the internationalization of production. In the socialist countries of Eastern Europe, for example, where planned economic integration is the counterpart of regional integration among market economies, this process is carried out at the public and interstate level through, *inter alia*, joint state-owned undertakings established by the member states of the Council for Mutual Economic Assistance. Moreover, these countries follow a selective, centrally planned, approach as regards the objectives, areas and forms of co-operation with multinational corporations (for example, co-production arrangements) employing the modalities of their economic and social system to protect national interest. In addition, there are countries which, on the basis of their political and social choices, may opt for different, self-reliant styles or models of development which leave little or no room for the participation of multinational corporations as they are currently organized.

National policy framework

Host Governments may affect the contribution of multinational corporations to development by their specific policies towards and their treatment of foreign direct investment, as well as by their general economic and social policies.

(a) Negotiating with multinational corporations. The terms on which multinational corporations gain entry into a host country are obviously a matter of considerable importance. Influenced by the view once widely held that developing countries should open their doors wide to foreign capital to enhance their development, many of these terms were not sufficiently carefully negotiated.

Many developing countries have felt that their bargaining position in dealing with multinational corporations is weak. There has been the assumption that multinational corporations, with the exception of certain resource-based industries, can choose their location for production according to the country offering them the most attractive environment and most favourable terms. The initial agreement concluded with multinational corporations thus tends to include a large number of special concessions. Later, as circumstances change, the concessions appear to be too onerous and the host country may deem it necessary to redress the situation. In such cases foreign affiliates could be treated in a discriminatory fashion or could even be expropriated. Such treatment, though it may be directed towards particular multinational corporations inevitably creates an atmosphere of distrust which operates against the long-term interests of both host countries and corporations. Moreover, concern about future unfavourable treatment may lead multinational corporations to attempt to extract the most out of their investment in the least possible time. These, and other uncertainties, make multinational corporations reluctant to invest in some developing countries unless their prospects are distinctly more attractive than those expected in developed countries.

In fact developing countries are not always, in the initial negotiations, in such a weak position. Those which possess valuable natural resources, for example, are beginning to realize their vital importance to multinational corporations and their increased bargaining power. Several others, by forming regional groups among themselves and enlarging their markets, have been able to secure the collaboration of multinational corporations on more advantageous terms. The abundance of relatively skilled labour is also being used to induce multinational corporations to set up export-oriented, labour-intensive manufacturers. Finally a number of developing countries have evolved careful planning policies and foreign investment regulations which not only enable them effectively to control and monitor the operations of multinational corporations, but also offer those enterprises a stable and balanced environment.

However, a number of further steps must be taken. Developing countries should indicate precisely, as an increasing number of them are already doing, what, in general, they expect of multinational corporations. They need to elaborate the ways in which multinational corporations can fit into their overall plans and priorities, and to identify the areas in which those enterprises should make a contribution. Governments should clarify questions of ownership and control as well as specify policies in respect of the activities of multinational corporations pertaining to the political field. When negotiating with a particular multinational corporation they should indicate more precisely the kind of policy that the affiliate should follow with respect to such matters as the choice of products to be manufactured, the degree of local processing, the employment of nationals, wage policy and other similar matters.

Among the particular point which should be covered in such an understanding is whether the multinational corporation should be treated differently from a national enterprise; for example whether special regulation will be introduced governing such activities of the corporation as the production and marketing of new products, the source and ways of finance, remittances of profits, royalties and capital, and the employment of expatriates. Maximum clarity on both sides is essential for better understanding and future good relations.

The Group recommends that host countries should specify as precisely as possible the conditions under which multinational corporations should operate and what they should achieve. They should also indicate the ways in which the activities of multinational corporations should be integrated into the local economy and fit into the overall priorities of the country.

In considering specific investment projects, developing countries should take the initiative in exploring possibilities of obtaining the kind of external contribution they want in the selected sectors. This means seeking competitive offers from multinational corporations which seem to have the requisite technology and skills. Simultaneously, alternative forms of foreign co-operation with international institutions or public or private entities should be considered.

In evaluating the terms proposed by multinational corporations, the ostensibly most attractive offer may not be the most advantageous, since the impact of these corporations on the local economy can be far-reaching. Therefore their true costs and benefits should be carefully analysed.

Experience and expertise are crucial elements in conducting negotiations of this kind successfully. Yet those elements are often lacking in developing countries. Experience can be gained more quickly if the same group of people handle all such negotiations. And the international community should assist developing countries in strengthening their expertise.

The Group recommends:

(1) That host countries should consider setting up centralized negotiating services or co-ordinating groups to deal with all proposals for foreign investment, especially from multinational corporations.

(2) That the United Nations should strengthen its capacity to assist host countries, at their request, in such negotiations with multinational corporations, as well as to train their personnel in the conduct of such negotiations.

While a clear understanding on various issues at the time of entry is vital, it has to be recognized that conditions change, and that what may have seemed to be adequate and fair at the time of entry may prove unsatisfactory to either party over time.

A large number of agreements made in the past lack comprehensiveness and contain no provision for renegotiation. Developing countries have, of course, the power, through legislation, to modify the terms of agreements. But sometimes such actions, if carried out unilaterally, entail disproportionately high costs in terms of future flow of investment. A willingness on both sides to renegotiate agreements which have been in force for more than, say, 10 years could help to avoid recourse to extreme measures.

The Group recommends that in the initial agreement with multinational corporations, host countries should consider making provision for the review, at the request of either side, after suitable intervals, of various clauses of the agreement. The review by the host country should be carried out by the negotiating services or co-ordinating groups recommended above.

In recent years, the multinational corporations themselves have done a great deal of rethinking about their role in developing countries. Many of them no longer insist on operating only through wholly owned subsidiaries, or even on a majority shareholding basis in the enterprises they set up. Yet many of them do wish to retain effective control over management, especially in the initial years.

The Group recommends that developing countries should consider including provisions in their initial agreements with multinational corporations which permit the possibility of a reduction over time of the percentages of foreign ownership: the terms, as far as possible, should also be agreed upon at the very beginning, in order to minimize the possibilities of future conflict and controversy.

Not only is there a need to review the terms and conditions of entry in the light of changing circumstances, it is also essential to keep under review the policies and performance of the multinational corporations. Knowledge of such conduct and performance would help to dispel mystery and distrust and constitute a basis on which developing host countries could formulate their policy.

The first requisite for a proper evaluation is the availability of information on a continuing basis.

We wish to make one final point in this subsection. The negotiating position of host countries is strengthened if broader options or alternatives are open to them. One alternative to the 'package deal', implicit in foreign direct investment, is for the individual components of the package to be purchase separately. There is evidence that some multinational corporations are ready to accept new forms of operation in which ownership rights are reduced. Management and service contracts, turnkey operations, limited-life joint companies, are all being actively explored.

The agreements that multinational corporations have made with several socialist countries of Eastern Europe are also worthy of consideration. Contractual joint ventures, or co-production agreements, are based on national ownership, limited duration and explicit provision for renegotiation, and involve a reduction of many of the risks usually attached to foreign direct investment.

Developing countries would also enhance their bargaining power if they identified alternatives outside the realm of the multinational corporations. Enterprises jointly owned by Governments or firms of several developing countries or joint enterprises with Governments of developed market or centrally planned economies are possibilities which could be further explored.

Each of these arrangements may or may not be suitable alternatives to the package provided by the multinational corporation. Each case should be assessed on its own merits.

(b) Treatment of foreign investment. As a general principle, we believe that the affiliates of multinational corporations should be encouraged to identify as closely as possible, with the interests of host countries, developed and developing. The links that multinational corporations maintain with their parent companies and home governments should not lead them to act in a way which conflicts with the national policy of the host countries. An essential counterpart is that the policies of host governments towards foreign affiliates should be fair, and as closely as possible similar to those which they apply to their national enterprises.

The phrase 'as closely as possible' is used because we recognize that there are many respects in which both the rights and obligations of multinational corporations or their affiliates cannot be identical with those of the national firms. Multinational corporations expect the right to repatriate their profits and, in certain circumstances, their capital. A national firm cannot be given the facility of transferring its profits abroad by countries which cannot afford the free outflow of funds.

Likewise, there may be areas in which host governments might find it desirable to introduce policies which are favourable or unfavourable to multinational corporations. Such discriminatory policies may be necessary because of the special features of foreign direct investment. For example, since a country can protect its infant industries from foreign competition through international trade, it cannot totally deny itself the possibility of sheltering such industries from competition by foreign affiliates established by multinational corporations. It may consider that mergers and acquisitions involving domestic firms should be allowed, or even actively promoted, while those involving foreign firms should be prohibited. On occasion, the host country may deem it justified to impose special requirements on its foreign affiliates, for example, in respect of profit remittances, access to capital markets, or labour conditions.

We believe that the cases in which relationships between multinational corporations and host governments have deteriorated sharply over time are often those in which clarity was lacking in host country policies or, no less important, those in which special exemptions from prevailing regulations and policies were sought and given as a price for the entry of the corporation. In general, we believe that if the framework of a country's policies is not acceptable to a multinational corporation, it may be better for it to stay out than to gain entry on exceptional terms.

To avoid these negative impacts, no less than to promote fruitful co-operation between themselves and multinational corporations, it is desirable for host governments to treat the affiliates of the corporation as indigenous companies, unless specific exceptions are provided.

The Group recommends that host countries should adopt policies towards affiliates of multinational corporations similar to those applied to indigenous companies, unless specific exceptions are made in the national interest.

(c) General policies. The capacity to deal effectively and successfully with multinational corporations depends on the total development effort, of which direct measures concerning those corporations, or their alternatives, form only a part.

The kind of products produced by multinational corporations are obviously influenced by import substitution measures, as well as income distribution policies, or the lack of such policies, in the host country. The balance of payments impact of multinational corporations is influenced by trade policy. If protective tariffs are levied, a high cost structure may be encouraged, and exports may be inhibited. The type of technology introduced and the employment impact may be adversely affected by inappropriate interest rate and tax policies or by veiled subsidies to imported capital goods. The incidence of transfer pricing depends, to a large extent, on the efficiency of exchange controls and rules concerning remittances, as well as intercountry differences in tax rates and systems.

Some of these specific issues are discussed elsewhere.[17] Here we would simply emphasize that a proper policy by host countries towards multinational corporations cannot be evolved in a vacuum, but must form part of a network of policies which is based upon a well-conceived development strategy with adequate support from national institutions.

This, in turn, will only be possible if the host country possesses the technology of choice.[18] In other words, the ability to make the appropriate decisions based on adequate information about the alternative policies open to it and the costs and benefits involved in adopting one policy rather than another. The misuse of these resources may well be the most serious true cost of development. The importance of choosing wisely is especially crucial today, since the assets with which many developing countries find that they can bargain best with the developed world and with the multinational corporations are non-renewable natural resources. It is thus not only important for developing countries to obtain a just price for their resources, but to spend the proceeds in a way which will generate long-term and continuing economic and social progress.

The general environment which host countries provide is sometimes influenced by the actual implementation and administration of policies as much as by the nature of the policies themselves. We are very conscious of the fact that ostensibly sound policies may be undermined by bureaucratic red-tape or even rampant corruption. Regulatory machineries and discretionary administrative powers, including those concerning multinational corporations, may be used as avenues for bribery. Vigorous anti-corruption measures should be introduced by all Governments. Host countries, both developed and developing, should examine carefully the possibilities of corruptive practices in granting special permissions or concessions to multinational corporations. In particular, multinational corporations should not be allowed to give direct or indirect gratuities to office holders of host governments and trade unions. Home countries could assist in this regard by strict measures against bribery committed by their nationals elsewhere. International efforts for exchange of experiences in the harmonization of anti-corruption provisions would also help.

Regional co-operation

Developing countries have a great deal to gain from measures of regional co-operation among themselves. Such measures would also greatly assist them in their dealings with multinational corporations.

The bargaining power of developing countries may be strengthened by co-operative action. Many of them in the past have engaged in competitive granting of tax concessions to multinational corporations and other incentives to attract foreign investment. Often these concessions, which involve a measure of sacrifice on the part of host countries, are not necessary to augment the flow of investment. Even the tax concessions transfer resources from poor host countries to rich home countries.[19] In other instances, they only reduce the benefits which could be expected to flow from the operation of multinational corporations.

Regional co-operation not only strengthens the bargaining position of developing countries but also helps them to evolve appropriate techniques for dealing with the problems to which the activities of multinational corporations often give rise. Where regional co-operation enlarges the market to which the multinational corporation gains access, the inducement to invest is enhanced. In order to gain access to large regional markets, multinational corporations have been willing to accept terms and conditions which they would reject from small countries. Developing countries in such conditions not only secure the co-operation of the corporations on better terms but can also benefit from the economies of scale. A number of developing countries have attempted to achieve these purposes by regional co-operation of various forms and degrees of comprehensiveness, although progress has been uneven on the whole.

The Group recommends that developing countries should intensify their efforts for regional co-operation, in particular the establishment of joint policies with regard to multinational corporations. The United Nations should study the experience of existing regional groups as it relates to multinational corporations and should disseminate relevant information to developing countries and provide technical assistance to them.

The international economic system

The multinational corporations in their present form and dimension are products of the international economic system within which they operate. Their basic strategies evolve in response to the existing world situation as well as to policies at national or regional levels. The rules of the game of the international system thus affect the activities of the multinational corporations, as well as national and regional policies. The growing importance of these corporations has in turn affected the functioning of the entire system.

The response of multinational corporations to the basic orientation of the existing system is most apparent in regard to trade. When capital and technology are mobile but labour is not, they tend to turn to countries where relatively skilled labour is abundant and inexpensive. Whether this will generate much employment in many developing countries where unemployment is endemic depends on the readiness of the developed countries to accept their products. if instead they choose to raise tariff and non-tariff barriers against such exports from developing countries, the potential of multinational corporations to contribute in this regard will necessarily be reduced. Improvements in the existing international trade régime will thus enhance the potential of the multinational corporations to contribute to development.

The international monetary system also has an important bearing on the operations of multinational corporations, in areas such as choice of location and financial flows. Apart from its influence on national and regional policies on production and trade, the degree of stability of exchange rates and the adjustment mechanism provided by the system evidently affects the policies of multinational corporations. Events in the recent monetary crisis have directed attention to the possible role of multinational corporations in the volatile short-term movements that have occurred, in addition to the fundamental disequilibria in the balance of payments of several major industrial countries. Although the current convulsions in the international monetary system may not be caused by speculative activities of multinational corporations, the ability of these enterprises to move massive amounts of funds across borders is unquestionable and such movements can undoubtedly aggravate the situation. This potential has been greatly enhanced by dramatic changes in international banking and consortia arrangements. A vigilant monitoring or surveillance by central banks of movements of funds of multinational corporations across borders is thus indicated. Moreover, in evolving a new monetary system, the role of multinational corporations will need to be taken seriously into account, in contrast to the benign neglect it has received so far.

While the international division of labour is influenced by the existing international trade and monetary régimes, it may be strongly affected, intentionally or unintentionally, by multinational corporations. Their large capabilities for moving products and inputs across borders are important instruments in affecting the actual division of labour. At the same time, the apprehension that host countries may be turned into 'branch-plant' economies may not be limited to developing countries. The organization, productive and distributive networks created by multinational corporations often assign a peripheral and dependent role to affiliates in many host countries, while the centres of top decision making and scientific research remain in a few highly industrialized countries. Although the locational pattern of multinational corporations reflects the uneven distribution of the factor endowments, it is also moulded in many cases by artificial administrative devices employed by home and host governments (tariffs, subsidies, and the like) as well as by the corporations themselves. There is no indication, as is sometimes suggested, that multinational corporations are evolving into real internationalized entities whose ownership, management and objectives are truly global, and within which all nations and their citizens are treated equitably and world welfare is truly maximized.

In today's complex economy, the 'invisible hand' of the market is far from the only force guiding economic decisions. To a considerable extent, conscious planning, both public and private, has played an increasing role in decision making. Increasingly, basic decisions on the allocation of resources with respect to what, how and for whom to produce are being concentrated in corporate planning mechanisms. The growth of multinational corporations gives them increasing control over resources and thus augments their capacity to re-allocate them. Such decisions, when taken exclusively from the point of view of the interests of the enterprise, again pose serious problems. The question of establishing public mechanisms, both national and international, to orient the planning of consumption, to choose among different alternatives and to generate awareness in respect of their implications for the strategy of development of a given country, or region, appears to be a basic problem demanding a solution.

Decisions regarding the rules of the game and the creation of institutions and machinery to deal with the operations of multinational corporations must therefore be made in addition to, as well as in the context of, current negotiations for the improvement of the existing international trade and monetary systems. For unless a serious and united effort is made to formulate policies and programmes in respect of multinational corporations, which are most directly related to the actual international division of labour, considerations of money and trade reform appear to be somewhat empty and the world economic order lacks any firm foundation. There is no substitute for consideration of the various parts of the system in the context of the entire interdependent network.

15.6 Some interesting facts

Comparing company sales with gross national product: similar sets of figures have often been published before. The justification for doing so again is that the facts here are more recent than any previously published and that the presentation highlights a wider spread of firms.

These figures are interesting to the reader as they give some impression of size. Figures which compared corporate budgets with those of national governments would also be interesting. They would show that senior financial executives of large numbers of companies handle more money than most government finance ministers: but of course this could be misleading, the amount of money handled by the finance minister depends on the politics of the country as well as its wealth. The figures given can also be misleading. They only refer to wealth, not to power. The reader may link the two, but the amount of power that wealth carries must vary with the circumstances. If the largest corporation invested all its wealth in the smallest country, no doubt that company would be very powerful there. But the situation described here is one of a global spread not a concentration.

The facts are: in 1974 there were 22 countries in the world with Gross National Products totalling over $40,000 m.[20] (Switzerland was the smallest of these with $43,000 m.) No companies had sales over $40,000 m.

There were two countries with GNP between $30–40,000 m (Austria and the Republic of Korea). A number of companies had sales between these figures including: General Motors, General Electric, Exxon, Ford, and Texaco.

There were four countries with GNP between $20–30,000 m (Yugoslavia, Hungary, Denmark, Norway). The companies which had sales between these figures included two European—Royal Dutch Shell and British Petroleum—as well as United States companies like Mobil Oil.

15.7 Suggestions for further reading

Papers on this subject appear somewhere in the world every day, and any recommendations must appear arbitrary. The following are selected because they make significant points or because they take a strong line, ranging from enthusiastic support for the companies to strong hostility.[21] For key to references see pp. 343–4.

General

(B) FAYERWEATHER, J., Ed. (1973) *International Business—Government Affairs: Toward an Era of Accommodation,* Ballinger: Cambridge, Mass.
(B) VERNON (1971).
(B) FARMER & RICHMAN (1976).
(A) HAYS *et al.* (1972).
(B) DUERR, Michael C. (1974).
(B) ROBINSON (1973). Introduction and chapter 7.
(A) DANIELS, OGRAM & RADEBAUGH (1976). Chapter 11.
(A) KAPOOR & GRUB (1972). Chapters 6 and 7.
(B) ROBOCK & SIMMONDS (1973). Chapters 7–10.
(B) BROOKE & REMMERS (1970). Chapter 10.
(A) MALAWER, S. S. (1974). Law and international business studies, pp. 81–83, *Journal of International Business Studies*, **5.2,** Autumn. This brief note gives the main subjects for investigating legal issues and foreign business together with some references.
(C) EITEMAN & STONEHILL (1973) Chapter 10. To be published.
(B) LLOYD, Bruce (1975). The identification and assessment of political risks, *Moorgate and Wall Street Journal*, Spring, pp. 49–76.
(B) NEGANDHI, A. R. & PRASAD, S. B. (1975). *The Frightening Angels*, Kent State University.
(C) DUNNING, J. H. (1973). Multinational enterprises and domestic capital formation, *Manchester School*, September.

The international framework

(B) *The Impact of Multinational Corporations on Development and on International Relations*, UN Sales Document E.74.11.A.J.. There are many other UN publications on the subject.[22]
(A) DANIELS, OGRAM & RADEBAUGH (1976). chapters 13 and 14.
(A) KAPOOR & GRUB (1972). Chapter 1.
(B) ROBOCK & SIMMONDS (1973). Chapter 14.
(B) THORPE, P. A. (1976). Transnational enterprises and international regulation: a survey of various approaches in international organizations, *International Organization,* **30.1.**
(C) LAUTER, G. P. & DEAKIE, P. M. (1975). Multinational corporations in Eastern European socialist economies, *Journal of Marketing,* October.
(C) JURAWICKI, Leon (1975). The Cooperation of the socialist state with the MNC's (1975). *The Columbia Journal of World Business,* Spring.
(A) DANIELS, OGRAM & RADEBAUGH (1976). Chapter 15.

The less developed countries

(A) KAPOOR & GRUB (1975). Chapters 6 and 7.
(C) SARUP, V. (1975). The Corporate problems of the MNC in India. Unpublished paper in possession of International Business Unit.
(C) WELLS, Lovis T. (1973). Economic man and engineering man: choice of technology in a low wage economy, *Public Policy*, Summer.
(C) MASSIAH, G. (1974). Multinational corporations and a strategy for national independence, *Conference paper*, Conference on Multinational Corporations in Africa (25 Sept.–5 Oct.). Dakar: United Nations African Institute for Economic Development and Planning.
(C) WIONCZEK, Miguel S. (1975). Rules for multinationals: the Latin American contest, *Worldview*, October.

The International Centre for the Settlement of Disputes was set up by the World Bank in 1966 to deal with disputes between investors and foreign countries. So far it has not been much used. For an account, see:

(C) RYANS, J. K. & BAKER, J. C. (1976). The international centre for the settlement of disputes (ICSID), *Journal of World Trade Law*, **10.1** Jan. Feb.

15.8 Exercises for this chapter

Case studies

Grangesberg, undated, (IMEDE GM—121, ICH 9–313–085 and 086) by Christensen, C. R., Scott, B. R.
These cases present two political issues; (i) the sale of stategic wide-diameter pipes to Soviet Union, including Premier Kruschev's inspection of company installations, (ii) the Company's position as Foreign Investor in Liberia and its role as exploiter of natural resources in an underdeveloped area.

Consolidated Industries Ltd., 1972. (IMEDE, ICH 9–373–887), by Aharoni, Y. and Baden, C.
A multinational enterprise president wants to measure the corporation's impact on society; he asks a young manager to compile a list of 'Social Indications'.

The London and Rhodesian Mining Co. Ltd., 1973. (Manchester Business School, CCH 374–042–1), by Channon, D. F.
This case deals with the management of a highly diversified multinational corporation, business government relations, the role of the Board of Directors, leadership style and the determination of political risk.

Problems of Complying with a host country's Conditions for the Establishment of a Manufacturing subsidiary, 1973 (University of Bradford Management Centre, CCH 376–023–1).
The List of Conditions with which a foreign-owned commercial vehicle assembler must comply in order to set up a plant in Nigeria.

Television Imports Controversy, 1972 (Harvard, ICH 9–373–836), by R. Moxon.
A consideration of the arguments involved in a request to the United States tariff commission to raise import duties on Japanese television sets.

Impact of Public Policy on Collaborative Ventures in Europe, 1974, (INSEAD, ICH 9–375–604).
A useful background to the subject.

15.9 Questions for discussion

(1) 'In all business operations, the enterprise has common interests and potential areas of conflict with governments and must recognize

governmental policies and actions as constraints in business decision-making' (Robock & Simmonds). Comment.

(2) Describe conflicts which might arise between a company's objectives and the public interest when the 'company' is the Italian subsidiary of a United States firm. Discuss, with examples, ways in which such conflicts may be resolved. Note: Any pair of countries can be subsituted for Italy and the United States.

(3) Discuss the view that a country should curtail—
either incoming foreign investment
or outward foreign investment—
when faced with balance of payments problems

(4) Consider the kind of economic criteria which in your view ought to be established in developing economies for determining the amount and nature of multinational activity in those countries.

(5) Critically, examine the statement that direct investment has quantitatively more to offer than equivalent amounts of portfolio investment and foreign aid to recipient countries.

(6) In what ways are governments sensitive about political and economic power in the multinational companies?

(7) Outline and discuss proposals being made to control the activities of multinational companies.

(8) Identify some of the criticisms that are likely to be made against a large foreign chemical company operating in Latin America. Write a memorandum to the Group Chief Executive from a confidential adviser giving an appraisal of these criticisms and the extent to which they should be expected to influence corporate policies.

(9) Evidence indicates that host country controls on multinational business are increasing. Give reasons for this development and consider the kind of problem likely to arise from an intervention policy.

(10) It has been said that: 'More than any other body the IMF can claim to have been the guardian of international financial probity since the Second World War'. Do you agree? Give reasons for your answer.

16 Culture and Education

16.1 The elusive differences

'The need for comparative, cross-cultural research has long been emphasized. Equally, the difficulties of conducting such work on a meaningful basis have become apparent. Though the potential for such projects seems unlimited, the reality has been disappointing and much of the difficulty has arisen from either (*a*) the lack of adequate conceptual frameworks or (*b*) the severe logistical difficulties of conducting such work'.[1]

Understanding the different cultural systems in which business is carried on is often considered the most important skill for the international manager; but the search for a key to this understanding, as the above excerpt suggests, is often frustrating and elusive. Everyone is aware of national differences, but this awareness is compounded of many half truths and stereotypes. Facts are more difficult, and it is hard to be precise even about the meaning of the word culture.

In this chapter the word is being used in a broad sense of the bundle of attitudes, perceptions, memories, prejudices, and other guides to action which can be identified as characteristics of a particular group and which condition the direction of change in that group. The most obvious thing about culture is that it is always changing and this fact alone increases the elusiveness. For the purposes of studying international business, the interest is concentrated on differences between the culture in particular countries. But how are these differences isolated? There is a strong suspicion that some generalizations which are alleged to represent national differences actually reflect company size or type of ownership or some other variable which has got inextricably mixed with others, and in any case the particular combination of influencing factors is itself part of the culture being studied. Further there are differences within a country (regional, occupational, class) which may be more noteworthy than the differences between countries. The English miner and the German miner, for instance, may have more cultural resemblances through their occupation than they have differences as a result of nationality. The same may occur with many occupations, including managers. The professional manager is becoming increasingly internationalized and a force for cultural change himself as his professionalism increases.

The difficulties of identifying the cultural differences are only exceeded by the problems caused by ignoring them. The subject has considerable implications for the development of international management skills and there are other reasons for interest. The international firm itself provides a focus of study for cultural change, a framework for controlled observation. If social anthropologists could use the international company as a laboratory, management scientists could certainly make more use of the work of social anthropologists. Some of the confusion could be reduced considerably if the evidence painstakingly collected by students of management could be interpreted in a more convincing framework of anthropological theory.[2] Meanwhile this chapter will try to trace a path through some of the subjects to be considered in investigating cultural differences and give some guidance on issues of concern to the international manager. If some of the guidance is still by 'rule of thumb', this stems from the present state of the art.

One writing[3] which surveys the management literature on this subject detects three schools of thought. One is called 'universality' where the view is taken that cultural differences are unimportant. The activity of management is the same throughout the world and so are the conditioning factors. Local variations are determined by differences of style or situation rather than culture. The second school is called 'cultural cluster' and takes the opposite view. Managers bring their beliefs and values to their activity and conduct it accordingly. The third school is labelled 'economic cluster' and claims that the level of industrial and economic development in a country is the main influence on managerial behaviour. Each school emphasizes points which have to be considered in constructing a general theory. The stage of economic development of the country and of the professional development of its management cadre are influencing factors, and the significance of some of the 'cultural clusters' are being reduced as managers in one country learn from another. The study in question shows a preference, nevertheless, for the latter approach. In the following pages little support is evidenced for the universalist assumptions which may produce more problems than are solved as superficial resemblances are pressed into support for minimizing the cultural differences. Undoubtedly there is much to be learnt by one culture from another in tackling the problems of industrialization, but the universalist view suggests that the learning is all one way. Who is to say with present evidence whether the American emphasis on individual responsibility is more effective than the Japanese on group decision-making in either or both countries? Or vice versa? It may be that one method or the other will eventually be found to be more effective for all mankind, but the more reasonable assumption in the present state of knowledge is that each is effective in its own cultural setting. There appears to be, however, a number of questions in the issues discussed in these pages that are related to the stage of development of an industrial society. If group responsibility is a culture bound characteristic the transition from family management, appointment by inheritance, to professional management, appointment by qualifications, does seem to be universal. Although there may be evidence that in some advanced industrial societies the divorce between ownership and management has not gone as far as is sometimes assumed, the trend is surely unmistakable.

Each subject listed below can be viewed in terms of a spectrum from extreme similarities between the way the particular subject is developed in one country or another to extreme differences; there is also a direction of change. A general summary of the most convincing evidence currently available is attempted in the rest of this chapter. But first it must be pointed out that the concern with cultural differences, apart from their interest in their own right, is related to both the problems of general management and those of marketing and that conceptually these are distinct. For general management cultural differences mean those issues that need to be recognized for the way they affect the motivation and control of subordinates in other countries; styles and techniques are both involved inasmuch as they impinge upon value systems. The marketing aspect is not just concerned with relations with subordinates abroad, even in the marketing function; the concept here is of a bundle of changing demands and expectations on the part of the consumer which again vary from country to country.[4] The effects of the demands and expectations may be difficult to assess and sometimes contradictory. For some products local prejudices are important, for other products a foreign label may be preferred. Food and drink is an industry which comes on both sides of that distinction, and success and failure may be closely related to identifying changing cultural attitudes. The obtaining of government contracts will often involve considerable perceptiveness as to what is important to the legislators and voters in the country. Most of the issues discussed below have both marketing and management implications. The issues have been chosen because they are both relevant and frequently mentioned: motivation including attitudes to work and money, authority and stratification, family and sex, and a whole range of social beliefs and practices.

Attitudes to work and money demonstrate motivations which affect both management and marketing policies. They also represent issues on which there are many beliefs which have no substance but prejudice. Some beliefs have no substance at all. Companies which have developed international productivity comparisons with some degree of sophistication have demonstrated to themselves that views deeply ingrained in managers about levels of work in different countries are untrue. But this does not mean that more effective management can change the approach to work at will in a situation where leisure is highly valued. Managers themselves appear to say 'enough is enough' at different levels of salary and of work load in different countries. Attitudes to leisure vary from country to country; higher incomes may produce more work or more spare time. The work ethic means in effect that excessive preoccupation with work is considered a virtue in some parts of the world and a vice in others. As a result different types of appeal, reward and penalty, are effective in different cultures; but even beside this cautious and general statement there must be placed some reservations. One is that studies of morale in different countries[5] show this to be a complex variable; motivation depends on numerous factors, some of which may be only slightly influenced by national cultural traditions. Another observation about attitudes to work and money is that the national situation must be considered. The willingness to work and the acceptability of certain products will be different in times of war than in peace, and may be affected by other national crises as well. Further the labour situation will affect the demand for labour-saving equipment both in factory machinery and in domestic goods.

Most managers everywhere regard themselves as pragmatic in outlook. This seems to be a generalization that a wide assortment of writers allow themselves, but even so the alleged pragmatic approach can lead to a number of different results. Three studies of Indian and United States managers showed, for instance, that the former opted for strategies which led to optimum results but with high risk; the American managers preferred lower risk and lower expected pay-off.[6] Other studies[7] show that managers rate their subordinates in contrasting ways in different countries. In particular the differences within an occupation are greater in Western countries than in some developing countries, although differences between occupations may be greater in the developing countries.

The second group of issues is covered by words like authority and stratification. The factors which determine a person's role and expectations in society vary considerably between cultures, but again the stage of industrialization may be as important as the cultural traditions; at least the two influence one another. Stratification is a word that is used as loosely as culture. It may refer to the prestige in a society of various groups selected because of their hereditary or religious standing or because of their wealth, occupation or education; any combination of these factors can be found. In considering the environment of international management information is required on the usual means of recruiting for different occupations within a particular country, the provision of education, the availability of suitable people for conducting the business, and the life styles of the people in the different classes. To this should be added the nature of the class distinctions, how rigid are they and how socially mobile is the population.

It has been pointed out that in a traditional industrialized society, the labour demand is roughly triangular.[8] There is a narrow peak of top management broadening rapidly with a wide base of semi-skilled and unskilled workers. During the process of the industrial revolution, the societies concerned developed a supply of labour which roughly corresponded to the demand. The peak of the supply triangle may have been narrower than the demand, and there may have been some identations lower down especially among the skilled occupations; but the labour required was usually available, albeit the reverse was not always true. In times of economic depression supply was ahead of demand especially at the bottom. The sizes of the triangles may have been different, but the shape was normally the same. The traditional non-industrialized society had a labour requirement which could be compared to an inverted T, with a narrow band of leaders and middle classes and a large number of peasants and workers at the bottom. The process of industrialization, as the country develops, produces a labour demand of the same triangular shape as that of the traditional industrialized countries, but some societies have much more difficulty than others in producing a labour supply that matches the new requirement. Countries in the Far East and in the socialist bloc seem to have found this transition easier than those in other parts of the world. There is a tendency in many cultures to produce bulges in the original upright of the T rather than a triangle. Thus there may develop a surplus of people with advanced qualifications and a total lack of skilled workers or even of people capable of filling lower managerial positions. Interestingly the labour supply in some of the industrialized countries, notably the United States but also to a certain extent in Britain, is beginning to acquire a similar shape. The triangular demand remains: the requirement exceeds the supply at the top, but a little lower the supply is exceeding the demand at least in certain professions. Below that again, among skilled workers and certain semi-professions, the demand runs ahead even in times of unemployment. At times of economic expansion the economy is increasingly constrained by severe shortages of trained electricians, mechanics, plumbers, typists and others. Among the unskilled, unemployment remains endemic in spite of forecasts to the contrary going back to the first days of compulsory education. The base of the demand triangle is narrowing all the time. Companies which have invested with inadequate knowledge of the type of labour available have met trouble.

Much has been written about the price of labour as an incentive to companies to move to certain countries; the availability of labour capable of exercising the levels of responsibility and skill required by the firm may be more important. If the home country can no longer supply the junior supervisors and skilled workers required, there may be few countries that can do so. Hence the search is limited.

The class structure of society and the factors by which it is shaped determine the respective status of different professions and with it the shape of the customer market as well as the allocation of jobs. A society without too many constraints on social mobility may give prestige to the teaching profession and a larger part of the national income will be spent on educational equipment than in a society which is more rigidly stratified. Educational institutions may be resented in countries where children are regarded as a source of income. Other countries, by no means always the same ones, will be opposed to welfare support for adults. The subject of education also brings up methods of managerial training; these have proved less transferable across frontiers than other management techniques. Some American techniques of sensitivity training, for instance, have been strongly criticized in Africa where they have been regarded as aimed at inhibitions which are irrelevant or non-existent. This is just one example of a culture-bound method of training.

There has been a tendency in some countries to a more participative management system which is also centralized. In countries where the military class has high prestige, a disciplined but decentralized system may prevail. Indeed the society where the armed forces are comparatively little integrated with the rest of the population has differences in management style and market development all too little studied. It is clear that military regimes incline to a paternalistic attitude; they do not favour the hire and fire outlooks they find in foreign firms, eager as they often are to co-operate with foreign businessmen.

A study quoted earlier also shed light on the exercise of authority by managers in different countries.[9] It shows that out of 90 comparative investigations of managerial styles carried out internationally before 1970, the overwhelming majority emphasized the differences rather than the resemblances; and some writers have specifically warned against the dangers of reading too much into the occasional success of a company which sets out to ignore the national differences or pretends that they do not exist.[10] The one common feature that many managers show under questioning is a preference for a less authoritarian system than the one they actually have, but there the resemblance ends. Questions about whether managers think their subordinates wish for more responsibility or not are answered very differently in different countries, as are questions about the reliability and trustworthiness of subordinates. Deference is a virtue in some countries, while phrases like 'to stand on your own feet' are used to express desirable attitudes in others. Favoured management styles are affected by such differences.

A characteristic that seems to be universal is the move from the family firm to professional management. Not only does this happen almost everywhere, but similar accounts of the problems involved creep into the literature as well as the legends of more and more countries. The professional manager is always described as having a hard struggle to establish himself against the entrenched family, however impoverished in mind and money. This is another example of a universal resemblance hiding numerous differences of which the international manager has to take account. Where the extended family [11] still provides its own social security system, business ownership and leadership will be serving many other purposes than providing income for shareholders. Foreign companies embarking on joint ventures in countries where this applies often misunderstand what is at stake. Alien managers may ridicule the need to find jobs for the family, they overlook the fact that they are dealing with a social unit that is not just a business concern. Equally labour costs will be higher where social security has to be paid for outside the firm, but wages may be lower in the totally paternalistic society. Expectations may also be lower and many consumer goods may be unsaleable.

Other cultures, besides those where the extended family is strong, may have prejudices against labour saving devices in the home and the spending power of the women and the young people will be limited. Strongly held social and religious beliefs resist changes which industrialization might otherwise be expected to bring. Different allocations of job by religion, sex, region, race, tribe or other such considerations and the pace and direction of change in different countries are a significant part of the international management environment. Tradition gives rise to a number of other subtle considerations which were discussed some years ago in a book called *The Silent Language*.[12] The phrase refers to the unspoken differences which identify cultural differences, from matters of observances and taboos to less significant but noticeable questions like the time taken to answer a letter. In some cultures an important issue is dealt with immediately; in others promptness is taken as a sign that the matter is regarded as unimportant, the time taken must correspond with the gravity of the issue. An aspect of the silent language may be the volume of communication that takes place between managers at all in a particular country. It has been shown, for instance, that there are considerable differences in the rate of interaction between managers in different countries.[13]

The discussion can be summed up by saying that there are differences in the cultural environment between one country and another which are hard to identify and constantly in a state of change. Nevertheless the skilled international manager understands and respects them. With all the prejudices and travellers' tales which bedevil the understanding, some key issues do need attention when framing an international management system or developing a market. The differences are as easily exaggerated as they are underestimated, and the reactions of companies vary from serious attempts to take the colour of their surroundings to brash efforts to be conspicuous. As with national frontiers, the boundaries of culture have a way of reasserting themselves even when they are expected to disappear.

16.2 Suggestions for further reading

There have been many studies of management across cultural boundaries, the reader may like to consult:

(C) BODDEWYN, J. (Ed.) (1970). *Comparative Management: Teaching, Training and Research*, New York University: Graduate School of Business Administration. A collection of essays giving a clear overview of existing work on the subject at the time of publication and setting lines for future development.

(C) FARMER, R. N. & RICHMAN, B. M. (1976). *International Management: An Operational Theory*, Cedarwood Press, 2nd edn. The first edition of this book was a landmark in such studies.

(C) HARBISON, F. & MYERS, C. A. (1959). *Management in the Industrial World: An International Analysis*, McGraw-Hill. This was a pioneer collection of management studies. It has been said that: 'their country chapters are deceptively simple but actually require very good knowledge of management and its environment in the country studied, as well as familiarity with the local literature, . . .' Boddewyn (1970) see above.

(C) NEGANDHI, A. R. & PRASAD, S. B. (1972). *The Frightening Angels*, Kent State University.

The reader may also like to refer to:

(B) HALL, D. *et al.* (1969). The European elite, pp. 45–55, *European Business*, October.

(C) LITVAK, I. A. & MAULE, C. J. (1976). Comparative technical entrepreneurship: some perspectives. pp. 31–38, *Journal of International Business Studies*, Spring.

(C) TOYNE, B. (1976). Host country managers of multinational firms: an evaluation of variables affecting their managerial thinking patterns, *Journal of International Business Studies*.

(C) VANSINA, L. S. (1971). Integrating different nationality groups, chapter VI of THIAGARAJAM, K. M. *et al.* (1971). *Managing the Multinationals: A Behavioural Approach*, Prentice-Hall: London & New York.

A survey of the literature on an important aspect of the subject is:

(D) HESSELING, P. (1971). *Organizational Behaviour and Culture: The Case of the Multinational Enterprise,* Van Gorcum.

For a thorough survey of management in different cultural systems, see:

(D) ENGLAND, G. W. *et al.* (1974), The Manager and the Man: A Cross-Cultural Study of personal Values, *Organization and Administrative Sciences,* **5.2**, Summer.

Management Education is an aspect of this subject not discussed in this chapter. The provision varies considerably even in industrialized countries as does the type of institution where management education is conducted. There is considerable international cross-fertilization. An account of management development in different environments is:

MASSEY, J. L. & LUYTJES, J. (Eds) (1972). *Management in an International Context*, Harper & Row: London & New York.

16.3 Questions for discussion

(1) 'Comparative management stands between theory and practice as:
   (*a*) it borrows from and contributes to our systematic knowledge of management and organization theory . . .' and
   (*b*) is relevant for the training and effectiveness of managers'.
   (Jean Boddewyn). Discuss this view of the value of studying management in different cultural settings.

(2) Outline the main features that should be noted about the local culture by a company going into a foreign country of your choice. Both management and marketing issues should be considered.

(3) 'And, at the same time, comparative management studies add to fundamental knowledge in the behavioural sciences by allowing for more diversity and variation in how problems are handled, decisions made and controls affected by managers from differing cultures'. Discuss.

(4) Discuss the development of international management, and the extent if any to which you think there is going to be a disappearance of cultural differences in the profession.

(5) Outline the provision for management education and the main differences between countries (select three specific countries for discussion).

(6) 'The multinational firm no longer has to pay any serious attention to the so-called *cultural differences*'. Discuss.

(7) Compare and contrast some of the evidence available on styles and

patterns of management in different countries.

(8) Identify and illustrate some of the main features that the marketing manager has to look out for when commencing operations in a new country in consumer goods.

17 The Reputation of the Multinational

17.1 An increasingly hostile environment

Criticism of multinational companies has become increasingly widespread in recent years, based on a wide spectrum of evidence ranging from the historical to the hysterical and from hard fact to pure fantasy. The hard-pressed manager may feel himself oppressed by critics who are implacably hostile without attempting to understand his approach to his job or the pressures under which he labours. He may feel himself misled by unhelpful and censorious criticism; he may, on the other hand, be equally misled by his friends who deny problems where they do exist and induce a deceptive complacency. From the managerial point of view, the climate of opinion can be discussed under three categories:

(1) The view of those who are hostile to business as such, and attack the multinational firm as a suitable target; no action on the part of managers would alter their opinions.

(2) The views of those who encounter or understand the problems and have things to say which can be translated into action by the companies.

(3) The views of those who are deeply committed ideologically to the support of big business and are not always sensitive to the difficulties.

The first two on the above list are not easy to disentangle. A senior executive of one of the best known of the multinationals[1] expressed the changing attitude of youth towards business thus:

'A corporation is a business structure whose sole reason for existence is the earning of profits by manufacturing products for as little as possible and selling them for as much as possible. It does not matter whether the product does good or evil, what counts is that it be consumed—in ever-increasing quantities. Since everything the corporation does has, as its ultimate goal, the creation of profit, it offers its workers no deep personal satisfactions, no feeling of contributing anything worthwhile to society, no true meaning to their activities. Go to work for a corporation and you are, through good salaries and various fringe benefits, installed as a faceless link in the lengthening chain—completing the circle by becoming one more consumer of all their junk. And, like all circles, the whole structure signifies nothing.'

The above approach is essentially ecological, emphasizing consumption of resources and the quality of life aspects of work. Another major approach is political in that it attacks not production and consumption themselves but the ownership of production and the distribution of the power to consume. It attacks business as primarily an exploiter of labour rather than resources.

Criticisms of business, capitalism or private ownership are thus both broad and well-known. The particular issues relating to multinationals are more narrow and, in many cases, more complex in terms of detailed understanding. Nevertheless a phrase like 'transfer pricing' can now evoke hostility in circles where it would have had no meaning at all a short time ago.

Multinationals are particularly vulnerable to criticism for obvious reasons: they are often pervasive and conspicuous, they are a readily identifiable group, they are owned by foreigners, and their use of expatriate managers identified with a headquarters overseas can arouse feelings of hostility in the host country. In short the multinational can provide a scapegoat for dissatisfactions or shortcomings in the domestic situation.

Criticisms include: absentee decision-making, inter-country conflicts of interest, exports of jobs, tax avoidance, transfer pricing, labour relations problems, lack of disclosure, tendencies towards monopoly, inappropriate technology transfer and bribery. The problem of categorization is clear from this list in that labour relations problems, lack of disclosure and anti-trust questions among other examples, are by no means exclusive to the multinationals but within these headings there are aspects which are unique to international operations.

The critics themselves differ markedly in outlook, motivation and influence but often raise the same points to substantiate their comments. Thus for any individual point of criticism, no one 'solution' could ever satisfy all the commentators. There are those on the left who would be dissatisfied with anything short of the overthrow of capitalism. In such a context the usual criticisms of multinationals invariably appear but international business is merely singled out as the ultimate form of capitalism and no amount of external affairs effort and expenditure on the part of companies will change such a view where it is firmly held. Similarly a minority on the right may criticise foreign ownership of industry on purely chauvinist grounds. Such an emotionally based attitude tends not to be receptive to countervailing arguments. Between these two extremes is a core of critics who seek changes short of total disruption, but not necessarily the same changes.

The broad case of multinational involvement in the third world provides a good example. A number of critics, notably church groups in America, are urging companies to increase their involvement in developing countries in order to help alienate the problems of poverty. Their capacity to do so is stressed by one authority[2]:

'The multinational company in a sense invents opportunities and, through its vision and its knowledge, creates projects by focusing resources of capital and technology where nothing existed before. There is no substitute for the crucible of experience, which only the multinational company can provide.'

There are plenty of examples of an opposing view, including:

'The multinationals, whether they know it or not, are firmly on the side of inequality, forming a deadly alliance with corruptible third world elites.'[3]

The increase in African infant mortality resulting from the introduction by multinationals of Western style baby foods is cited as one example of the harm which can result from international business activity in developing countries. Qualifying the criticism somewhat, the same author believes that asking multinationals:

'to contribute positively to the development of the Third World is to ask them to perform a task for which they were not designed. They are motivated by money and yet we critics are asking them to develop goods for a part of the world which is still predominantly outside the market economy.'

More radical critics go even further, arguing that there is no place for western multinationals in the underdeveloped world.

'Les pays sous-developpés ont tout à perdre en collaborant avec le "social-impérialisme".'[4]

Multinationals are damned if they do not involve themselves in the Third World and equally damned, by others, if they do.

Critics on the left of centre have expressed concern over the financial power of multinationals to manipulate currency fluctuations to the detriment of government interests. However, we also find a right wing critic stressing the weakness of individual governments in terms of staffing and capacity for action in contrast with the control and sophistication available to companies.[5]

Technology transfer raises different points from different critics. An executive of the Inter-American Development Bank accuses multinationals of selling to developing countries:

'processes which elsewhere are being abandoned or on the verge of being abandoned.'[6]

Others take the line of the Intermediate Technology Group which criticises the transfer of modern, capital-intensive technology since it does not create the jobs needed in the Third World. In this case it is important to identify the real issue, which is the price asked by the companies for technology which may be obsolete in the industrialized world.

Yet other critics condemn what they call 'runaway companies': those which move from one country to another seeking cheap labour. These critics fall into groups around those whose concern is to improve the wages, working conditions and trade union representation of the host country workers and those seeking protection for the home economy of the multinational. In the latter group, none are more vociferous than the AFL–CIO[7] which has described the multinationals as

'a modern day dinosaur which eats the jobs of American workers.'

These examples serve to illustrate the point that the critics are far from homogenous as a group. A similar situation obtains with governments, both home and host, and their views on the ideal relationship with the multinationals. The United States government in particular has had a contorted relationship with international business from antitrust to security considerations on the negative side whilst seeking to use some elements of multinationals in a quasi-ambassadorial role or as an extension of foreign policy on the positive side.

Many criticisms have a very poor basis in fact, but lack of evidence has more often played into the hands of the critics, as have historical precedents. The onus is clearly on the side of the companies to prove that times have changed since the 1920s when a United Fruit manager in Honduras could write:

'We must produce a disembowelment of the incipient economy of the country in order to increase and help our aims. We have to prolong its tragic, tormented, and revolutionary life; the wind must blow only on our sails, and the water must only wet our keel.'[8]

Indeed today the task of the critics is made, on the surface at least, easier than it might otherwise be by their ability to quote a small number of celebrated examples in support of their arguments. This area of business behaviour and attitudes raises the most difficult and controversial questions in the field of multinational company reputation. Some company names have come to act as trigger phrases to some of the critics: ITT in Chile and Gulf Oil in Angola have evoked ideas of excessive political interference. Lonrho is associated with the use of tax havens. Hoffman-LaRoche sparks off the transfer pricing debate. Rio Tino Zinc antagonizes the environmental lobby. Kodak, Nestlé or IBM are associated with questions of trade union recognition. Oil companies have been in the forefront of the bribery debate as have aircraft manufacturers like Lockheed, whilst electronics companies raise the issue of exporting jobs to countries where labour is cheap.

Many critics look no further than these few cases in their attacks on multinationals. Many audiences are satisfied with these few names as evidence that multinationals should be the objects of suspicion, investigation or legislation. It could be argued that these examples conceal the most important criticism. This is not that companies involve themselves in occasional subversive activity but that they constantly influence national economic policies by accident or by design (see chapter 15). Within a climate of suspicion it is far from easy for companies to defend themselves convincingly.

Some undertakings are particularly vulnerable:

'Why then is RTZ so unpopular? The answer probably lies in the remark by Duncan . . ., that "taking wealth out of the soil is an emotional business". The mining and smelting of minerals appears as theft of the soil. It is clearly visible and, in the case of smelting, all too smellable. Not all Duncan's charm and public relations advisors will ever make RTZ loved.'[9]

Public relations activities have also backfired badly. In late 1973 ITT placed an advertisement in *Business Week* proclaiming:

'Jobs make people independent and secure.'
'Creating jobs for people is what we do best.'
'And that, we submit, is our first and most important social responsibility.'

The same issue of the magazine carried a major article on ITT analysing its activities, subsidiary by subsidiary, including repeated references to 'massive lay-offs', 'whittling down employment' and redundancies at worker level. The article further stressed that managers are rarely fired but kept on the payroll often in honorary or consultant functions as are directors of acquired companies.[10]

It is difficult enough for named companies to defend themselves, it is a doubly formidable task for other multinationals who suffer from implied attacks. A 'thin end of the wedge' situation applies in which the sins of the few are attributed to many since multinationals are such a readily identifiable group. If some multinationals are *known* to use bribes, others are *assumed* to do so. A multinational is guilty until proved innocent.

Whilst corporate social responsibility programmes are clearly laudable in themselves, their contribution to the overall reputation of multinationals is strictly limited. Such programmes can be dismissed by critics as public relations exercises or diversionary tactics to steer attention away from other, less reputable, activities.

Increased disclosure, of a meaningful kind, is the cornerstone of a number of proposed codes of conduct for multinationals and could provide the key to future corporate reputation. It can be argued that the real significance of the Securities Exchange Commission investigation into bribery is not the evidence that payments were made but the fact that the funds involved, often considerable, never appeared in the accounts of the companies concerned. Again the 'thin end of the wedge' might be assumed: if secret accounts can be maintained for one purpose, they can exist for others. How can shareholders, governments or other interest groups support or condemn the activities of corporations if the information at their disposal is inadequate or distorted?

The impact of access to both information and personalities on one professor making a study tour of multinationals has been described:

'Well, he said, when I started this project I was convinced that the multinational companies were indeed a serious threat to world peace and to the soveriegnty of nations, but in the course of the interviews I've had in Europe and the US I've changed my mind completely.'[11]

The final, and perhaps most important, question is the attitude of business to business itself:

'What impresses me most in examining intercorporate relationships is not centralized control, banker or otherwise, but the network of personal and business affiliations and contacts and the mutually supportive character of so much of the business system ... One can deduce that activities carried out by substantial business firms, no matter how odious, will not be subject to open criticism by important businessmen who are part of the corporate-banking network. If Dow, General Electric Honeywell, North American Rockwell and other major Vietnam war suppliers were to produce gas chambers under contract with the Pentagon, their decisions would be accepted in silence by the community of leading business firms.'[12]

Corporate responses to criticisms of multinationals have tended to concentrate on the benefits which companies can bring to host and home countries, on social responsibility projects undertaken by companies and on denials by individual companies that they are involved in activities like tax evasion or abuse of transfer prices. As we have seen, there is a credibility problem with all of these strategies and the tide of criticism is still rising. As suggested above the business community has consciously or unconsciously relied on a united front of group solidarity in the face of its critics. When commenting on the positive aspects of international business, company spokesmen refer to multinationals as a group in the same way that critics do in their attacks. The negative aspects of the behaviour of some companies are ignored, implying tacit acceptance by business commentators. This approach may no longer be viable for a company concerned to behave as a 'good citizen' and to be seen as such. It will, in future, be necessary not only to deny bad corporate behaviour on the part of one's own organization but also to condemn that behaviour on the part of others.

This may seem unrealistic at a time when many see a closing of ranks on the part of business as the optimum strategy in a hostile world. It can never be easy in a world economy where many companies supply goods and services to other companies and many congolmerates have highly diversified interests, for an individual enterprise publicly to comment on or dissociate itself from the activities of another. It is, however, the concerted power of multinationals working together which is the prime cause of concern to many political and economic commentators as well as an increasing number of host governments. Some fragmentation of international business solidarity may well occur if there is a rise of the kind of political power suggested by a French socialist leader:

'Il est certain que, face à un pouvoir economique multinational, seul un pouvoir politique de même envergure est en mesure de proposer un système, d'abord de défense, ensuite de conquête et de pouvoir pour l'ensemble des travailleurs . . .'[13]

This might be regarded as wishful thinking.

The points made above suggest some reasons why even companies capable of commanding the most skilled public relations services in the world have acquired such a dubious reputation. Part of the answer must be to interpret the criticisms in the way this chapter does and thus isolate those on which action can and should be taken. Another part of the answer lies in the decision-making process in the firm. Intentions are not translated into facts and unnecessary problems are caused by too little attention to formal and informal communications. A particular problem is the role of top management in the foreign subsidary. If a needlessly difficult position is created here, then the company's natural champions will speak without conviction. Action at this point might be the most significant single contribution a company could make to improving its reputation. Meanwhile some companies have taken action to establish better relations with their environment, the next section describes the new measures.

17.2 The corporate response

Managers have grown increasingly bewildered by the climate of opinion.

They have been put on the defensive by their critics, but also feel that they are working hard and at great self-sacrifice to enrich the general public, including those critics. The managers feel that the benefits that their corporations are bringing in improved life-styles are not sufficiently recognised or publicized. They know that the popular picture of monolithic and faceless corporations does not fit the facts of the life they live—underestimating the human and individual elements as well as the inhuman pressures. Even trade union leaders are known to demand information from companies, the collection and assembly of which would increase these pressures and cause discontent among their white collar members working for the same companies.[14]

Senior managers in foreign subsidiaries find themselves exercising considerable ingenuity to avoid conflict with local interests. Nevertheless they are often conscious of conflicting demands, which come from inside the company as well as from outside. The manager knows that if he falls seriously foul of the local government, for instance, he will lose his job; on the other hand he is working for an organization geared to the interests of the centre, so his career equally depends on taking actions which cannot always favour his country, or the country of his temporary adoption if he is an expatriate. The manager is also likely to believe that the advantages his business brings to the country outweigh many of the drawbacks that he also knows about. As a result his opinion inside the company will favour two responses: the adoption of a 'good citizen' policy in support of the local community and public relations exercises aimed to present the company in a favourable light.

A few large companies have institutionalized this response in a new department. This development has occurred mainly in American firms, and with some false starts and teething troubles. The department may have a name like Corporate External Affairs; its function is to deal with the non-commercial aspects of the environment, and to deal with them in a more comprehensive manner than a publicity department would. Indeed external relations absorbs public relations in a wider concept as marketing does sales or finance accounting. The making of a new department to integrate and develop all those previously fragmented decisions which included company patronage for educational, charitable or leisure activities as well as publicity and the improvement of the corporate image. But the new function goes further in attempting to feed back into the company relevant messages picked up from the 'climate of opinion' discussed in this chapter. The collection of these 'messages'—the *non-market research* as it might be called—can itself be a difficult task, demanding a considerable exercise of judgment. Available evidence is inadequate and ranges from public opinion polls, reflecting what may be a transitory view of a specific and slanted issue, to exercises in futurology which are substantial even if based on inadequate tools.[15]

The external affairs function recognizes the significance of the fact that the company exists in multiple environments, and that the long-term interests of the company involve establishing satisfactory relationships with the interest groups which make up the various environments. Once again this can be compared with the emergence of the marketing function based, as it was, on insights into the need for a new relationship between the company and the customer. It is now recognized that business normally starts from what the customer wants to buy rather than what the company wants to sell, and that competitive advantages flow from this attitude. Similarly the future operation of companies will depend upon starting from what the community wants or needs, and that the very ability to continue to do business depends upon this insight. The analogy with marketing breaks down at some point; for ineffective marketing normally only affects the company concerned; external relations affect multinational companies as a group.

17.3 One company's case

A lucid presentation of a company case was made by a director of BASF in evidence before a German parliamentary committee.[16] His points may be summarized:

(1) The companies bring advanced technology, capital and organizing ability to their host countries; by this means they are able to add much greater value to host country resources of materials and manpower than would otherwise have been the case. The bulk of this added value stays in the host country in the form of wages and purchases of materials and services from local suppliers. Relatively little is exported as dividends and interest payments.

(2) The companies provide host countries with access to overseas markets which local business would be unable to reach.

(3) The technology and management skills which the companies bring to the country spread to competitors and to government.

(4) International companies pay high wages—at least relative to the prevailing local standards and may often provide the only chance of secure well paid employment in a region. Welfare, medical care and safety standards are high, often far above those enjoyed by the rest of the population. These standards are eventually forced on local employers. In remote areas companies often provide housing, roads and schools—which eventually pass to the host country.

(5) International companies are generally law abiding, often more so

than the local business community. They not infrequently have to deal with corrupt governments.

(6) Native born staff are progressively trained and promoted into virtually all levels in the affiliates. They are given experience in other countries.

(7) Standards of safety, product quality and environmental protection are heavily influenced by home country practice. A company making technically advanced items which has to move intermediate products from one country to another simply cannot afford the confusion which would arise from multiple standards.

The same company was involved in a celebrated case in the United States. The State of South Carolina, as part of its policy of encouraging foreign investment to help cure a problem of chronic unemployment, persuaded BASF to consider building a large chemical complex on the coast. The proposal was strongly opposed by property developers in an area which contained an expensive holiday resort and also by fishermen. In support was the State government, which was to provide necessary communications in the form of roads and a railway, and the local authorities in an area of high unemployment. Eventually the controversy became national with organizations like the Friends of the Earth against and the National Association for the Advancement of Coloured Peoples strongly in favour. In face of the controversy the company withdrew.[17]

17.4 Suggestions for further reading

Many of the books on company-government relations are also relevant to this chapter.

Among the constructive critics, those making points about which action can be taken, the most readable are:

(B) BARNET, R. & MUELLER, R. (1975). *Global Reach*, Simon & Shuster (English edition Jonathon Cape: London).
(B) GEORGE, Susan (1976). *How the Other Half Dies,* Penguin.
(B) SERVAN-SCHREIBER, J. J. (1967). *Le Défi Amèricain*, Editions Denöel.
(B) TUGENDHAT, C. (1971), *The Multinationals*. Penguin.

The publication of *Global Reach* produced numerous replies, including:

(B) *A Critical Commentary on 'Global Reach'*, (1975). Center for Multinational Studies.

Among critical commentaries see also:

(C) *Multinational Enterprises and Social Policy*, (1973). International Labour Office.

Among defences by businessmen are:

(B) SPENCER, W. I. (1975). Who controls MNC's? *Harvard Business Review*, Nov. This article takes the form of an interview with Mr Spencer of Citicorp.
(B) VELMANS, L. A. (1976). Multinational corporations: target for attack, *Financial Executive*, Feb. Mr Velmans is vice-president of the Hill and Knowlton International Corporation.

Writings on the External Affairs Department include:

(B) BODDEWYN, J. J. (1974). The development of external relations by American multinational enterprises, in Sethi & Holton (1974).
(C) BODDEWYN, J. J. (1975). Organizing for corporate external affairs in Europe, *Business International.*

Two research surveys could also be consulted:

BODDEWYN, J. J. (undated). *The External Affairs of Transnational Firms: A Research Note.* Baruch College, City University of New York. This paper surveys the relevant literature.
WEBER, J. A. (1975). Notes on the External Relations Function of US Based Multinational Corporations, *Conference Papers.* Academy of International Business Annual Meeting.

17.5 Questions for discussion

(1) Suggest and evaluate reasons why international business is more likely than domestic to be affected by changes outside the company.
(2) What are criticisms of the companies currently being made which might be expected to influence corporate policies?
(3) Suggest some guidelines for the establishment of a corporate external affairs department.
(4) Discuss the advantages and disadvantages of establishing an external affairs department.
(5) Comment critically on the use of the phrase 'corporate social responsibility'.

18 The Future of International Business

The *Global Shopping Centre*[1] is a phrase that will continue to be heard. Indeed the one safe prediction about international business is that its volume will continue to increase. Short of a holocaust which will render any prediction meaningless, the movement of goods and money around the world in ever larger quantities is an irreversible trend which will only ultimately be limited by transportation and other communications problems. Every other prediction is hazardous. In this chapter a number of subjects are listed which are likely to change within the next twenty years. The approach here is to identify and discuss some landmarks of the future; the more fashionable approach through scenarios is not used because it would carry the discussion beyond the confines of this book. Nevertheless the landmarks can be more meaningfully discussed in groupings which show their interactions, and readers may well like to devise their own scenarios from the issues suggested:

18.1 Rich and poor: a new division of labour

It now seems less likely than it did in 1974 that there are going to be radical changes as between the rich and poor nations. No doubt some will move up the list of countries arranged in order of gross national product per head and others will move down; but major reshuffles are unlikely to be caused by oil and other commodity price changes. Long term world dependences on one substance seems unlikely; even if the commodity was inexhaustible, substitutes are likely to be found, and the process of industrialization usually proves slower than the expectation. But, given the first point about rich and poor, a new international division of labour does seem probable. This will be ensured by a combination of government action to encourage local manufacturers, in industrial as well as less developed countries, and of corporate policies to cut the costs of manufacture. Even if labour costs do rise relatively fast in countries which currently manufacture labour intensive electronic equipment, and even if the manufacturing process becomes less labour intensive, the skills and aptitudes will have been built up in the new centres of production. agriculture as well as industry is likely to share in the redrawing of the economic geography maps of the future. Indeed new methods of food production and changing tastes are likely to make some dramatic changes; already questions about feeding the world's population are changing into questions about selling the world's food.

18.2 Government and intergovernmental intervention: the fragmenting of international business

The trend to greater official intervention is likely to prove as irreversible as the trend to an increased volume of international business. But government intervention is a phrase which covers a number of different activities. Presumably the work being done on trade, currency exchange, investment codes and commodity prices will become more institutionalized and the flow of goods and money will be regulated accordingly. The main new element will be an increase in regional and other treaty organizations in an attempt to enrich or strengthen countries whose governments see themselves as having common interests. There is no reason to expect that this form of internationalism, which will affect marketing and logistic projects, will have any effect on those aspects of nationalism which will continue to influence management policies. There is the further consideration that, whatever happens to tariffs, non-tariff barriers are likely to become more important still. In particular health and safety laws will vary from country to country inhibiting the movement of an increasing range of goods from automobiles to pharmaceuticals, from sweets to machinery. More important, perhaps, will be rules about priority imports and part local manufacture which are one element of the increasing government intervention.

If some stabilization of the various international market places with intergovernmental bodies as arbitrators is likely, the direct intervention of governments is certain to increase. This will not only be in connection with the increasing regulation of national economies leading to the non-tariff barriers just mentioned; also involved will be more state enterprises and state support for national companies competing in the international field.

This trend, together with that towards stricter laws enforcing competition, will lead to a greater number of companies in international business; the greater interest of the socialist bloc, as well as the beginnings of foreign investment from less developed countries will ensure that there will be more investors as well as more traders. In the merger years of the 1960s the opposite trend was forecast. It was widely assumed that world business would be dominated by a limited number of companies[2]. Government pressures, in addition to the operation of powerful incentives to foreign investment within companies, are likely to make international business more fragmented. The giants may not disappear, although their relative growth will be limited, the proportion of business obtained by smaller firms will increase. The reaction to size and the questioning of the growth ethic are likely to be increasing features of the future. And this questioning, on commercial as well as on social grounds, is likely to be translated increasingly into corporate as well as national policies. The national policies of less developed countries, especially where strengthened by regional organizations, are likely to be increasingly hostile to the unregulated operation of the large organization. The rules will be different from the Anti-trust laws of the industrialized countries, they will concern conditions of investment and trade. This is said in spite of suggestions in chapter 15 that more countries were opening their doors to foreign investment. Liberalization and regulation will increasingly go together, and business strategies will need to accept this. The less developed countries are going to become more attractive as markets and so they can afford to fix more rigorous conditions. It must be recognized that phrases like 'the economies of scale' and 'the laws of comparative advantage', which western writers have elevated to the dignity of theories, are regarded as no more than crude political propaganda by many thinkers in the Third World. But the reaction against bigness is growing in the west, too, and with it a growing likelihood that relatively small companies in an increasing volume of activity are the pattern of the future. To provide these companies with the information and the strategic thinking needed to penetrate complex world markets, there will be a further increase in the demand for service industries.

18.3 Corporate policies: greater variety

The pressures are such that foreign investment is sure to increase along with trade. Companies will continue to follow competitors and customers, as suggested in chapter 3, even if they find the discouraging factors there described sufficient to prevent them starting abroad before others have led the way. These factors will ensure, however, an increasing use of other means of penetrating foreign markets, especially those which are designed to gain the advantages of investment without actually having to commit equity outside the home country. Management contracts are likely to spread rapidly and licensing and franchising arrangements will increasingly resemble these contracts with their total packages. This increasing use of the 'package' will lessen the gap, if it still exists, between the profitability of investment and that of licensing and is a corollary of the larger total number of companies already forecast. An increasing number of these will be small, specialist firms providing a system rather than a product. Part of the international division of labour will be an intensified swing to the service industries in the most industrialized countries. Their lead in technical and managerial knowhow will increase, thus making consultancy based on these countries saleable but absorbing even more of the skills which would otherwise go into production management.

The division of labour will be reflected in contractual arrangements by which companies in one country provide management, advisory and research services for companies in another, and in the siting of different units in a multinational group. Under both these arrangements there is likely to be a greater concentration of knowledge and decision-making. This may have political implications, there will certainly be implications for company organization. The foreign company, whatever its legal and financial relationship with the parent or contract partner, will have to have a more clearly defined place in the managerial system to compensate for loss of independence and autonomy. Another corollary of this development is greater attention to personnel policies which identify reward and locate able managers. Where the relationship is one of parent to subsidiary, the porportion of local shareholders will increase and policies will have to take account of this too.

The general dominance of more sophisticated policies, developed at the centre of a group however held together, will be especially true in the finance function. All the observable trends—greater inflation, higher interest rates, fluctuating currencies, higher corporate taxes—add up to advantages in the skilful sourcing of funds that will become even greater in the future. The global view will not grow less because of the critics, it will grow more subtle.

The above points are briefly stated because they summarize the main themes already discussed in this book. The future includes an increasing regulation of international business through international agreements and an increase of direct intervention by governments. One consequence of this intervention, and of the operation of normal commercial pressures as well, will be the increasing use of a variety of means of conducting foreign business especially the growth of knowledge agreements. Another consequence of government action, this time in part running counter to commercial considerations, will be the fragmentation of international firms and the emergence of larger numbers in an increasingly competitive environment. The companies themselves will need to react with growing sophistication in formulating strategies to take advantage of the widening range of opportunities, in framing systems of organization and communications more suited to the changing environment and especially in developing decision-making processes that meet both the opportunities and the problems.

18.4 Suggestions for further reading

Most of the general books on the subject risk only brief references to the future, but see:

(A) DANIELS, OGRAM & RADEBAUGH (1976) chapter 26. This deals with both trade and investment.

A specialized approach is provided by:

(C) BUCKLEY, P. J. & CASSON, M. (1976). *The Future of the Multinational Enterprise*, MacMillan. This book, like most of the articles on the subject, deals with the issues facing the investor rather than the trader.

The following is interesting from both points of view:

(B) HASS, H. van der (1967). *The Enterprise in Transition*, Tavistock: London.

18.5 Exercises and questions for this chapter

Early in the chapter it is said that 'readers may well like to devise their own scenarios from the issues suggested'. Groups of readers or course members may like to consider situations like:

(1) A future with accelerating inflation rates in most countries (nowhere less than 8% and an average of 15% in the main trading nations) and interest rates, increasing protectionism between trading blocs, and increasing foreign manufacture by companies and trade between subsidiaries. The effects on the environment, especially government reactions, and the effects on the corporate management system should be considered.

The probable effect if any one of the above factors does not increase or accelerate could also be discussed.

(2) A future with intense competition between trading blocs (the EEC, COMECON, North America, Latin America, East Africa, West Africa, the Middle East, South East Asia, for example) should be considered. Assume that each bloc will be offering constraints and incentives for trade and investment both outwards and inwards designed to further the commercial and personal interests of citizens of member countries.

(3) Assume that the relative positions of different countries remain the same and that the international framework would not alter greatly,

and assess likely changes in company and government policies in a situation of limited change. Estimate the conditions which could make the limited change situation untenable.

Then make assumptions of radical change in individual countries and see how these are likely to change the scene.

(4) Identify one issue which, in your opinion, can reasonably be considered a 'landmark of the future' with regard to international business. Present a general review of the selected issue.

Appendix I
Courses on International Business

For convenience of presentation each course has been divided into ten sessions. The length of each session can be varied to suit the particular teacher of the class, from a one hour presentation to a six month simulation exercise. Similarly the level of sophistication can be varied through the whole range from the most elementary to the most advanced courses: this book contains cross-references at most levels, although more concerned with strategy than routine.

Each session entry contains a cross-reference to the chapter in this book where the subject is discussed; at least the Suggestions for Further Reading, and the Questions for Discussion attached to the chapter should be useful. Parts of most of the courses can be used for seminars for middle managers or trainees. A separate proposal is included for senior executive seminars.

International business strategy—I

(1) Introduction: What happens to business strategy when the company goes international? (chapter 1).
(2) The international transmission of resources (chapters 2 and 3).
(3) Relations with foreign cultures: issues and conflict resolution (chapter 16).
(4) National interest, sovereignty and identity (chapter 15).
(5) Trade and investment: the international dimension (chapters 2, 3, 14).
(6) Integrated versus fragmented strategies (chapter 5).
(7) Structure (chapter 9).
(8) Planning, communication and control (chapters 5 and 11).
(9) Decision-making (chapters 1 and 9).
(10) The future of international business (chapters 17 and 18).

International business strategy—II

(1) Introduction. The transition to international business. Some useful concepts. Plans for the course.
(2) Aspects of the environment of international business (chapters 14–16).
(3) Multinational corporate planning (chapter 5).
(4) Foreign trade (chapters 2 and 6).
(5) Foreign investment (chapters 3, 6, 7).
(6) The role of the international executive (chapters 12 and 16).
(7) The structure of the international firm (chapter 9).
(8) International production, sourcing and logistics (chapter 8).
(9) Communications (chapter 11).
(10) Summary and overview: The future of international business (chapters 17–18).

International corporate planning

(1) Introduction: The international dimension (chapters 1 and 5).
(2) The route abroad, methods of entry and operation (chapters 2 and 3).
(3) The changing environment: monitoring, information (chapters 11 and 14).
(4) The changing environment: economic and political implications (chapters 14–17).
(5) Central planning and local initiative (chapters 5 and 9).
(6) Policies for geographical diversification (chapters 1–5).
(7) Policies for product diversification (chapter 5).
(8) Policies for control (chapters 6–10).
(9) The role and organization of the central planning function.
(10) The activities of the central planning function. The techniques. Summary and conclusion.

International trade and marketing

(1) Introduction: the product customer relationship, a survey of the special issues which distinguish international from domestic marketing; assignment of general reading and coursework (chapters 1–6).
(2) The environment of international marketing: purchasing power,

government intervention, terms of trade, cultural conditions (chapters 14–16).

(3) The organization of the marketing function and the decision-making process (chapters 6 and 9).

(4) The communication of messages across frontiers. Advertising and publicity. The physical means of communication and distribution (chapters 6 and 11).

(5) Legal aspects of international marketing: taxation, tariffs, patent rights, trade marks, cartels, price-fixing, resale price maintenance. Incentives and hindrances to trade (chapter 15).

(6) The route abroad, methods of entry and operation (chapters 2 and 3).

(7) Financing the foreign sales and trade (chapter 7).

(8) The insurance and protection of foreign trade (chapters 2, 3, 6).

(9) Market research and the collection of data. Although this activity logically comes first, it is placed at the end of the course because the student will gain a better appreciation of the information required as the course proceeds (chapters 6 and 11).

(10) An integrating case study to bring the course together in the context of the total subject (chapter 6 or 8).

A course on international finance and control

(1) Introduction. Company finance and accounting. The special issues which come to the surface when the company and the finance function go international (chapter 7).

(2) The environment—international financial institutions and sources of funds (chapters 14 and 15).

(3) The environment: constraints and legal issues (chapters 14 and 15).

(4) Taxation.

(5) Comparative Accounting.

(6) Export and import financing.

(7) Cash management: sources and uses of funds (chapter 7).

(8) Financial control (chapter 10).

(9) Capital structure, and how this changes as the company develops abroad.

(10) Case study (chapter 7).

A course on the international business environment

(1) Introduction. The interaction between business and the three main aspects of the environment: economic, legal, cultural.

(2) International trade theory (chapter 14).
(3) International monetary theory (chapter 14).
(4) International economic institutions and agreements (chapters 14 and 15).
(5) The effect of foreign direct investment on the economies of both the home and the host countries (chapter 15).
(6) The causes that prompt the development of multinational corporations (chapter 3).
(7) Legal issues and taxation (chapters 7, 14, 15).
(8) The international company and the nation state (chapter 15).
(9) Managing across cultural boundaries (chapters 16 and 17).
(10) The changing environment of international business (chapters 14–18).

This course, like the others, assumes an interdisciplinary approach, but can easily be turned into an international economics course by taking out 8 and 9.

Equally chapter 15 could be the basis of a course on company–government relations by itself.

A course on international management

(1) Introduction. A brief survey of relevant issues from social anthropology. An overview of international management (chapter 16).
(2) Comparative management. Different assumptions, views of life, motivations, in different countries (chapter 16).
(3) Comparative management. Different theories (chapter 16).
(4) Staffing the foreign assignment (chapter 12).
(5) Managing staff abroad (chapter 12).
(6) Sensitivity to the cultural differences (chapter 16).
(7) International communications (chapter 11).
(8) Labour relations across frontiers (chapter 13).
(9) Personnel policies (chapter 12).
(10) The international executive (chapter 12).

Programme for a senior executive seminar on profitable international policies

(1) International corporate planning. How to get to grips with the

problems and to fix the priorities of steering the foreign side of the business.

(2) The decision-making process. How to determine what decisions must be reserve to the centre and what delegated to the subsidiaries in a complex multi-dimensional corporate system. How to ensure that the system is understood and not too cumbersome. How to exercise appropriate surveillance of what is happening.

(3) Financial policies: the sources and uses of funds. The general appraisal of financial policies.

(4) Selecting and appraising the key executives, including the subsidiary chief executives.

(5) The changing environment of international business.

Suggestion for further reading

The Academy of International Business periodically publishes a review of international business courses. At the time of going to press, the latest was:

DANIELS, J. D. & RADEBAUGH, L. H. (1974), International Business Curriculum Survey, Academy of International Business.

Of the 272 academic institutions listed as running courses on the subject, the following were the levels and subjects:

	Undergraduate	Graduate
Finance and Accounting	93	86
Marketing	151	97
Management	62	84
Area Studies	20	19
General Overview	65	68

Appendix II
Research on International Business

by Hans Schollhammer

During the past fifteen years international and comparative management issues have become the focus of an intensive research effort. This effort is reflected in the growing membership of professional organizations[1] and especially in the ever increasing flow of publications on international management (concerned with the management and operations of multinational firms) and comparative management (concerned with cross-cultural or cross-institutional similarities and differences of management issues).[2]

Any field of interest that undergoes such a rapid expansion requires (*a*) a period assessment of the state of knowledge, (*b*) a dissemination of information about current efforts on gaining new knowledge, and (*c*) an exchange of ideas or opinions about the future directions of the field among those who are interested in it. There exist a few publications which deal with all or some of these three broadly stated requirements.[3] This study deals with those stated under (*b*) and (*c*); i.e., it is an attempt to provide in summarized form information about the current research

---

*Reproduced, with passages omitted, from SCHOLLHAMMER, H. (1975) The survey on international and comparative management research, *Management International Review*, Feb.–March. Reproduced by permission.

Dr. Hans Schollhammer is Associate Professor at the University of California, Los Angeles, Graduate School of Management, Los Angeles, USA.

The paper represents a survey among the members of the International Management Division, The Academy of Management and The Academy of International Business, prepared for the 34th Annual Meeting of the Academy of Management, Seattle, Washington, August 1974.

[1] The Academy of International Business (previously named Association for Education in International Business) had approximately 100 members in 1965 as compared to almost 600 members in 1974. The International Management Division of the Academy of Management has approximately 200 members in 1974.

[2] The most extensive reference guide on international/comparative management publications is *The International Executive*, an abstract published three times a year.

[3] Significant contributions in this regard are: Richard D. Robinson, 'Research needs in international business', mimeographed report to the AEIB meeting, December 1965; Lee C. Nehrt *et al.*, *International Business Research: Past, Present and Future*, Bloomington: Bureau of Business Research, Indiana University, 1970; Jean Boddewyn and Raghu Nath, Comparative management studies: an assessment, *Management International Reviews*, vol. 10, no. 1, 1970, pp. 3–11; Sperry Lea and Simon Webley, *Multinational Corporations in Developed Countries: A Review of Recent Research and Policy Thinking*, British North American Committee, 1973; Hans Schölhammer, Strategies and Methodologies in international business and comparative management research, *Management International Review*, vol. 13, no. 6, 1973, pp. 17–41.

effort on international and comparative management issues and on future research priorities as viewed by the members of the International Management Division of the Academy of Management and the Academy of International Business.

The survey on international and comparative management research

Among the very substantial number of people actively engaged in international and comparative management research, there is a need for becoming aware of research in progress. A survey on international/comparative management research was intended to provide answers to questions such as: What subjects are currently under investigation? What research strategies and methodologies are used to gain new knowledge? What are some prospective research subjects to which researchers may devote more attention in the future? What are the opinions on desirable research priorities that deserve more protracted study and analysis. For these purposes a questionnaire was mailed during April 1974 to the 521 members of the Academy of International Business and 185 members of the International Management Division of the Academy of Management. Because of duplicate membership, a total of 618 questionnaires was mailed and by 1 July 1974, 103 useable replies had been returned, i.e., a response rate of about 17%.

Table 1
Characterization of the respondents

Respondents. professional orientation:	Respondents' association with US institutions	with non-US institutions	Total
Academicians (faculty members of universities or colleges and members of academic research institutes)	70	20	90
Doctoral candidates	5	0	5
Practitioners (business executives and members of business research centres)	6	0	6
Government Officials	1	1	2
Total	82	21	103

Of the 20 academicians associated with non-US educational institutions, 8 are in Canada, 7 in Europe, 4 in Japan and 1 in Central

America. The response rate of the non-US members of the two professional organizations that were surveyed is thus higher than that among the US membership. The 70 responding academicians associated with US educational institutions represent 54 different institutions.

The 'devotion' to international and comparative management research

The respondents to the survey were asked to indicate what percentage of their total research activities are related to international and comparative management and what percentage to other fields. Among the 90 respondents associated with educational institutions, 22 (i.e. 25%) indicated that all their research efforts are in the area of international/comparative management; the others (i.e. 75%) divide, in varying degrees, their research activities between international/comparative management and other fields of endeavour. Table 2 summarizes the results on the question about the respondents research effort devoted to international/comparative management.

Table 2
Average percentage of respondents' total research activities

	Related to international or comparative management (%)	Related to other fields (%)
Academicians	68	32
Doctoral candidates	100	0
Practitioners	48	52
Government officials	90	10

These findings suggest that the large majority of those engaged in international and comparative management research are conducting research to a substantial degree in other fields as well. For an interdisciplinary field such as international/comparative management this situation may be viewed as a desirable state of affairs since it provides for cross-stimulation and a closer linkage to related fields. On the other hand there is the drawback of a divided loyalty and the inherent danger of an opportunistic approach to research that this situation may reflect. Although in numerical terms the research output in international and comparative management is very substantial, the quality of a large portion of it has been criticized. One may speculate whether the lack in quality of a relatively high proportion of the international and comparative research that is published could be due to the fact that a substantial proportion of the researchers in this field are also conducting research in other areas. For instance, 15% of the respondents indicated that only 30% or less of their total research activities are related to international and comparative management. In these cases, international or comparative management research may only be a 'by-product' of other research endeavours. Having one's feet in more than one camp may have certain strategic advantages; in the case of a concerted research effort such a situation may, however, not necessarily be conducive to generating the best possible results.

Independent versus collaborative research

International and comparative research projects are frequently very complex and large in scope. For this reason it may be appropriate to carry out the research in co-operation with others. In order to get information on this issue, the questionnaire included the following question: To what extent are your current research activities a joint effort with others? The response to this question shows that 18 (i.e. 20%) of the responding academicians do only independent research and are not collaborating with others on their research in progress. The remaining 80% of the respondents engage—to varying degrees—in co-operative research endeavours. The following Table 3 summarizes the survey results in this regard.

Table 3
Independent versus collaborative research (average percent of total research effort)

	Independent research effort (%)	Collaborative research effort (%)
Academicians	611	39
Doctoral Candidates	100	0
Practitioners	75	25
Government Officials	30	70

These results reflect a high degree of willingness among the researchers on international and comparative management issues to join forces with others and to co-operate with them in carrying out the research.

International and comparative management research in progress

It is not surprising that a large majority of the respondents to the survey are actively engaged in one or more research projects. However, one fourth of the responding academicians (23) stated that they are not at present involved in any research endeavour dealing with international or comparative management issues. The remaining three fourths of the responding academicians (67) provided information on their research in progress, although a few of them in only very broad, general terms such as 'research on personnel management in multinational corporations'.

Those survey respondents who listed only one research project as being under investigation and those listing more than one project are equally divided. The 50% of the respondents with several research projects in progress generally listed two or three projects.

Dominant subjects of research

International and comparative management offer remarkable opportunities for new explorations and, as a result, the range of subjects currently under investigation shows a great variety. There are, however, a few dominant themes which receive broad attention, and a considerable amount of research is under way on these issues. Concerning international management issues the following subject areas are studied by a relatively large number of researchers and thus may be characterized as dominant subjects of research:

(1) The interaction of multinational enterprises with governments and related policy issues.

(2) Economic nationalism and its effect on multinational business operations.

(3) The growth and international expansion of non-US multinational firms, their business strategies and management approach. Particular attention is paid to the operations of non-US multinational firms in the United States.

(4) Operational problems of multinational enterprises with emphasis on organizational, personnel management and communication issues.

Concerning comparative management, current research is dominated by two broad areas of investigation:

(1) Cross cultural differences in management styles, their causes and consequences.

(2) Comparisons of managerial issues under a socialist-type economy with western management practices.

The interaction between multinational enterprises and host- as well as home-country governments has traditionally been an area of rather intensive exploration[4] and it seems that this area is at present even more widely investigated. Impressive numbers of researchers with admirable publication credentials are concentrating their research endeavours on multinational business—government relations.

For the purpose of categorizing international and comparative management research according to its research orientations, the following scheme may be adopted:[5]

INTERNATIONAL/COMPARATIVE MANAGEMENT RESEARCH
Basic Orientations

THEORETICAL-ABSTRACT ⟷ EMPIRICAL

THEORETICAL-ABSTRACT	EMPIRICAL
○ Conceptualizing	○ One-Dimensional — descriptive — analytical-interpretive — generalizing-normative
○ Synthesizing	○ Multi-Dimensional — descriptive — analytical-interpretive — generalizing-normative

This typology suggests that, as a first approximation, one may distinguish between two basic research orientations: (*a*) a research effort that aims primarily at the establishment of a theory by advocating various models, conceptual frameworks or typologies for developing and testing hypotheses; and (*b*) a research effort that aims primarily at the accumulation, explanation and evaluation of empirically-derived, factual data. Each of these two major research orientations has in turn various sub-categories. On the theory-building side one may distinguish between a conceptualizing research endeavour (i.e. an effort to develop theoretical constructs as an aid for the systematic detection, explanation and evaluation of international/comparative management phenomena), and a research endeavour that can be characterized as a *synthesizing*

[4] See, e.g., David Burtis, Farid Lavipour, Stephen Ricciardi, and Karl Sauvant (Eds), *Multinational Corporation—Nation-State interactions: An Annotated Bibliography*, Philadelphia: Foreign Policy Research Institute, 1971; Jack Behrman, *National Interests and the Multinational Enterprise*, Englewood Cliffs, NJ: Prentice Hall, 1970, and *US International Business and Governments*, New York: McGraw-Hill, 1971; Raymond Vernon, *Sovereignty at Bay*, New York: Basic Books, 1971; John Fayerweather, *Foreign Investment in Canada—Prospects for National Policy*, White Plains, NY: International Arts and Sciences Press, 1973; J. J. Boddewyn, *Western European Policies Toward US Investors*, New York: Institute of Finance, New York, University, 1974.

[5] See Schöllhammer, Strategies and methodologies in international business and comparative management research, *Management International Review*, vol. 13, no. 6, 1973, p. 19 ff.

effort (i.e. a systematic integration of relevant pieces of existing knowledge to provide a broad, general perspective on the subject under study). Empirically-oriented research can be subdivided, depending on the scope of the research project, into *one-dimensional*, focusing on one, narrow subject without regard for related issues; and *multi-dimensional*, focusing on several related issues. Within each of these two sub-categories one can distinguish three approaches: (*a*) descriptive research studies aiming at the presentation of empirically verified facts without much concern for analysis or interpretation or cause and effect relationships; (*b*) analytical-interpretive studies focusing on an evaluation of empirically verified data, and (*c*) generalizing-normative studies using selected empirical data primarily as a means for generalizing or for making normative, prescriptive assertions.

A systematic review of the international business and comparative management literature published between 1959 and 1972 reveals that three-fourths of the publications could be classified as 'empirical' and the rest as 'theoretical'. Among the empirical studies about two-thirds are one-dimensional, and one-third are multi-dimensional. Thirty-five per cent of all the empirical studies are essentially descriptive, 45% can be characterized as analytical-interpretive, and the remaining 20% as generalizing-normative.[6]

In spite of the somewhat skimpy information provided by many survey respondents on their current research projects there is evidence that the pattern characterizing published international business research between 1959 and 1972 continues to prevail as far as the on-going international and comparative management research is concerned. One notices, however, some minor shifts in emphasis. As far as the reported research in progress is concerned about 85% can be characterized as 'empirical', whereas theoretical-abstract research endeavours account for the remaining 15%. A majority of the current international/comparative research projects that can be characterized as empirical are one-dimensional, i.e. focusing on one or a narrowly defined set of issues. Whether the results of the current research efforts, once they are published, will be primarily descriptive, analytical-interpretive, or generalizing-normative is difficult to assess on the basis of the information provided by the survey respondents. There are, however, indications that studies which can be characterized as generalizing-normative are on the rise. Very little of the current international/comparative management research effort goes into the development of case material.

---

[6] Hans Schöllhammer, Strategies and Methodologies in International Business and Comparative Management Research, *op. cit.*, p. 24.

Research methodologies

It has already been pointed out that about one third of the respondents to the survey provided no information at all as to the research methodologies they are using on their research in progress. Forty per cent gave only a very rudimentary response, for example stating that data are being sought by means of questionnaires and interviews. Only one fourth of the respondents were relatively specific about their research efforts from a methodological point of view. A large percentage of the researchers on international and comparative management issues seem to show little concern for a systematic planning of their research effort. They seem to develop their research strategies either on an *ad hoc* basis or simply from the point of view of expediency. For example, a well-known contributor to the international and comparative management literature stated flatly: '. . . we figure out our methodologies as we go'. This seems to be a very prevalent attitude.

Among those survey respondents who were explicit about research methodologies on their projects that are under investigation, almost 50% mentioned only interviews as the sole sourse for accumulating empirical data. Thirty per cent indicated the use of interviews in combination with questionnaire surveys, and 20% use only questionnaire surveys as a source of information. The use and re-interpretation of available secondary sources of information were mentioned by only a few respondents, and only three respondents indicated in-depth case studies and observations over a period of time as the data base of their research. Interviews are thus the prevalent research methodology, although the indicated sample size is almost invariably rather small.

One recommendation that can be drawn from the survey results concerned with the scope and methodology of current international/comparative management research is that, given the willingness of researchers to collaborate with others, it would be desirable to plan a number of large scale research projects to which researchers associated with different institutions could contribute. The results of such an effort may well outweigh those of numerous small studies that are published but whose impact is negligible from the point of view of advancing the state of knowledge on international and comparative management issues.

Future research priorities

An investigation of international and comparative management research in progress would be incomplete without also soliciting information on perceived current research gaps and future research priorities. For this purpose the survey included the question: 'In your opinion, what research needs in international and comparative management should be given priority?' Of the 103 survey respondents, only 47 answered this question with varying degrees of detail.

There is little unanimity about existing research gaps and future research priorities. Many researchers seem to believe that their current research effort is precisely on a subject that warrants a high priority. There are, however, a number of issues which in the opinion of several respondents should become the focus of a concerted effort:

(*a*) Economic nationalism and the interaction between multinational enterprises and governments were mentioned by several respondents as a priority area for future research. In this general domain research projects that were specifically proposed are: the possibilities for mediation in the case of MNC—government conflicts together with an inquiry into supranational approaches to MNC accountability, the role multinational corporations play in political affairs, an investigation of administrative, informal government practice (analogue of non-tariff trade barriers) aimed at hindering foreign direct investments and multinational business operations. In addition to these subjects, a range of other issues with 'political overtones' was mentioned as warranting research priority; for instance, the internationalization of ownership of multinational enterprises, or the impact of terrorism and kidnapping of international executives on multinational firms' operations.

(*b*) The intra-company transmission of managerial and technical know-how is another set of research issues that in the opinion of several respondents should be investigated with priority.

(*c*) A comparative analysis of different forms of employee participation in management and/or ownership. Another proposed priority research subject is an analysis of the effects of a multinationalization of labour unions and the emergence of company-wide unions in multinational enterprises.

(*d*) Indicative of a widespread belief that international and comparative management are in need of a greater consolidating and synthesizing effort is the recommendation by several respondents that a priority research effort should focus on an analysis of existing research.

(*e*) For some respondents priority in international and comparative management research is not a matter of selecting certain significant topics and making them the subject of a concerted research effort, but the way in which research is carried out. For example, among the desirable priorities in international and comparative management research is a greater commitment to a collaborative, international research effort (as contrasted with an individual effort).

The general conclusion to be drawn from the survey on current and prospective research on international and comparative management issues is that there is little uniformity in thrust and limited consensus about research issues to be dealt with on a priority basis. There is, however, a substantial amount of research under way which is indicative of a further dynamic development of the international and comparative management fields.

International and comparative management research: some evaluative conclusions

Since 1959 international and comparative management issues have become the focus of an intensive research effort by a growing number of scholars, business executives and government officials. This effort has led to a steadily increasing flow of publications. A large portion of it has, however, been criticized as:

(i) merely descriptive of empirical phenomena and lacking in analytical rigour,
(ii) episodic and produced on an *ad hoc* basis,
(iii) reflecting substantial methodological deficiencies,
(iv) self-centred in the sense that already existing studies are frequently ignored.

If one analyses the survey information on the international and comparative management research that is in progress, one gets the impression that the above criticisms also hold true for a sizable part of it. On the one hand one notices and is impressed by the range of research projects that are currently under investigation and by the strong orientation toward empirical research. On the other hand, one cannot overlook significant shortcomings:

(1) Insufficient attention is frequently paid to the planning of the research effort. It seems that empirical evidence is often gathered without much concern for the representativeness of the data and without a well developed, appropriate methodological instrumentarium.

(2) A sizeable portion of the on-going international and comparative management research is not aimed at theory-building in the sense that certain hypotheses are tested. There is evidence of an inadequate linkage between empirical research and existing theoretical constructs. Theoretical and empirical research in current international and comparative management research seem to be largely independent of each other instead of interdependent and mutually supportive.

(3) A very substantial percentage of the research in progress is one-dimensional, i.e. narrow in scope and directed to 'small' problems, with

an emphasis on shortrun research results. This situation would not have to be viewed critically if at the same time a comprehensive synthesizing or integrative research effort were made. This is, however, not the case. International and comparative management still consists of a variety of theories, paradigms and a substantial volume of empirical studies in search of a synthesizer.

An awareness of these shortcomings in current international and comparative management research should ideally lead to a resolution to reduce them as much as possible. In reality, this may be difficult to achieve since some of the shortcomings are indigenous, i.e. a consequence of the character of the fields and their rather short history. However, there is certainly room for improvements and the professional societies (Academy of Management and the Academy of International Business) should play an active role in this regard. A first essential step is to conduct periodic suveys of on-going international and comparative management research and to make the resultant information quickly available to those interested in the fields. In fact, this is an old recommendation and it would seem appropriate now to implement it. In 1965 Robinson stated at a meeting of the Association for Education in International Business: 'I would urge that we get out a simple card form on which each member would report annually his own research and that of his graduate students, the AEIB to complete, duplicate and distribute this information. In fact, we might make the annual report a condition of membership.'[7] This suggestion is still very relevant since its implementation would provide a better awareness about the research in progress, and a certain linkage or even a co-operative research effort on related research topics with a possibly synergistic effect.

Another area in which the professional societies could become more active is in the organization of large-scale, collaborative research projects in which interested researchers associated with different institutions could participate. Such a collaborative, large-scale research effort could well have a more noticeable impact on advancing the state of knowledge on international and comparative management than the numerous isolated, small-scale studies.

It is obvious that the professional societies can play only a facilitating role in an attempt to improve the state of international and comparative management research. What is really needed is a commitment by each individual researcher to contribute to a reduction in the identified shortcomings. In addition, the analysis of the information provided by the survey on current international and comparative management research

---

[7] Richard Robinson, Research Needs in International Business, *op. cit.*, p. 2.

Number of Publications Referenced in *The International Executive* per Reference Guide Heading, 1959–1973

	1959	1960	1961	1962	1963	1964	1965	1966	1967	1968	1969	1970	1971	1972	1973
General Management	77	114	148	131	189	203	253	296	257	296	336	391	424	395	307
Marketing	143	220	283	226	398	309	329	300	286	253	230	196	207	161	97
Public Relations	43	29	45	25	26	30	41	33	49	26	22	20	27	24	19
Industrial Relations	172	174	182	165	247	202	263	276	210	289	233	278	310	280	250
Law	51	43	68	75	82	98	142	106	106	161	124	147	106	98	124
Finance, Accounting, Tax	165	177	175	150	215	259	293	269	219	259	196	261	246	170	197
Banking and Insurance				53	85	92	84	71	84	108	74	72	120	91	89
Transportation						72	61	55	48	58	58	52	53	47	45
Economic Relations:															
World Trade	152	154	136	102	126	95	122	105	88	105	87	105	101	112	104
Regional Ec. Groups				74	109	80	82	75	65	73	52	48	59	84	48
Ec. Development & Aid	101	85	150	152	217	258	237	213	210	201	174	190	164	158	154
Monetary Affairs	45	55	112	100	125	131	171	138	119	147	115	121	145	131	115
Trade Restrictions	17	20	39	40	32	37	38	27	46	59	53	66	70	50	62
Background:															
General	29	44	42	58	40	56	59	45	50	21	34	30	28	46	39
Western Hemisphere	107	112	145	160	163	167	167	163	135	157	110	87	132	149	142
Western Europe						178	173	193	173	170	125	86	120	128	93
Eastern Europe & Sov. U.						38	65	49	48	63	43	28	45	39	58
Africa	57	123	130	128	97	132	113	108	103	112	60	51	81	76	53
Middle East	55	65	40	39	36	36	44	32	35	44	20	20	29	28	31
Far East	153	213	109	195	147	171	195	196	217	212	146	103	146	150	160
Oceania				28	30	42	35	35	47	38	22	19	34	32	23

Source: Schöllhammer, Hans, Strategies and methodologies in international business and comparative management research, *Management International Review*, **13,** no. 6, 1973, p. 18.

leads one to emphasize three criteria as guidelines for future research endeavours in these fields:

(1) A better linkage of new international and comparative management research with the already existing knowledge of these fields as well as with the body of knowledge in general management.

(2) A greater effort in bridging the gap between normative theories and empirical studies.

(3) A greater emphasis on analytical and synthesizing research endeavours to the detriment of merely descriptive empirical studies.

Research endeavours with these characteristics will provide a basis for further dynamic growth of international and comparative management knowledge.

Appendix III
A Library on International Business

Among the literature on the subject, the following books are readable and interesting. Students and businessmen wishing to build up their libraries would do well to consider this as a list of recommended texts. For key to references see page 9.

(B) BROOKE, MICHAEL Z. & REMMERS, H. L. (1972). *The Multinational Company in Europe*, p. 194, Longman: London.

(B) BROOKE, M. Z. & REMMERS, H. L. (1970). *The Strategy of Multinational Enterprise: Organisation and Finance*, Longman: London. 2nd edn. Pitman: to be published 1978.

(C) BROOKE, M. Z. & VAN BEUSEKOM, M. *Multinational Corporate Planning*, Pitman: London. To be published 1979.

(A) DANIELS, J. D., OGRAM, E. W. & RADEBAUGH, L. H. (1976). *International Business: Environments and Operations*, Addison-Wesley: London.

(B) DUNNING, J. H. (1972). *International Business*, Penguin: London.

(C) DUNNING, John H. (Ed.) (1971). *The Multinational Enterprise*, Allen & Unwin: London.

(C) DUNNING, J. H. (1974). *Economic Analysis and the Multinational Enterprise*, Allen & Unwin: London.

(A) DYMSZA, W. A. (1972). *Multinational Business Strategy*, McGraw-Hill: London & New York.

(C) EITEMAN, David K. & STONEHILL, Arthur I. (1978). *Multinational Business Finance*, Addison-Wesley: London. To be published.

(B) FARMER, R. N. & RICHMAN, B. M. (1976). *International Business: An Operational Theory*, 2nd edn, Cedarwood.

(B) FAYERWEATHER, J. (1969). *International Business Management*, McGraw-Hill: London.

(B) GRUB, P. D. & KASKIMIES, M., Eds (1972) *International Marketing in Perspective*, Sinien Kirja Oy.

(D) GUNTER, Hans, Ed. (1972). *Transnational Industrial Relations*, MacMillan: London.

(A) HAYS, Richard D. *et al.* (1972). *International Business: An Introduction to the World of the Multinational Firm*, Prentice-Hall: London & New York.

(B) KAPOOR, Ashok & GRUB, Phillip D. (1972). *The Multinational Enterprise in Transition*, Darwin Press.

(B) KOTLER, P. (1972). *Marketing Management*, 2nd edn, Prentice-Hall: London & New York.

(A) RICKS *et al.* (1974). *International Business Blunders*, Grid.

(C) ROBBINS, Sidney M. & STOBAUGH, Robert B. (1973). *Money in the Multinational Enterprise: A Study of Financial Policy*, Basic Books: London.

(B) ROBINSON, R. D. (1973). *International Business Management: A Guide to Decision-Making,* Holt, Rinehart & Winston: London & New York.

(B) ROBOCK, S. H. & SIMMONDS, K. (1973). *International Business and Multinational Enterprise*, Irwin: Illinois, USA.

(B) SALERA, V. (1969). *Multinational Business*, Houghton Mifflen: New York.

(B) SETHI, S. P. & HOLTON, R. H. (1974). *Management of the Multinationals*, Free Press.

(C) STOPFORD, T. M. & WELLS, L. T. Jnr (1972). *Managing the Multinational Enterprise*, Longman: London.

(B) TERPSTRA, V. (1972). *International Marketing*, Holt, Rhinehart & Winston: London & New York.

(B) THORELLI, H. B., Ed. (1973). *International Marketing Strategy*, Penguin: London.

(B) VERNON, R. (1971). *Sovereignty at Bay*, Longman: London.

(B) VERNON, Raymond & WELLS, L. T. (1976). *Manager in the International Economy*, 3rd edn, Prentice-Hall: London & New York.

Periodicals

Most management journals have articles from time to time devoted to international business. The most important specialist journal on this subject is:

The Journal of International Business Studies, published for the Academy of International Business by Rutgers University.

For a list of over 3000 titles of recent books and papers on the subject, see:

BROOKE, M. Z., BLACK, M. & NEVILLE, P. (1976). *A Bibliography of International Business*, MacMillan: London.

Notes to Chapters

Where references are by author and date only, full particulars can be found in Appendix III unless otherwise stated.

For key to references see p. 9.

2 Foreign business without foreign investment

(1) Organizational learning is a phrase derived from the work of Cyert & March, see (D) CYERT, R. M. & MARCH, J. G. (1963). *A Behavioural Theory of the Firm*, Prentice-Hall. This book, which brings together economic and sociological theories of organization provides much of the underlying theory of this chapter and the next. See also chapter 3, note 8.

(2) These notes on the selection and appraisal of agents are taken from research notes in the possession of the International Business Unit. A similar outline could be produced for any of the collaborative methods of doing business abroad which the ingenuity of businessmen has produced.

(3) For an example of a typical problem with agents see page 36.

(4) By 'control' in this case is meant the establishment of a system of communications between the agent and the company to keep the latter regularly and fully informed about the development of the business. As is pointed out in the text careful and skilful negotiation with the agent is required.

(5) For a discussion of licensing failures due to lack of marketing skills in the subsidiary see (B) GRUB & KASKIMIES (1962), p. 346. See the following pages in that book for further discussion of both licensing and franchising.

(6) Although it should not be overlooked that more countries are taxing royalty income more highly than before. There is a substantial withholding tax in India, for example.

(7) Adapted from: (B) ELLISON, R. (1975). Management Contracts, an unpublished paper of the International Business Unit. The following quotation is from GABRIEL, P. P. (1967). *The International Transfer of Corporate Skills*, Harvard. See also

ELLISON, R. J. T. (1976). Management contracts, *Multinational Business*, March, pp. 19–28.

(8) In GABRIEL (1967). See above note.

(9) Source: *Trade and Industry,* 11 April 1975, p. 101.

(10) Source: Franchising in the Economy, 1974–5, US Department of Commerce Publication.

(11) In 1973 world exports and production by foreign subsidiaries of multinational companies were *each* equal to 12.5% of gross world product (for these figures we are indebted to Professor Warren J. Keegan, George Washington University).

3 Foreign investment

(1) This is known as the Hecksher-Olin theory from those who first put it forward. The Leontieff paradox was a reply which said that countries with high labour costs exported labour-intensive products. The controversy is discussed in many of the writings recommended for further reading. See also below section 14.2 and note 5 to chapter 14.

(2) See (C) DUNNING, J. H. (1974). The future of the multinational enterprise, *Lloyds Bank Review*, **113,** July, pp. 15–32.

(3) See (C) PENROSE, E. T. (1959). *The Theory of the Growth of the Firm*, Blackwell: Oxford & New York.

For references to Portfolio Theory mentioned in the following paragraph see (C) DUNNING (1974), pp. 64–6 and note 38.

(4) See (B) VERNON & WELLS (1976), chapter 11.

(5) There is a vast literature on this subject. The most illuminating single book is (D) ETZIONI, A. (1976), *Comparative Analysis of Complex Organizations*, 2nd edn, Collier-MacMillan: New York.

(6) See also back chapter 1, Fig. 1.1.

(7) For the historical approach see (B) FRANKO, L. (1976). *The European Multinationals*. See also (C) STOPFORD, J. M. (1974). The origins of British-based multinational manufacturing enterprises, *Business History Review* **48.3,** Autumn, pp. 303–335.

(8) See (D) CYERT, R. M. & MARCH, J. G. (1963), *A Behavioural Theory of the Firm*, Prentice-Hall: London & New York. See also above chapter 2, note 1.

(9) Most of the works on international management listed in the bibliography of this book take some variant of the commercial theory view. Not all the authors refer to the underlying theories briefly described in the text. For the distinction between aggressive and defensive strategies see BROOK & REMMERS (1970), chapter 9.

(10) See KINDLEBERGER, C. F. (1969). *American Business Abroad*, Yale, and DUNNING, J. H. (1958). *American Investment in British Manufacturing Industry*, Allen & Unwin. The Swedish study mentioned is reported in (D) JOHANSON, Jan & VAHLNE, Jan-Erik (1974). The Internationalization Process of the Firm, Department of Business Administration, University of Uppsala.

(11) Chapters on international investment appraisal are contained in books mentioned in chapter 7.

For a textbook on investment appraisal in general, see (D) MERRETT, A. J. & SYKES, A. (1973). *The Finance and Analysis of Capital Projects*, 2nd edn, Longman: London.

(12) This subject has been the subject of research by Mr H. J. Ruff in the International Business Unit, Manchester. For a preliminary report of his findings see: (D) RUFF, H. J. (1974). Ground rules for the establishment of foreign selling subsidiaries, *Indian Administrative and Management Review*, July/Sept.

(13) For the advantages of operating across different national economies see (C) BROOKE & VAN BEUSEKOM (1978), chapter 2.

(14) See (C) STOPFORD & WELLS (1972). See above, note 7, and (B) BROOKE & REMMERS (1972), chapter 5; these and other writings on joint ventures are mentioned under Further Reading.

(15) See below, chapter 8. See also (B) BROOKE & REMMERS (1970), chapters 6 and and 7.

(16) One example of this, Wilmot Breeden Co. Ltd., is mentioned as a suitable case study towards the end of this chapter.

4 Disinvestment

(1) Adapted from: (B) SACHDEV, J. C. (1976). Disinvestment: a corporate failure or a strategic success, *International Studies of Management and Organization*, Spring–Summer, pp. 112–130.

(2) (C) HAYES, R. H., New emphasis on divestment opportunities, *Harvard Business Review*, July/Aug. 1972; (C) LOB, J. C. & CHARLES, D. E., Corporate surgery: how divestment can boost profits by cutting sales, *Corporate Financing*, May/June 1970.

(3) No published data on the number of cases of British foreign disinvestment is available. These statistics are compiled by monitoring various newspapers and other business journals. The American figures are from (C) BODDEWYN, J. J. & TORNEDEN, R. L. US Foreign divestment: a preliminary survey, *Columbia Journal of World Business*, Summer 1973, pp. 25–29. The subsequent defini-

tion also comes from this source.

(4) (B) ROSE, Sanford, Multinational corporations in a tough new world, *Fortune*, pp. 52–7, August 1973.

(5) (B) WIDING, J. W. 'Reorganising your world-wide business', *Harvard Business Review*, May/June 1973, pp. 153–5.

(6) (D) TRUITT, J. F., Expropriation of Private Foreign Investment: A Framework to Consider Post World War II Experience of British and American Investors, Ph.D. Thesis, Indiana University, Graduate School of Business, 1969.

(7) (B) SACHDEV, J. C., 'Disinvestment: a new challenge to multinationals and a new threat to developing countries', *Multinational Business*, September 1974, pp. 22–30.

(8) (C) SACHDEV, J. C., British private disinvestment in India and the neighbouring countries, *Indian Administrative & Management Review*, July/September 1974, pp. 36–8.

(9) See below, chapter 9.

5 International corporate planning

(1) Section 5.2 is by David P. Rutenberg, Associate Professor, Graduate School of Industrial Administration, Carnegie-Mellon University. This section is modified from an article under the same title published in *Long Range Planning*, December 1969, pp. 24–6, and reproduced with permission. The word *synergy* is used by corporate planners to indicate the working together of more than one factor for the mutual improvement of all the factors mentioned.

(2) A 'block diagonal' matrix is one where one side of the diagonal line is blocked out—i.e. symmetrical.

(3) See (D) RUTENBERG, David P. (1970). Organizational archetypes of a multinational company, *Management Science*, **16**.6, February.

(4) This paragraph neatly represents some interesting paradoxes, but naturally not every country or government fits all the situations described; indeed with some the position may be reversed.

(5) (D) *Long-Range Planning*.

6 International marketing management

(1) This point is well made by one writer on the subject: See (C) BUZZELL, R. D. (1968). Can you standardize multinational marketing?, pp. 102–113, *Harvard Business Review*, November–December. An adapted version can be found in THORELLI (1973), pp. 325–339. Table 1 (p. 333 in Thorelli) is

especially useful, although this is a table of 'obstacles to standardization' only. It is not always realistic to separate the obstacles from the pressures as explained in the next passage in the text. See also the other entries included in the Further Reading for this chapter.

(2) The possible international product strategies are well presented in (C) KEEGAN, Warren J. (1969). Multinational product strategy: strategic alternatives, *Journal of Marketing*, January. This article has been reprinted numerous times with revisions. See *European Business,* Jan. 1970. See also ROBOCK & SIMMONDS (1973). Chapter 19, KAPOOR & GRUB (1972). Chapter 14, THORELLI (1973). Chapter 17. It should be noted that all the examples given in this article are of consumer goods.

(3) A number of blunders in product adaptation are listed in RICKS *et al.* (1974), pp. 16–20. Pages 11–16 in the same book describe some advertising errors.

(4) Adapted from an article by Graham Buxton, lecturer in marketing science, Management Centre, University of Bradford, in the *European Journal of Marketing*, **7,** no. 1 (1973), reproduced with permission.

(5) See: (C) FELDMAN, Laurence P. (1971). Societal adaptation: a new challenge for marketing, *Journal of Marketing*, July.

(C) KOTLER, Philip (1972). What consumerism means for marketers, *Harvard Business Review*, May–June.

(C) DAWSON, Leslie M. (1971). Marketing science in the age of aquarius, *Journal of Marketing*, July.

(6) See: (B) DRUCKER, P. F. (1955). *The Practice of Management*, p. 44, Mercury Books.

(7) See: (C) LAZER, William (1969). Marketing's changing social relationships, *Journal of Marketing*, January.

(8) See: (D) WIND, Yoram, and DOUGLAS, Susan P. (1972). International Marketing Segmentation, *European Journal of Marketing,* **6,** no. 1, Spring, pp. 17–25.

(9) See: (C) COOKE, Peter (1972). Market analysis utilizing cultural anthropological indicators, *European Journal of Marketing*, **6,** no. 1, pp. 26–34.

(10) See: (C) CARSON, D. (1967). *International Marketing: A Comparative Systems Approach*, preface, p. vi, John Wiley: New York.

(11) See: (C) SHARRO, Stanley J. (1963). Comparative marketing and economic development, in SCHWARTZ, George, (Ed.), *Science in Marketing*, chapter 14, John Wiley: New York. This is an excellent evaluation of work in this field.

(12) See: (C) DAWSON, Leslie M. (1971). Marketing science in the age of aquarius, *Journal of Marketing*, July.

(13) See: (C) BARTELS, Robert (1968). Are domestic and international marketing dissimilar?, *Journal of Marketing*, July. Figs 5.1 and 5.2 are based on this work.
(14) See: (B) FISK, George (1967). *Marketing Systems: An Introductory Analysis*, p. 739, Harper International: New York.
(15) See: (C) HILLIER, Terry (1972). Shopping centres: the struggle ahead, April, p. 55, *Marketing*.
(16) This list is known as Rostow's classification. See: (C) ROSTOW, W. W. (1971). *The Stages of Economic Growth: A Non-Communist Manifesto*, p. 4, Cambridge University Press.
(17) See: (C) BARTELS, Robert (1968). Are domestic and international marketing dissimilar?, *Journal of Marketing*, July, 9. 59.
(18) See: (B) DICHTER, Ernest (1962). The world customer, *Harvard Business Review*, July–August. This may well be regarded as an optimistic classification. More realistic, perhaps, is the view of FARMER & RICHMAN (1976) discussed briefly below in chapter 16.
(19) See: (B) FISK, George (1967). *Marketing Systems: An Introductory Analysis*, p. 739, Harper & Row: New York.
(20) See: (C) WINICK, F. (1961). Anthropology's contribution to marketing, *Journal of Marketing*, 1961.
(C) LAZER, William & KELLEY, Eugene J. (1962). Interdisciplinary contributions to marketing management, in LAZER & KELLEY (Eds), *Managerial Marketing: Perspectives and Viewpoints*, Irwin: Illinois, USA.
(C) ENGEL, James F., KOLLAT, David T. & BLACKWELL, Roger D. (1968). *Consumer Behaviour*, Especially parts 2, 3 and 4, Holt, Rinehart & Winston: London & New York.
(21) See (C) WIND, Yoram & DOUGLAS, Susan P. (1972). International market segmentation, *European Journal of Marketing*, Spring. Table 6.2 is adapted from this work.
(22) See: (C) FELDMAN (1971), p. 57, see above, note 5.
(23) See: (C) FISK (1967), p. 709, see above, note 14.
(24) See: (C) KOTLER, Philip & ZALTMAN, Gerald (1971). Social marketing: an approach to social change, *Journal of Marketing*, July.

7 International financial management

(1) This chapter has been written specially for this book by Gunter Dufey, Professor of International Business and Finance. Graduate

School of Business Administration, University of Michigan. The author wishes to thank Professor Ian H. Giddy, University of Columbia, for helpful comments while accepting responsibility for any errors.

(2) Source: SMITH, D. T. (1966). Financial variables in international business, *Harvard Business Review*, January.

(3) This section is based on: DUFEY, G. & GIDDY, I. H. (1975). Forecasting exchange rates in a floating world, *Euromoney*, p. 28, November. International currency exchange is discussed below in chapter 15.

(4) For examples see: ANKROM, R. K. (1974). Top-level approach to the Foreign Exchange Problem, *Harvard Business Review*, July–August pp. 79–90. DUFEY, G. (1972). 'Corporate finance and exchange rate variations', *Financial Management*, Summer, pp. 51–7. HOYT, N. (1972). The management of currency exchange risk by the Singer company, *Financial Management*, Spring, pp. 13–20. TECK, A. (1974). Control Your Exposure to Foreign Exchange, *Harvard Business Review*, Jan.–Feb., pp. 66–75.

(5) ALIBER, R. Z. & STICKNEY, C. P. (1975). Accounting measures of foreign exchange exposure: the long and the short of it, p. 44, *The Accounting Review*, January.

(6) See: GIDDY, I. H. (1976). Exchange Risk: Whose View? University of Chicago, Center for Mathematical Studies in Business and Economics, Report 7646.

(7) LESSARD, D. R. & LORANGE, P. (1976). Currency Changes and Management Control: Resolving the Centralization/Decentralization Dilemma Through the Use of Internal Forward Exchange Rates, M.I.T., Sloan School, Working Paper 849–76, April.

(8) For the many varied aspects of multinational strategy see: BROOKE & REMMERS (1970).

(9) See: RODRIGUEZ, R. M. & CARTER, E. (1976). *International Financial Management*, chapter 9, Prentice-Hall: London & New York.

(10) The following is based on: GIDDY, I. H. (1976). 'The cost of capital in the international firm', unpublished note, Graduate School of Business, University of Chicago.

(11) For details see: RODRIGUEZ & CARTER (1976), see above note 9, chapter 10 & 11; see also SETHI & HOLTON (1974), p. 272.

8 Production, supply and location

(1) This statement does not, of course, include the many writings on the reasons for foreign investment (covered in chapter 3) nor those on comparative management (referred to in chapter 16). There are also numerous books on production in different countries. But writings on the actual management of production across frontiers are very limited in number and are mostly in case study form. See, for example, the case studies suggested later in this chapter.

(2) This subject is discussed above in chapter 5 and in (C) BROOKE & VAN BEUSEKOM (1979). An article which sets out a matrix scheme for answering some of the main questions is (C) STOBAUGH, Robert B. (1969). Where in the world should we put that plant?, *Harvard Business Review,* **47.1,** Jan.–Feb., pp. 129–136. Reprinted in KAPOOR & GRUB (1972).

(3) It's noticeable that an authority like R. D. Robinson devotes most of a chapter on 'supply strategy' to discussion of the implications of tariffs, see (B) ROBINSON (1973), chapter 2; this chapter also includes a list of issues that are likely to be raised by operating in different legal systems.

(4) Adapted from MATTSON, L. G. (1972. Multinational customers' influence on the industrial goods manufacturer's marketing organization and competitive position. Unpublished paper, University of Linkoping, Sweden. Reproduced by permission. The full paper should be read, the excerpts used here are those that concern buying; some important research proposals are included in the original article.

Professor Mattson is Professor of Business Administration, Centre for International Business Studies, University of Uppsala. At the time of writing this paper he was at the European Institute for Advanced Studies in Management, Brussels.

(5) Some qualification needs to be placed beside this paragraph. See the article by DAVIS, EPPEN & MATTSON (1974) listed in the Suggestions for Further Reading at the end of the chapter.

9 Decision-making and organization

(1) For a fuller discussion of this subject, with examples, see BROOKE & REMMERS (1970), chapters 2 and 3.

(2) A body of theory has been built up around this subject. See the writings of A. Etzioni which are especially prominent.

(3) The paper by JENNEGREN (see Suggestions for Further Reading

at the end of the chapter) denies any link between decentralization and efficiency.

10 Communications and control

(1) Excerpted from McINNES, J. M. (1971). Financial control systems for multinational operations: an empirical investigation, *Journal of International Business Studies*, Fall. The quotation in the first paragraph is from (C) HAWKINS, D. F. (1965). Controlling foreign operations, *The Financial Executive,* **33**.2, Feb. At the time he wrote this paper, Dr McInnes was a senior lecturer at the Manchester Business School. He is now in Business.

(2) This statement contains an implicit criticism of 'exception reporting' as it is commonly used. In practice it is difficult, even impossible, to define beforehand what is an 'exception' worthy of management's attention.

(3) But it evades the issue of choosing an appropriate price level index. The problem of choosing an index arises from the fact that inflation affects different sectors of an economy to different degrees.

(4) Although companies are now accustomed to living with these differences, the range of problems involved in foreign control gets more complex and less like the domestic (editorial note).

11 Communications, information and the transfer of knowledge

(1) This point comes up repeatedly in interview reports in the possession of the International Business Unit in Manchester.

(2) This is not, of course, intended to minimize the importance of language training for executives. The recognition of the need for such training is among the factors that lie behind the phrase 'so much anticipated' used in the text.

(3) See above, chapter 9. A full discussion of this subject can be found in (B) BROOKE & REMMERS (1970), chapter 2.

(4) See (D) PRITLOVE, J. H. (1968). The Communication of Technical Change in International Companies, unpublished paper, International Business Unit, Manchester.

(5) See (D) PARKER, J. E. S. (1974). Research Intensive Activities and the Multinational Enterprise, Reading Occasional Papers no. 15.

(6) By (C) PAVITT in DUNNING (1971). Chapter 3. See in the text under further reading.
(7) This excerpt on information sources used by multinational companies is modified from KEEGAN, Warren J. (1974). 'Multinational scanning: a study of the information sources utilized by headquarters executives in multinational companies', *Administrative Science Quarterly*, Sept. Reproduced by permission. W. J. Keegan is Professor in the School of Government and Business Administration at the George Washington University.
(8) See (C) BAUER, R. A. *et al.* (1964). *American Business and Public Policy*, p. 155, Atherton Press.
(9) (D) AGUILAR, F. J. (1967). *Scanning the Business Environment*, p. 94, MacMillan: London.
(10) (C) ALLEN, T. J. (1965). The differential performance of information channels in the transfer of technology, in (C) GRUBER, W. H. & MARQUIS, D. G. (Eds) (1965). *Factors in the Transfer of Technology*, pp. 137–154., M.I.T.
(11) See (C) HAAS, H. van der (1967). *The Enterprise in Transition*, Tavistock: London.
(12) See (B) DRUCKER, P. (1966). *The Effective Executive*, p. 13, Harper & Row: London & New York.
(13) See FOURAKER, L. E. & Stopford, J. M. (1968). Organizational structure and multinational strategy, pp.47–64, *Administrative Science Quarterly*, June.

12 Staffing the multinational firm

(1) For a discussion of the so-called 'rational' and 'natural' processes in company management, see BROOKE & REMMERS (1972), chapter 7.
(2) For a fuller discussion of the subject of this paragraph (the International Grade) see later in this chapter, and 214–6 in BROOKE & REMMERS (1970), chapter 5.
(3) The two statements are not, of course, irreconcilable. The foreign subsidiary can adopt methods used in the parent company without actually being instructed to do so. Some of the evidence used in this section is derived from a study of personnel practices in foreign companies in Britain undertaken in the International Business Unit by Mary Black & Paul Neville; the report is unpublished.
(4) See GENNARD, J. (1974). The impact of foreign-owned subsidiaries on host country labour relations: The Case of the United Kingdom, in FLANAGAN, R. J. & WEBER, A. R. (Eds), *Bargaining Without Boundaries*, University of Chicago Press.

(5) This passage is based on a research paper presented to the International Business Unit by Michael Ng in October 1975.

(6) In fact that sentence oversimplifies a complex problem—sometimes a management style which is in conflict with the local culture can be effective. See (B) BROOKE & REMMERS (1970). (1970).

(7) This point is strongly made in (B) BARNET, R. J. & MUELLER, R. E. (1974), *Global Reach,* p. 62. Simon & Sluster and Jonathan Cape: London.

(8) The cost factor for managers is notoriously a difficult one to assess. If the scheme is working well and genuinely ensuring that experienced managerial talent is available at the point of need, then the expense is irrelevant.

(9) Recruitment from outside the company is normally through an executive recruitment agency.

(10) See MILLER, E. (1973), The international selection decision, *Academy of Management Journal*, **16**.2.

(11) The motives for transferring managers abroad are discussed in (C) EDSTROM, A. (1974). Beliefs About International Transfers and their Implications for Transfer Policy, *Conference Papers*, Seminar on Recent Research on the International Firm, European International Business Association, Jouy-en-Josas, Dec.

The point about executive wives is made in: (B) ALEXANDER, William (1970). Mobil's Four-hour Environmental Interview, p. 18, *Worldwide P. and I. Planning,* Jan.–Feb.

(12) For the re-integration of expatriates see:
(C) MURRAY, A. J. (1973). International personnel repatriation: cultural shock in reverse, pp. 59–66, *MSU Business Topics*, Summer.

(B) SMITH, Lee (1975). The hazards of coming home, pp. 71–3, *Dun's Review*, Oct.

(C) NOER, D. M. (1974). Integrating foreign service employees to home organisation: the godfather approach, *Personnel Journal,* Jan., pp. 45–51.

(13) Reprinted by special permission from the October 1976 issue of International Management. Copyright ©. McGraw-Hill International Publications Company Limited. All rights reserved.

13 International industrial relations and trade unions

(1) Bruno Kreisky, quoted in the *New Statesman*, 17 October 1976,

reproduced by permission.

(2) Notably in Günter (1972) in which many of these points are made.

(3) See above, chapter 9. The second half of the statement is justified by evidence in the possession of the International Business Unit.

(4) For statements to the contrary, which do emphasize the emergence of international trade union organisation, see: ROBOCK & SIMMONDS (1973), pp. 533–7, ROBINSON (1973), pp. 189–190 (where twelve examples are given of international trade union action). See also (C) BLAKE, D. H. (1972), 'The Internationalization of Industrial Relations', *Journal of International Business Studies,* Autumn, p. 32.

(5) For a list of the international bodies and their affiliates, see *The Journal of Industrial Relations*, June 1972, p. 159.

(6) Excerpts from KUJAWA, Duane (1975), Transnational industrial relations and the multinational enterprise, *Journal of Business Administration*, **7.1,** reproduced by permission. For the same author's expanded study see the reading list to this chapter. This excerpt shows the obstacles to international negotiations in the light of the established procedures in four countries. It also shows how international union activity may develop. Duane Kujawa is Professor of International Business at Florida International University.

(7) See KASSALOW, E. M. (ed.) (1963). *National Labour Movements in the Postwar World*, Northwestern University Press.

(8) See (D) KUJAWA, D. (1972). Foreign sourcing decisions and the duty to bargain under the NLRA, *Law and Policy in International Business*, **4.3,** pp. 499–501.

(9) See (C) ROBERTS, B. C. & ROTHWELL, S. (1974). Recent trends in collective bargaining in the United Kingdom, in *Collective Bargaining in Industrialised Market Economies*, International Labour Office.

(10) Quoted from (D) STURMTHAL, A. (1972). *Comparative Labor Movements: Ideological Roots and Institutional Development*, Wadsworth, pp. 141, 166–7.

(11) See (D) KAMIN, A., Ed. (1970). *Western European Labor and the American Corporation*, Washington D.C.: The bureau of International Affairs.

(12) See KAMIN (1970). As above in note 11, pp. 259, 263.

(13) See KUJAWA (1971). Details under suggestions for further reading.

(14) Quoted from STURMTHAL (1972). See above, note 10.

(15) See (D) SEYFARTH, *et al.* (1972). *Labor Relations and the Law in France and the United States*, University of Michigan. This volume is one of a series on labour relations in various countries which has been used extensively in preparing this paper. The

authors are members of the Chicago law firm of Seyfarth, Shaw, Fairweather & Geraldson.

(16) See (C) DELAMOTTE, Y. (1974). *Collective Bargaining in Industrialised Market Economies*, International Labour Office.

(17) See (C) BLAKE, D. H. (1972). The internationalization of industrial relations, *Journal of International Business Studies*, **3**.2, Autumn.

(18) See (C) GENNARD, J., *Multinational Corporations and British Labour: Review of Attitudes and Responses*, p. 47, British North-American Committee.

(19) See the original article from which this passage is excerpted for details of the studies the author made in the automobile industry.

(20) See *The Wall Street Journal*, 5 Nov. 1974.

14 The economic environment

(1) The BankAmericard is an example of a credit card arrangement which involves several banks in different countries who make one another's cards available to their customers. American Express, on the other hand, is operated internationally by direct foreign investment.

A list of some recently established international consortia to provide general banking facilities is given in (C) EITEMAN & STONEHILL (1973), p. 85. On the following page the same book points out the savings in interest charges through an international bank which can transfer funds instantaneously.

(2) See, for example, (C) SALERA (1969), chapter 21–2. Also EITEMAN & STONEHILL (1973), pp. 94–105.

(3) Quoted from (A) *The World Bank Atlas* (1975), p. 3. For a detailed list of sources of foreign funds and development aid institutions, see (A) DANIELS, OGRAM & RADEBAUGH (1976), chapter 9.

(4) This brief paragraph oversimplifies a complicated subject. A comprehensive discussion of the subject is to be found in (D) CHOWN, J. F. (1974). *Taxation and The Multinational Enterprise*, Longman. The reader should also refer to: (C) EITEMAN & STONEHILL (1973), chapter 7 and (C) ROBBINS & STOBAUGH (1974) chapter 5.

(5) Excerpts from HELLEINER, G. K. (1973). Manufactured exports from less-developed countries and multinational firms, *The Economic Journal*, March, pp. 21–47. The whole article should be read. G. K. Helleiner is Professor of Political Economy in the University of Toronto and author of *A World Divided* (1976). Cambridge University Press.

(6) The is referred to above in chapter 3. See also (C) VERNON, R., (Ed.) (1970). *The Technology Factor in International Trade, A Conference of the Universities—National Bureau Committee for Economic Research*, pp. 145–231, New York: National Bureau for Economic Research. This passage discusses the various theories.

(7) See (D) CAVES, R. E. (1971). International corporations: the industrial economics of foreign investment, *Economica*, **38**.149, Feb., pp. 1–27.

(8) See (D) LITTLE, I. *et al.* (1970). *Industry and Trade in Some Developing Countries: A Comparative Study*, Oxford University Press.

(9) This represents an increase in manufactured exports from $7000 m in 1970 to $28,000 m in 1980 (see Robert McNamara's speech to the Annual Meeting of the Governors of the International Bank for Reconstruction and Development, Sept. 1971).

(10) See (C) *Development Assistance, 1971 Review*, p. 89, OECD.

(11) (C) *The Economic Survey 1970–1* (1971). Dar-es-Salaam: The United Republic of Tanzania.

(12) See (B) VERNON (1971), pp. 102–6, 245.

(13) See (C) LARY, H. D. (1968). *Imports of Manufactures from Less-Developed Countries*, National Bureau of Economic Reseach.

(14) See *The Times*, London, 31 October 1971.

(15) For a good summary of the arguments on this point see (D) MASON, R. H. (1971). *The Transfer of Technology and the Factor Proportions Problems: The Philippines and Mexico*, UNITAR Research Report no. 1.

(16) See VAN DAM, A. (1971), The world's work: who needs it most?, pp. 24–30, *Columbia Journal of World Business*, **vi.** 5, September–October.

(17) (C) AHARONI, Y. (1966). *The Foreign Investment Decision Process*, p. 318, Harvard.

(18) (C) HYMER, S. & ROWTHORN, R. (1970). Multinational corporations and international oligopoly: the non-American challenge in (C) KINDLEBERGER, C. P., (Ed.) (1970). *The International Corporation: A Symposium*, M.I.T. Press.

(19) The opposite is widely believed among industrialists. There is a passing reference to this point in chapter 11 (editorial notes).

(20) The President of Magnavox 'offered' to manufacture all his television receivers in the US in return for a tariff increase from 6% to 35% (*The Times*, 8 Oct. 1971).

(21) *Economic Factors Affecting the Use of Items 807.00 and 806.30 of the Tariff Schedules of the United States* (1970). Washington: United States Tariff Commission.

(22) 807.00 is a US tariff regulation allowing concessions on the re-

import of goods part manufactured abroad.

(23) VERNON (1971), pp. 107–8.

15 The political and legal environment–national

(1) See, for example, BROOKE, M. Z. (1972). Problems of the Multinational Company, chapter 13 in SAMUELS, J. M. (Ed.). *Readings in Mergers and Takeovers,* Elek: London.

(2) This phrase is discussed in a perceptive book aptly entitled (B) *The Enterprise in Transition.* See HAAS (1967), full details are given under 'further reading' in chapter 18. An example of legislation enforcing competition is Article 86 of the Treaty of Rome which concerns abuse of a dominant market position: the first three cases brought were GEMA (1971), Continental Can (1971) and Zoja (1972). Article 85 prohibits agreement between companies which restrict or distort competition.

(3) Set up by the Federal Government as part of Roosevelt's New Deal in the 1930s. Now mainly generates electricity and manufactures fertilizers. For a study of the United States' most famous nationalized industry see (C) SELZNICK, P. (1949). *TVA and the Grassroots*, University of California Press.

(4) See (C) HUFBAUER, G. C. & ADLER, F. M. (1968). *Overseas Manufacturing Investment and the Balance of Payments,* US Treasury Department for the United States, and (C) REDDAWAY, W. B. (1968). *Effects of UK Direct Investment Overseas: Final Report,* Cambridge University Press.

(5) For a report that denies that any jobs have been lost in the United States through US based foreign investors, but that on the contrary there has been a net gain in jobs, see *Business International.* For the contrary view see BARNET, R. & MUELLER, R. (1975). *Global Reach,* Simon & Shuster: New York.

(6) See *Barrons,* 8, March 1976, p. 8.

(7) In 1974 only the United States, Brazil and Mexico had larger populations than 30,000,000 on the whole American continent.

(8) See (C) BENOIT, E. (1966). Interdependence on a small planet, *The Columbia Journal of World Business,* Spring, p. 9.

See also the statement that the multinational corporation is: 'a modern concept designed to meet the requirements of a modern age: the nation state is a very old fashioned idea and badly adapted to serve the needs of our present complex world', BALL, G. W. (1967). The promise of the multinational corporation, *Fortune,* June.

(9) The late Professor György Ádám made a detailed study of statements writing off the nation state. See (B) ÁDÁM, G. (1971). The World Corporation: problematics, apologetics and critique, *Trends in World Economy*, **5**, Hungarian Scientific Council for World Economy.

(10) This summary is taken from a list agreed at a Conference of the International Institute of Management in Berlin, Sept. 1974. See (C) BROOKE, Michael Z. & GOLDBERG, Walter H. (1974). *The Multinational Firm and National Policies*, Berlin: International Institute of Management. Walter Goldberg is Director of the Institute.

(11) The description of the GATT, UNCTAD and the IMF is based on notes compiled by C. Cragg of the International Business Unit.

(12) The OECD resolution and its annexes were passed on 21 June 1976. Member governments published the documents. The British statement is *International Investment: Guidelines for Multination Enterprises* (1976). HMSO: Cmnd. 6525. See also *Recommendation of the Council Relating to the Improvement of Information on the Activities of Multinational Enterprises* (1976, April 6) OECD C (76) 43.

(13) For the Andean Pact rules see: (C) WEEKLY, J. K. (1971). The Andean Common Market foreign investment code, pp. 19–24, *MSU Business Topics*, Autumn. See also (C) pp. 69–74, *The Journal of International Business Studies*, Spring, 1972.

(14) The excerpt is taken with modifications from (B) The Report of the (C) Group of Eminent Persons (1974). *The Impact of Multinational Corporations on Development and on International Relations*, pp. 25–7, 36–44, United Nations Sales Document E.74.II.A.5. Reproduced by permission. The reader is advised to consult the full text of this important report.

(15) UN Publications, Sales no. 73.11.A.11.

(16) (C) *International Development Strategy: Action Programme for the Second United Nations Development Decade*, para. 50, UN Publication, Sales no. E.71.11.A.2.

(17) In part II of the Report from which this excerpt is taken (see above, note 14).

(18) See chapter VI of the same Report.

(19) See chapter XI of the same Report.

(20) The GNP figures were taken from *The World Bank Atlas*. The World Bank has 101 members of whom 73 had a gross national product below $20,000 m and therefore less than the companies named.

(21) Not all these papers are easy to obtain. Some are held by the International Business Unit.

(22) See especially *Transnational Corporations: Issues Involved in the Formulation of a Code of Conduct* (1976). UN Publications, Sales no. E/C.10/17.

16 Culture and education

(1) Quoted from a notice issued by the European Institute for Advanced Studies in Management about a meeting on organization and industrial cultures, 26 May 1976.

(2) One example of the possibility of doing this is briefly indicated in BROOKE & REMMERS (1970), chapter 5 where the theory of the *intercalary* position is used to interpret some puzzling evidence about role problems among senior executives in the foreign subsidiary of an international company. The *intercalary* position is that of the local national official who represents a foreign power to his subordinates and a foreign response to that power to his superiors. See (D) GLUCKMAN, M. (1959). *Custom and Conflict in Africa*, Blackwell.

(3) See BARRETT, G. V. & BASS, B. M. (1970). Comparative Surveys of Managerial Attitudes and Behaviour in BODDEWYN, J. (Ed.) (1970), *Comparative Management,* chapter 8, New York University. This book has a detailed discussion of the subject. One example of each school of thought is: Universality: (C) LIKERT, R. (1967). *The Human Organization*, McGraw-Hill: London & New York.

Cultural Cluster: (D) HAIRE, M. *et al.* (1966). *Managerial Thinking: An International Study*, Wiley: London & New York.

Economic Cluster: (D) KERR, C. *et al.* (1964). *Industrialism and Industrial Man* (2nd edn), Oxford University Press.

Barrett & Bass prefer the Cultural Cluster approach.

(4) A well-known bank advertisement hinges on knowledge about the significance of colour in clothing in Nigeria. Another example, as several firms have discovered to their cost, is that of trade marks of brand names which sell well in one country but turn out to have hidden meanings in another. In addition to these errors of judgment which damage the marketing effort, there are examples of successful marketing where damaging side effects have resulted. The best known of these was the sale of powdered milk to housewives who could not read the instructions with the resultant injury to the children. Another illustration is the high pressure selling of food and drink with little nutritive value in areas of great poverty to the detriment of people's health.

(5) There have been numerous studies of industrial moral over the years. A seminal example is CROZIER, M. (1964). *La Phénomène bureaucratique,* Seuil, (English edn Tavistock: London).

(6) At the least, their 'pragmatism' leads them in different directions. The facts referred to are quoted in (C) BODDEWYN (1970). See above note 3, from: (D) THIAGARAJAN, K. M. & BASS, B. M.

(1969). Differential preferences for long versus short-term payoffs in India and the United States, *Proceedings, xvith International Congress of Applied Psychology*, pp. 440–6, Swets & Zeitlinger: Amsterdam.

See also: (C) NEGANDHI, A. R. & PRASAD, S. B. (1971). *Comparative Management*, Appleton Century Crofts: New York.

(7) Also quoted in BODDEWYN (1970). See above note 3, p. 201.

(8) In FARMER & RICHMAN (1976). This perceptive book should certainly be referred to by students of the subject. See advice for further reading later in this chapter.

(9) See above, note (3).

(10) See (C) GRANICK, D. (1962). *The European Executive*, Doubleday.

(11) The 'extended family' is a phrase used to describe a society where a high degree of interdependence between the members is normal, and where members in several degrees of relationship live together. The 'head' of an extended family may take responsibility for several generations and numerous cousins within a generation. This contrasts with the 'nuclear' family, consisting of a husband and wife and their children, which is considered normal in most western societies. The strength of the extended family can vary considerably from the situation where the head of the family has quasi-judicial powers to that where only a shadow of the institution still exists.

(12) See (B) HALL, E. T. (1959). *The Silent Language*, Doubleday.

(13) Several studies have made this point. For an example see BROOKE & REMMERS (1972), chapter 8, a report on work by T. Weinshall which also asserts that management education in an international school can change inherited outlooks. Weinshall's work demonstrates both the differences and the change process.

17 The reputation of the multinational

(1) Jacques Maisonrouge, then President of IBM World Trade, see: *Growth of the Business World*, 13 November 1969 (Quoted in *Global Reach*, p. 24, see suggestions for further reading, p. 317. Much of the research for this chapter was carried out by Paul Neville, International Business Unit.

(2) (D) FREEMAN, O. L. (1975). The underdeveloped nations: victims—and victors—of commodity price increases, p. 39, *Conference Report*, Chicago World Trade Conference.

(3) See (C) TURNER, L. M. (1974). There's no love lost between mul-

tinational companies and the Third World, *Business and Society Review,* **11,** Autumn, pp. 75–8.

(4) 'The Under-developed countries have everything to lose from collaborating with "social imperialism". See (B) AMIN, S. (1975). Le tiers monde doit larguer les amarres. *Les Cahiers du Club de 'Nouvel Observateur',* **6.**

(5) See (A) TUGENDHAT, C. (1971). *The Multinationals,* Penguin. At that time, Christopher Tugendhat was a Conservative member of the British Parliament.

(6) José Epstein.

(7) The American Federation of Labor—Congress of Industrial Organizations, the United States body to which most of the major unions in that country are affiliated.

(8) Quoted by (B) TURNER, L. M. (1973). *Multinational Companies and the Third World,* Hill & Wang (English edn, p. 21, Allen Lane 1974).

(9) (B) WEST, Richard (1975). British multinationals in hot water, *Business and Society Review,* **13,** Spring, p. 79.

(10) See *Business Week,* 3 Nov. 1973.

(11) From a statement by Carl Gerstacker of Dow Chemicals. See: (B) GERSTACKER, C. A. & KIRKLAND, L. (1974), Worldcorps: job makers or job takers?, *Business and Society Review,* **11,** Autumn, p. 90.

(12) Prof. E. S. Herman of the Wharton School of Finance. Quoted from BARGET & MULLER (1975), p. 241, see Suggestions for Further Reading at the end of the chapter.

(13) 'It is certain that, faced with an economic power of the multinationals, only a political power with a similar scope is in a position to put forward a system firstly of defense and then of conquest, of power for the workers . . .', François Mitterand. See: (A) *Les cahiers du Club 'Nouvel Observateur'* (1975), p. 21, no. 6.

(14) It is easier for United States unions to make general demands for 'information' than European ones precisely because white collar unionism is less developed in the States and so the unions do not have to worry so much about the complications of such demands for their members.

(15) For a critique of available intelligence on the environment see: (C) BEHRMAN, J. M., BODDEWYN, J. J. & KAPOOR, A. (1975). *International Business-Government Communications,* Heath-Lexington. See also Boddewyn (1975) in Further Reading for this chapter.

(16) Presentation by Erich Henkel, Overseas Director of BASF, published in *European Chemical News,* German Supplement, 13 December 1974.

(17) The story would make a good case-study for use in connection with this chapter. See WOOD, O. G. *et al.* (1971), The BASF Controversy: Employment vs. Environment, University of South Carolina, *Essays in Economics*, **25**, November.

18 The future of international business

(1) See (B) BARNET, R. and MUELLER, R. (1975), *Global Reach*, Simon and Shuster (Eng. ed. Cape).
(2) See (B) PERLMUTTER, H. V. (1968), super-giant firms in the future, *Wharton Quarterly*, Winter.

Index